WORD ORDER AND WORD ORDER CHANGE

LIST OF PARTICIPANTS

EMMON BACH
Department of Linguistics
University of Massachusetts

ALAN BELL
National Science Foundation

CHARLES J. FILLMORE
Department of Linguistics
University of California (Berkeley)

SUSAN FISCHER
Salk Institute

TALMY GIVÓN
Department of Linguistics
University of California (L.A.)

JOSEPH H. GREENBERG
Department of Anthropology
Stanford University

ROBERT HETZRON
Department of Eastern Languages
University of California (S.B.)

GROVER HUDSON
Department of Linguistics
University of California (L.A.)

LARRY M. HYMAN
Department of Linguistics
University of California (L.A.)

WINFRED P. LEHMANN
Department of Linguistics
University of Texas

CHARLES N. LI
Linguistics Program
University of California (S.B.)

EDITH MORAVCSIK
Department of Linguistics
University of California (L.A.)

MAURINE B. PHELPS
Oregon College of Education

GERALD SANDERS
Department of Linguistics
University of Minnesota

ARTHUR SCHWARTZ
Linguistics Program
University of California (S.B.)

ROBERT STOCKWELL
Department of Linguistics
University of California (L.A.)

SUSAN STEELE
Department of Anthropology
University of New Mexico

WALRIN SWIECZKOWSKI
Department of Linguistics
Lublin University

SANDRA A. THOMPSON
Department of Linguistics
University of California (L.A.)

ROBERT UNDERHILL
Department of Linguistics
California State University (S.D.)

THEO VENNEMANN
Department of Linguistics
University of California (L.A.)

WORD ORDER AND WORD ORDER CHANGE

edited by

CHARLES N. LI

UNIVERSITY OF TEXAS PRESS   AUSTIN AND LONDON

For reasons of economy and speed this volume
has been printed from camera-ready copy
furnished by the Editor, who assumes full
responsibility for its contents.

International Standard Book Number 0-292-79002-3
Library of Congress Catalog Card Number 74-17620
Printed in the United States of America

To Joseph H. Greenberg

CONTENTS

PREFACE

The Conference on Word Order and Word Order Change was held at the University of California, Santa Barbara, California, January 26-27, 1974. This volume is composed of twelve of the thirteen papers presented at the Conference. Grover Hudson spoke on Amharic preposition embedding and relative clause history but decided against publishing his findings because of certain gaps in his data. The papers fall into two groups: the first eight are concerned with the diachronic aspect of word order, the rest with the synchronic aspect of word order. The stimulating and productive discussions which took place during the Conference are not included in this volume. However, subsequent to the Conference, a number of the papers have been revised because of the comments and the discussions.

The cornerstone in the study of word order is unmistakably Joseph H. Greenberg's Some Universals of Grammar with Particular Reference to the Order of Meaningful Elements. It serves as a starting point for most of the papers in this volume. The empirical facts amassed by Greenberg have made it possible to study the WHY and HOW questions concerning the synchronic nature of word order and the diachronic processes of word order change. However, during the Sixties, the field of syntax in the United States was almost exclusively the domain of those who researched the synchronic structure of English, as if there were an operational synonym between 'theoretical significance' and 'transformational study of English.' Thus, in the years immediately following the publication of the Universals of Language, the immense potential for theoretical investigation offered by Greenberg's cross-language study was accorded with little attention. Not until the Seventies have attempts been made to understand and explain those WHY and HOW questions which are the obvious consequences of Greenberg's universals. The Conference on Word Order and Word Order Change was organized in the hope that the empirical basis for the study of word order, both synchronic and diachronic, could be extended beyond what is already available in the extant literature and that the explanations of the empirical facts, i.e., answers to the theoretical questions posed by the data, could be provided at least partially if not in total.

I wish to thank all the participants, who made the Conference productive and stimulating. I am grateful to Dr. Bruce Rickborn, Dean of the College of Letters & Science, for his support of the Conference, to Professors Larry Hyman and Arthur Schwartz for their advice and aid in organizing the Conference.

Charles N. Li

INFLUENCES ON WORD ORDER CHANGE IN AMERICAN SIGN LANGUAGE [1]

by

Susan Fischer

1. <u>Introduction</u>

Until quite recently, research in linguistics has confined itself, often intentionally,[2] to languages which are either currently spoken, or were spoken at one time, and I here stress the word <u>spoken</u>. Virtually everyone recognizes written language as derivative from spoken language, and except for occasional forays by some into animal communication, channels other than the oral-aural have been ignored, particularly in the case of human languages. In the instance of research on word order and the kinds of conclusions which we draw from research on that topic, it seems to me that an examination from the perspective of a different modality could shed a great deal of light on the subject. This is particularly relevant since speech is such a linear, time-bound phenomenon that it would be at least theoretically possible to establish a strong link between this linearity and the use of word-order to express grammatical relations.

Sign language in general, and American Sign Language as an example of a sign language, while it certainly has linear components--one sign succeeds another, two sentences are separated by time--in other aspects is much more simultaneous than linear. Thus, the components of a sign (at the word level)--i.e., the shape of the active hand or hands, the location, on the body or in space, where the sign is made, and the movement involved,[3] all work together simultaneously, unlike the sequence of phones which go to make up a spoken word, although there is some overlap. Furthermore, a great deal of information which might be spelled out in some linear fashion in spoken language is simultaneously incorporated into a sign (usually a verb, see the discussion below, section 2.1). Given this brief characterization, the examination of word-order phenomena, and also of word-order change in the American Sign Language (hereafter abbreviated ASL) may have a special bearing on general investigations of the role of word order in natural language.

The fact that there do exist word-order restrictions in ASL, despite the difference in modality, is already significant. The fact that they are apparently different from what they were a hundred years ago is intriguing. In this paper, I shall discuss present word-order restrictions in ASL, the evidence for different ones a hundred years ago, and then I shall try to elucidate the reasons for this change, and to speculate both

on the path it could have taken, and on why the change may not yet be
complete. Some of the explanations I shall propose are quite familiar,
but some really depend on the difference in the channel of communication.

2. The Syntax of Present-day ASL[4]

2.1 Some unfortunately necessary preliminaries

I hope that eventually explanations such as this will no longer be
necessary, but for now it may be a good idea to clear up some rather common misconceptions that many people, even otherwise aware linguists, have
about sign language or about ASL. Many people think that sign language
is all pantomime. An obviously related misconception is that signs are
tied to the concrete world--i.e., that it is impossible to discuss ab-
stractions in a sign language. Neither of these is, of course, true.
While it is true that some signs were originally analogic, they have become more and more arbitrary over time (see Frishberg, 1973) and many
signs never had any iconic base. There are signs for all the abstract
ideas that deaf people use, including some that are as subtle and difficult to translate into English as gemütlichkeit. These myths are somewhat reminiscent of the kinds of things that used to be said about so-
called "primitive" languages.

Related to these myths is the idea which many have that sign language is universal. In our work, we have encountered or seen deaf people
from France, Germany, Hong Kong, Japan, and Great Britain, and their sign
languages are all different, not only at the level of having different
signs for different concepts, but also having different morpheme structure constraints and "phonetic" outputs. Just as one can posit a universal phonetics from which individual languages select their particular
sound repertoires, so there may be a set of "universal" gesture types
from which sign languages choose subsets to form their sign repertoires.
As in the case of spoken languages, the subsets chosen differ from language to language.

At the other extreme from the myth of universality of sign language
is the idea that any sign language is merely a degenerate form of the
spoken language which surrounds it, or that it is based on that spoken
language in some way. While it is true that there is going to be some
influence on the language from the surrounding community, the "degeneracy"

accusation probably has roots in the difficulty one has in trying to write down sign language. If one gives a rough English gloss for every sign in a sentence, the result may well look like a primitive pidgin. When one gives an <u>adequate</u> gloss, however, one soon realizes how much is missing from English. Just as an example to give little of the flavor of a good ASL sentence, let us take an English sentence (1), and its ASL translation.

(1)...They (two people mentioned previously) got on the trolley.

When we translate this sentence into ASL, one way to gloss it might be

(2)...GET-ON TROLLEY.

Now, while one does translate this sentence with just two signs, there is really a great deal of information packed into it, and indeed, a better gloss would be (3):

(3) TWO-PEOPLE-GET-ON-SOMETHING-HIGHER-THAN-THEY-AND-SIT-DOWN-TOGETHER TROLLEY.

Clearly, this is <u>not</u> just "bad English."

2.2 Word Order in Present-day ASL

The basic word-order in ASL is Subject-Verb-Object (SVO). This is the order one finds in a sentence with reversible subject and object[5] which are full noun phrases and not "appositivized" with pronouns. It is also the order one gets in subordinate clauses with <u>any</u> two full noun phrases for subject and object. Any other order will have intonation breaks. If we have a sentence like (4), other possible orders are those in (5) and (6).[6]

(4) MAN NOTICE CHILD. (SVO) ["The man noticed the child"]

(5) CHILD, MAN NOTICE. (OSV) ["As for the child, the man noticed it"]

(6) NOTICE CHILD, MAN. (VOS) ["He noticed the child, the man did"]

In sentence (5), the object is topicalized, and in sentence (6) the subject or perhaps the verb phrase is topicalized. In more complicated sentences, the subject of an embedded sentence can be fronted when topicalized, as well as its verb phrase, object, or indeed the entire embedded sentence:

(7) V-P DENY PRESIDENT CHEAT CONGRESS. ["The vice-president denies that the president cheated Congress."]

(8) PRESIDENT, V-P DENY CHEAT CONGRESS. ["As for the president, the vice-president denies that he (prexy) cheated Congress."]

(9) CONGRESS, V-P DENY PRESIDENT CHEAT. ["As for Congress, the vice-president denies that the president cheated it (them?)."]

(10) CHEAT CONGRESS, V-P DENY PRESIDENT (FINISH). ["As for cheating Congress, the vice-president denies that the president (did)."]

(11) PRESIDENT CHEAT CONGRESS, V-P DENY. ["As for the president cheating Congress, the vice-president denies it."]

Intonation breaks are accomplished by pauses, head tilts, raising of eyebrows, and/or probably numerous other cues that I as a non-native, non-deaf signer have yet to learn to pay attention to.

The above are the only orders of subject, verb, and object allowed in ASL if the subject and object are reversible. Another way of looking at these data is to turn them around. If one has sequences like noun-verb-noun, verb-noun-noun, or noun-noun-verb, how will such sequences be interpreted? In the case of native signers, especially those who do not rely a great deal on speech, NVN is subject-verb-object, NNV is either conjoined subject+verb or object-subject-verb, and VNN is either verb+ conjoined object or verb-object-subject. By contrast, hearing people tend more often to invariably interpret the first noun as the subject and the second as the object, regardless of the two nouns' positions with respect to that of the verb.

The important thing to emphasize here is that nowhere, when we have reversible nouns, do we have subject-object-verb sequences in present-day ASL. One can either say that such sequences are disallowed or that sequences of NNV are always interpreted as OSV (or SSV).

3. Word Order in ASL 100 Years Ago

There are three kinds of evidence that basic word-order in ASL was quite different as recently as 100 years ago from what it is today. Specifically, we have evidence for SOV order from external evidence,

historical evidence, and internal evidence. The external source consists
of texts of French Sign Language. The historical source consists of texts
of American Sign Language of 100 years ago, and the internal sources are
certain fixed idiomatic expressions which are felt to be archaic relics
of an older time.

3.1 Evidence from French Sign Language

In section 2.1, I claimed that French Sign Language is quite different from American Sign Language. How, then, one may ask, can I use FSL
as evidence for what ASL used to be? The answer lies in the history of
ASL as far as we know it. Briefly, just before the French Revolution,
the first school for the deaf which used sign language was established in
Paris by the Abbé de l'Épeé. The American Gallaudet in the early 1800's
was in England looking for a teaching method for the deaf in the United
States and encountered l'Épeé's successor at the school, l'Abbé Sicard.
Sicard's star pupil, Clerc, returned to the United States with Gallaudet
and taught the French sign system in the first school in the United
States, though there were some changes made in the crossing, and also
probably some native influences from signs which undoubtedly already existed here. This, however, was the first attempt at any sort of stan-
dardization of sign languages. Since about 1870, sign language has been
forbidden in the schools for the deaf in France, which has resulted in
rather sweeping changes in French sign languages. Ironically, from the
evidence we have from sign books published in France 100 years ago and
longer, Old French Signs, at least at the word level, are closer to present-day American signs than they are to present-day French signs, at
least from my limited experience.

In 1865 the Abbé Lambert published La Clef du Langage de la Physionomie et du Geste (Extrait de la Méthode Courte, Facile, et Pratique
d'Enseignement des Sourds-Muets Illettrés) (The Key to the Language of
the Body and Gesture--Extract of the Short, Easy, and Practical Method
of Teaching Illiterate Deaf-Mutes.) Like l'Épeé, Lambert was concerned
with giving the deaf enough of a conceptual base that they could understand and accept Christianity. The book includes a dictionary of signs,
with some illustrations. Also included is the parallel text of a catechism. (On the right is the French sign, and on the left is the French).
Typical examples are given below with English translations.

French	(French) Sign
moi, etant mort, j'aurai encore des yeux, mais je ne verrai plus. (I, being dead, will still have eyes, but I shall no longer see.)	MOI, MORT, YEUX AVOIR? OUI (MAIS) VOIR? FINI. Me dead, eyes have? Yes, (but) see? Finished.
Tu vois ce livre, tu vois cette table, tu vois cette chaise. (You see this book, you see that table, you see that chair.)	TOI LIVRE VOIR--TOI TABLE VOIR-- TOI CHAISE VOIR. You book see, you table see, you chair see.
Toi, tu me vois, moi je te vois. (You see me, I see you.)	TOI, MOI VOIR--MOI, TOI VOIR. You me see--me you see.

There are some exceptions to this order, which we shall discuss below, but by and large, this is the most predominant form. The last example, if seen by a present-day ASL signer, would be interpreted as having the opposite meaning--i.e., it would be interpreted as meaning "I see you, you see me."

This order extends even to some embedded sentences. We thus get examples like: (fr.)Peux-tu toucher ton âme? ["Can you touch your soul?"] (FSL) TOI ÂME TOUCHER, POUVOIR? ["You soul touch, can?"] which would be consistent with SOV structure. Similarly, we have (fr.)Moi, j'entends parler, j'entends sonner la cloche--j'entends battre le tambour. [me, I hear speak, I hear sound the bell, I hear beat the drum] (FSL) MOI, PARLER ENTENDRE--MOI, SONNER LA CLOCHE, ENTENDRE--MOI, BATTRE LE TAMBOUR, ENTENDRE. [Me, speak hear--me, sound the bell, hear--me beat the drum, hear] (=I hear talking, I hear the bell ring, I hear the drum beat.) Except for pronoun enclitics, spoken French is predominantly SVO just as English is, so that it is somewhat of a mystery why FSL should ever have had SOV order. We may have clues to this mystery below.

3.2 American Sign Language in the 1870's

A more direct historical line to present-day ASL comes from the ASL of a hundred years ago; presumably, modern ASL is a direct descendant of this language. Here, too, we have written texts giving English glosses of signed stories. In particular, from the American Annals of the Deaf of 1871 we find an ASL text of the story of the Prodigal Son (Keep, 1971). A few sentences from that text will suffice, I think, to show the consistent SOV order of ASL at that time.

> ...Days few after, son younger money all take, country far
> go, money spend, wine drink, food nice eat. Money by and
> by all. Country everywhere food little: son hungry very.
> Go seek man any, me hire. Gentleman meet. Gentleman son
> send field swine feed: son swine husks eat, see--self
> husks eat want--cannot--husks him give nobody.

Here again we note, not only the SOV order, but also the use of post-positions (ASL now has a mixture of prepositions and post-positions), postposed adjectives (again, modern ASL is mixed, and uses different orders
of adjective and noun for different topicalization effects), and even adverbs postposed after the adjectives they modify. Perhaps one can make
this difference clearer if one juxtaposes this extract with a modern ren-
dition of the same paragraph (courtesy of Bonnie Gough).

> LATER-ON, SECOND-OF-TWO YOUNG SON DECIDE, GATHER, PACK,
> LEAVE HOME, GONE. TRAVEL, GOOD TIME, SPENDTHRIFT, FOOLISH-
> LIVING. BROKE. HUNGRY. NEG.GROW FOOD FIELD NONE. PATIENT,
> WORK OVER-THERE, COUNTRY FARM, FEED PIG HERD. PIGS GRAZE.
> LOOK-AT-THEM. "NEG. ME RATHER ME GRAZE WITH THEM, FILL-UP,
> FAT-BELLY. (HIM [FARMER]) NOT FEED-ME ENOUGH, NEG."

(Neg. is a headshake which is a suprasegmental feature that can by itself
negate a sentence.)

In the modern extract, verbs come before objects (including embedded sentences or verb-phrases), prepositions come before their objects, and adjectives come before the nouns they modify. Clearly something rather
drastic has transpired in a short hundred years.

3.3 Internal Evidence from ASL

In section 2, I claimed that one never gets SOV order in ASL if the
subject and object are reversible, i.e., if they could be reversed and
one would still have a semantically plausible utterance. However, in
general there is a great deal more freedom of word order if subject and
object are not reversible. It thus becomes possible to have SOV word
order--indeed even OVS becomes possible--when there is only one plausible
way to interpret the grammatical relations in the sentence. It is all
right to say sentence (12) in ASL, though a sentence like (13) is not

possible if the intended interpretation is that the first noun be the agent, and the second the patient.

(12) MAN MUST B-I-L-L-S PAY.

(13) * MAN MUST WOMAN PAY.

Sentences like (12) are not really the issue in this argument, since it is just as possible (even better) to say (14) as (12).

(14) MAN MUST PAY B-I-L-L-S.

Sentences (12) and (14) show the flexibility of ASL order under conditions of non-reversibility. However, there exist other cases, often idioms or near-idiomatic expressions, where only OV order is permitted. Examples of this include:

(15) SHOES RESOLE (=resole shoes)

(16) WATER TURN-FAUCET (=turn on water)

(17) MOVIE FLASH-FLASH (= Take movies)

(18) MONEY EXCHANGE EXCHANGE (=balance the budget)

(19) NECK CUT-OFF (=slaughter, as a chicken)

All of these phrases are ungrammatical if the order of verb and object is reversed. These are felt by native signers to be unusual, fixed expressions. I think that one can argue that these are relics of an older time when it was more common to have the object occurring immediately before the verb. The independent evidence we have from the last century supports this view.

4. The Why's of Change

What seems to have changed in ASL in the last hundred years is, most importantly, that the object, which previously preceded the verb, now follows it (unless something else gets in the way), and concomitantly, the postposition is now generally a preposition, the adjective can precede or follow the noun, where before it could only follow, and the adverb precedes an adjective (as in VERY HUNGRY, where 100 years ago it was HUNGRY VERY).

All of these changes can be viewed as occurring in one direction, namely, toward a closer approximation to, if not English grammar, at least English word order. In this section we shall examine the reasons for this direction of change. Some of these reasons will sound all too familiar to the student of languages in contact. Some relate to the unique problems and complications of deafness.

When two languages come into contact, there is bound to be an influence in at least one direction, apparently in general from the more to the less prestigious language. This is a form of linguistic imperialism, really, where the more powerful wins out. English and ASL are two such languages. There is indeed an island (or, rather, many small islets) of ASL within oceans of English--after all, the deaf population in the United States is probably not much more than 2 hundredths of a percent. Furthermore, most hearing people do not come into contact very much with deaf people, whereas it is almost impossible for a deaf person to avoid hearing people. The pressure of numbers also makes one wonder why ASL didn't cave in long ago.

A more subtle factor lies in the way sign language tends to be learned. All of us probably know of immigrant children who learned English in the streets and in the schools and not from their parents. In present-day America this is the exception; in the case of ASL, it is the rule. Only about 10% of all deaf children have deaf parents, if that many. Since most hearing parents of deaf children do not know ASL, this means that most deaf children will learn ASL 1) fairly late, and 2) from their peers, for the most part. Even if their parents learn signs, which is a fairly recent development, it is very difficult for an adult to learn ASL, and parents will tend, whether in principle or just in practice, to sign English. This will tend to be true of most people who learn signs fairly late in life. Thus, the input to the deaf child may be at least a mixture of ASL (from deaf people) and a signed version of English.[7]

If exposure is one influence on this change, specific linguistic imperialism is certainly another. In an article criticizing the one in which the Prodigal Son extract appeared, E. G. Valentine (1872) concludes:

> It would seem, then, that the sign-language, not only is
> not perfect, but that it is an inferior language, and that
> a "wide gulf" exists between this and the English language,

>since the latter is one of the "refined and cultivated"
>languages. It is further acknowledged that this language
>will never be much farther advanced than it now is.
>
>...if the sign language is acknowledged to be an inferior
>and deficient language, incapable of expressing thoughts
>beyond the grasp of children, and if the excessive use
>of this language is shown to be positively injurious,
>then we are justified in protesting against its being
>placed on an equality with the English language.

This argument remains basically unchanged 100 years later. It is not my aim to argue for or against this position, but merely to point out that this kind of attitude on the part of educators of the deaf was apparently quite widespread at the time of the writing of this article, though both sides must have had their advocates. The reader should notice that these disputes are independent of the oral-manual controversy, which has been raging for 300 years, and has yet to be resolved.

At any rate, attitudes such as those expressed in Valentine's article serve to make the deaf person ashamed of his/her language when it isn't English. Furthermore, the consequence of this attitude, namely the use of English word order in classroom signing, will add to the child's exposure to the use of this order.

All of these factors go to suggest why sign language should have changed from SOV to SVO. However, they cannot tell us by what dynamic process this change has taken place over time. This question will be discussed in the next section.

5. The Hows of Change

On the surface, at least, the change from SOV to SVO, and more particularly the change in interpretation of NNV sequences from SOV to OSV, seems rather drastic. In this section, we shall discuss first, some of the factors which help to mitigate this drasticness, and secondly, some of the mechanisms in ASL which may make this change appear more "natural", in some parsimonious sense of that word.

5.1 Narrowing the Gap at Both Ends

In the interests of exposition, I have up until now painted a slightly less than accurate picture of ASL past and present. The situation is in fact a bit more muddy than the simple facts I have presented so far would indicate. As a matter of fact, ASL (and FSL) 100 years ago was not totally consistently SOV, and present-day ASL is not always consistently SVO, although there are certainly strong tendencies in both cases. Perhaps one should conclude that the change from SOV to SVO had already begun in the 1870's and that in the 1970's it is not yet complete. We have, after all, the example given at this Conference (Li and Thompson) of a change which is not complete after 2000 years. At any rate, these inconsistencies help to make the change more plausible.

5.1.1 The Earlier Stage--FSL and Old ASL

Even if we limit ourselves to cases of reversible noun phrases, we find inconsistencies in the century-old texts available to us. Turning first to FSL, we find that although the overwhelming majority of cases are SOV, we have one example of SVO and another of OSV. The SVO is:

> (FSL)   TOI VOIR RIEN.   (Fr.)   Tu ne vois rien.
> [= You see nothing.]

The example of OSV is:

> (FSL)   DIEU TOI AIMER IL-FAUT.   (Fr.)   Tu dois donc aimer Dieu.
> [= It is necessary that you love God, or you must love God.]

This second example is somewhat interesting. It occurs in a context where Dieu is definitely the topic of the discourse--every sentence begins with Dieu, apparently regardless of its grammatical function in the sentence. This would appear, then, to be the beginnings of topicalization by a left-dislocation rule. One wishes one had better descriptions of the intonational patterns used in the utterance of these sentences.

In the old American Sign Language evidence, there are also two counter-examples to SOV. One is from the text of the Prodigal Son:

> (20)   GO SEEK MANY ANY, ME[8] HIRE.   [(He) went to seek any man who would hire him.]

This sentence is interesting, since the reason for its order may well be some sort of heavy noun phrase constraint of the type proposed by Ross (1967). For the second example, which is OSV, it is worth, I think, quoting the entire context in which it occurs.

> Suppose that the deaf-mute at the very beginning of his

efforts to learn language, has come to know the words
<u>cat</u>, and <u>catch</u>, and <u>boy</u>. Making the sign for cat, which
we do by putting the thumb and forefinger of each hand
to the mouth as if taking hold of whiskers, and then
stroking the back of the left hand to indicate the fur;
then locating the animal; then, having made the sign
for boy, we represent him as catching the cat, and
write for the child the sentence, "A boy catches a cat."
Does he not know what it means, and is there any difficulty in his modeling other sentences after this form?
None whatever.

(From Keep, 1871)

We shall return later to the notion of "locating the animal", which is
crucial for the grammar of ASL, but for now, we should just note that if
one deletes all the verbiage, the order of the signs in the sentence which
translates "The boy catches the cat", would seem to be CAT BOY CATCH,
which is indeed OSV.

We thus find that in both the French and American Sign Languages of
the 1870's there exist already the seeds of this change--quite sparse, but
there nonetheless.

5.1.2 SOV in Modern ASL

There are two cases in which one can have the order SOV in modern
ASL. I qualified my original statement of the lack of SOV in modern ASL
by saying that this held for reversible noun phrases which were full noun
phrases and not pronouns. So, logically the two exceptions to this rule
are non-reversible noun phrases and pronouns, though a very special type
of pronoun which we shall discuss in 5.2.

In general, subjects and objects in ASL have a great deal more freedom of occurrence when they are non-reversible than when they are reversible. We have already seen (see above, section 3.3) cases in which the
object <u>must</u> precede the verb. There are many, many more in which it <u>can</u>
but does not have to, if it is non-reversible with the subject. Thus, in
present-day ASL the basic sentence BOY LIKE GIRL can occur, preserving
the grammatical relations, only as LIKE GIRL, BOY or GIRL, BOY LIKE, and
not as BOY GIRL LIKE with the intended reading. However, in a case of a
sentence like BOY LIKE ICE-CREAM, we <u>can</u> also have BOY ICE-CREAM LIKE,
and perhaps even ICE-CREAM LIKE BOY, as well as the two perturbations

allowable in reversible cases.

The reasons for this greater freedom are obvious--there is only one way to interpret the non-reversible cases plausibly, whereas in the case of the reversibles there could be two.[9]

The upshot of this is that the change from SOV to SVO is not as great a leap as one might think.

5.2 The Path of Change

Since changes in languages tend to take place over time, rather than instantaneously, it becomes necessary to attempt to account, not only for the direction of change, but also for the actual path by which that change could have taken place. We shall present a hypothesis on that path for our case now.

5.2.1 Grammatical Mechanisms in ASL, or How to Get From One Place to Another

In order to understand the path of linguistic change in ASL, it is necessary first to understand the mechanisms, in addition to word order, which ASL uses to express grammatical relations. These mechanisms are really unique to a spatial, visual modality, although imperfect analogues can be found in speech. Not only are they unique to a spatial modality, but they also take unique advantage of the manual-visual channel. I should probably emphasize that these mechanisms do indeed serve grammatical functions in ASL, even though they may be used in spoken language in a paralinguistic way. As an example of what I mean, in English it is strange to say "I don't understand that," while smiling. In ASL it is ungrammatical.

Facial expression, the tilt of the head, the muscular tension in the body, the angle of the body with respect to the line between signer and viewer, all play roles in the grammar of ASL.[10] What I want to concentrate on here, however, is the use of a very special property of verbs in ASL to convey grammatical relations.[11]

I should hasten to point out that this is a special property not only of verbs in ASL, but also of people. People are very good at remembering the locations of things. In fact, some people use location as a mnemonic device for remembering ordered sets of unrelated items (such as lists of unrelated nouns). Thus, if I am signing in a discourse (i.e., not an i-solated sentence), I can establish the location of a referent, by point-ing, making a sign in that location, or some other device (this is used

for referents which are not physically present), and for the rest of the
discourse, I can use that location to refer to that referent. A signer
and his/her interlocutors can keep quite a number of referents apart.

So far as this particular mechanism goes, this is probably close to
an equivalent of pronominalization in ASL, a device to obviate the necessity for repeating names all the time.[12]   This, however, is only the
first step, the roughing out, as it were, in the sculpting of space. We
can refine it a great deal further.

It is interesting to note that while nouns and adjectives in ASL tend
to be made primarily, though of course not totally, on the body, verbs,
even some stative verbs like HATE, are made out in the space in front of
the body. This gives the sign a great deal of freedom of movement, and
this is crucial.

What verbs in ASL can do is, once the location of referents has been
established, to move or orient the hands between them, thus indicating
clearly and unambiguously the grammatical relations involved. Let us take
an example. The citation form of the ASL verb meaning "to give a present"
is made by two "X" hands (see Figure 1), palms facing each other, first
held upright and then twisting at the wrist such that the hands move down
and away from the body. If we wish to sign "someone gives me a present",
then the starting position is the same, but the hands, instead of moving
down and away from the body, move down and toward it, often even touching
the chest at the endpoint of the sign. This sign, then, always moves
toward the recipient--if none is specified, the citation form is used.
If one is specified, the sign moves toward it (as long as the recipient
isn't physically located behind the signer, in which case, (s)he will
probably turn around before signing), be it to the side, straight in front,
or toward her/himself.

Figure 1. "X"

This sign can, in addition, show, in one of two different ways, the donor as well as the recipient. One way is for the hands to start, not in the upright position, but with the knuckles stretched back toward the location, real or established, of the donor. Another way is to exaggerate the starting point of the sign, locating it very precisely, perhaps with a downward movement so that the addressee will notice the precise path of the sign--the signer is thus saying "this whole path, not just the endpoint, is important here". I must re-emphasize here that the verb does not have this flexibility unless locations have been established, either by mentioning the referents first and then "finding a place for them", or by actual demonstratives for things or people that are actually present. Another way of saying the same thing is to say that verbs incorporate the location only of pronouns, or that they cliticize only pronouns, which is what this process most closely resembles.[13]

The notion of setting up locations and then later referring to them is not new. We find a particularly vivid example of this in Lambert (1865). Again, as with the catechism, this is a parallel text. I shall give first, the normal French, then the FSL translation with a word-by-word English gloss.

(21) En ce temps-là, on amena un sourd-muet à Jésus qui
     allait par la ville de Sidon vers la mer de Galilée, et
     on le pria de lui imposer les mains. Jésus lui mis les
     doigts dans les oreilles et de la salive sur la langue,
     àpres l'avoir retiré de la foule; puis, ayant soupiré et
     levant les yeux au ciel, il dit: Ouvrez-vous.

(22) In that time, a deaf-mute was brought to Jesus as he was
     going through the city of Sidon toward the sea of Galilee,
     and he was asked to lay his hands on him. Jesus put his
     fingers in the deaf-mute's ears, and saliva on his tongue,
     this after having drawn him away from the crowd. Then,
     having signed and lifting his eyes to heaven, he said,
     "Open up."

(23) AUTREFOIS, VILLE SIDON ICI,   MER GALILÉE   LÀ--
       Before, city   Sidon here,   sea Galilee   there--

     JÉSUS VILLE SIDON   LÀ   TRAVERSER, MER GALILÉE
     Jesus city Sidon there   cross , sea Galilee

```
VERS -- HOMME SOURD-MUET UN ICI -- HOMMES
toward-- man deaf-mute one here -- men

PLUSIEURS SOURD-MUET PRENNENT AU BRAS, JÉSUS À
many deaf-mute take by the arm, Jesus to

CONDUISENT, -- HOMME PLUSIEURS PRIENT: SOURD-MUET LÀ,
lead, -- man many pray deaf-mute there

JÉSUS MAIN IMPOSER À LUI -- HOMMES PLUSIEURS ICI,
Jesus hand place to him -- men many here

JÉSUS SOURD-MUET RETIRER DE -- JÉSUS, SOURD-MUET
Jesus deaf-mute retire from -- Jesus, deaf-mute

ICI, LES DOIGTS OREILLES TOUCHER DU -- SALIVE
here, the fingers ears touch some-- saliva

BOUCHE SUR DU -- JÉSUS-CHRIST YEUX AU CIEL,
mouth on some -- Jesus Christ eyes to sky,

SOUPIRER, DIRE: MOI ORDONNER: OREILLES ENTENDRE,
sign, say me order : ears hear,

BOUCHE PARLER.
mouth speak.
```

In this example, all those "ici's" and "là's" are establishment of location, and I am willing to bet, though it doesn't show up explicitly in this text, that the verbs traverser, prennent, conduisent, imposer, and possibly toucher were all variants of the citation forms of those respective signs which were changed to show the location of their arguments.

This use of so-called directional verbs is one of the particular ways in which ASL (and probably other sign languages as well) takes advantage of its channel of communication. It has been shown previously (Bellugi and Fischer, op. cit.) that signs require more time to utter than spoken words, so that in order to get ideas across efficiently, ways must be found within the modality that are "natural" to a visual channel. The use of directional verbs enables one to compact a great deal of information into one sign, and in a way which does not exist in spoken language.

The fact that nouns have to be pronominalized before they can be cliticized onto the verb provides a very strong countervailing pressure to the English influence on the change from SOV to SVO (though not, I hasten to point out, on the change from SOV to OSV, which we shall return to in a moment.) Thus, if we take a sentence like (24), there are two ways one could translate it into ASL.

> (24) The girl kicked the boy.

The most straightforward way of doing so would be in (25). This would also be the most usual way if the sentence occurs in isolation.

> (25) GIRL KICK BOY.

If, however, the sentence occurs in a more extended discourse, especially if one will wish to refer to the boy and/or the girl again, the most natural way to sign the meaning of (25) is with (26).

> (26) BOY (HERE)   GIRL (HERE)   SHE-KICK-HIM.
>   (right hand)   (left hand)   left "kicks" right, from
>   direction of location of girl to location of boy.

The sentence of (26) gives us an OSV structure. It would be possible, however, to reverse the order of the subject and object and, in this case, because there are other cues, retain the meaning--the verb remaining constant. This would give us a sentence like (27).

> (27) GIRL (HERE)   BOY (HERE)   SHE-KICK-HIM.
>   (left hand)   (right hand) left "kicks" right (from girl
>   to boy)

Sentences with the order and grammatical relations of (26) are preferred over sentences like (27) by native signers, though (27) is certainly acceptable. One possible reason for this has been pointed out to me by Allen Munro, whom I would like to thank for this observation. A sign like KICK moves from the location of the agent to the location of the patient. If the agent is mentioned after the patient (i.e., if we have OSV order), then the least amount of transition time between signs is used. If, on the other hand, the order is SOV, an additional step of moving the hands from the location of the patient back to the location of the agent, in order to start the verb sign, is required.

There are a few directional verbs, such as TAKE, BORROW, and INVITE in which the movement is from the patient or dative to the agent. The vast majority, however, are in the class of KICK or GIVE-A-PRESENT, and move away from the location of the agent toward the location of the

patient or dative (these locations being either actual or established by
convention). If, then, one has a situation where either order is possible
but SOV is preferred over OSV, this situation may tend to be somewhat unstable. That both possibilities existed in the 1870's is shown by the
example cited earlier about the boy catching the cat: "making the sign
for cat...then locating the animal; then, having made the sign for a boy,
we represent him as catching the cat...".

5.2.2 The Threefold Way, or "How to Get From One Time to Another"

I am going to try in this section to present a plausible account of
how ASL got from SOV to SVO in a hundred years. I think that an important first step lies in the change in probability of occurrence between
sentences like (26) and sentences like (27). Let us represent sentences
like (26) with Figure 2., where (1) represents the item which is uttered
and located first, and (2) the item which is located and uttered second.

(1)   (2)

←---------------------

Figure 2.

Figure 3. would then represent sentences like (27).

(1)   (2)

---------------------→

Figure 3.

The arrows represent the direction of movement in a verb like KICK.

Since schemata like Figure 2. are more efficient than those in
Figure 3., they are going to win out. Both schemata are possible in both
time periods, but over time the probability of occurrence of 2. increases
and the probability of the occurrence of 3. decreases. This much will
give us a change from SOV to OSV as the unmarked order, at least for NNV
sequences where locations are established within a discourse. The next
step might be to extend this to sequences of NNV where locations are not
established.

This, however, is, in and of itself, an unstable situation. Often
in a language, though of course not always, one wants the subject to be
the topic, and generally the topic comes first in a sentence. However,
if one fronts the subject in an OSV sequence one gets SOV. Unfortunately,
if the change from SOV to OSV has already taken place in NNV sequences

where locations are not established, then this will automatically be re-
interpreted as OSV, thus apparently making it impossible to topicalize
the subject.

Here the influence of English comes in. One alternative to the dilemma in the previous paragraph would be to "right-dislocate" the subject
instead of fronting it. Notice, however, that this solution would give
us an OVS structure, which is (a) at least rather unusual for a natural
language, and (b) in direct contradiction to English structure, especially
for reversible subject and object. One can certainly say, "Well, who
cares about English?", but in this special case, this is easier said than
done. Leave us not forget that even in the 1870's there existed advocates
of a Signed English, and indeed probably there were people for whom signing in the order of the English language was the only kind of signing they
knew. There are many people like that today as well. If one has two
groups of people trying to communicate and for one NVN means SVO and for
the other NVN means OVS, then a certain amount of confusion could be expected to arise as to what people mean when they utter NVN. So the solution of right-dislocation is out.

The path of least resistance would then seem to be using the SVO
structure when one wished to topicalize the subject. The last step in
the change would then be the change in emphasis from OSV to SVO as to
which was more marked, OSV finally becoming a structure where the object
has been topicalized.

This entire change must take place within the constraints of the
kinds of minimization of functional ambiguity first suggested by Klima
(1970). This theory allows us to account for the continued greater freedom of order in the case of a non-reversible subject and object,[14] and
will constrain the co-occurrence of SOV and OSV structures to just those
where there is something else, such as the establishment of location, to
disambiguate the grammatical relations.

6. Summary

The American Sign Language, that language used by the deaf in the
United States, has a basic word order of SVO. Other orders are allowed
under the circumstances that (a) something is topicalized, (b) the subject and object are non-reversible, and/or (c) the signer uses space to
indicate grammatical mechanisms. Even with these qualifications, ASL has

a different basic word order (and derived word order) from what existed 100 years ago, both in France and the United States. I have tried to suggest that there has been a great deal of pressure from English to conform to the syntax of the spoken language of the community. At the same time, however, there are countervailing pressures arising from the fact that ASL is a sign language, produced in space rather than sound, and perceived by the eye rather than the ear. In order to use space to indicate grammatical relations, it is necessary to have a different order of elements from English. These two pressures have interacted to produce a language which is still different from English, but conforms more to it than it used to.

NOTES

1. Research for this paper was supported by Grant #NS-09811; I should like to thank René Bernard and Ursula Bellugi for guiding me to the historical materials and Sharon Neumann and Bonnie Gough for patiently answering my incessant questions. All errors are, of course, my own.

2. See, for example, Hockett's "design features" in Greenberg (1963).

3. See Stokoe, Casterline, and Croneberg, (1965), for a more complete and detailed description of these parameters.

4. This section is based on Fischer, to appear, which the reader should refer to if (s)he wants more detail.

5. Reversible NP's are those which could be reversed without changing the semantic acceptability of the sentence.

6. Glosses for signs will be given in capital letters. When more than one English word is needed, as in (3) above, hyphens will be used to connect the words of the gloss of the sign. Hyphens are also used to connect the letters of a fingerspelled word.

7. Some signed English consists of just signing English word order. Some signed English signs English word order and fingerspells functional morphemes (such as of, the, or, etc.). Others, fairly recently introduced, attempt to have a consistent sign for every English morpheme. Attempts to tie sign language to the syntax of the spoken language surrounding it were first made by l'Épée. This sign language was modified for English in the early 19th century, and has eventually disappeared in about a generation after its introduction.

8. The use of direct rather than indirect speech is a striking difference between ASL even now and English.

9. This is not to say that ASL could not express the idea of something semantically anomalous, but simply that in order to do so, something special, such as the use of exaggerated intonation, would have to be used.

10. Some of these are discussed in Bellugi and Fischer, 1972.

11. A more detailed description of the behavior of verbs under these conditions can be found in Fischer (to appear).

12. There are other means of pronominalization in ASL, namely deletion.

13. See my "Verbs in American Sign Language" for more detailed descriptions of the actual "phonological" realization of these processes. (In Klima and Bellugi, to appear.)

14. Indeed, there can be reversibility and non-reversibility between two objects. In my dissertation (Fischer, 1971) I showed that there is greater freedom of movement for English datives and direct objects if they are non-reversible than if they are reversible.

BIBLIOGRAPHY

Bellugi, U. and S. Fischer, (1972). "A Comparison of Sign Language and Spoken Language," Cognition, 1, pp. 173-200.

Fischer, S. (1971). The Acquisition of Verb-Particle and Dative Constructions, unpublished doctoral dissertation, M.I.T.

----------- (to appear). "Sign Language and Linguistic Universals", to appear in the Proceedings of the Franco-German Conference on French Transformational Grammar, Berlin, Athaenium.

----------- (to appear (a)). "Verbs in American Sign Language", to appear in Klima and Bellugi.

Frishberg, N. (1973). "Arbitrariness and Iconicity: Historical Change in American Sign Language", paper presented at the 1973 Winter Meeting of the Linguistic Society of America.

Greenberg, J. (Ed.) (1963). Universals of Language, Cambridge, M.I.T. Press.

Hockett, C. (1963). "The Problem of Universals in Language", in Greenberg (1963).

Keep, J. R. (1871). "The Sign Language", in American Annals of the Deaf, 16, pp. 221-234.

Klima, E. (1970). "Regulatory Devices Against Functional Ambiguity", paper presented at IRIA Conference, 1970.

--------- and U. Bellugi (to appear). The Signs of Language, Cambridge, Harvard University Press.

Lambert, L'Abbé de (1865). La Clef du Langage de la Physionomie et du Geste (Extrait de la Méthode Courte, Facile, et Pratique d'Enseignement des Sourds-Muets Illettrés).

Ross, J. R. (1967). Constraints on Variables in Syntax, unpublished doctoral dissertation, M.I.T.

Stokoe, W., D. Casterline, and C. G. Croneberg (1965). A Dictionary of American Sign Language on Linguistic Principles, Washington, Gallaudet College Press.

Valentine, E. G. (1872). "Shall We Abandon the English Order?" American Annals of the Deaf, 17, pp. 33-47.

DYNAMIC ASPECTS OF WORD ORDER IN THE NUMERAL CLASSIFIER

by

Joseph H. Greenberg

Some of the synchronic hypotheses proposed in Greenberg (1973) regarding the numeral classifier construction will serve as a point of departure for the present more diachronically oriented study.[1]

Among the conclusions of the earlier discussion which will prove to be relevant in this connection are the following:

1. There are many indications that in the tripartite construction consisting of quantifier (Q), classifier (Cl) and head noun (N), Q is in direct construction with Cl and this complex construction, which will be called the classifier phrase, is in turn in construction with N.[2] We may symbolize these relationships as follows: $((Q \longleftrightarrow Cl) \longleftrightarrow N)$, where the notation $\longleftrightarrow$ is used to indicate the possibility of both orders of the items connected by it.

2. In consonance with the world-wide favoring of the word order QN in language without numeral classifiers, there is a heavy statistical predominance of the order Q-Cl as against Cl-Q in the classifier phrase of languages with the numeral classifier construction.[3]

3. In accordance with the first principle, that of immediate constituency of Q and Cl, orders in which N separates Q from Cl nowhere occur as regular word order types. The remaining possibilities, then, all of which are found, are: 1/ (Q-Cl)-N; 2/ N-(Q-Cl); 3/ (Cl-Q)-N; 4/ N-(Cl-Q). In conformity with the second principle, however, orders 1/ or 2/ are far more frequent than 3/ or 4/ in numeral classifier languages.

4. A further observation is that, whereas the order within the classifying phrase $Q \longleftrightarrow Cl$ is, for any language, almost invariably fixed, there is considerable variation in many languages in the order of the Head Noun $\longleftrightarrow$ Classifier Phrase construction. Thus, many languages have both N-(Q-Cl) and (Q-Cl)-N as regular possibilities in apparent free variation (e.g. Malay).

5. The favoring of Q-Cl over Cl-Q in the classifying phrase does not find its parallel in a corresponding favoring of the order $(Q \longleftrightarrow Cl)$-N over N-$(Q \longleftrightarrow Cl)$. The order in which the classifying phrase is postposed to the noun is at least as frequent as the preposed order. Because of this fact, the Classifier $\longleftrightarrow$ Head Noun construction was not considered a subtype of the Quantifier $\longleftrightarrow$ Head Noun construction in regard to word order properties in Greenberg (1963).

6. In numeral classifier languages the numeral classifier construction is almost always identical with the measure construction including rules of word order. This is so much the case that many grammars of such languages consider the numeral classifier construction as merely a subvariety of an overall construction type which includes measures. For example, if the order is five-flat-object-book, a classifier language will almost invariably have the order five-pounds-cheese.

7. It is generally the case that numeral classifier languages will apparently lack a classifier in nouns indicating periods of time, units of distance and the word 'time' in such phrases as 'five times'. It was hypothesized that in these cases, the correct interpretation was not that the classifier is omitted but that words like 'day', 'mile' and 'time' are themselves measures of verbal action so that we have to do with a subtype of the overall classifier or measure phrases. In other words, such phrases as 'five days' are rather to be identified with $(Q \longleftrightarrow Cl)$ than $(Q \longleftrightarrow N)$.

8. Finally, it was noted that many classifier languages have constructions in which the classifier appears without a quantifier. The meaning here is invariably singular, and is in some languages specified as definite, in others indefinite and in still others neither. In some grammars it is explicitly noted that this occurs through deletion of 'one' (the most unmarked number).

The preceding purely synchronic observations suggest certain diachronic hypotheses which may be stated as follows.

First, we may posit that the synchronic order of the $Q \longleftrightarrow Cl$ classifier phrases is not only synchronically basic but represents diachronically the normal order $Q \longleftrightarrow N$ before the introduction of the noun classifier construction. It is normally still present in expressions of time, distance and frequency of verbal action in isolated form and in incorporated form in the measure construction. Since, in fact classifiers are always nouns and in a great many instances still function as head nouns, we deduce that the classifier phrase at the beginning is simply a quantifier-noun phrase with a particular syntactic use. It was noted, under 2. above, that in regard to word order properties, $Q \longleftrightarrow Cl$ within the classifier construction conforms to generalizations characteristic of $Q \longleftrightarrow N$ in non-classifier languages.

Secondly, the great variability of order within languages of the classifier phrase itself in construction with the head noun as against the virtual fixity of Q ←→ Cl (point 4 above) suggests that the order of N in relation to the classifier phrase is often in the process of undergoing a shift.

Thirdly, we may further hypothesize that it is likely that in such cases the earlier order is N-(Q ←→ Cl) rather than (Q ←→ Cl)-N. This is because the postposing of the classifier phrase, viewed as a quantifying expression, is deviant in relation to the general tendency of quantifiers to precede nouns. We may conjecture that in later stages with the spread of the general classifier to the point where the language is close to or in some cases reaches a situation in which there is only a single 'classifier', the construction comes to be treated more and more as simply a quantifier and hence moves to the more normal order Q-N as now represented by (Q ←→ Cl)-N.

We may now consider the evidence bearing on the validity of these hypotheses. The most cogent will be direct historical documentation. Here Chinese represents a uniquely valuable case as a numeral classifier language with historical records extending over at least three millenia. At present all Chinese dialects have this construction and also have, as far as I know, the order (Q-Cl)-N. As a further point it is to be noted that they also use classifiers in the demonstrative construction in the singular (Dem-Cl)-N.

The following brief account of the history of the classifier construction in Chinese is based chiefly on Wang Li (1958) and the various works of Dobson on different stages of early Chinese (Dobson 1959, 1962, 1964, 1968).

The earliest written Chinese is that of the only partially deciphered oracle bones of the Shang dynasty (1401-1123 B.C.). Wang Li (1958:II.236) cites two examples from this period in which the classifier is a noun identical with the noun classified, e.g. rén shí-yoù-liù rén "man ten-and-six man" i.e. 'sixteen men'. This "autonymous" construction is found in Burmese, Thai and other Southeast Asian languages at the present time. However, there is also the use of rén 'man' as a classifier in qiang shí rén "Qiang (a tribal name) ten man" i.e. 'ten Qiang'.

As scanty as the evidence is from the Shang period it shows substantial agreement with that of the next period, Early Western Chou, and indicates that the basic pattern of early Chinese in this matter was already

established. The points of agreement include the existence of the autonymous construction, the use of rén as a classifier and the word order N-Q-
C1.

The texts of Early Western Chou (11th and 10th centuries B.C.) are of
two types which agree in their essential linguistic features. The first
of these consists of inscriptions on bronze vessels and the second of certain archaic portions of the Shu Ching (Book of Documents); Dobson (1962)
calls this language Early Archaic Chinese (EAC). His work contains both
a summary grammar and a set of texts with translation constituting about
one third of the extant corpus of this period.

EAC has a limited set of classifiers and the autonymous construction
of the Shang period continues to be frequent. Unlike contemporary Chinese,
classifiers do not occur in the demonstrative construction. While the
present paper is concerned primarily with word order, it may be pointed
out that the later appearance of the demonstrative construction confirms
a diachronic hypothesis in Greenberg (1973), namely that the classifier
construction starts with expressions of quantity and, if it spreads syntactically, does so first by occurring with demonstratives.

In all, according to Dobson, EAC has three constructions: N-Q-C1,
N-Q and Q-N. The evidence of this period and of the preceding Shang period confirms our hypothesis insofar as the postposed order N-(Q-C1) rather
than (Q-C1)-N as in present day Chinese. An examination of the texts edited by Dobson reveals certain other pertinent facts not considered in
the grammatical sections of his book. We might expect on the basis of our
earlier stated hypotheses that the order Q-C1 incorporated in the full
classifier phrase N-(Q-C1) reflects the earlier basic Q-N order. This is
supported by the exclusive occurrence of the order Q-N in time, distance,
measure and currency expressions in EAC. In fact, with countables the
Q-N construction without classifiers is still the most usual one. In
other words the classifier is not required. It remains then to explain
the occurrence of N-Q expressions. An examination of the texts edited by
Dobson shows that at least in this part of the corpus, the order N-Q only
occurs in lists, e.g. from the Sheau Yu Diing: reward /Yŭ/?/?/bow/one/,
/arrow/hundred/, /decorated/bow case/one/, /metal/mail/one/, etc. Forrest
(1948:112) notes this usage of N-Q without classifiers as being specifically in lists in the "Proto-Chinese" language of the Book of Odes, equivalent to Dobson's Middle Archaic Chinese.

It is noted by Chao (1968:272-3) in his grammar of contemporary Mandarin that the order N-(Q-Cl) is found in lists. In Banggais, an Austronesian language (Van der Bergh, 1953:81) in which the normal order is (Q-Cl)-N, lists have the order N-(Q-Cl). The rule is illustrated by the example of a list of contents of a bride price payment. Among non-classifier languages, Biblical Hebrew may be cited in this connection. An interesting example is I Kings 5-7, which contains a detailed description of the building work done for Solomon by Hiram, King of Tyre. Throughout this description the numerals consistently precede the noun. But in 7:40-45 there is a summary which begins, "So Hiram made an end of doing all the work that he made for King Solomon on the house of the Lord: the two pillars..." etc. In this summary all the numerals follow the noun. The further significance of this construction will be discussed in a later section.

To summarize, in EAC, outside of the N-Q list construction we have Q-N and N-(Q-Cl). We interpret Q-N as a survival of the earlier non-classifier stage and N-(Q-Cl) as reflecting this form in its Cl-Q constituent.

The "Classical Chinese" literary language of the fourth and third centuries B.C. is called Late Archaic Chinese by Dobson. This language does not use classifiers and the usual construction is Q-N.[4] The Book of Odes (11th-7th century B.C.) shows, according to Dobson (1968), an intermediate situation in which all of the EAC alternatives appear but the classifier construction is limited to rén 'man'.

The indications are that the classifier construction did not disappear from the spoken language during this period but its non-occurrence is part of the stylistic emphasis on brevity and the omission of redundant items. It reappears in the written language of the Han dynasty (202 B.C.-221 A.D.) but still with the old word order. After the Han period the modern order Q-Cl-N begins to occur. Wang Li conjectures from the frequent appearance of the classifier construction in poetry of the T'ang dynasty (618-907 A.D.) that by this time the construction was compulsory. The shift to the contemporary state of affairs was probably complete by the ninth century, to judge from certain Buddhist texts qualified by Maspero as "popular" (Maspero, 1915). These texts are probably specifically Mandarin. They exhibit not only the modern order (Q-Cl)-N but also the use of the classifier with the singular demonstrative and the frequent use of ko, the Mandarin general classifier. On the other hand a more literary text of the same period analyzed by Schafer (1948) shows basically the same alternative constructions as those of EAC, namely N-Q-Cl, Q-N and N-Q.

Further historical evidence comes from Khmer. Modern Khmer has the order N-(Q-Cl); Old Khmer has the same order. This case is then compatible with our hypothesis in that it does not show (Cl-Q)-N which would contradict it by implying a shift from prenominal to postnominal position.

A somewhat more ambiguous case is Burmese. The present Burmese order is N-(Q-Cl). According to Hla Pe (1965),from the 15th century on, Pali exercised an intensive influence on Burmese, resulting among other things in a construction (Q-Cl)-(linking particle)-N. Presumably, the native Burmese construction is found earlier and has persisted into modern times; the case is thus like that of Khmer except for the intrusion of Pali influence.

Important evidence for a shift of the classifier phrase from postnominal to prenominal position, not based on direct historical evidence, is furnished by Gilyak. In this language there is a rule that with the numbers 1-5 inclusive Q-Cl follows the noun while for numbers larger than 5 the order is (Q-Cl)-N. In the speech of the younger generation, according to Panfilov (1962:191), the construction with 1-5 now usually exhibits the order (Q-Cl)-N so that this order has been generalized to all numerals. Thus we see the shift from postnominal to prenominal position in actual process in Gilyak at the present time. The hypothesis that this is the last stage of a shift from an earlier general postnominal position, in which the smallest, most unmarked numerals have shown the greatest resistance to an innovation in word order is strengthened by the existence of other similar cases in non-classifier languages. It was earlier suggested that as the general classifier spreads the classifier construction gets treated more and more like an ordinary numeral construction. In Gilyak the younger generation has also virtually accomplished the reduction to a single classifier.

It is planned to treat in more detail in a separate paper cases of the type just referred to. The following examples will indicate what is meant. In the Basque of San Sebastian, the number 'one' always follows the noun, 'two' may precede or follow and numbers larger than 'two' always precede. In the Basque dialects of France, only 'one' follows. Gavel (1929:116) notes that in certain dialects in Spain, however, all cardinal numbers are postposed, and he remarks, "Tel était peut-être primitivement l'usage basque général." In Classical Arabic 'one' and 'two' follow the noun, 3-10 may either precede or follow and for numbers greater than 10, the numeral always precedes the noun. Modern dialects show varying stages of a shift to exclusive Q-N order in Gutman scale or implicational chain fashion as shown in the following table in which underlining indicates the more frequent occurrence of a particular alternative and F and P mean "follows noun" and "precedes noun" respectively.

	1	2	3-10	>10
1.	F	F	F ~ P	P
2.	F	F	P	P
3.	F	F ~ P	P	P
4.	F ~ P	P	P	P
5.	P	P	P	P

Examples of stage 1 are Classical, Hassania (Mauretania) and Zanzibar, incidentally a good example of survival at the periphery. Stage 2 is exemplified by Fellahin dialects of Syria (Bauer) and Palestine (Driver). Stage 3 is found in Iraqi (Erwin) and Syrian (Cowell). Stage 4 is Moroccan and stage 5 is Meccan (Schreiber).

Another interesting example is Umbundu, a Bantu language of Angola, described in Valente (1964). The order N-Q is practically universal in Bantu languages and can be confidently reconstructed for Proto-Bantu. In Umbundu, with 1-5 the only permitted order is N-Q; with 6-99 the alternative constructions N-Q and Q-N are found. With numbers >99 only Q-N occurs.

The foregoing examples contribute towards the establishing of the hypothesis that when a sequence of the lowest numbers follow the noun, while the higher numbers precede in the same language, it is the former which represents the earlier rule which applied to all numerical phrases. Hence, it also serves to strengthen the hypothesis of a historical change from noun+classifier phrase to classifier+noun phrase in the case of Gilyak.

Thus far, all the evidence adduced for the shift from postposed to preposed classifier phrase has been directly historical or, in the case of Gilyak, an actually observed generational shift. Generally, however, in deciding such questions the most copious source is reconstruction based on the comparison of related languages. There are indeed language families within which some languages have preposed and other postposed order.

But to reconstruct postposed order would, of course, be in the present
context circular, for this is precisely what we are trying to verify. In
phonology we can often reconstruct phonetic features of proto-phonemes because we have independent evidence concerning the relative plausibility of
changes. But in the present instance, it is precisely the plausibility of
these processes which is at issue.

Two comparative cases of this sort are worth considering here, even
if no decisive conclusion can be drawn. One is that of the Thai language
family. In respect to word order in the classifier construction disre-
garding minor variations, these languages may be divided into two groups.
One, consisting of Thai proper (Siamese), Laotian, Shan of Burma and the
geographically isolated Khamti of Assam, postposes the classifier construction to the noun. The other group, containing Thai languages of
northern Vietnam near the Chinese border and also languages in China proper (e.g. Dioy of Kweichow province), has the preposed order. I shall
with slight arbitrariness call these the Southern and Northern type respectively. The question is whether it is possible to tell which type em-
bodies the earlier pattern. According to our general thesis it should,
of course, be the Southern type.

There is one further interesting and relevant fact. All Thai languages exhibit the same pattern of 'one' following while other numbers
precede the quantified item which was noted earlier in Basque and Arabic,
but within the classifier construction. For example, Laotian has 'orange
round-object one' for 'one orange', but for numbers larger than one,
'orange two round-object'. Correspondingly, expressions of time and distance, and others without a noun head show this same pattern, e.g. 'year
one' = one year, but 'two year' = two years. Our hypothesis here is that
the Thai classifier construction arose at a time before a shift from N-Q
to Q-N was complete, i.e. while the most unmarked number still followed
the noun. After that it remained, as it were in a fossilized state within
the classifier construction. A language of the Southern type will therefore regularly have 'orange round-object one' and 'orange two round-
object' as illustrated above for Laotian. The Northern languages have
'two round-object orange' with the preposed classifier phrase, as described earlier. However, for "one orange" they do not have '*round-object one orange', as might have been expected, but 'round-object orange
one'. The Northern languages have, however, the same pattern as the

Southern ones in expressions of time, distance, etc., e.g. 'year one', 'two year'.

The argument might be advanced that it is simpler to derive the Northern pattern from the Southern rather than vice versa. In the former instance 'orange two round-object' would change to 'two round-object orange', while 'orange round-object one' would put the classifier before the noun. Given once more a hypothesized greater resistance of the un-marked 'one', the position of 'one' would be unchanged and perhaps also be resistant because of the pattern 'year one' found throughout Thai.

The opposite course of change seems more complex and less plausible. If the Northern pattern were original, 'two round-object orange' would become 'orange two round-object', but 'round-object orange one' would become 'orange round-object one' with the classifier 'round-object' in-serted between 'orange' and 'one'. This seems less likely, though I hardly consider the argument decisive.

Another relevant comparative case is that of the Indo-Aryan lang-uages, whose classifier constructions are considered by Emeneau (1956) to be the source of similar constructions in Dravidian and Munda lang-uages. The construction is widespread in Indo-Aryan although absent from many of them. It is particularly prominent in the "Gaudian group" (Ben-gali, Assamese, Oriya, Bihari). In Bengali, as described in Ferguson (1962), the "classifiers", generally called determinatives in the gram-mars of Bengali and closely related languages, have the following main uses. They are suffixed to nouns and other substantival words such as adjectives and demonstratives to express determination (hence the name "determinative", e.g. boĭ-khana 'book-the'). In this usage the meaning can only be singular. For the plural definitive there is only a single possibility, the suffix -gulo, which does not figure as a classifier in the numeral construction. The singular definitives are chosen by the criteria common in numeral classifier systems, e.g. shape, human vs. non-human, etc. and also appear with the noun in numeral constructions, e.g. pāc-khana boĭ 'five flat-object book' with the same classifier khana as in boĭ-khana 'book-the' cited above. In this construction both Q-Cl-N and N-Q-Cl are possible with the latter being definite, e.g. boĭ pāc-khana 'the five books'.[5] Chatterji (1926) has discussed the earlier history of these classifying determiners. Since the determinative use is confined to the singular, one could conjecture that its suffixing

reflects the hypothesized earlier postposed order N-Q-Cl with as elsewhere the deletion of 'one'. Chatterji's historical data, however, give
no evidence of the former existence of an actually expressed 'one'. His
material does, however, seem to show a greater frequence of the postposed
construction in the numerical construction in the earlier literature. It
would require a careful examination of these texts to verify whether the
meaning, when postposed, was always definite in earlier times. In the
closely related Assamese, Babakaev (1961) cites the determinative construction as in Bengali, but only refers to Q-Cl-N in the numeral construction. Kakati (1941), however, gives with the numeral one expressed
and in the indefinite meaning both Q-Cl-N and N-Cl-Q. This suggests in
line with the earlier thesis regarding the greater stability of word order in the most unmarked numeral 'one', the last stages of the posited
shift from postposed to preposed position, with 'one' showing free variation while the other numerals precede. All this is admittedly precarious
and requires further research, particularly with informants, in these
languages.

We may summarize our results on this point, then, by asserting that
there are a number of cases of varying probability in which the evidence
points to a historical shift from postposed to preposed position and no
cogent counterevidence. It should be noted, however, that it is not
claimed that the construction always arises in the postpositive form.
Outside of probable cases of borrowing in the preposed form, there are
other instances in which the preposed form is found and in which there is
nothing to show that it was ever otherwise (e.g. Iranian languages).

It remains, however, to consider the factors involved in the synchronic favoring of the postposed classifier construction such that even
consistent SOV languages with preposed nominal modifiers, such as Japanese, have the postposed order as usual or exclusive. Diachronically,
also, as has been seen, there is evidence that the construction sometimes
originates with this order even though in the non-classifier construction
the quantifier precedes the noun.

One line of investigation is to consider languages in which variant
orders occur and to investigate what, if any, differences of function are
found. The evidence unfortunately is very fragmentary, but there are
some useful indications which might be pursued further.

In Palaung, an Austroasiatic language of Burma, described in Milne

(1921), there are two quantifier constructions: Q-N, or N-(Q-Cl), e.g. ār kū 'two fish' or kū ār tō 'fish two classifier'. As can be seen, these are the two basic constructions of Early Archaic Chinese if we exclude the N-Q list construction. No account is given concerning different meanings or functions of the two constructions. However, an examination of accompanying sentences and texts shows a further syntactic difference. In the Q-N construction Q always immediately precedes the noun, being indeed the only modifier which precedes. In contrast, the classifier phrase may follow the noun at a considerable remove, being separated from the noun by intervening elements which are not part of the noun phrase. The following is an example (Milne, 1921:39), Ta-ang gē leh Yang-ngūn sa-ram ō ār uaī kū, literally "Palaung they go Rangoon year this two three classifier.", i.e. 'A few Palaung are going to Rangoon this year.' The classifier phrase can be here viewed as adverbial, as though one said, 'The Palaung go to Rangoon this year fewly, or in small numbers.' It could seem natural also to have a pause between 'this' and 'two three classifier'.

In Standard Malay the classifier phrase is compulsory and may precede or follow the noun. Thus one may say either lima ekor ikan 'five classifier fish', or ikan lima ekor 'fish five classifier'. In general the grammars I have consulted seem to treat this as 'free variation'. I did, however, encounter a statement concerning this in one grammar of Malay, namely Pierce (1944), which contains the following statement (p. 34): "These coefficients (sci. classifiers) precede the noun except in the case where emphasis falls upon the numeral." Thus: ikan, lima ekor, 'fish, five of them'. Note that here the postulated pause is indicated by a comma.

Although Hungarian does not have numeral classifiers in the usual sense, alongside of the common set of numerals is one which is used optionally, but only with persons. This second set has a suffix -an or -en depending on vowel harmony considerations. This personal set usually follows rather than precedes the noun. Thus one can say either három ember jött, 'three man came' or az emberek hárman jöttek. In the latter case, unlike the usual numeral construction which governs the singular, 'man' is morphologically plural and the verb is also plural in agreement with it. Moravcsik (1971) notes that the suffix -an, -en is the usual one which forms adverbs from adjectives in Hungarian and that this con-

struction shares the same word order possibilities as the adverbial manner phrase. One can also say hárman jöttek az emberek just as one says
gyorsan jöttek az emberek, i.e. 'quickly came the men'. She seeks to
convey the feeling of the Hungarian numeral with -an or -en which she
calls adverbial by translating "the people three-ly came", etc.

Japanese has two alternative constructions in quantifier expressions.
One of these involves the classifier expression, a fused word with the
order Q-Cl, joined to the following noun by the marker no, e.g. sambiki
no inu 'three-animal no dog'. Otherwise no is a genitive marker and has
a variety of other uses, e.g. it can sometimes be paraphrased 'who is',
'which is'. In the other construction no is not involved and the Q-Cl
combination usually follows but is much freer in its word order properties.
It may, for example, be sentence initial but it usually precedes the verb.
Martin (1956:175) calls this latter type adverbial and tries to convey its
peculiarities into English by phrases like 'to the extent of ...'. It may
be further noted that grammars generally say that the no construction is
more definite in meaning.

Wang Li (1958) notes that where as in the Ts'o Chuan both the preposed and postposed constructions occur, the first is more closeknit while
in the latter the noun may be separated from the classifier by additional
items, e.g. mǎ níu jīe bǎi pī "horse cow all hundred classifier", in
which jīe 'all' separates the nouns from the classifier phrase.

In a general way, then, there seems to be a parallelism in the languages just discussed in the existence of two constructions. In one of
them the quantifying expression precedes the noun. The other is freer in
word order, tends to follow, to be associated with the verb or the sentence as a whole and may have a pause before it. I will hereinafter call
the first of these prenominal and the second adverbial.

Where there is a distinction within the language between a classifier
and non-classifier construction, the classifier construction is to be
ranged with the adverbial. Ainu is such a language. Either the numeral
precedes the noun directly without a classifier or it follows with the
classifier. In their grammar, Kindaiti and Tiri (1936) regularly translate the Ainu classifier construction by the Japanese pronominal no
phrase. Unfortunately, they give no account of the difference between
the two. Batchelor (1905) states that in Ainu the classifier construction
occurs only in an answer to questions and that there it is compulsory.

We hypothesize that the adverbial construction is, at least in those
languages in which the classifier construction arises through internal
processes, the basis for this construction. Essentially, the classifier
expression is in origin a quantifying phrase which serves as comment to
the head noun functioning as topic. This is seen most clearly in the
list construction where, for example, in Mandarin, Chao describes it as
involving a pause and supplying "under one's breath" of shr 'is', e.g.
'the oranges, (are) two round-objects; the bananas, (are) three long-ob-
jects, etc.' (the example is invented). Chao classifies this 'list construction' as S-P (subject-predicate).

The use of a classifier in these instances can be viewed as a device
which avoids the bare predication of numerals which is disfavored in many
languages. For example, in English one says 'there are two tables' rather
than 'the tables are two'. Dawson (1968:63) in his work on Classical
Chinese, commenting on a passage from Chuang-Tsu, makes the following observation: "Notice the word order here. Instead of saying 'the Brigand
Chih had nine thousand followers' the normal word order is as here 'the followers (of) the Brigand Chih (were) nine thousand men'." Here 'men' has the
role which develops into the classifier in the classifier construction.

The stages would be parallel to the hypothesized sequences of deep
structures in some generative accounts of the adjective phrase: 1) predication, 2) relative clause, 3) adjective follows noun, 4) adjective precedes noun. I do not mean to assert this represents a diachronic sequence in which each is a stage in which one of these constructions pre-
dominates. Several may coexist. The relative clause which has not thus
far been exemplified here is found in Gilbertese, a Micronesian language
which has both N-Q-Cl and Q-Cl-N where related languages have only N-Q-
Cl. Alongside of Q-Cl-N is a relative construction: 'book which two flat-
object'.

Finally, it may be conjectured that possessive classificational systems arise in much the same way as numeral classifier systems. In the
languages, all of them Austronesian or Amerind, which have such systems,
it is built on a division between alienable and inalienable possession
in which for inalienables (typically body parts and/or kinship terms) we
have a direct construction without classifier expressed by possessive
affixes, e.g. 'head-my', whereas alienable possession is expressed by a
superordinate possessed noun in apposition to the noun designating the

actual possessed object, e.g. 'dog my-animal'. One cannot in such language say 'my-dog' directly. For 'the dog is mine' one says 'the dog is my-animal'. The inalienables here play much the same role as time and length expressions in classifier languages. They retain the earlier construction. There is no "normal" expression such as *'the nose is mine' in answer to the strange hypothetical question *'Whose nose is this?'. These languages all have bound possessives. Hence there is difficulty in expressing possessive predication and this is circumvented by saying 'This dog is my-animal.' In principle the same factors are involved in languages without possessive classification where a single word, usually one meaning 'thing' or 'possession' is used here. An example is the construction in Egyptian Arabic with bitā9 'possession'. We have parallel to possessive classifier languages, elbēt bitā9i 'the house possession-my' but with kin terms ab-ī 'father-my'.

It is realized that the account given here is in many respects conjectural and that more investigation of these questions is needed. I hope, however, that the testing of the hypotheses advanced here will help to stimulate further work on these questions.

NOTES

1. The present study was supported by the Stanford Project on Language Universals founded by the National Science Foundation. I am also indebted to Charles Li for calling to my attention Wang Li (1958) and to Vicky Shu for providing a translation of the relevant chapter on the history of the classifier construction in Chinese.

2. There are, however, a few instances in which the classifier goes with the noun, but these usually involve the deletion of the numeral 'one'. An example is the Bengali and Assamese 'definitive' mentioned later in the paper, e.g. Bengali boi-khana "book-the", in which khana functions as a numeral classifier in other constructions. Efik seems to have an incipient classifier system in which the classifier is prefixed to the noun which itself is followed by a numeral. This case seems to involve something like English two grease spots as against two spots of grease.

3. See especially Greenberg (1963), Universal 18 which includes AN → DN with far greater than chance frequency.

4. Wang Li cites some examples of the classifier construction from the classical language but these are all from the Ts'o Chuan. However, its traditional date is disputed and it is generally now assigned to the Han period. It would seem that the occurrence of classifier constructions in it lends linguistic support to the hypothesis of its relatively late date. In fact the occurrence of the preposed order as an alternative suggests that it is even post-Han.

5. According to Chatterji (1926), Bengali can have in addition both N-Q-Cl with the connotation of definiteness, and to Q-Cl-N, which is the usual construction, additional constructions in which the classifier phrase has the internal order Cl-Q rather than Q-Cl. In this case the meaning is approximative, e.g. 'about three'. This is parallel to the Russian usage čelovek p'at' 'about five men' versus p'at' čelovek 'five men'.

BIBLIOGRAPHY

Babakaev, V. D. 1961. Assamskij jazyk. Moscow.

Batchelor, J. 1905. Ainu-English-Japanese dictionary. 2nd ed. Tokyo.

Bergh, J. D. van den. 1953. Spraakkunst van het Banggais. The Hague.

Chao, Y. R. 1968. A grammar of Spoken Chinese. U. C. Press, Berkeley and Los Angeles.

Chatterji, S. K. 1926. The origin and development of the Bengali language. Calcutta.

Dawson, R. 1968. An introduction to Classical Chinese. Oxford.

Dobson, W. A. C. H. 1959. Late Archaic Chinese; a grammatical study. Toronto.

------------------. 1962. Early Archaic Chinese. Toronto.

------------------. 1964. Late Han Chinese. Toronto.

------------------. 1968. The language of the Book of Odes. Toronto.

Emeneau, M. 1956. India as a linguistic area. Language, 32. 3-16.

Ferguson, C. A. 1962. The basic grammatical categories of Bengali. Ninth International Congress of Linguists, Cambridge. 881-90.

Forrest, R. A. D. 1948. The Chinese language. London.

Gravel, H. 1929. Grammaire basque. Bayonne.

Greenberg, J. H. 1973. Numeral classifiers and substantival number: problems in the genesis of a linguistic type. Working Papers on Language Universals, 9. 1-39. Stanford.

---------------. 1963. Some universals of grammar, in J. H. Greenberg, ed. Universals of Language. Cambridge.

Hla Pe. 1965. A re-examination of Burmese 'classifiers'. Lingua, 15. 163-85.

Kakati, B. 1941. Assamese, its formation and development. Gauhati.

Kindaiti, K. and Tiri M. 1936. Ainu-go hô gaisetsu. (Introduction to Ainu grammar). Tokyo.

Martin, E. 1956. Essential Japanese. Rutland, Vt.

Maspero, H. 1915. Sur quelques textes anciens de chinois parlé. BEFEO, 14.

Milne, L. 1921. An elementary Palaung grammar. Rangoon.

Moravcsik, E. 1971. Observations on cardinal numbers in Hungarian. Unpublished MS.

Panfilov, V. Z. 1962-5. Grammatika nivxskogo jazyka. Moscow.

Pierce, J. 1944. A simple but complete grammar of the Malay language. Singapore.

Schafer, E. H. 1948. Noun classifiers in Classical Chinese. Language. 24. 408-13.

Valente, J. F. 1964. Gramática umbundu. Lisbon.

Wang Li. 1958. Hàn-yǔ shǐ-gǎo. (Outline of the History of the Chinese language). Peking.

SERIAL VERBS AND SYNTACTIC CHANGE: NIGER-CONGO

by

Talmy Givón

1. Preamble[1]

This is an attempt to understand the great syntactic diversity
found in the Niger-Congo family in terms of diachronic syntactic change.
At the same time it is also an attempt to use the Niger-Congo data to
illuminate a number of universal principles governing complex changes
in grammar. Like most works of its kind, this is a first stab rather
than the last word on the subject. This is especially true in an area
where written records frequently do not exist or else seldom reach back
beyond a century or two. Nevertheless, I believe, interesting questions may be asked and specific hypotheses may be--albeit tentatively--
formulated.

The bulk of the paper will deal primarily with two diachronic processes. The first is the demise of SOV syntax in Niger-Congo and the
diverse syntactic typologies resulting from it. One of these typologies,
I would like to show, is verb serialization of a highly specific type.
The second diachronic process involves two mutually-linked changes which,
in combination, affect the lexico-syntactic typology of the language
in a rather profound fashion: The lexical re-analysis (or 'grammaticization') of verbs as prepositional case markers, and the correlated
change from a serializing to a non-serializing VP typology. This compound diachronic change has been shown (see Li and Thompson 1973a, b, c)
to introduce features of SOV syntax into an erstwhile SVO verb-serializing language.

I would begin by summarizing the evidence for reconstructing Proto-
Niger-Congo as an SOV language.

2. Evidence for SOV syntax in Niger-Congo

Of the major sub-groups of Niger-Congo, I have some data for all
except the Adamawa-Eastern group. All the others (Mande, West-Atlantic,
Benue-Kwa, Bantu) reveal unmistakable traces of earlier SOV syntax,
either in their current syntax or in their morphology.

2.1 Mande

For this group I have data from two languages, Kpelle[2] and
Bambara.[3]

2.1.1 Kpelle

This language has retained in part SOV syntax in its verb phrase. Thus for the accusative one finds:

(1) è   kâli   kaa   (SOV)
    he   hoe   saw
    'He saw the hoe.'

Locative, instrumental and manner phrases, however, follow the verb:

(2) è   lì   naa   (SVO)
    he   went   there
    'He went there.'

(3) è   wúru   tèe   à   bóa   (SVO)
    he   stick   cut   with   knife
    'He cut the stick with a knife.'

(4) è   tíi   kè   à   ńélɛɛ   (SVO)
    he · work   did   with   it's-good
    'He worked well.'

The benefactive and dative phrases also follow the verb:

(5) è   tíi   kè   k̂âloŋ-mi   (SVO)
    he   work   did   chief-for
    'He worked for the chief.'

(6) è   sɛŋ-kâu   tèe   k̂âloŋ-pə́   (SVO)
    he   money   sent   chief-to
    'He sent the money to the chief.'

In the noun-phrase syntax, all modifiers in Kpelle follow the noun with the exception of genitives and genitive-derived N-N compounds. Thus, the noun modifier which is most directly correlated to OV syntax in the verb-phrase -- the genitive[4]-- conforms to SOV pattern.

All case markings in Kpelle are post-positional, historically derived from nouns through the genitival N-N compound pattern. The list includes:

(7) | suffix | meaning | meaning as noun |
    | --- | --- | --- |
    | -sû | 'inside' | 'inside' |

-lá	'into'	'mouth'
-pôlu	'behind'	'back'
-túe	'toward'	'front'
-ŋá	'up'	'upside', 'top'
-kɔlɛ	'near'	'vicinity'
-mù	'down-into'	'lower part of house'
-pɔ́	'to', 'at'	'presence'
-mâ	'on'	'surface'
-mî	'for'	?
-yée	'from'	'hand'

The verb morphology shows an interesting mix. Modality notions
are marked by combinations of verb suffixes (suggesting an SOV origin
and verb prefixes (actually subject suffixes); suggesting an SVO origin).
Those are:

(8) prefixes: ˋ, ì , nì

suffixes: -ˊ, -a, -à, -aâ, -ì, -fá

While the relative size of the morphemes does not allow speculation as
to which -- prefix or suffix -- is the older pattern, one should note
that currently sentential complements in Kpelle follow modality verbs
(i.e., verbs such as 'begin', 'end', 'succeed', 'fail', 'want', 'refuse'
etc.). Since modality verbs are the most common universal source for
modality morphemes,[5] one may tentatively conclude then that the modality
suffixes of Kpelle represent a survival of the older SOV syntax in the
verb phrase, a pattern that is now limited to only the accusative.

2.1.2 Bambara

The syntactic situation in Bambara is almost identical with that
of Kpelle, and may be summarized as follows:

(a) Of nominal objects, only the accusative precedes the verb, while
     the benefactive, instrumental and locative follow;

(b) Of the four types of sentential complements ('know', 'order',
     'inform', 'begin'), only that of modality verbs ('begin') precedes
     the verb, while the others follow. This is clearly a more com-
     plete SOV pattern compared to Kpelle, where all four types follow
     the verb;[6]

(c) Three tense-aspect markers are prefixal to the verb, but they do not derive from modality verbs. Rather, they arise from a <u>locative</u> source (i.e. <u>be</u> 'be at', <u>bě-nà</u> 'be-at-come', <u>yě</u> 'be';

(d) Only one tense marker is verb suffixal, the past tense -<u>la</u>;

(e) All case-markings are post-positional. A number of those are clearly relatable to existing nouns, following the same genitival N-N compound pattern as in Kpelle;

(f) Of the noun modifiers, only <u>genitivals</u> precede the noun, again conforming to the pattern of nominally-derived post-positions, see (a) above.

One may tentatively conclude that the Mande group represents a slowly-receding SOV pattern, which is still strongly evident in the nominal and verbal morphology, but is otherwise confined -- in the syntax -- to the perennial 'hard core' of <u>accusative</u> objects, <u>genitive</u> modifiers and <u>infinitival</u> complements of modality verbs. A mere hint of serial-verb constructions is found in Bambara, and only in the <u>manner-instrumental</u> pattern, where the following variations may be observed:

(9) cὲ' yě waraba fàgà niń mùrú <u>yě</u> (non-serial)
   man past lion   <u>kill</u> <u>with</u> knife <u>be</u>
   'The man killed the lion with a knife'

(10) cὲ' yě mùrú <u>kὲ</u> <u>kà</u>   waraba fàgà ('serial')
    man past knife <u>do</u> <u>and</u>   lion   <u>kill</u>
    'The man took the knife and killed the lion'

(11) cὲ' yě waraba fàgè kègùn-yá <u>là</u> (non-serial)
    man past lion   <u>kill</u> clever-ness <u>at</u>
    'The man killed the lion cleverly'

(12) cὲ' yě kègùn-yá <u>kὲ</u> <u>kà</u>   wáraba <u>fàgà</u> ('serial')
    man past clever-ness <u>do</u> <u>and</u>   lion <u>kill</u>
    'The man used his cleverness and/to kill the lion'

The best guess is that the 'serial-looking' pattern in (10) and (12) above represents a more recent innovation. The presence of the consecutive marker <u>kà</u> in these constructions clearly attests to this.[7]

2.2 West-Atlantic

For this group I have data from two languages, Dyola (from Sapir, 1965) and Fula (from Arnott, 1970).

2.2.1 Dyola

In the synchronic syntax of Dyola, SVO is the overwhelmingly prevalent order. Thus accusative, benefactive, locative and dative nominal objects follow the verb, in both nominal and pronominal forms:

(13) inję   i-buję   ę-jam-ęn[8]
     I   A-killed   P-goat-the
    'I   killed the goat'

(14) si-tęy-ǫm
    they-ran-me
    'They ran for me'

(15) u-ja   u-walǫa di   ę-kǫlǫ-ŋ
    we-go   we-enter loc P-well-the
    'We will enter the well'

(16) na-sęn-ǫm-ǫ
    he-gave-me-him
    'He gave him to me'

(17) ni-sęn-ǫ e-be
    I-gave-him P-cow
    'I gave him a cow'

The complements of all modality verbs I could find, with the exception of 'finish', follow the verb -- and thus conform to the prevailing VO pattern:

(18) ni-mam-maŋ   tu-ri
    I-want   P-eating
    'I want to eat'

(19) na-nǫ: ęn   ą-kan dǫ
    he-can   P-doing it
    'He can do it'

(20)　na-tǫŋ　ʒ-lʉ
　　　he-started P-laughing
　　　'He started to laugh'

However, the OV pattern in the case of 'finish' suggests the older SOV syntax:[9]

(21)　ni-ri　i-ban
　　　I-eat　I-finished
　　　'I finished eating'

(22)　ba-rǫgǫr-ul　i-ban
　　　P-speaking-you I-finished
　　　'I finished speaking to you'

The current VO syntax of modality-verb complements is clearly attested from the fact that modality morphemes more recently derived from verbs comes as verb-prefixial:

(23)　u-ja　u-walǫa <u>di</u>　ǫ-kǫlǫ-ŋ　　（'go' > 'FUTURE'）[10]
　　　we-<u>go</u>　we-enter <u>loc</u>　P-well-the
　　　'We <u>will</u> enter the well'

(24)　na-lakǫ　a-jaw　　　　　　　　　　（'sit', 'live' > 'PROGRESSIVE'）
　　　he-<u>sit</u>　　he-go
　　　'He <u>is</u> going'

(25)　na-lankǫn a-kan dǫ　　　　　　　　（'continue' > 'CONTINUOUS'）
　　　he-<u>continue</u> he-do it
　　　'He <u>continued</u> doing it'

(26)　pa-ni-mạn　bu-rǫk　　　　　　　　（'be full' > 'CONTINUOUS'）
　　　FUT-I-be <u>full</u> P-working
　　　'I will <u>keep</u> working'

Other modality prefixes which precede the subject-agreement morpheme on the main verb (as in (26) above) are: <u>pan</u>- 'FUTURE', <u>lǫt</u>- 'NEG-FUTURE,[11] <u>takun</u>- 'NEG-IMPER', <u>mamb</u>- 'IMPER, OBLIG'. This is clearly the current, innovative pattern in the modality system, and the prefixal morphology is predictable from the V-COMP (VO) syntax of the verb phrase.

On the other hand, the presence of a number of modality <u>suffixes</u> in Dyola clearly suggest an older SOV syntax. These suffixes are the

'neutral' -ǫ, the perfective -į, the habitual-pase -ǫ:n, the negative
-ut: and the negative -erit. From the size of these morphemes one may
infer that the OV stage of the language is not far removed, at least
so far as sentential complements of modality verbs are concerned (this
again conforms to the fact that 'finish' follows its complement).

Another relic of the previous SOV syntax is, I believe, the extensive system of verb-deriving suffixes. Both semantically and morphologically this system is extremely reminiscent of the P-Bantu verb suffixes. Some of the representative examples are:

(27) Passive: ni-bon-i bon
                I-send-PASS-REDUP
                'I was sent'

(28) Causative: ǫ-posit-ǫy ǫ-jum-en-i
                 P-post-the A-stop-CAUS-PASS
                 'The post has been finished'

(29) Reciprocal: pa-nu-jm-ǫr-al
                 FUT-you-forget-RECIP-INCL
                 'You (inclusive) will forget each other'[12]

(30) Instrumental/means: pǎ-ni-rįben-ɰm u-jaama-w w-ǫla
                         FUT-I-follow-INST P-tracks-the A-his
                         'I will follow by means of his tracks'

(31) Recursive: -lo:p 'tie'   -lo:p-ɰl   'untie'
                               tie-REV

(32) Prepositional: pǎ-nǎ-rįn Dakar
                    FUT-he-arrive
                    'He will arrive in Dakar' (speaker not in Dakar)

                    pǎ-nǎ-rįn-ɰ Dakar
                    FUT-he-arrive-PREP Dakar
                    'He will arrive in Dakar' (speaker is in Dakar)

(33) Negative: -baj 'have',   -bǎj-ǎtį 'lack'
               -lak 'cook'   -lǎk-ǎtį 'refuse to cook'[13]

In the noun phrase syntax of Dyola, all modifiers--including the
genitive--follow the noun, as in:

(34) ę-jam-ęn mǫ
      P-goat-the my
      'my goat'

(35) si-jam-ęnas   s-eti   Alasan
      P-goat-the-pl A-of   Alasan
      'the goats of Alasan'

The verb 'be' -ęn and a locative preposition di are used for
locative-related functions, as in:

(36) injǫmę di burǫk
      I   be-with work
      'I am working', 'I am at work'

(37) bu-rǫk n-ęn di bǫ
      P-work I-be with it
      'I am working'

(38) u-nęŋ   ji-ñil-aj di ę-tabul-ęy
      you-put P-baby-the loc P-table-the
      'Put the baby on the table'

Another locative particle, bę, is also used in locative-dative contexts:

(39) na-jajaw bę ba:ba
      he-went loc there
      'He went (to) there'

The same particle bę may be also used as dative/purposive:

(40) na-sęsęn a-ñil-aw Bakari bę kakur
      he-gave   P-child-the Bakari for upbringing
      'He gave the child to Bakari for upbringing'

These patterns are quite reminiscent of those discussed by Lord (1973),
where erstwhile verbs meaning 'be at' or 'be with' become prepositions.
However, in general one finds no traces of real verb serialization in
this language, at least according to the available data. Something
resembling a serial pattern may be seen in:

(41) pą-nu-nąr-ul ka-ful u-gu:b
      FUT-you-take-you P-cloth you-cover
      'You will cover yourself with cloth'

I doubt that this item reflects more than the universal tendency, see discussion later on, for a language lacking many prepositions to begin a serial pattern which, eventually, may result in the re-analysis of many verbs as prepositions.

2.2.2 Fula

The current VP syntax of Fula closely resembles that of Dyola, above, with complements -- both nominal and sentential -- following the main verb. Similarly, all noun modifiers, including the genitive, follow the head noun. The innovative pattern in the grammar of nominals, as compared to Dyola, is the use of nominally-derived locative prepositions, obtained through the genitival-compound channel, with an overt possessive construction (surviving at least with pronouns):

(42) ba maa-ɗa   yeeso Bello
      like of-you   front Bello
      'like you'   'in front of Bello'

      haro maa-ɗɗe   dow maa-re
      presence of-them   top of-it
      'in their presence'   'on it'

Most of the relics of the erstwhile SOV syntax appear in the frozen morphology of Fula. The verb-deriving suffixes are of the same type as found in Dyola. Most modality markers appear as verb suffixes, with the sole exception of one or two. Frozen/bound noun morphology, in particular derivational morphology and compounds, again attest to an older MOD-N pattern. Thus in nominalizations one finds:[14]

(43) suud- 'hide'   > suud-ki 'hiding'
      juul- 'pray'   > njuul-ndam 'Islam'
      suk-a 'a youth' > sukkaa-ku 'youthfulness'
      mah- 'build'   > mah-oo-wo 'a builder'

Several kinship-term compounds strongly suggest a MOD-N syntax:

(44) mawn-iraa-wo 'older brother'
      miny-iraa-wo 'younger brother'
      jamw-iraa-wo 'owner'

In addition, several MOD-N compounds are attested in the lexicon:

woojagite- 'brave'   (wooja- 'be red', gite 'eyes')
hoyagikku- 'easy going' (hoya- 'be easy', gikku 'character')
jeeɗookuugal- 'silent' (jeeɗo- 'be silent', kuugal 'work')
mawnahoore- 'big-headed' (mawna- 'be big', hoore 'head')

To sum up, then, while the syntax of these languages is almost
entirely SVO, their bound morphology, in both the nominal and verbal
systems, clearly suggests an earlier SOV stage.[15]

2.3 Gur (Voltaic)

The data I have on Gur languages comes from Mooré (Peterson, 1971),
Sup'ide (Welmers, 1950), Baribe (Welmers, 1953) and Ware (Prost, 1968).
While in the first the evidence for an earlier SOV stage is confined to
the bound morphology, the last three exhibit a number of SOV traits in
their syntax as well.

2.3.1 Mooré

In the verb phrase of Mooré the syntax is VO, as in the <u>accusative</u>
and <u>dative</u> cases below:

(46) m̄ kóó   dáw   wamde
     I   gave man   calabash
     'I gave the man a calabash'

Further, one finds the distinct beginnings of serialization. Thus, for
the <u>dative-benefactive</u> case one may have either the non-serial (47) or
the serial (48):

(47) a <u>kõo</u>   aKulga   ligdã
     he <u>gave</u> Kulga   money
     'He gave the money to Kulge'

(48) a <u>dïka</u> ligdã n <u>kõ</u> (a) aKulgã
     he <u>took</u> money cons. <u>gave</u> (it) Kulga
     'He gave/brought the money to Kulga'

A similar variation is found in the <u>instrumental</u> case:

(49) a <u>wagã</u> nemdã   <u>ne</u> sᵾugã
     he <u>cut</u> the-meat <u>with</u> the-knife
     'He cut the meat with the knife'

(50) a djka syugã   n   wãg   nemdã
      he took the-knife cons. cut the-meat
      'He cut the meat with the knife'

A similar variation is found in the locative:

(51) a dygda   zak-ẽ
      she cook   compound-at
      'She is cooking at the compound'

(52) a bee   zak-ẽ   n   dygda
      she is   compound-at cons. cooking
      'She is at the compound cooking'

The use of the verb 'give' to mark the benefactive case is further
illustrated in:

(53) a tumda me   n   kõ   naabã
      he work   prt. cons. give the-chief
      'He is working for the chief'

(54) a kyu noaag n   kõ   naabã
      he killed chicken cons. give the-chief
      'He killed a chicken for the chief'

The presence of the co-existing serial and non-serial variants, as well
as the presence of the consecutive marker n in the serial constructions,
suggest that serialization is a relatively new phenomenon in Mooré.

    A number of facts about the language attest to an earlier SOV
syntax:

(a) The locative post-position -ẽ;

(b) The pre-noun position of genitival modifiers, as in:

(55) dáw   wamdé
      man   chicken
      'the man's chicken

(c) In the verbal morphology, auxiliaries with 'adverbial' meaning and
     larger size are verb prefixes, conforming to the current SVO syn-
     tax. But the tense-aspect markers, phonologically much more re-
     duced (usually to a single vowel), are suffixal.

2.3.2 Sup'ide

In this language SOV syntax is still attested for <u>accusative</u>
objects:

(56) mi <u>á</u> bili <u>nyá</u>
      I <u>past</u> slave <u>see</u>
      'I saw a slave'

(57) mi <u>ná</u> baga <u>wìì</u>
      I <u>prog.</u> house <u>look-at</u>
      'I am looking at a house'

In 'have' and 'bring' expressions the copular/prepositional particle
<u>ní</u> 'at', 'with' is used, and the syntax is SVO:

(58) mì ná <u>nyá</u> <u>ní</u> mpàè
      I prog. <u>be</u> <u>with</u> sheep
      'I have a sheep'

(59) mi â <u>pa</u> <u>ní</u> mpàè
      I perf. <u>come</u> <u>with</u> sheep
      'I brought a sheep'

In the verb morphology a number of modalities are prefixal, as
<u>ná</u> 'progressive', <u>â</u> 'perfective', <u>a</u> 'past' and <u>ma</u> 'remote past'. But
modal suffixes are also attested in the negative <u>-mḗ</u> and the present-
habitual <u>-li/-ni/-dí</u>.

In the noun-phrase syntax, while adjectives follow the noun, both
demonstratives and genitivals precede it:

(60) kàkǫ̀ bó?á
      lizard big
      'a big lizard'

(61) ñgé ǹkùù-ŋi
      this chicken-def
      'this chicken'

(62) mì-bíli-ŋi
      my-slave-def
      'my slave'

Bariba shows virtually the same situation, with accusative objects preceding the verb, genitivals preceding the nouns but demonstratives already follow it. In the modality system one again finds some modal prefixes: rӑ 'perfective', rӑ 'habitual', kú 'negative', n 'negative', but also a number of modal suffixes: -ӑ 'past', -e 'subjunctive', -ȅ 'habitual', -mǫ 'continuous', -re 'frequentative'.

2.3.3 Wara

In the verb-phrase syntax here accusative nominals still precede the verb, as in:

(63) i   laabo   lie:ni
      he   cow   kill-asp
      'He is killing a cow'

Modalities are all suffixal, including: -:ni 'progressive', -ni 'perfective past' (probably the copula ni 'be at/with'), -bo 'negative', -yi 'yesterday', -aa-ni 'future'. Some examples are:

(64) ninana nu i-pa yi   bo
      man   this A-come yest. neg.
      'This man did not come yesterday'

(65) ni   u   wan-aa-ni
      I   it   eat-fut.-perf
      'I will eat it'

In the noun-phrase, genitivals precede the noun, as in:

(66) i-klepie   n-tya   i-yibube
      it-fingers   I-it(pos)   he-eyes
      'its fingers'   'mine'   'his eyes'

(67) si-tӑ   kpi-usu-mӑ
      tree-root   chicken-eggs-P
      'the root of the tree'   'chicken eggs'

While adjectives and determiners follow the noun:

(68) pi   kamiya   ninana ngbe
      child good   man   the
      'a good child'   'the man'

While relative clauses follow the head noun, the demonstrative which functions as the subordinating particle comes <u>at the end</u> of the relative clause, as in:

(69) ninana ngbe pa <u>nu</u>
     man   the   came <u>that</u>
     'the man who came'

(70) ninana ngyeye mi nya pe   <u>nu</u>
     men   the   I   saw them <u>that</u>
     'the men that I saw'

As I have argued elsewhere (see Givón, 1972a), a clause-final position of a relative subordinator is a typical feature of a language in which the relative clause <u>precedes</u> the head noun. This feature in Wara may thus be viewed as another relic of the earlier MOD-N (SOV) syntax.

Copulative expressions also preserve traces of SOV syntax:

(71) n-tya <u>kę</u>   kpie <u>kę</u>   kpie <u>bo</u>
     I-of <u>is</u>   boy <u>is</u>   boy <u>neg.</u>
     'it's mine'   'it's a boy'   'it's not a boy'

(72) tumu-so kamu <u>ni</u>
     cultivation good <u>is</u>
     'cultivation is good'

(73) sambie n-gle <u>ni</u>
     knife my-hand <u>is</u>
     'I have a knife' (lit.: 'a knife is in my hand')

Locative complements of the copuli <u>ni</u> precede the copula. Further, Wara has developed a system of noun-derived locative <u>post</u>-positions, as in:

(74) i siyo <u>tu</u> ni   i siye <u>ngi</u> ni
     he tree <u>under</u> is   he tree <u>top</u> is
     'he is under the tree'   'he is on the tree'

Other post-positions used in Wara are -<u>ki</u> 'inside', -<u>solo</u> 'behind', -<u>ku</u> 'near', -<u>gle</u> 'for'. They are all nominally derived through the genitival compound pattern, as in the use of <u>gle</u> 'hand' as the bene-factive-dative 'for'/'to':

(75) i   na   simile   n-gle ni
      he   give dress   my-hand past
      'He gave me a dress'

While older modalities are all verb suffixal, arising presumably,
from the older OV syntax, sentential complements currently follow the
verb, for both cognition and modality verbs:

(76) i   waa ni   a   mi-fi   tamã
      he say past that you-buy dolo
      'He said that you bought dolo'

(77) i   suma   tumu-se   ni
      he know   cultivation asp.
      'He knows how to cultivate'

Given this VO syntax, it is not an accident that the language is beginning to develop modality prefixes from verbs, as seen in the auxiliary
use of 'go' in:

(78) i   laa   tumuse   ni
      he go   cultivation asp.
      'He went to cultivate', 'he cultivated'

To sum up the situation in Gur languages, one may say the following:

(a)   Clear traces of an older SOV syntax are attested in all these
      languages;

(b)   All of the languages studied here seem to be moving slowly away
      from SOV syntax, but at a different rate and in different manner;

(c)   Mooré seems to be developing verb serialization as a way of replen-
      ishing its now-largely-extinct suffixal case markings:

(d)   Wara, on the other hand, seems to go on replenishing its case-
      marking system through the genitival noun-compound pattern. Since
      genitives still precede the head noun in Wara, the currently inno-
      vated case markers are post-positional, thus still conforming to
      the older SOV (MOD-N) syntax.

2.4 Benue-Kwa

While the bulk of Benue-Kwa languages are currently SOV verb-
serializing languages, it is easy to spot in their morphologies as well

as syntax clear survivals of earlier SOV syntax. Thus, for example, Welmers (1970) reports a number of modality suffixes in Igbo, as well as a large number of verb-deriving suffixes, many of which indicate, semantically, a main-verb origin, much like the Bantu verb-suffixes.[16] Stahlke (in private communication) reports a number of SOV relics in Ewe, where some genitive modifiers (mostly pronominal) may precede the head noun. Further, some lexical compounds in Ewe preserve the older OV syntax of the verb phrase:

(79) agble-de-lá   'farmer'   tó hehe 'ear pulling'
      farm-go-agent   ear pulling

      nú-fyá-lá 'teacher'   alã dídí 'search for meat'
      thing-show-agent   meat search

      Tógó-tǫ́ 'person from Togo'
      Togo-person

This is also evident from the presence of SOV syntax in one tense-aspect:

(80) me-le suku yím   'I am going to the market'
      I-be   market go-prog.

Ewe also has nominal-genitive derived post-positions, as in:

(81) élè kplǫ la dzí   'It's on the table'
      it's table the sky

      medze gbedé gbǫ́ 'I am staying near the blacksmith's'
      I-stay blacksmith near

      wò áɸé le pósu lá megbé   'Your house is behind the
      your house is post the back   post office'

      wò nkú-me   'in front of you'
      your front-loc.

Further evidence for SOV relics in Benue-Kwa may be found in Hyman (1974). In the next section I will present the evidence from Bantu, a sub-branch of Benue-Kwa.

2.5 Bantu

In Givón (1971b) I have suggested that there exist strong indications that P-Bantu had undergone a stage of SOV syntax. Let me briefly recount the type of evidence which suggests this.

(a)   The pre-verb position of the bound object pronoun can best be
        explained by assuming that it is a frozen relic of an earlier SOV
        syntax. This closely parallels the case of Indo-European.[17]

(b)   Both semantic and morphemic arguments strongly suggest that the
        Bantu verb-suffixes are _verbal_ in origin.[18] Their suffixal
        position can only be explained by hypothesizing an earlier SOV
        syntax.

(c)   The more recent modality markers in P-Bantu languages are all
        prefixal. Their connection to modality-verbs is easy to estab-
        lish, the change from modality-verbs to 'auxiliaries' and tense-
        aspect markers is an ongoing process in all P-Bantu languages,
        and the verb-prefixal position corresponds well to the current
        VO syntax in the verb phrase. Most P-Bantu languages have any-
        where between 7-20 modality prefixes of this kind, but of those
        only 4-5 may be reconstructed to Proto P-Bantu.[19] This suggests
        that before the split of P-Bantu, it was already an SVO dialect.
        However, P-Bantu languages also have a number of modality suf-
        fixes. Their small size (in most cases only a vowel) and the
        fact that they are all reconstructible to Proto P-Bantu, strongly
        suggest that they represent the older pattern. But that pattern,
        in order to yield modality _suffixes_, must have been a stage of
        SOV syntax.[20]

(d)   Some evidence exists to suggest that relative pronouns in Proto
        P-Bantu were verb-suffixal. As I have argued in Givón (1972a),
        this is a feature typical of a MODIFIER-NOUN syntax in the noun
        phrase and an OV syntax in the verb phrase.[21]

(e)   A number of Bantu languages show a relic locative _post-position_.
        Historically this morpheme could have only arisen during a stage
        of SOV syntax.[22]

        To sum up, then, it seems that relics of an earlier SOV syntax
may be found in all sub-groups of Niger-Congo.

3.   The demise of SOV syntax in Niger-Congo
        In this section I would like to discuss the various syntactic
typologies that arose in the wake of the shift from SOV syntax in the

Niger-Congo family. Since verb-serialization, found mostly in languages
of the Benue-Kwa sub-group, is one of the major typologies which evolved
following the split of the family, I would like to begin this section
with an exposition of serial-verb constructions in Benue-Kwa.

3.1 Verb serialization in Benue-Kwa

In the past few years a protracted debate has been going on in
African Linguistics concerning the synchronic grammatical status of
serial verb constructions (for representative examples see Stahlke,
1970, Hyman, 1971, Bamgboṣe, 1972, 1973, Awobuluyi, 1967, 1972, 1973,
Lord, 1973, Elimelech, 1973, Williams, 1971). The argument has ranged
along three separate dimensions:

(a) Whether serial verbs are synchronically verbs or prepositions;

(b) Whether -- if they are analyzed as verbs -- they represent syn-
     chronically a coordinate or subordinate structure;

(c) Whether diachronically serialization arises from conjunction or
     from subordination.

While this paper will not concern itself directly with seeking answers
to these questions, it will nevertheless have some bearing on the manner
in which the questions themselves are asked.

In this section I would like to first illustrate some of the more
representative types of serial verb constructions in the Benue-Kwa
(henceforth BK) branch of Niger-Congo.[23] The languages are mostly of
the Kwa sub-group, with the exception of Bamilake (Fe'fe') which is of
the semi-Bantu sub-branch of Benue-Congo, and Efik which is presumably
of the Benue-Congo branch as well. The examples below are grouped
according to their case-functional label.

(82) ìywi <u>abà</u> utsì <u>ikù</u>   (Yetye, Stahlke, 1970)
      child ACT   door <u>shut</u>
      'The child shut the door'

(83) ìywi awá   utsì ikù   (Yatye, Stahlke, 1970)
      child <u>took</u> door shut
      'The child shut the door'

(84) wó <u>lá</u> shnáknû <u>bā ya</u> (Gwari, Hyman, 1971a)
he <u>took</u> pot <u>broke</u>
'He broke the pot'

(85) a̍ ka̍ <u>láh</u> ca̍k <u>nsá?</u> (Bamileke, Hyman, 1971a)[24]
he past <u>took</u> pot <u>come</u>
'He brought the pot'

(86) a <u>kò</u> <u>ncāk</u> wúzā (Bamileke, Hyman, 1971a)
he <u>take</u> <u>seek</u> food
'He is looking for food'

(87) ū <u>lá</u> dùkǔ <u>là</u> (Nupe, Hyman, 1971a)
he <u>took</u> pot <u>break</u>
'He broke the pot'

(88) bɔ́lá <u>mú</u> adé <u>wá</u> (Yoruba, Elimelech, 1973)
Bole <u>took</u> Ade <u>come</u>
'Bola brought Ade'

(89) adé <u>gbà</u> ajá <u>là</u> (Yoruba, Elimelech, 1973)
Ade <u>got</u> dog <u>save</u>
'Ade rescued the dog'

(90) <u>mén</u> òkpókoro ókò <u>dí</u> (Efik, Welmers, 1968)
<u>take</u> table that <u>come</u>
'Bring that table!'

<u>instrumental</u>

(91) ìywi <u>awá</u> òtsi <u>ikù</u> utsì (Yatye, Stahlke, 1970)
child <u>took</u> stick <u>shut</u> door
'The child shut the door with a stick)

(92) mo <u>fi</u> àdé <u>gé</u> igi (Yoruba, Stahlke, 1970)
I <u>took</u> machete <u>cut</u> wood
'I cut the wood with a machete'

(93) ū <u>lá</u> èbī <u>bā</u> nàkǎ (Nupe, Hyman, 1971b)
he <u>took</u> knife <u>cut</u> meat
'He cut the meat with a knife'

68

(94) ó <u>wèrè</u> ḿmà <u>bèé</u> ánù̩   (Igbo, Hyman, 1971b)
      he <u>took</u> knife <u>cut</u> meat
      'He cut the meat with a knife'

(95) ó <u>jî</u> ḿmà <u>bèé</u> ánù̩   (Igbo, Lord, 1973)
      he <u>used</u> knife <u>cut</u> meat
      'He cut the meat with a knife'

(96) á̩ ká̩ <u>láh</u> piě <u>ncwēe</u> mbá̩a (Bamileke, Hyman, 1971b)
      he past <u>take</u> knife <u>cut</u> meat
      'He cut the meat with a knife'

(97) ə <u>de</u> poma bəə me   (Twi, Christaller, 1875)
      he <u>?</u> stick <u>strike</u> me
      'He struck me with a stick'

(98) <u>dá</u> àkuri <u>sìbé</u> éto   (Efik, Welmers, 1968)
      <u>take</u> axe <u>cut</u> tree
      'Cut the tree with an axe!'

(99) <u>dúk</u> mótò ámì <u>ka</u> óbyò   (Efik, Welmers, 1968)
      <u>use</u> car this <u>go</u> town
      'Go to town with this car!'

(100) mō <u>mú</u> ìwé <u>wá</u> īlé [25]   (Yoruba, Lord, 1973)
      I <u>took</u> book <u>come</u> house
      'I brought the book home'

(101) ū <u>bīcī</u> <u>lō</u> dzūká   (Nupe, Hyman, 1971b)
      he <u>ran</u> <u>go</u> market
      'He ran to the market'

(102) ó̩ <u>gbàrà</u> ó̩só̩ <u>gáa</u> áhyà (Igbo, Hyman, 1971b)
      he <u>ran</u> <u>go</u> market
      'He ran to the market'

(103) ó̩ gà <u>àlá</u> <u>nà</u> Àbá   (Igbo, Lord, 1973)
      he future <u>return</u> <u>be-at</u> Aba
      'He will return to Aba'

(104) á̩ ká̩ <u>khẃa</u> ndw̄a <u>ngén</u> ntee (Bamileke, Hyman, 1971b)
      he past <u>run</u> <u>go</u> market
      'He ran to the market'

(105) ìywi <u>awá</u> ínyahwè <u>awa</u> ìtywi   (Yatye, Stahlke, 1970)
       child <u>took</u> book   <u>went</u> house
       'The child took the book home'

(106) ù <u>lá</u> dùkǔ <u>bě</u>   (Nupe, Hyman, 1971a)
       he <u>took</u> pot <u>come</u>
       'He brought the pot (over)'

(107) ó <u>jìri</u> ite <u>byá</u>   (Igbo, Hyman, 1971a)
       he <u>held</u> pot <u>come</u>
       'He brought the pot (over)'

(108) <u>mén</u> òkpókoro ókò <u>di</u>   (Efik, Welmers, 1968)
       <u>take</u> table   that <u>come</u>
       'Bring that table (over)!'

(109) <u>mén</u> òkpókoro ɛmì <u>kǎ</u> úfək m̄mə̀ (Efik, Welmers, 1968)
       <u>take</u> table this <u>go</u> house their
       'Take this table to their house!'

<u>benefactive-dative</u>

(110) mo <u>mú</u> ìwé <u>wá</u> <u>fún</u> ę   (Yoruba, Stahlke, 1970)
       I <u>took</u> book <u>come</u> <u>give</u> you
       'I brought the book for you'

(111) à ká <u>láh</u> càk <u>nsǎ?</u> hǎ ā (Bamileke, Hyman, 1971a)
       he past <u>take</u> pot <u>come</u> <u>give</u> me
       'He brought the pot for/to me'

(112) mo <u>sǫ</u> <u>fún</u> ǫ   (Yoruba, Stahlke, 1970)
       I <u>said</u> <u>give</u> you
       'I said to you'

(113) Òyé <u>mú</u> ìwé <u>wá</u> <u>bùn</u> mí (Yoruba, Stahlke, 1970)
       Oye <u>took</u> book <u>come</u> <u>present</u> me
       'Oye brought the book for me'

(114) mo bá ǫ <u>mú</u> ìwé <u>wá</u> ilé (Yoruba, Stahlke, 1970)
       I <u>benefited</u> you <u>take</u> book <u>come</u> house
       'I brought a book home for you'

(115) n<u>ám</u> útom ɛ̀mì n<u>ɘ̀</u> mì   (Efik, Welmers, 1968)
      <u>do</u> work this <u>give</u> me
      'Do this work for me!'

(116) y<u>ét</u> ùsan n<u>ɘ̀</u> ɛỹé   (Efik, Welmers, 1968)
      <u>wash</u> dishes <u>give</u> him
      'Wash the dishes for him!'

As argued by Stahlke (1970), Pike (1967, 1970) and Lord (1973),
there are strong grounds for believing that many serial verbs in Niger-
Congo cannot any more be analyzed synchronically as verbs. That is, in
many instances the diachronic process through which some verbs in a
series are re-interpreted as prepositional case-markers is already well
under way. I will return to this subject further below.

3.2 Strategies of syntactic change from SOV

Vennemann (1972) has suggested that when SOV languages lose their
original post-positional case markings, they would tend to shift to SVO
syntax. The Niger-Congo data surveyed above suggests that the situation
may be a bit more complex. To begin with, the one case-marker conspicuously absent in pre-serialization Niger-Congo languages is the <u>accusative</u>.
But as seen above, the accusative object is the most persistent SOV survival in languages which have otherwise shifted to SVO. On the other
hand, the locative, dative and instrumental, which are usually more
marked in the older Niger-Congo suffixal morphology, are the first ones
to shift to post-verbal (SVO) syntax. Hyman (1974) has suggested an
interesting explanation to this phenomenon. In his view SOV syntax is
limiting since, once the verb is uttered, no further <u>after-thoughts</u> may
be added. Since the accusative is the most prominent member of the <u>new-</u>
<u>information</u> in the verb phrases, it is not likely to be left behind for
an afterthought. On the other hand, locatives, adverbials, instruments
or benefactives, which are all part of the <u>circumstances</u> of the verb
phrase, are more likely to be forgotten and then picked up as afterthoughts. Hyman thus claims that one of the driving forces in the
syntactic change SOV > SVO may be the post-posing of after-thought
clauses.

On the other hand, much of the Niger-Congo data tends to support
Vennemann's (1972) hypothesis, though in addition the data also fur-
nishes further insights into the actual mechanisms involved in the change.

Thus, for examples, in all the erstwhile SOV languages surveyed above, those which retained a GENITIVE-NOUN syntax in the noun phrase and have used it, further, to create an extensive post-positional system derived from nouns, seem to have resisted the change away from SOV syntax much more than languages which did not develop post-positions. One may thus argue that a more viable development of case-markings here retarded the move to SVO. Further, one may thus view serialization and post-position development as two alternatives which a 'mature' SOV language (which lost most of its suffixal case markings) may take -- in order to re-stabilize the case-function marking system. While it is true that most serializing languages in Niger-Congo are currently SVO languages, at least one language, Ijo (Williamson, 1965) is both strongly SOV in its current syntax and strongly serializing, along a model extremely close to the other serializing KBC languages described earlier above. One may thus conceive of at least four alternative scenarios for a 'mature' SOV language, all of which seem to be attested in Niger-Congo:

(i)   A 'mature' SOV language may first shift to SVO (cf. Vennemann, 1972) and then develop verb-serialization as a means of marking case functions of nominals (most BK, Moreé);

(ii) A 'mature' SOV language may first shift to SVO and then develop prepositions via the genitival noun-compound pattern in a N-POSS syntax (Fula, P-Bantu[26]);

(iii) A 'mature' SOV language may re-develop a new generation of noun-derived post-positions via the genitival pattern and this will considerably retard the move toward SVO or even completely arrest it (Mande, Wara);

(iv) A 'mature' SOV language may develop serialization directly, without changing first to SOV (Ijo);

We are thus dealing with two independent processes which may either combine or appear quite separate from each other. Both are presumably motivated by the need, in a 'mature' SOV language, to cope with the perceptual problems arising from the attrition of post-positional case markings. The first, suggested by Vennemann (1972), involves a change in word order. The second alternative involves the morpho-lexical system of the language, by which new case markings are introduced either through the nominal system (pre- or post-position via the genitival pattern) or the <u>verbal system</u> (pre- or post-positions via verb serialization).[27]

3.3 Serialization, SOV and language classification

In this section I will discuss two language clusters which are, each in its own way, somewhat of an exception within Benue-Kwa. The first, Kru, is presumably a Kwa language. The second, Ijo, is either Kwa or Benue-Congo.

3.3.1 <u>Kru</u>[28]

Kru is classified by Greenberg (1963) as a Kwa language, though its exact link within Kwa has never been clear. In examining the syntax of Kru, one finds that in unembedded sentences as well as in most embedded environments SVO syntax prevails in the verb phrases:

(117) nyeyu-na   bla nyino-na
      man-the   beat woman-the
      'The man beat the woman'

(118) ni-jipwe <u>ka</u> nyeyuna bla nyinona
      I knew   <u>that</u> man-the beat woman-the
      'I knew that the man beat the woman'

(119) nyeyu-na <u>o</u> blaa nyino-na
      man-the PRO beat woman-the
      'The man who beat the woman'

(120) nyino nyeyu-na bla <u>na</u>
      woman man-the   beat <u>the</u>
      'The woman that the man beat'

(121) nyo-be <u>o</u>-bla nyino-na
      who-be <u>who</u>-beat woman-the
      'Who (is it that) beat the woman?'

However, in complements of modality verbs, as well as in other modality-related environments,[29] one finds the survival of SOV order:

(122) nyeyu-na <u>jilá</u> <u>boy</u> nyino-na bla
      man-the <u>want</u> <u>M</u> woman-the beat
      'The man wants to beat the woman'

(123) nyeyu-na mũ nyino-na bla
  man-the <u>go</u> woman-the beat
  'The man will beat the woman'

(124) nyeyu-na <u>si</u> nyino-na bla
  man-the <u>neg</u> woman-the beat
  'The man did not beat the woman'

(125) nyeyu-na bə́é nyino-na bla
  man-the <u>M</u> woman-the beat
  'The man may beat the woman'

(126) n-pni nyeyu-na bə́é nyino-na bla
  I-squeeze man-the <u>M</u> woman-the beat
  'I forced the man to beat the woman'

(127) nyeyu-na <u>yo</u> nyino-na bla
  man-the <u>M</u> woman-the beat
  'If the man beats (will beat) the woman...'

Possessive modifiers <u>precede</u> the head noun, as in:

(128) ná-ara   Seyŏ-<u>ŏ</u>-sra   nyeyuna-a-sra[30]
  my-house   Seyon-<u>of</u>-house   man-the-<u>of</u>-house
  'my house'   'Seyon's house'   'the man's house'

And the language has a viable system of case-marking post-positions derived from nouns via the genitival compound pattern, as in:

(129) sra-<u>kpŏ</u>   sra-<u>bweti</u>
  house-<u>top</u>   house-<u>under</u>
  'on top of the house'   'Under the house'

  tu-na-<u>sonti</u>   blokũn-<u>kli</u>
  tree-the-<u>under</u>   box-<u>inside</u>

  'under the tree'   'inside the box'

  sra-<u>ju</u>   sra-<u>de</u>
  house-<u>front</u>   house-<u>back</u>
  'in front of the house'   'behind the house'

  sra-<u>wakaey</u>
  house-<u>side</u>
  'near the house'

There is no serialization in Kru for the <u>locative</u>, <u>comitative</u>, <u>dative-benefactive</u> or <u>accusative</u> cases. A number of older affixes, some pre-positional and some post-positional, are used to signal these cases. The only case in which verb-serialization seems to exist is the <u>instru-mental/manner</u> case, where it co-exists together with two other patterns, one using no marking (only for manner adverbs), the other using an older instrumental suffix on the <u>verb</u>:

(130) o-<u>nu</u>   faka o-cyẽ swa   (serial$_i$)
       he-<u>use</u> knife he-<u>cut</u> meat
       'He used the knife to cut the meat'

(131) o-<u>nu</u>   faka   o-<u>ye</u>   swa-<u>cyẽ</u>   (serial$_{ii}$)
       he-<u>use</u> knife he-?   meat-<u>cut</u>
       'He used a knife in order to cut meat'

(132) o-<u>cyẽ</u>   swa-na   wula-wula   (unmarked, non-serial)
       he-<u>cut</u> meat-the speed
       'He cut the meat fast'

(133) o-<u>cyẽ-ne</u>   swa-na   faka   (verb-suffix, non-serial)
       he-<u>cut-INST</u> meat-the knife
       'He cut the meat with a knife'

That the verb-suffix pattern is the older, SOV-derived one, is evident from instrumental compounds, where it is obligatory on the verb. Thus:

(134) cyẽ-<u>ne</u> faka   ka-<u>ne</u>   klabasẽ
       cut-<u>INST</u> knife   draw-<u>INST</u> calabash
       'a cutting knife'   'water gourd'

It thus seems that in some case areas, where the old morphology of a 'mature' SOV language has become sufficiently eroded, Kru is innovating case markers via serialization. While in the case of locative markers it is innovating via the genitive compound, nominal route. The language, to quite an extent, is reminiscent of the Mande group or the Wara-like lan-guages in Gur, but it has gone much further along in changing to SVO syn-tax in the verb phrase. Further, the seeming viability of many of its SOV derived case markers helps explain the almost total lack of verb seriali-zation, which is definitely a new, limited pattern in the language so far. The implications of such a typology is that verb serialization may be introduced <u>gradually and partially</u>, invading first the specific areas where the older case-marking system has been lost. The situation in Mooré, see above, was quite reminiscent of such a pattern.

In terms of its genetic relationships, Kru may indeed be an early split off BK, and perhaps it may not even be a Kwa language altogether.

3.3.2 Ijo

To my knowledge Ijo is, so far, the only Benue-Kwa language found in which the old SOV syntax remained almost intact -- but in addition verb serialization has also developed. Williamson (1965) suggests that Ijo is equally close to Kwa and Benue-Congo. Thus the question of how its syntactic typology has become as unique as it seems to be is rather intriguing. Let me first illustrate some of the more typical serial-verb constructions in Ijo. All the data are taken from Williamson (1965).

Instrumental

(135) erí ogidi akị́-nị indi pẹị-mị́
      he machete take-asp. fish cut-asp
      'He cut a fish with a machete'

(136) áràụ́ zu-ye ákị buru teri-mí
      she basket take yam cover-asp
      'She covered a yam with a basket'

Manner

(137) ayá bara-ki àkị dúma tun
      new way take song sing
      'Sing a song in a new way'

Dative/benefactive

(138) dúma tun-nì a-pịrị
      song sing-asp her-give
      'sing a song for her'

(139) egberi gbá-nị ụ-pịrị
      story say-asp him-give
      'tell him a story'

(140) yé gba-nị ụ-dịá
      thing say-asp him-show
      'say a thing to him'

Accusative

(141) yé   akį-nį ụ-bęę́
       thing take-asp him-say
       'say a thing to him'

(142) wo-ákį   dúma tun
       him-take song sing
       'sing a song about him'

(143) óru   akį-nį ụ-karį-mọ
       deity take-asp him-invoke-dir[31]
       'invoke a deity against him'

Locatives/pattern i

(144) áru-bį   àkį tįn kaka-mọ
       canoe-the take tree tie-dir
       'tie the canoe to a tree'

(145) tarį-amá àkį-nį a-gbána-mọ
       blessings take-asp her-place-dir
       'bestow blessings upon her'

Locative/pattern ii

(146) erí amá dùo yọụ   bo-mí
       he   town go   paddle come-asp
       'he came paddling from town'

(147) erí ụwọ́ụ dùo wẹ́ni-mį
       he   road go   walk-asp
       'he walked along the road'

(148) erí utuú dùo kóro mu-mí
       he   roof go   fall go-asp
       'He went down from the roof'

(149) erí okí mu tọrụ   bẹįn-mį
       he   swim go river cross-asp
       'He went swimming across the river'

(150) erí árụ-bį   òki yọrọ-mį
       he   canoe-the swim round-asp
       'He swam around the canoe'

(151) ofóni-bi tọ́rụ fìn bẹ̀jn-mị
       bird-the river fly cross-asp
       'The bird flew across the river'

While the current serial-verb system is extremely productive in Ijo in creating surface markings for case relations, the remnants of the old post-positional system, drastically reduced, can still be seen. Thus, an old locative post-position -ọ is still used in some contexts:

(152) apu arụ́ ụ̀kụlọụ-bi-ọ sụ́o-kụmo-èé
       big canoe hold-the-loc enter-don't
       'Don't enter into the hold of the big canoe'

(153) wónì wo timi yọ́-bị̀-ọ mú-mị
       we   his stay place-the-loc go-asp
       'We went to the place where he stayed'

(154) ọmịnị wárị-bị̀-ọ̀ tími-mị
       they   house-the-loc stay-asp
       'They stayed at the house'

(155) kị́mị-bị déin-bi-ọ̀ bó-mị
       man-the   night-the-loc come-asp
       'The man came during the night'

This single locative post-position is, of course, semantically quite un-marked and perceptually rather small. So that the development of a new pattern, particularly of the type in (146) - (151), is to be expected.

The language also has two old comitative post-positions. The first, -mọ(mọ̀), is still used as a comitative case marker, as in:

(156) erí wo bịna ówèri-mọ bó-mị
       he   his relative man-with come-asp
       'He came with his (male) relative'

It is used in a variety of other subordinate-conjunction capacity, as in:

(157) wó warị là-mọ
       our house reach-with
       'as soon as we reached our house'

(158)   ọrọ   andaá   timị-mịnịịˆˋ-mọ
        they wrestle asp...-<u>with</u>
        'while they wrestle'

The post-position -<u>mọ</u> is also, not unpredictably, used in noun-phrase
conjunction, where it is suffixed to <u>both</u> conjuncts, the second one also
taking optionally the post-position -<u>kpọ</u>:

(159)   iwiˊri-<u>mọ</u>   nbẹle-<u>mọ</u>-<u>kpọ</u>   bóˊ-dọụ
        Tortoise-<u>with</u> Lizzard-<u>with</u>-<u>with</u> come-asp
        'Tortoise and Lizzard have come'

The post-position -<u>kpọ</u> is also used in other contexts as a sentence
subordinator:

(160)   i   tiˊmi-mi-ebe-<u>kpọ</u>
        you stay-asp-even-<u>if</u>
        'even if you stayed'

(161)   kẹnị   kịˊmịˋ-kpọ   ụwụ-ẹrịˋ-a
        one   man-<u>even</u> him-see-not
        'not one man (even) saw him'

(162)   bịsáˊ   òwei-kpọ
        that   man-<u>too</u>
        'that man too'

The use of -<u>kpọ</u> in both conjunctions and subordinations strongly suggests
that it came originally from a meaning such as 'with', and perhaps even
from a verb such as 'join', 'meet' etc.. Its phonological shape is extremely reminiscent of a similar radical discussed in detail by Lord (1973).
At any rate, even if both -<u>mọ</u> and -<u>kpọ</u> were initially comitative particles,
they probably did not participate in the marking of the <u>instrumental</u> and
<u>manner</u> cases, so that the latter are now marked by the verb 'take', 'use'
in serialization.

All noun modifiers in Ijo precede the noun, including relative
clauses and genitives. The language thus has the potential of developing
post-positions via two channels: The genitival-nominal channel, and the
serial-verb channel. As I shall argue below, many of the serial verbs in
Ijo as in other BK languages are well on their way to becoming case-marking
morphemes. One could perhaps claim that the noun 'way', as used in (163)
below, is already functioning as a manner post-position:

(163)   yé   nimi-a   bara-kị̣ mị̣e
        thing know-not way   act
        'act foolish<u>ly</u>', 'act <u>in a</u> know-nothing <u>way</u>'

Similarly, one could easily foresee the development of a post-position
from the noun 'top', as in:

(164)   wárị̣ ọgọnọ-bị́-ọ̣
        house top-the-loc
        'on top of the house'

     The more than 10 tense-aspect modalities in Ijo are verb-suffixal
and mostly sentence final, conforming to the verb final or COMP-V syntax
of an SOV language. The language is undergoing change in this respect,
however, since all modality verbs with the sole exception of 'want' currently <u>precede</u> their complement, as in:

(165)   ọmị̣nị́ barị́-nị̣ andá-mị̣
        they <u>repeat</u>-asp wrestle-asp
        'They wrestled again'

(166)   srị́ <u>kụrẹị́</u>-nị̣ eke fị̣-á
        he   can-asp   rat eat-not
        'he couldn't eat Rat'

(167)   erị́ <u>séri</u> you-mi
        he   <u>begin</u> cry-asp
        'He began to cry'

(168)   arị́ <u>lá</u> bo-mi
        I   <u>succeed</u> come-asp
        'I succeeded in coming'

Similarly, in causative expressions, the verb 'cause' precedes its complement, as in:

(169)   wónị̣ u-<u>mị̣ẹ́</u>-nị̣ indi <u>dị̣ẹ</u>-mị́
        we   him-<u>make</u>-asp fish <u>share</u>-asp
        'We made him share the fish'

Here, however, one may wish to argue that the conjunctive origin of verb
serialization explains the seeming violation of the OV pattern, so that
in (160) and (161) the order of the verbs in the series follows the

logical time-order, with the 'complement' verb being the result of
'cause':

(170)   wónì uru ak<u>í</u>-n<u>ì</u> <u>ч-mịẹ́-nì</u> uru <u>bou-mí</u>
        we   wine <u>take</u>-asp him-<u>make</u>-asp wine <u>drink</u>-asp
        'We made him drink the wine'

3.3.3 <u>Syntactic typology and genetic classification</u>

Within the Benue-Kwa sub-family, almost all sub-groups are currently
SVO verb-serializing languages. The three conspicuous exceptions are:

(a)   Kru (non-serializing, some stable SOV features surviving);

(b)   Ijo (almost total SVO syntax);

(c)   Bantu 'proper' (no verb serialization);

While Kru may be a more early offshoot of Kwa, the same may not be said
of Ijo and Bantu. The closest relatives of Bantu 'proper' in Benue-Kwa,
the so-called Semi-Bantu languages (Bamileke), show verb-serialization
of the general Kwa type. So does Tiv, of the Bantoid sub-branch. One is
thus forced to conclude that, if the present linguistic classification is
indeed correct, the split of Bantu from the Bantoid group occurred <u>prior</u>
to the development of verb-serialization. Further, since Ijo has developed
verb serialization but retained an almost complete SOV syntax, the split
of Ijo from Benue-Kwa must have occurred when the group was still largely
an SOV dialect. Thus, as Hyman (1974) has suggested, verb-serialization
in Benue-Kwa must be viewed as an <u>areal</u> phenomenon which developed in most
of the sub-groups of BK <u>independently</u>, after their split. Similarly, the
change from SOV to SVO within Benue-Kwa occurred largely <u>after</u> the major
sub-branches have split from each other.

4.   <u>Gradual change away from verb serialization</u>

In this section I would like to show that the verb-serializing languages of Benue-Kwa may be undergoing a gradual syntactic-lexical change,
from SVO verb-serializing syntax towards a non-serializing verb phrase in
which erstwhile verbs are re-analysed as prepositions. By way of introducing the subject, I would like to cite some recent work by Charles Li
and Sandra Thompson.

4.1   The Chinese connection

Li and Thompson (1973a,b,c) have recently described an interesting
case of syntactic change in Chinese, from an older SVO stage to the current largely SOV of Mandarin.   The situation may be summarized as such:

(171) | stage | syntax | VP type | case marking | verb-morphology |
|-------|--------|---------|--------------|-----------------|
| Archaeic (12-14th Century BC) | SVO | serial | by verbs | monosyllabic (simple) |
| Mandarin | SOV | non-serial | by prep. | polysyllabic (complex) |

The hypothesis concerning the syntactic change involved then runs as
follows:

(a)   The first verb in a series was re-interpreted as a 'grammatical
       particle' or prepositional case marker, as eg. the active-verb
       marker ba (erstwhile 'take'), the passive marker bèi (erstwhile
       'receive', 'submit') as well as a large number of so-called 'co-
       verbs, to be mentioned later on;

(b)   As a result, the object NP which followed the erstwhile first verb
       in the series, now precedes the main verb (which used to be the
       second in the series).   SVO thus changed to SOV;

(c)   Syntactically (though not necessarily semantically)[32] this may be
       also interpreted as a change from a complex (embedded) VP to a
       simplex (unembedded) one;

(d)   In Chinese, these syntactic-lexical changes seem to have also been
       linked with the rise of complex (polysyllabic) verbs as against the
       previous simplex (monosyllabic) ones.   While many of the complex
       verbs represent the compounding or re-lexification of V-N combina-
       tions, others also represent the compounding of V-V combinations.[33]

Parts (a), (b) and (c) of the hypothesis may be illustrated as follows:

82

(172)   serializing-SVO   non-serializing-SOV

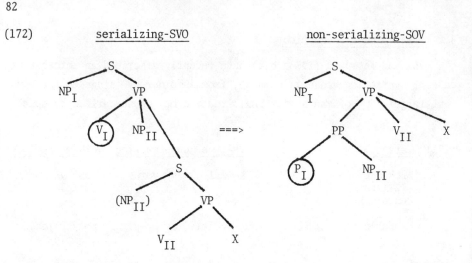

In the space below I would like to suggest that both the re-analysis of
serial verbs as prepositions (or, in Ijo, post-positions) and the subsequent introduction of some SOV syntactic features into the verb phrase are
currently underway in Benue-Kwa. While these two processes, one lexical
and the other syntactic, are linked, they should nevertheless be considered in isolation, since the first does not automatically precipitate
the second

      Li and Thompson (1973c) have discussed a large class of morphemes
in Chinese labeled 'co-verbs', which are clearly derived from erstwhile
serial verbs. In many respects they already 'behave like prepositions'.
I would first like to outline the reasons why a diachronic change of this
type should be expected to go gradually, rather than be a 'one shot'
affair.

4.2   Criteria for verb ---> preposition re-analysis
      One should consider three types of criteria:

(a)   Semantic criteria.- The shift from verb to preposition usually in-
      volves the depletion of some semantic material out of the erstwhile
      verb. For example, while 'take' in (173) below may be interpreted
      almost literally, the same 'take' in (174) may not:

(173) ma   fi   àdá   gé   igi   (Yoruba, Stahlke, 1970)
       I   took machete cut tree
      'I cut the tree with a machete'

(174) mo <u>fi</u> ǫgbǫ̀n <u>gé</u> igi   (Yoruba, Stahlke, 1970)
       I <u>took</u> machete <u>cut</u> tree
       'I cut the tree cleverly'

Similarly, when the verb 'give' is used as the <u>benefactive</u> case-marker,
it may be interpreted more or less literally in (175) below, but much
less so in (176):

(175) mo <u>mú</u> ìwé <u>wá</u> fún ǫ   (Yoruba, Stahlke, 1970)
       I <u>took</u> book <u>came</u> gave you
       'I brought the book for you'

(176) mo <u>sǫ</u> <u>fún</u> ǫ   (Yoruba, Stahlke, 1970)
       I <u>said</u> <u>gave</u> you
       'I said to you'

For the same case in Mooré, 'give' may be still interpreted literally in
(177) but not at all so in (178):

(177) a <u>dika</u> ligdã n <u>kõ</u> aKulga   (Mooré, Peterson, 1971)
       he <u>took</u> money-the cons. <u>give</u> Kulga
       'He gave the money to Kulga'

(178) a <u>tumda</u>-me n <u>kõ</u> naabã   (Mooré, Peterson, 1971)
       he work-asp. cons. <u>give</u> chief-the
       'He worked for the chief'

Similarly, while the use of 'take' above in the instrumental case may
retain some of its literal meaning in (179), its used in the accusative
case in (180) has lost much of the meaning of 'take':

(179) ìywi <u>awá</u> òtsi <u>ikù</u> utsì   (Yatye, Stahlka, 1970)
       child <u>took</u> stick <u>shut</u> door
       'The child shut the door with a stick'

(180) ìywi <u>awá</u> utsì <u>ikù</u>   (Yatye, Stahlke, 1970)
       boy <u>took</u> door <u>shut</u>
       'The boy shut the door'

In the same vein, while <u>abà</u> in Yatye may have once held a verbal meaning
such as 'take', 'act' or 'cause' that meaning is not necessarily evident
in its use for the accusative case:

(181) ìywi <u>abà</u> utsì <u>ikù</u>   (Yatye, Stahlke, 1970)
child <u>?</u> door <u>shut</u>
'The child shut the door'

The same is true of the 'splitting-verb' <u>gbà</u> in Yoruba, which may have
originally had the meaning of 'get' or 'take', but that meaning is not
evident in its use for the accusative case in:

(182) bọ́lá <u>gbà</u> adé <u>gbọ́</u>   (Yoruba, Elimelech, 1973)
Bola <u>?</u> Ade <u>believe</u>
'Bola believed Ade'

Finally, while the literal meaning of 'go' (something like 'move by foot')
may be still discernible in (183) below, it is much less discernible in
(184) and (185), using the same locative <u>dùo</u>:

(183) erí amá <u>dùo</u>-mi   (Ijo, Williamson, 1965)
he town <u>go</u>-asp
'He went through town'

(184) erí bení <u>dùo</u> yọụ-mị   (Ijo, Williamson, 1965)
he water <u>go</u>   paddle-asp
'He paddled through the water'

(185) erí utuú <u>dùo</u> <u>kóro</u> mu-mi   (Ijo, Williamson, 1965)
he roof <u>go</u> <u>fall</u> go-asp
'He went down from the roof'

Many other examples of this type may be found in Lord (1973) and Li and
Thompson (1973c).

(b)   <u>Morphological criteria</u>.- One of the first things that may happen to
erstwhile serial verbs, as suggested in Li and Thompson (1973c) and Pike
(1970) is loss of ability to take normal verb affixes, such as modalities,
subject agreement or object pronouns. This process is obviously gradual,
so that a verb may lose its ability to take some affixes but not all at
the same time.

(c)   <u>Syntactic criteria</u>.- When a verb is semantically reanalysed as a
preposition or a conjunction, quite often it remains, for a long time after
wards, at its original serial-verb position. A good example for this is
the sentence conjunction <u>sì</u> in Yoruba, as in:

(186) John jẹ ẹ̀wà Bill sì jẹ ẹran   (Yoruba, Elimelech, 1973)
      John <u>ate</u> beans Bill <u>and</u> <u>ate</u> meat
      'John ate beans and Bill ate meat'

While nowhere in the language is <u>sì</u> currently used as a verb, its position
is clearly that of a serial verb, with a presumed original meaning such
as 'join', 'add', 'repeat' etc. Its frozen serial-verb syntactic position
has a number of syntactic consequences. Thus, as Elimelech (1973) points
out, neither VP conjunction nor gapping may be done in Yoruba. That is,
it is impossible to delete the verb under identity (gapping) or conjoin
it under subject identity (VP conjunction). This is most likely the result of <u>sì</u> , while semantically a conjunction, still retaining the 'frozen' syntactic behavior of a verb.

     Another example, again from Yoruba, involves the topicalization of
verbs through fronting. As Elimelech (1973) points out, if the serializing verbs <u>gbà</u> '≠get' and <u>mú</u> 'take' are used, the second verb in the series
cannot be fronted. But if the serializing <u>ti</u> 'hold' is used, the second
verb may still be fronted.

     Similarly, Elimelech (1973) also shows that constructions with
<u>gbà</u> '≠get' don't show conjoined variants any more, while those with <u>mú</u>
'take' and <u>ti</u> 'hold' still do:

(187) bọ́lá gbà adé gbọ́
      Bola <u>acc.</u> Ade <u>believed</u>
      'Bola believed Ade'

(188) ≠bọ́lá gbà adé, bólá sì gbọ́ ọ
      Bola <u>acc.</u> Ade, Bola <u>and</u> <u>believed</u> him

(189) bọ́lá mú ìwé wá
      Bola <u>took</u> book <u>came</u>
      'Bola brought the book'

(190) bọ́lá mú ìwé, bọ́lá si wá
      Bola <u>took</u> book, Bola <u>and</u> <u>came</u>
      'Bola took the book and (then) came'

The three serial verbs thus show a definite gradation as to which one behaves 'less like a verb' syntactically: <u>ti</u> > <u>mú</u> > <u>gbà</u>. While they may
have arisen from a very similar semantic background, <u>gbà</u> is much further
along the way to becoming a preposition.

Finally, Lord (1973) cites a number of cases where the NP conjunction arises, historically, from the serial verb 'join', 'meet', 'be with', 'be at', and is still also used as the subordinating preposition 'with'. In these situations, the violation of Ross's Co-ordinate-Structure-Constraint is allowed. That is, a structure that may be semantically already co-ordinate, behaves syntactically like a sub-ordination. This clearly reflects the verbal origin of the conjoining morpheme.

4.3 The case for a gradual shift from serialization

Given the situation outlined above, one could indeed argue that:

(a)   It is highly unlikely that a verb would change suddenly into a preposition by all semantic, morphological and syntactic criteria at once. One thus expects to find, for a long time, many different types of intermediate cases in the language, whereby some criteria a 'particle' is already a preposition, while by other it is still 'a verb'. In particular, morphological and syntactic behavior is likely to lag behind the more progressive semantic re-analysis, and thus quite often represent vacuous relics of the older semantic situation.

(b)   Different serial verbs may enter the verb > preposition re-analysis at different times and perhaps at different pace, so that one may find a whole range of mixed type in a language in which serialization is slowly being re-interpreted. This is precisely what Li and Thompson (1973c) have shown in Chinese, and undoubtedly also the situation in the serializing languages in Niger-Congo (see also Pike, 1970).

All this, of course, makes the synchronic analysis of the grammar of serializing languages rather messy, and it is not an accident that the argument concerning the current status of serial verbs in various languages has been lengthy and, largely, unresolved. But this is precisely the situation one expects when a language is in the middle of a protracted diachronic change.

Another type of argument which is, in my mind, rather futile, is the one undertaken in Hyman (1971b), Williams (1971), Stahlke (1970) and Li and Thompson (1973b) concerning the co-ordinate vs. sub-ordinate status of serial-verb constructions. While Hyman (1971b) makes a strong

case for the co-ordinate <u>diachronic origin</u> of serial-verb constructions,
it is quite clear that languages do proceed to re-analyse <u>semantically</u>
the relationship between two erstwhile coordinate ('consecutive')
clauses, so that eventually a non-coordinate semantics prevails. But
for a long time afterwards, as I have shown above, the very same language
may retain the <u>morphological</u> evidence of the earlier 'consecutive' structure in the form of a conjunction or a consecutive/infinitival form of
the second verb. They may also retain a number of co-ordinate <u>syntactic</u>
traits. And while the presence of these morphological and syntactic
relics is useful in the diachronic argument concerning the origin of
these constructions, it is often misleading when used in the synchronic
argument concerning their current status.[34]

4.4 Shift from serialization and shift to SOV syntax

One should also point out that the lexical-semantic re-analysis of
verbs as case markers does not automatically result in the introduction
of a total SOV syntax into the language. Rather, the results may often
be a <u>mixed</u> syntactic typology. For example, if the <u>first</u> verb in the
series gets re-analyzed as a preposition, one indeed gets a situation
in which at least one nominal object phrase now precedes the second --
main -- verb. In the case of (191) below this results in a new syntax
with <u>instrumental</u> objects preceding the now-main verb, while in (192)
the result is an <u>accusative</u> preceding the verb:

(191) mo <u>fi</u> àdá gé igi   (Yoruba, Stahlke, 1970)
       I   took machete <u>cut</u> wood
       'I cut the wood with a machete'

(192) ìywi awá utsi <u>ikù</u>   (Yatye, Stahlke, 1970)
       child <u>took</u> door <u>shut</u>
       'The child shut the door'

On the other hand, it is equally common to find the <u>second</u> verb in the
series being re-analyzed as preposition. In which case, while the semantic process of making one verb a preposition and making the other verb
in the series <u>more complex</u> semantically may be of exactly the same
general type, the lexical-semantic re-analysis does not result in the
introduction of SOV syntax into the language. This may be seen in the
<u>dative</u> and <u>locative</u> cases below:

(193) mo sǫ fún ǫ   (Yoruba, Stahlke, 1970)
       I said gave you
       'I said to you'

(194) ū bīcī lō dzūkó   (Nupe, Hyman, 1971b)
       he ran go market
       'He ran to the market'

As suggested by Lord (1973), the choice as to which verb will be
re-analyzed as a preposition and which one will remain the main verb
depends on the relative semantic prominence within a particular construction. That is, the evaluation of one component of the event as 'the
main event' and the rest as 'the circumstances'. Thus, the very same
verb 'take' may be in one construction re-analyzed as the instrumental
or accusative preposition, ceding the center of the stage to the other
verbs, as in (191) and (192) above. But it may also, in the case of a
construction such as (195) below, be retained as the main verb and increase its own syntactic complexity, while the other verb -- in this
case the locative one -- is re-analyzed as a preposition:

(195) mo mú ìwé wá ilé   .   (Yoruba, Lord, 1973)
       I took book come house
       'I brought the book home'

Finally, the very same case-marking verb may appear either as the
first or the second verb in the series, presumably in a way initially
determined by considerations of discourse structure and semantic prominence. As a result of this, one may find in a serializing language
cases in which the same case-object may either precede or follow the
main verb:

(196) ìywi abà òtsi ikù utsi   (Yatye, Stahlke, 1970)
       child took stick shut door
       'The child used the stick to shut the door'

(197) íywi ikù utsì ni òtsi   (Yatye, Stahlke, 1970)
       child shut door with stick
       'The child shut the door using a stick'[35]

Similarly:

(198) mo mú ìwé wá fún ẹ   (Yoruba, Stahlke, 1970)
       I took book came gave you'
       'I brought the book for you'

(199) mo bá ẹ mú ìwé wá ilé   (Yoruba, Stahlke, 1970)
       I benefited you took book came house
       'I benefited you by bringing a book home'

Similarly:

(200) a dʉgda zak-ẽ   (Mooré, Peterson, 1971)
       she cook compound-at
       'She is cooking at the compound'

(201) a bee zak-ẽ n dʉgda   (Mooré, Peterson, 1971)
       she is compound-at cons. cooking
       'She is at the compound cooking'

Clearly, then, the lexical-semantic re-analysis of verbs into prepositions in a serial-verb construction is likely to create semantically more-
complex verbs in all cases (see discussion further below), and is also
likely to introduce some SOV syntax into an erstwhile SVO-serializing
language. But it is not likely to introduce a complete SOV syntax into
the language. For one thing, it has no effect on the syntax of the
noun-phrase (see discussion below). For another, it is not clear what
the effect would be on the order of sentential complements within the
verb phrase (i.e., complements of modality and cognition verbs in particular).

5. Discussion

In the remaining space I will discuss a number of more general
implications for diachronic syntax arising from the data and syntactic
changes described above.

5.1 On the relation between VP and NP word order

One of the universals proposed in Greenberg (1966) is that languages with an OV syntax in their verb phrase would also tend to show
MOD-N syntax in their noun phrase. It has been generally assumed (as
e.g., in Vennemann, 1972b) that this is the work of analogy. It seems
to me that this assumption is open to a number of challenges, and that

in fact there exists a much more explanatory hypothesis to account for this syntactic parallelism.

By far the most common survival of 'OV traits' in the noun phrase of erstwhile SOV languages is the pre-nominal position of <u>genitival</u> or <u>genitive-derived</u> modifiers. In Givón (1971a) I have suggested that the genitive modifiers may be viewed as the <u>spearhead</u> of the invasion of OV syntax into the noun phrase. I have further suggested that this is the result of VP nominalization rules, which create OBJECT-VERB nominal compounds (eventually re-analysed, in many languages, as NOUN-NOUN compounds). Thus, for example, the compound-pattern in English responsible for the likes of 'chimney sweep', 'lion tamer', 'street cleaning' or 'garbage disposal' is a relic of the old OV syntax of English. The process by which the OV order in the verb phrase is transferred to a GEN-N order in the noun phrase may be summarized as:

(202)

```
        VP                          NP
       /  \          ==>           /  \
    (NP)    V                  (GEN)    N
```

From here on analogy becomes a more viable concept. That is, if a language has 'real possessive' nominals involving the same genitive case marker as the one used in the nominalizations described above (as is indeed the case in Indo-European, Semitic, Bantu as well as many and maybe most other languages), then the analogy from the genitive derived by nominalization on to the 'true possessive' genitive is a more viable hypothesis. Further, if the morphology of adjectives involves a nominal-genitive typology, then perhaps it is easier to extend the analogy on to adjectival modifiers.

A second possible pattern connects adjectives directly to the verb phrase syntax, again via nominalizations. In many languages adverbs of manner are based directly on adjectival stems, as the case is certainly for many English adverbs of the type "knowingly', 'knowledgeably', 'hard', 'good', 'perversely' etc. Now, if in an SOV language manner adverbs precede the verb, then when verb phrases containing those adverbs are nominalized, the resulting nominal construction is likely to yield an ADJ-N combination, as in the English pattern seen in 'hard working', 'long suffering', 'later arrival', late comer' etc. This process may be again summarized as:

(203)

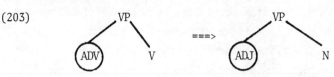

Finally, one should point out that another nominalizing channel may also explain how relative clauses get to precede the head noun in an OV language. This channel involves the transmission of sentential verb complements into noun complements, accounting for current English patterns such as:

(204) 'his refusal to surrender the tapes to the committee'
'arguments about the propriety of firing Cox'
'knowing that compliance with the courts mean disaster'
etc.

In this fashion, large clauses which have retained much of their sentential syntactic structure are introduced as modifiers to the noun which is derived from nominalization of the erstwhile verb. The old preposition used in the old verb-complement structure is quite often changed to the genitive 'of' or its equivalents, as in:

(205) 'giving books to children' ∿ 'the giving of books to children'
'his knowledge about Watergate' ∿ 'His knowledge of Watergate'
'his tendency to run away' ∿ 'his tendency of running away'
etc.

Further, if a language uses the same subordinator (as in English that, Hebrew she, Spanish que etc.) for both complements of cognition verbs ('know') and relative clauses, then the nominalization of cognition verbs together with their complements would further enhance the syntactic-morphological similarity between noun-complements derived from nominalizations and embedded, true relative clauses is further enhanced, thus further opening the door for possible analogy. Thus:

(206)

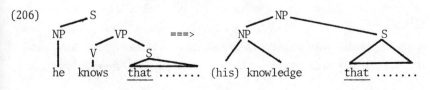

In fact, one may wish to argue that nominalization patterns of this type
may be one possible channel through which erstwhile V-COMP subordinators
are transferred or spread into the morphology of relative clauses.   At
any rate, it is quite clear that there is no need to resort to direct
analogy between the HEAD-COMPLEMENT order in the verb phrase and the
HEAD-MODIFIER order in the noun phrase in order to explain the parallel-
isms. The nominalization model is much more explanatory, on one hand,
and makes much weaker claims, on the other.[36] Further, it is also clear
that the analogy is _unidirectional_ -- from VP syntax to NP syntax -- but
not vice versa.[37]

An interesting corroboration of the dependent status of NP syntax
vis-a-vis VP syntax may be found in Amharic, a language which has undergone a change VSO > SOV as a result of contact with the Cushitic substratum in Ethiopia (for details, see Hudson, 1974). In this language
the definite article is a noun suffix, but if a modifying adjective precedes the noun, the definite article is suffixed to that adjective:

(207) mäkina-w   'the car'
       car-the

       tilig-u mäkina   'the big car'
       big-the car

In Ge'ez, the closest attestation to the VSO pre-Amharic, one finds the
modifying adjective -- with the definite suffix -- _following_ the noun.
One may thus conclude, as is indeed attested in Ge'ez, that the definite
article -u was an NP-final morpheme. In time it became _bound_, and when
the older N-ADJ order changed to ADJ-N, the definite article moved with
the adjective to which it was bound. Now here is the rub -- in Amharic
the definite article appears as a _verb suffix_ when a noun is modified by
a (preceding) relative clause:

(208) mäkina yä-gazzä-w säw   'The man who bought a car'
       car   that-bought-the man

Since we know that the definitizer -u/-w was an NP-suffix in pre-Amharic,
the only way of explaining its verb-suffix position in relative clauses
is by assuming that there existed a stage in Amharic in which N-MOD was
still the prevailing order within the noun phrase, but the VP syntax has

already changed to SOV, so that in relative clauses the verb was positioned clause-final, and therefore also NP-final:

(209)

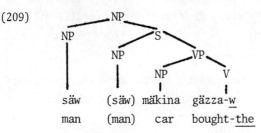

		mäkina	gäzza-w
säw	(säw)	mäkina	gäzza-w
man	(man)	car	bought-the

NP syntax is thus shown to lag behind VP syntax.

If the model presented above is indeed valid, then one suggestion
made by Li and Thompson (1973a) cannot be supported. This concerns the
supposed role of relic SOV syntactic patterns in the NP of Archaeic
Chinese in facilitating the later change to SOV via the serial-verb re-
analysis channel. If the relation of VP and NP syntax is indeed unidi-
rectional, and if the causal determination is from VP syntax to NP syntax,
then this suggestion is untenable.

5.2 The diachronic drift along universal semantic rivers

The data from both Niger-Congo and Chinese show an amazing consistency as to what verbs may give rise to what prepositions. This may be
summarized as in the following table:

(210)

case	verb(s)	preposition sense
accusative	'take', 'get', 'do'	ACC.
locative	'go', 'come' 'exit', 'leave' 'enter' 'be at', 'live', 'sit' 'rise', 'climb' 'fall', 'descend'	'to' 'out', 'from' 'into', 'in' 'in/at/on' 'up' 'down'
dative/ benefactive	'give', 'present', 'send'	'to/for'
benefactive	'benefit', help'	'for'
Instrumental	'take', 'hold', 'use', 'be with'	'with'
Associative	'be at', 'be with', 'join', 'meet'	'with'
Conjunction	'be at', 'be with', 'join', 'meet' 'add', 'repeat'	'with', 'and' 'and'

At this point it should be noted that the re-analysis under consideration involves <u>two</u> opposite processes:

(a)   As discussed above, the <u>depletion</u> of much (though not all) of the semantic contents of a verb in the series (or all verbs except one), so that it becomes 'a preposition';

(b)   The parallel <u>enrichment</u> of the semantic contents of the remaining verb, so that it becomes -- both semantically and syntactically -- more complex.

The overall semantic complexity of the entire construction remains virtually unchanged, so that (211) and (212) below, for example, carry the same information, roughly[38] (Yatye, Stahlke, 1970):

(211)   ìywi <u>abà</u> utsi <u>ikù</u>   (before re-analysis)
        child <u>took</u> door <u>be-shut</u>
        'The child caused the door to shut'

(212)   ìywi <u>abà</u> utsi <u>ikù</u>   (after re-analysis)
        child <u>ACC,</u> door <u>shut</u>
        'The child shut the door'

Similarly, (213) and (214) carry roughly the same information (Nupe, Hyman, 1971b):

(213)   ū bīcī <u>lō</u> dzūkó   (before re-analysis)
        he <u>run</u> <u>go</u> market
        'He ran (going) to the market'

(214)   ū bīcī <u>lō</u> dzūkó   (after re-analysis)
        he <u>ran</u> <u>to</u> market
        'He ran to the market'

However, in (211) the verb <u>ikú</u> 'be broken' is an intransitive/stative verb, while in (212) the same verb -- as a result of the depletion of <u>abà</u> 'take' -- has become a causative, transitive verb, syntactically requiring an accusative object. Similarly in (213) the verb <u>bīcī</u> 'run' is an intransitive verb of the 'be at motion' type, while in (214) the same verb -- as a result of the depletion of <u>lō</u> 'go' -- has become a more complex motion verb, semantically 'motion in relation to a target' and syntactically requiring a locative object.

Finally, it is also possible to show cases in which the erstwhile verb does not only get depleted -- but also completely disappears, leaving the surviving verb visibly more complex. In Ijo, for example (see Williamson, 1965), one finds the following alternation, in which the serial verb 'take' gets deleted altogether in one variant:

(215) erì   opuru-mǫ   àki   tǫbǫ́ų́ pìrì-mi
      he   crayfish-the take   boy give-asp
      'He gave the crayfish to the boy'

(216) erí   opuru-mǫ-ni tǫbǫ́ų́   pìrì-mi
      he   crayfish-the boy   give-asp
      'He gave the crayfish to the boy'

The causative 'make' may be also deleted (or 'incorporated') completely, as in:

(217) erí   uru   akí-nì̧ u-mì̧ȩ́-nì̧ uru bou-mí
      he   wine   take-asp him-cause-asp wine drink-asp
      'He made him drunk with wine', 'He made him drink the wine'

(218) erí   uru   akí-nì̧   u-bou-mǫ́-mì̧
      he   wine   take-asp him-drink-cause-asp
      'He made him drink the wine'

In (218) above the lexical 'make', 'cause' was deleted while the verb bou 'drink' acquired a causative-suffix (-mǫ). That suffix is not always a replacement of the deleted 'make', but in other instances co-exists with it, as in:

(219) erí   árų-bì̧ mì̧ę̧ bilemǫ-mi
      he   canoe-the make sink-asp
      'He made the canoe sink'

(221) erí   árų-bì̧ bìlemǫ-mí
      he   canoe-the sank-asp
      'He sank the canoe'

Thus while the verb "sink" in (219) is an intransitive verb, the verb 'sink' in (220) -- following the deletion of 'make' -- is a transitive, causative verb.[39] It may well be that the accusative-marking serial verb is the one that would tend most to 'incorporate' in this manner (i.e., disappear entirely rather than remain as a case marking). This is in keeping with the more univerally known tendency for the nominative and accusative cases to be morphologically less-marked than the other cases in a fixed order SVO or SOV language.

One may offhand argue that an opposite process than the one outlined above, i.e., a process of prepositions becoming semantically enriched until they turn into verbs, is at least in theory possible. For this I find only rare, sporadic examples, such as in English 'up' as in 'to up the ante', or 'off' as in 'off with his head', or 'away' as in 'away with the rascal'. There are a number of reasons why such a process should be extremely rare. To begin with, when a verb loses much of its semantic contents and becomes a case marker, in due time it also loses much of its phonological material, becomes a bound affix and eventually gets completely eroded into zero. It is thus unlikely that a more crucial portion of the information contents of the utterance -- i.e., the semantic contents of a verb -- will be entrusted to such a reduced morpheme. Further, while the process of change through depletion is a predictable change in language, its opposite -- enrichment or addition -- is not. The argument here is rather parallel to the uni-directionality of transformations of deletion in syntax. It also closely parallels arguments in phonology, concerning the relative feasibility of strengthening/addition vs. weakening/deletion of, say, consonants.

5.3 Creolization and universals of diachronic semantics

In the preceding section I suggested that the process by which serial verbs become prepositions (or post-positions) is a highly predictable one, where certain types of verbs always give rise to certain semantic 'cases'. In this section I would like to cite a unique body of evidence which, to my mind, further supports the hypothesis outlined above. The evidence is derived from Krio (Williams, 1971), a Creole language spoken in Sierra Leone (for further discussion of this, see Williams, 1971 and Givón, 1973b). The grammatical substratum for this language is probably of the verb-serializing Kwa type. The vocabulary is largely derived from English, and the most exciting thing about it is the way in which this vocabulary has been integrated into Kwa-type serial-verb constructions. What we see is a rather systematic re-interpretation of certain, complex English lexical verbs into serial constructions, to

eventually yield more simplex prepositions, of the type found in Kwa languages. Thus, consider the following cases:

locative

(221) a bin <u>tek</u> di buk <u>go</u> na skul
     I past <u>take</u> the book <u>go</u> loc. school
     'I <u>brought</u> the book <u>to</u> school'

(222) <u>fes</u> di kəpə <u>kam</u> <u>ət</u> na di tebu
     <u>fetch</u> the money <u>come</u> <u>out</u> loc. the table
     '<u>Bring</u> the money <u>from</u> the table'

(223) i de <u>waka</u> <u>go</u> na tən
     he prog. <u>walk</u> <u>go</u> loc. town
     'He is <u>walking</u> <u>to</u> town'

(224) wi de <u>kəl</u> di dəkta <u>kam</u>
     we prog. <u>call</u> the doctor <u>come</u>
     'We are <u>sending</u> <u>for</u> the doctor'

dative/benefactive

(225) <u>kɛri</u> di kəpə <u>go</u> <u>gi</u> am
     <u>carry</u> the money <u>go</u> <u>give</u> him
     '<u>Take</u> the money <u>to</u> him'

instrumental

(226) di man <u>tek</u> di tIk <u>bit</u> di bobo
     the man <u>take</u> the stick <u>beat</u> the boy
     'The man beat the boy with the stick'

Thus, even though English has no verb-serialization of this type, and
even though English had all the available prepositions to mark these
cases, the Kwa speakers chose to borrow from English exactly the same
verbs which in a Kwa language would contribute -- via semantic depletion --
to the rise of the very same prepositional case markings. Since it is
rather obvious that no explicit instruction in this use of English vocabulary was ever given to these speakers, it seems to me that this pattern of borrowing can only be explained by assuming that the 'universal
patterns of semantic drift' discussed in the preceding section were indeed present in the competence of the Krio speakers, together, of course,

with their serial-verb grammatical competence as speakers of Kwa languages.

5.4 Serialization in SOV languages

Among all verb-serializing languages Ijo stands as a lone exception. It certainly shows that the combination of almost a complete SOV syntax together with an extensive pattern of verb-serialization is not only possible, but is indeed attested. This combination is nevertheless rare, and one would like to know why. That is, why should a 'mature' SOV language, which has largely lost its old post-positional case-marking inventory (and has resisted the Vennemann-predicted change to SVO), choose to regenerate its case system most commonly via the genitive-nominal channel, rather than via the serial-verb channel?

It seems to me that, in part at least, the answer lies in the potentially great syntactic perceptual complexity of a serializing SOV language. This is already evident in Ijo itself, where in a number of serial constructions a string of verbs/post-positions appear together at the end of the sentence, as in:

(227) erí ama dùo yọụ bo-mí
      he town go paddle come-asp
      'He came paddling from town'

(228) sụ arụ́-mọ̀ bo-yemi yọ-bị ụ-mịẹ́ tamamaa ká-mị
      war canoes-the come-asp fact-the him-take surprise be-much-asp
      'The coming of the war-canoes surprised him very much'

(229) erí utuú dùo kóro mu-mi
      he roof go fall go-asp
      'He went down from the roof'

(230) eri wílií akanaj tịẹmo-mị
      he wheel turn stop-asp
      'He stopped the wheel from turning'

(231) erị̄ tọrụ tẹịn di-mi
      I river flow look-at-asp
      'I looked at the river flowing'

This type of syntax resembles in many ways the perceptual properties of self-embedded structures, and would have been further compounded if it

were also maintained in the complements of modality verbs. But, while
the verb final and sentence-final position of all tense-aspect modalities
strongly suggests that at an earlier stage the complements of modality
verbs used to <u>precede</u> the verb in a full SOV pattern, modality verbs in
Ijo nowadays -- with the exception of 'want' -- precede their complements.
The language, it seems, has taken a definite step toward rectifying --
in part -- the perceptual complexity arising from the combination of verb
serialization and SOV syntax.

Another complement type also follows the verb -- that of 'make'/
'cause', as in:

(232) wóni u-<u>mi̩e̩</u>-ní̩   indi <u>di̩e̩</u>-mí̩
       we him-<u>make</u>-asp fish   <u>share</u>-asp
       'We made him share the fish'

If a conservative SOV order had prevailed, one would have expected the
perceptually much more complex order of:

(233) we him fish <u>share</u> <u>make</u>

In fact, the presence of a causative verb-suffix in Ijo (see (218), (219),
(220) above) strongly suggests that at some earlier stage in its history
the verb 'make'/'cause' <u>followed</u> its complement. But in the current
serial-verb stage 'cause' precedes its complement verb. Here one may
argue, however, that if serial-verb constructions arise from consecutive-
conjunction sources, then the syntax in which the result verb follows the
causation verb is a natural consequence of the temporal order of consecutivization. Indeed one finds a similar order in Ijo when verb serialization is of the cause-result type, as in:

(234) erí bé̩le̩ sù̩ru̩ pám-mo̩-mi̩
       he   pot   <u>wash</u> <u>be-clean</u>-cause-asp
       'He washed the pot clean'

(235) áràu̩ fí̩ai̩-mo̩   tù̩o̩ bin-mo̩-mi̩
       she   foods   <u>cook</u> <u>be-plenty</u>-cause-asp
       'She cooked plenty of food'

The stative verbs <u>pám-</u> 'be clean' and <u>bin</u> - 'be plenty' again require here
the old causative suffix -<u>mo̩</u>, reminiscent of the older, more strictly OV
syntax. But currently the result clause follows the causation verb.

If SOV verb-serializing languages are rare, then it should be equally rare to find a language in which case-marking post-positions are derived directly[40] from verbs. Ijo is the only one I know of. It thus seems that while prepositional case markings arise from either nouns or verbs, post-positional ones are likely to arise mostly from nouns -- given the low probability of SOV-verb-serializing languages.

NOTES

1. I am much indebted to Charles Li, Sandy Thompson, Bill Welmers,
Larry Hyman, Russ Schuh, Carol Lord, Baruch Elimelech, Ọladele Awobuluyi
and A. E. Meeussen for many helpful comments on earlier versions of
this manuscript. The opinions expressed below remain strictly my own,
as well as the possibly many ways in which I inadvertently misinterpreted data derived from the work of others.

2. For the Kpelle data I am indebted to Bill Welmers (in personal
communication).

3. For the Bambara data I am indebted to Karen Courtenay and Ibrahima
Coulibaly (in personal communication).

4. The relation between OV syntax in verb phrases and MOD-N syntax in
noun phrases will be discussed later on.

5. For a general discussion of this process, see Givón (1971a, 1973a).

6. While the 'classical' SOV languages, such as Amharic, Japanese or
Navajo show a 'complete' pattern, with the verb being the last element
in the verb phrase, it is not altogether clear whether a language is
'only a trace/receding SOV language' when only the accusative precedes
the verb. However, when complements of modality verbs conform to an
SVO pattern (i.e., follow the verb) while bound modality morphemes are
verb suffixes, it is reasonable to assume that at an earlier stage the
complements of modality verbs preceded the verb (i.e., conformed to a
more complete SOV syntax). The Kpelle situation clearly suggests that.

7. What I am really assuming here is that all serial constructions
ultimately arise, historically, from conjoined or 'consecutive' constructions. Hyman (1971a) claims that the presence of overt 'consecutive' morphemes in constructions somehow differentiate them, at the
synchronic typological level, from 'true' serial constructions. In my
mind the proper context in which to view this survival is diachronic
rather than synchronic. That is, a construction which initially arises
from a conjoined ('consecutive') source may retain evidence to this
effect in its bound morphology long after it has been semantically
re-analysed as a single action/event.

8. In the orthography I will use here the five tense (higher) vowels
will be rendered as: i, e, a, o, u, while the corresponding lax (lower)
vowels will be rendered as į, ę, ą, ǫ, ᶙ. Vowel length is indicated by
/:/. The symbol A- stands for subject agreement on the verb. P- stands
for the noun-class prefix. The noun suffix in this language is used as
the definitizer.

9. Hyman (in private communication) has suggested the presence of the
verb 'finish' after its (sentential) complement does not necessarily
indicate an OV syntax, since a temporal order could easily explain this
sequence, i.e., 'I ate and/until I finished' for (58), and 'I spoke to
you and/until I finished' for (59). This is certainly possible.

10. The use of 'go' as a future modality marker is probably facilitated
by the purposive use of 'go'--which syntactically places it in the same
class as modality verbs, e.g.: na-ja   a-rambęe ǫm

                                 he-go   he-help-me
                                 'He went to help me'

The same pattern is also observed with -jǫm 'come'. For further discussion of the role of this intermediate pattern see Givón (1973a).

11. The NEG-FUTURE modality lęt- is still attested as a verb meaning
'not be', as in: fu-ri-af   fu-lęt
                  P-food-the A-not-be
                  'There is no food'

In general one would expect here the older modality prefixes to precede
the subject agreement, as pa- in (63), and not carry a subject agreement of their own. While the more recent 'auxiliaries', as in (60),
(61), (62) and -męn 'be full' in (63) still behave more like verbs,
that is, they take a subject agreement morpheme. Note also that while
the complements of modality verbs in (55), (56), (57) and (59) come in
an infinitival/nominal form, the complements of the 'auxiliaries' in
(60), (61), (62) and (63) come in a finite, subject-marked form. One
can clearly see here the categorical transition: modality verb >
'auxiliary' > modal prefix.

12. The form of the suffix -ǫr 'each other' here suggests a <u>pronominal</u> origin in Dyola (rather than the comitative-conjunctive origin suggested earlier for the P-Bantu <u>na</u> suffix).

13. This is further evidence that complements of modality verbs, in this case 'refuse', used to precede the verb, i.e., SOV syntax.

14. While it is true that Fula has only noun-class suffixes, their systematic use in nominalizations is often related to an erstwhile MOD-N syntax in the noun phrase. For a more general discussion of this, see Givón (1971a).

15. Bill Welmers (in private communication) has informed me that in Gola, a West-Atlantic language from Liberia, while accusative object follow the noun, accusative object pronouns precede the noun. Thus: wò nan yɛmê <u>wo-jəuñ</u> 'He saw a-woman', but: wò nan <u>min</u> yɛmê 'He saw me'. This may indeed represent a relic of the ACCUSATIVE-VERB order of earlier times.

16. A number of the compound verbs cited by Welmers (1970) seem reminiscent of the Mandarin resultative compounds (see Thompson, 1973), e.g.: -kwàcì 'push shut' from -kwà 'push' and -cí 'be shut', or -méqhe 'open', from <u>mé</u> 'make' and -<u>ghé</u> 'be open'. The semantic relation between the two verbs in the compound here strongly suggest that the compound arose from a serializing SVO syntax, i.e., from the current syntactic pattern of Igbo. On the other hand, compounds such as -rísị̣ 'finish eating' from -rí 'eat' and sị̣ '*finish?', -lụ́cí 're-marry' from -lụ́ 'marry', -cí '*repeat?', -gáwá 'get going' from -gá 'go' and -wá '*begin?', -gáhyè 'go the wrong way' from -gá 'go' and -hyè '*miss?' or -rụ́gíde 'keep on working' from -rụ́ 'work' and -gídé '*continue', all strongly suggest that the second member of the compound was a modality verb and that the first member represents its erstwhile complement in an SOV syntax.

17. Meeussen (in personal communication) has suggested that an alternative explanation may be found in the relative size of pronouns as against the main verb (compared to the larger size of the non-anaphorized noun phrase itself), thus paralleling the syntactic behavior of verb-particle combinations in English ('give-up'). It seems to me that this

explanation is unacceptable in this case. As I have shown in Givón (1971a), the similar Indo-European case is clearly traceable to earlier SOV syntax. Further, in Semitic languages where an earlier VSO syntax is attested, the frozen, bound pronouns reflect that historical order to this day, in both Amharic (currently SOV) and Hebrew (currently SVO).

18. One obvious exception is the reciprocal/associative suffix -ana, where both morphemic and semantic grounds suggest that is originates from the comitative conjunction na. However, it may well be that na itself, currently meaning 'with', 'by', 'and', may have originated from a serial verb 'be at', along the model suggested by Lord (1973).

19. Meeussen (in personal communication), suggests at least -à- , -á-, -kí- , -kà- . Their semantic value cannot be reconstructed with con-fidence, tho it is possible that -à- represented a past tense, -á- a recent-past or present/habitual tense, -kí- some type of a progressive aspect.

20. Here one could enumerate the 'neutral' a, the subjunctive -e, the negative -i, the modified base -ile (which is possibly a compound) and perhaps also a perfective -e. Another verb suffix -u may have also existed, since it is currently attested in adjectives derived from erstwhile verbs and thus semantically may be reconstructed as another perfective suffix (roughly on the semantic pattern of 'the burn-ed house').

21. Larry Hyman (in personal communication) has suggested to me that Bamileke also has evidence for a relative-marker (pronoun) as a verb suffix, in this case a floating low tone. Further, Igbo, a Kwa lan-guage, has a floating high tone suffixed to the verb in relativization. The import of these facts may be to fix this feature as a remnant of the Proto-Niger-Congo SOV syntax.

22. This suffix is restricted mostly to the Eastern-Bantu and Southern-Bantu, tho Meeussen (in personal communication) suggests it is also pre-sent in Mongo. In the Eastern and Southern zones it has supplanted the pa,ku,mu prepositions either completely or partially in many environ-ments. Normally it is not claimed to have been in Proto P-Bantu. However, it seems to me that it is highly unlikely for an SVO language

to borrow a locative post-position or innovate it. I see thus no reason for not assuming that it is in fact a Proto P-Bantu relic, again reflecting an innovation which arose during an SOV syntax.

23. A table of relative chronology of the various splits within the Niger-Congo sub-family is given in the appendix. It roughly corresponds to Greenberg's (1963) classification, tho for some of the details I am indebted to William Welmers (in personal communication).

24. In all the Bamileke-Fe'fe' data, taken from Hyman (1971a, 1971b), I have taken the liberty to slightly simplify the original's orthography.

25. Carol Lord (in private conversation) also suggests that this sentence is more likely to yield a commitative construction, i.e., eventually correspond to the gloss 'I came home with the book'.

26. P-Bantu languages have developed, during the current SVO syntactic stage, a supplementary system of noun-derived prepositions through the genitival channel (for further discussion see Givón, 1971a).

27. One may further suggest that the change SOV > SVO is by itself not enough to resolve the perceptual difficulties of a language which lost its case markings during its 'maturation' as an SOV language. So that either one of two mutually-exclusive additional steps may be taken: (a) The language may add pre-positions through its nominal system, in which case it need not develop serialization. This seems to have happened in Fula. Or (b) The language may resort to serialization and thus derive case makings through its verbal system, in which case it need not develop preposition through the nominal system (KBC).

28. For the Kru data I am much indebted to Seyõn Jackson.

29. These environments form a natural class, both semantically and historically. For further discussion of the relation between modal verbs and modalities, see Givón (1973a).

30. The possessive link is an unmarked vowel which totally assimilates to the preceding vowel of nouns and names. It is absent if the possessive modifier is a pronoun. It is also absent in post-positions which derive initially from this compound pattern, a reduction that is not unexpected (see discussion in Givón, 1971a).

31. The directional suffix -mǫ is probably part of an older, non-serial pattern for locative expressions, having been semantically depleted to quite an extent, much like the locative post-position -ǫ. Tho it is quite conceivable that -mǫ originated from an erstwhile verb, as is strongly suggested from its syntactic position in an SOV language.

32. While one may argue that a serialized sentence such as 'He took pot broke (it)' is syntactically 'complex' while it's non-serial, re-lexified equivalent 'He ACC-pot broke' is 'simplex', it is doubtful that in terms of the overall semantic contents ('message') of the sentence there is any real change. Rather, the erstwhile verb 'take' has been depleted of some semantic contents, while the erstwhile verb 'break' has become semantically more complex. For further discussion of this see later on.

33. It is an open question whether the rise of polysyllabic ('compound') verbs in Chinese is a direct result of the change SVO-serializing to SOV-non-serializing. It could simply reflect the general tendency of OV syntax to create more agglutinative morphology than VO syntax.

34. There are, further, agent grounds for believing that even though a syntactically co-ordinate ('consecutive') construction may have been always used to initiate serial-verb constructions, the semantic relationship between the clauses in series is probably sub-ordinate (i.e., structured, hierarchized) to begin with. So that the clauses presenting the agent and patient are considered 'the main event', while the instrumental, adverbial, locational, benefactive can be considered as 'satelites' of the main event. The eventual syntactic re-analysis to approximate this underlying semantic fact more closely, may be thus viewed as a predictable consequence of verb-serial constructions from the very onset.

35. While the instrumental preposition ni in Yatye may not be presently traced to a specific verb, it is not unlikely that it originated from a commitative verb such as 'be at', 'be with', meet', etc., along the model suggested by Lord (1973).

36. In essence, the claim of 'direct analogy' is really a claim that speakers, and in particular children during first-language acquisition, are able to analogize along Chomsky's X̄ convention. That is, they are able to see the modifier standing in the same relation to the head noun as the complement or object to the main verb. I think this is a most unlikely possibility. It further would require that the acquisition of noun modification coincide with the acquisition of verb complementation, again a proposition that is not at all supported by current studies on the acquisition of language.

37. Further arguments for this unidirectionality may be found in Lehmann (1972). The survival patterns of SOV syntax in the noun phrases of erstwhile SOV languages long after the verb-phrase syntax has changed to VO further suggests that the noun phrase syntax is the dependent, derived pattern, while the VP syntax is the innovative one. The fact that the survival is normally confined to the 'smaller' modifiers, such as genitivals, genitive-derived nominal compounds and--less frequently-- adjectives, further enhances the credibility of the hypothesis concern- ing the relationship between nominalized verbs-cum-complements and rela- tive clauses. Indeed both relative clauses and noun complements tend to echo the current VP syntax much more--and present the older syntactic position much less--than do the 'smaller' noun modifiers.

38. There is a difference of some sort in the overall semantic con- tents of the construction, involving the relationship of relative seman- tic prominence between the erstwhile phrasal constituents. One may thus view the semantic re-balancing--between the two serial verbs in the sentence--as a mere continuation of an earlier re-analysis, namely the re-analysis through which two separate consecutive/coordinate actions or events have become re-interpreted as a one-event subordination. Once one of them is viewed as the semantically-more-prominent part of the overall construction, the other is a prime candidate for the deple- tion process shown above--as the more prominent, surviving verb becomes semantically more complex.

39. Similar instances of the incorporation of the 'cause' serial verbs are shown in Stahlke (1970) for Yatye. This process and its implica- tions to the typology of verb phrases is discussed in Givón (1972b).

40. A verb may become a case-marking post-position in an SOV non-
serialising language by first going through a nominalizing channel, and
then via the normal genitival-compound channel. It was pointed out to
me by Theo Vennemann (in private communication, see also Venneman, 1972)
that the equivalents of the English 'concerning NP', 'regarding NP',
etc., are post-positional in German. In Ijo one finds the verb mié
'make', 'cause' giving rise to the post-position 'because', as in:
osuó-bi-m̳ęį́-kò
rain-the-make-P
'because of (the) rain'
In this construction m̳ęį̂ itself appears in a nominal form, as is evident from the fact that it is suffixed by an older post-position -kò.
This may suggest that m̳ęį̂ developed into a post-position via the
genitival-noun channel, perhaps before Ijo started serializing, since
if 'rain' above were the subject of the serial verb 'cause', an object
would have intervened between 'rain' and 'cause' in an SOV language and
would have prevented this suffixation pattern from arising.

REFERENCES

Awobuluyi, Ọ. (1967), Studies in the syntax of the standard Yoruba verb, Ph.D. Dissertation, Columbia University.

---------- (1972), "Splitting verbs in Yoruba", Annales de l'Université d'Abidjan, Serie H: Linguistique, 1:151-164.

---------- (1973), "The modifying serial construction: A critique", SAL, 4.1:87-111.

Arnott, D.W. (1970), The nominal and verbal system of Fula, London: Oxford University Press.

Bamgboṣe, A. (1972), "On serial verbs and verbal status", to appear in JWAL.

---------- (1973), "The modifying serial construction: A reply", SAL, 4.2:207-217.

Christaller, J.B. (1875), A grammar of the Asante and Fante language, called Tshi, republished (1964), London: Gregg Press.

Elimelech, B. (1973), "Conjunction reduction and splitting-verbs in Yoruba", UCLA (mimeo).

Givón, T. (1971a), "Historical syntax and synchronic morphology: An archaeologist's field trip", in Papers from the Seventh Regional Meeting, University of Chicago: Chicago Linguistic Society.

---------- (1971b), "On the verbal origin of the Bantu verb suffixes", SAL, 2.2:145-163.

---------- (1972a), "Pronoun attraction and subject post-posing in Bantu relativization", in Papers from the Eighth Regional Meeting, Parasession volume, University of Chicago: Chicago Linguistic Society.

---------- (1972b), Studies in ChiBemba and Bantu grammar, SAL, Supplement #3.

---------- (1973a), "The time-axis phenomenon", Language, December 1973.

---------- (1973b), "Prolegomena to any Creology", to appear in B. Heine (ed.), African-Based Creoles and Pidgins, special issue of JAL.

Greenberg, J. (1963), The languages of Africa, IJAL, II,29.1, Publication #25.

---------- (1966), "Some universals of grammar with particular reference to the order of meaningful constituents", in J. Greenberg (ed.), Universals of Language, Cambridge: MIT Press.

Hyman, L. (1971a), "Some diachronic aspects of serial verbs", Institute of Nupe Linguistics (mimeo).

---------- (1971b), "Consecutivization in Fe'fe'", JAL, 10.2:29-43.

---------- (forthcoming).

Lehmann, W.P. (1972), "Converging Theories in Linguistics", Language, 58:266-275.

Li, C.N. and S. Thompson (1973a), "Historical change of word order: A case study of Chinese and its implications", UCLA and UCSB (mimeo).

---------- (1973b), "Serial verb constructions in Mandarin Chinese: Sub-ordination or co-ordination", in Papers from the ninth regional meeting, Parasession volume, University of Chicago: Chicago Linguistic Society.

---------- (1973c), "Co-verbs in Mandarin Chinese: Verbs or prepositions", UCLA and UCSB (mimeo).

Lord, C. (1973), "Serial verbs in transition", SAL, 4.3. (in press).

Peterson, T. (1971), Mooré structure: A generative analysis of the tonal structure and aspects of the syntax, Ph.D. dissertation, UCLA.

Prost, R.P.A. (1968), Deux langues Voltaiques en voie de disparition: Le Ware et le Natioro, Université de Dakar, Documents Linguistiques.

Sapir, D. (1965), A grammar of Dyola-Fogny, West African Language Monograph #3, Cambridge University Press.

Stahlke, H. (1970), "Serial verbs", SAL, 1.1:60-99.

Thompson, S. (1973), "Resultative verb compounds in Mandarin Chinese: A case for lexical rules", Language, 49.2:361-379.

Vennemann, T. (1972), "Explanations in Syntax", in J. Kimball (ed.), Syntax and Semantics, Vol. II, New York: Seminar Press.

Welmers, W. (1950), "Notes on two languages of the Senufo group", Language, 26.4:495-531.

---------- (1952), "Note on the structure of Bariba", Language, 28.1: 82-103.

---------- (1968), "Efik, Occasional paper #11, Ibaden University: Institute for African Studies.

---------- (1970), "The derivation of Igbo verbs", SAL, 1.1:49-59.

Williams, W. (1971), "Serial verb constructions in Krio", SAL, Supplement #2.

Williamson, K. (1965), A grammar of the Kolokuma dialect of Ijo, West African Language Monographs, #2, Cambridge University Press.

ADDED REFERENCES

Hudson, G. (1974), "Amharic preposition embedding and relative clause history", in these proceedings.

Hyman, L. (1974), "On the change from SOV to SVO: Evidence from Niger-Congo", in these proceedings.

Li, C. and S. Thompson (1974), "The semantic function of word order", in these proceedings.

Pike, K. (1967), "Grammar as wave", Georgetown Monograph Series #20, 1-14.

---------- (1970), Tagmemic and matrix Linguistics applied to selected African Languages, Summer Institute in Linguistics.

Vennemann, T. (1972b), "Analogy in generative grammar: The origin of word-order", Proceedings of XI International Congress of Linguistics, Bologna, August-September, 1972.

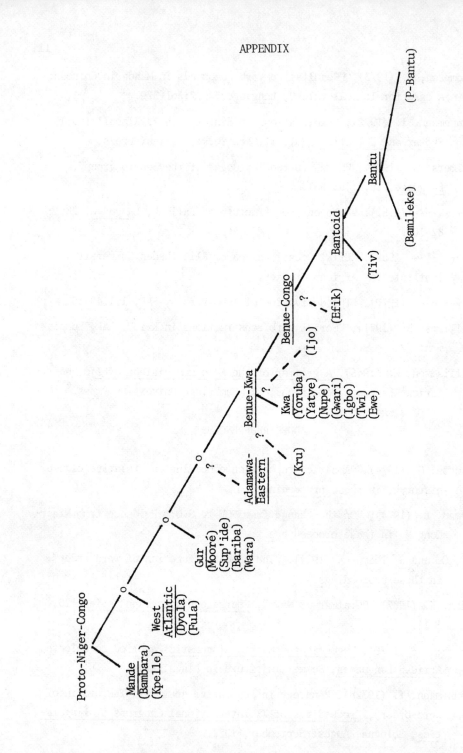

ON THE CHANGE FROM SOV TO SVO: EVIDENCE FROM NIGER-CONGO

by

Larry M. Hyman

1. Introduction

Although introductory texts and more advanced treatises of historical linguistics have relatively little to say about syntactic change, the past few years have seen several significant advances in the study of the evolution of word order. The synchronic foundation laid by Greenberg (1966) has provided a framework in which important generalizations on the nature of word order change can be made. Recent interest in this topic is seen in such works as Givón (1971), Lehmann (1972a,b; 1973a), Vennemann (1972, 1973a,b,c) and Li and Thompson (1973), as well as in the various papers presented at this symposium. In this paper I should like to address myself to the various factors which may contribute to the change of an SOV to an SVO word order. Particular emphasis will be placed on the nature of this change in several languages of the Niger-Congo family. I shall begin by addressing myself to the kinds of explanations which have been proposed to account for word order change. I shall then turn to the facts of Niger-Congo.

2.0 Approaches to Word Order

The four proposed explanations for word order change which I shall discuss in this section are 1) contact, 2) disambiguation, 3) grammaticalization and 4) afterthought. These are now discussed in the order in which they were proposed in recent literature.

2.1 Contact

In the various publications of Lehmann, it is suggested that word order changes come about through contact--that is, languages borrow alien word orders and gradually give up their own inherited syntax. It is well-known that the syntax of a language is readily affected by the external influence of neighboring languages, and I shall provide further evidence for this from West African languages. There are several instances which are sometimes mentioned where a language has "borrowed" the word order of a contact language. Thus, Amharic owes its present day word order to prolonged contact with Cushitic (Talmy Givón, personal communication). While it is sometimes suggested that the contact language may be completely lost (in cases where there is no clear sign of borrowing), it appears more likely that other factors are involved

in such cases. If all word order changes could be shown to have resulted from contact, this would be a strong argument for the monogenesis
of language--for, for each word order (e.g., SOV, SVO, VSO) there would
have to be a separate proto-human language reconstructed. Rather than
seeking lost contact languages, one should expect to find _internal_
causes of syntactic change, just as phonetic processes such as assimilation, owing their existence to articulatory and perceptual constraints
imposed by man's speech organs, constitute an internal cause of phonological change. In the following three sub-sections, three such internal causes are discussed.

2.2 Disambiguation

The analysis of word order change found in the works of Vennemann
represents a considerable step forward. In Vennemann (1973a) he argues
that word order changes result from the levelling of morphological case
markings, which in turn are lost through phonological change, e.g., the
dropping of sounds at the ends of words. It has of course often been
noted in the literature (e.g., Sapir 1921) that case marking provides
the same function as rigid word order--and that there is a frequent correlation between complex noun declension systems and relatively free
word order. In this view word order change is triggered by sound changes which threaten to disrupt the grammar.

In later works (e.g., Vennemann 1973b,c) a more elaborate theory
involving topicalization is developed. In the change from SOV to SVO,
three stages are recognized: 1) an original SOV stage with word order
serving a "pragmatic" function, i.e., topical material comes earlier
in a sentence than comment material; 2) an intermediate TVX stage
(topic-verb-everything else), with word order serving in second position the "semantic" function of separating the topic from the comment
of the sentence; and 3) an SVO stage, with word order serving the "grammatical" function of keeping the subject separated from the object (and
the rest of the sentence). What is important in this development is
that the change from SOV to TVX is seen as resulting from the reduction
of case markers (typically suffixal), which in turn is effected by the
general loss of word-final segments. With the case markings falling,
and with word order serving the pragmatic function of establishing
topic-comment relationships, ambiguity is likely to result as to what

the subject vs. object of a sentence is. The verb therefore pops into the second position to disambiguate. Modern German is seen as a TVX language, while English is an SVO language.

Some of the problems which I see in this proposal are the following. First, there are SOV languages which have no trace of case marking on nouns--and which have never had any. The Niger-Congo family, which in its proto days was SOV, is a case in point, with present-day Ịjọ having retained the SOV order of the proto language (Williamson 1965). Second, there are many languages which have already imposed fairly rigid word orders, but which have not lost their case markings, e.g., Russian. In particular, there seems to be evidence that the rigidification of an SVO word order in many languages temporally precedes at least the major case levellings. This should not be surprising, since case markings do not drop overnight--they weaken gradually through time.

If Vennemann's theory is correct, there should be transitional languages supporting his position. One possibility is outlined as follows. At a certain point a language has case markings and an SOV syntax. It happens that the case markings are in certain situations not able to fully distinguish between subject and object unambiguously (as in Standard German, whose morphemes I borrow in the following hypothetical examples). Thus, while the case markers in (1) unambiguously mark the object (and therefore also the subject) of the sentence,

(1) die Mutter den Sohn liebt   'the mother loves the son' (den = acc.)

the sentence in (2) should, intonation being equal, be ambiguous:

(2) die Mutter die Tochter liebt   'the mother loves the daughter'
         (die = nom., acc.)   'the daughter loves the mother'

If word order serves a disambiguating function, as suggested in Vennemann's model, there should be a language where an unambiguous sentence such as (1) is left as is, but where an ambiguous sentence such as (2) is modified to SVO, as seen in (3):

(3) die Mutter liebt die Tochter   'the mother loves the daughter'

     die Tochter liebt die Mutter   'the daughter loves the mother'

That is, we should have "mixed" syntaxes where the occurrence of SVO

rather than SOV is dictated by considerations of avoiding ambiguity.
While I can dismiss the possibility of such a language only on intuitive grounds, it should be clear that its existence follows from Vennemann's theory, and that the discovery of such a language would constitute dramatic confirmation of his general approach.

2.3 Grammaticalization

A third proposal to handle the data of word order change is owed
to Li and Thompson (1973). They show from Chinese data that word order
change can be the result of the "grammaticalization" of a lexical item--
here, a verb. In order to illustrate, consider the following sentence of
Ịjọ (Williamson 1965) in (4):

(4) erí, dúma tun-nì, a-pịrị   'he sang a song for her'
     he song sang her-give

As seen in this example, Ịjọ is an SOV language. In (4), however, it is
observed that the second verb (pịrị 'to give') is used as a benefactive
marker, though it still maintains its morphological identity as a verb.
If pịrị were to lose its verbal status, as has happened in many cases of
serialization in West Africa (see below), instead of analyzing the above
sentence as in (5), representing its diachronic source,

(5)

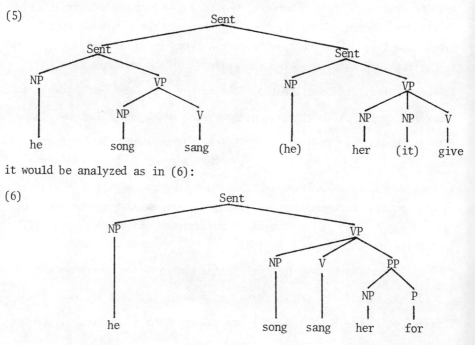

it would be analyzed as in (6):

(6)

It is noted in (6) that through the grammaticalization of the verb 'to give' we now have a main verb 'to sing' with a postpositional phrase after it. Now, if what Li and Thompson report for Chinese were to happen to Ịjǫ, this new SOV-PP word order would provide the new model for analogical syntactic change--since certain elements of a sentence appear after the verb, a precedent is set for further elements to start moving out as well. This analogical change would be impossible as long as speakers maintained cognizance of the verbal status of the benefactive 'to give'. It should be noted that <u>semantic</u> reanalysis of 'to give' to mean 'for' takes place prior to the complete loss of the verbal etymology of pịrị. Such a development has already been reported for a number of West African languages (Pike 1967, 1970; Lord 1973; Givón 1974).[2]

The examples which Li and Thompson (1973) discuss, and which I have artificially constructed for a future day in Ịjǫ, depict a strategy by which grammaticalization provides a new pattern, which becomes the basis for analogical word order changes elsewhere in the grammar. A second possibility should, however, not be overlooked. In particular, it may be possible that (4) will develop as in (7):

(7) he song sang her give > he song sang her-for > he song her-for sang

That is, after the grammaticalization process represented in the first change, the postpositional phrase 'her-for' may be pulled in to the left of the main verb, so that the original SOV word order can be maintained. Of course, in accordance with the universals presented by Greenberg (1966), we might further expect that if the course in (6) were preferred over that in (7), the ultimate word order will be 'he sang song for her', since prepositional (as opposed to postpositional) constructions are preferred by SVO languages.

2.4. Afterthought

The fourth and last approach to word order change I term <u>after-thought</u>. While this term is not entirely adequate (primarily because it is used as a cover term for a number of different--though related--phenomena), what I should like to argue is that one constantly present force contributing to word order change is the conflict between <u>syntax</u> and <u>pragmatics</u>. That is, speakers, in the course of using a language, sometimes find it necessary to break the syntax and <u>add</u> grammatical

elements in positions where they normally should not appear. Consider
the following relative clause in Standard German, where the observed
word order is SOV:

(8) der Mann, den ich gesehen habe   'the man whom I saw'
     the man   whom I   seen have

While Bartsch and Vennemann (1972) and Vennemann (1973a) have argued
for a semantic principle of "natural serialization", according to which
the most highly valued word order is SOV, this syntactic pattern presents one important practical inconvenience which speakers have to cope
with. Namely, once the speaker has put the verb down, it is no longer
possible to add anything (in a strict SOV language). However, the
speaker may forget to say something in the course of his utterance; or
he may find that it is necessary to add something, because his inter-
locutor has not understood; or he may realize that the sentence he has
just uttered is unclear or ambiguous. In all of these cases (and doubt-
less others), he may wish to add something after the verb-final utterance. Let us say with respect to the German relative clause in (8) that
the speaker forgot to include the important information that he had seen
the man the preceding night. Normally, the well-thought-out sentence
would be as in (9),

(9) der Mann, den ich gestern Abend gesehen habe

where gestern Abend 'yesterday evening' precedes the final verbal complex. However, once the speaker has said gesehen habe in (8), he can't
back up and insert gestern Abend. Instead, what is necessary is that
he take a pause and then say gestern Abend--but with a new intonation
curve, as in (10):

(10) der Mann, den ich gesehen habe... gestern Abend

I should like to claim that no language ever requires a speaker to start
the whole sentence over again in order to put forgotten information into
the correct pre-verbal slot. Instead, the afterthought material can be
tacked on at the end (in defiance of the "verb at the end" syntax), with
the pause and intonation signalling in effect that the speaker is aware
that he "shouldn't" be doing this--at least from a syntactic point of

view. Of course, the final step is the erasure of the pause and the incorporation of gestern Abend into the intonation curve of the preceding clause, as in (11):

(11) der Mann, den ich gesehen habe gestern Abend

As also noted by Vennemann (1973c), this construction is already well on its way to acceptance in spoken German. While I shall give further examples of this phenomenon in the next section, let us simply take note of the fact that this approach predicts that there will be intermediate stages between SOV and SVO, i.e., the verb does not zap into second position in one step, as it were. Rather, the grammatical elements between the S and the V move out in accordance with the likelihood of their serving as afterthoughts. In other words, this rightward movement of forgotten or added information may take place along a hierarchical scale, with such things as adverbial phrases being more subject to this "Ausklammerung" effect (Theo Vennemann, personal communication) than, say, the direct object of the verb.

3.0. Word Order Change in Niger-Congo

Like Givón (1974), I assume that Proto-Niger-Congo was an SOV language. Morphological and/or syntactic traces of the old order are preserved in each sub-group of this macro-family covering much of the African continent (see Givón 1974 for a survey of the relevant data as well as references). In this section I should like to consider what kind of evidence there is for each of the four possible explanations for word order change discussed in the previous section, focusing on the SOV to SVO changes which have taken place in Niger-Congo.

3.1. Contact

As mentioned in section 2.1, contact as a cause of syntactic change has received considerable attention in the works of Lehmann. In all of the other cited studies of word order change (Vennemann, Li and Thompson, Givón), it is either not mentioned, or is underestimated. In this section I shall show that many word order phenomena must be studied as "waves", just as phonological changes are best seen in this light. Thus, consider the following map of the West African coast in (12):

122

(12)
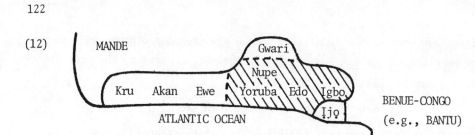

The encircled languages (Kru, Akan, Ewe, Yoruba, Nupe, Gwari, Edo, Igbo)
belong to the Kwa subgroup of Niger-Congo. To the West of them is the
Mande group, and to the East, the Benue-Congo group (of which Bantu is
the major representative). As already stated, Proto-Niger-Congo had
the word order SOV; in noun phrases it also had the Greenberg-predicted
order poss-N (possessor preceding noun possessed). The proto word orders, e.g., I yams bought and my yams, are still found in the Mande
languages to the Northwest of Kwa, as well as in Ịjọ (an isolate which
is sometimes included in the Kwa group). On the other hand, in Bantu,
to the East of Kwa, these proto word orders have both been modified,
since the only occurring orders are SVO and N-poss (i.e., I bought yams
and yams my). The languages of Kwa are somewhat intermediate between
the original SOV/poss-N and the innovative SVO/N-poss, as their geogra-
phic position may suggest. All Kwa languages show SVO in simple declarative sentences (see below for complications in Kru). However, the area
shaded in on the map (i.e., Yoruba, Nupe, Edo, Igbo) has changed poss-N
to N-poss, while the non-shaded-in area (i.e., Gwari, Ewe, Akan, Kru)
maintains the proto poss-N order. What is interesting in the word order
differences in the noun phrase is that the distribution of poss-N and
N-poss does not correspond to genetic linguistic boundaries, since Nupe
and Gwari, which differ in this respect, as seen in (13),

(13)   Nupe   ēyā ′mǐ`   'boat my'

       Gwari   mi ōyā   'my boat'

are closely related in the Niger-Kaduna sub-branch of Kwa. In other
words, Nupe is genetically much more closely related to Gwari than it
is to, say, Yoruba or Ewe. In addition, Westermann (1927) reports that
Gũ, a dialect of Ewe spoken in Dahomey (i.e., where Yoruba and Ewe dialects meet) has the order N-poss, although the more standard dialects
have poss-N, as indicated on the map. Although Westermann offers a
structural reason for the change of poss-N to N-poss (see section 3.5),

I suggest that this change results from heavy contact with Yoruba, which has N-poss. As further evidence for the areal nature of the split between poss-N and N-poss languages in Kwa, notice that those languages neighboring Kwa on the West, namely Mande, are also characterized by poss-N, while those languages neighboring Kwa on the East, namely Benue-Congo (e.g., Cross-River and Jukunoid) have N-poss. Since all of Bantu has SVO and N-poss, even though Bantu covers an immense geographical region, these word order changes are conceived in the following way: 1) an initial wave swept from Bantu changing SOV to SVO throughout Benue-Congo and Kwa (missing only Ịjọ); and 2) a second wave also starts from Bantu changing poss-N to N-poss. As was seen in the map in (12), this second wave is incomplete in Kwa, since it is stopped in the North by Gwari and in the West by Ewe (hitting only the Gũ dialect).

We must therefore conclude that contact is a very real force in syntactic change. Since we are dealing with word order changes within one linguistic family, Niger-Congo, we still are in need of an explanation for the first syntactic change--the one which presumably diffused from Bantu westwards. Notice, however, before turning to the remaining three approaches to word order change, that we should be careful not to indiscriminately attribute all such changes to contact. For example, it is conceivable to me that West Atlantic, another branch of Niger-Congo which, as pointed out to me by Joseph Greenberg (personal communication), has the order N-poss (see also Givón 1974), may have developed this order independently of the changes in Eastern Kwa. It is interesting to note that West Atlantic has a fairly consistent SVO syntax, unlike the Mande languages which separate West Atlantic from Western Kwa. Unless we are to attribute this to the VSO of neighboring Arabic and Berber to the North, this very well may have been an independent development--motivated by one of the three theories now to be discussed.

3.2 Disambiguation

The model of syntactic change outlined by Vennemann (1973a) involving loss of case markers, and problems associated with topicalization, is not readily adaptable to the facts of Niger-Congo, since Proto-NC was not characterized by case markings on nouns. While I shall suggest a possible role ambiguity may play in afterthought in section 3.4, it appears that the raising of topicalized material had no say in the word order changes that took place in Niger-Congo.

3.3. Grammaticalization

Givón's (1974) discussion is organized into two parts: first, he shows that Proto-Niger-Congo was SOV and that various Niger-Congo languages have become (or are becoming) SVO; second, he shows that this newly developed SVO with serialization (see section 4 below) is subject to the grammaticalization process discussed by Li and Thompson (1973), and may eventually lead SVO back to SOV again, as in Chinese. There is no doubt that grammaticalizations of the type discussed by Givón have occurred. Verbs can become auxiliaries or prepositions and eventually lose all traces of their verbal origin (cf. Pike 1967, 1970; Lord 1973). However, grammaticalization, though logically applicable, does not appear to play any role in the change from SOV to SVO in Niger-Congo.

That it could very well have played such a role is seen from the derivation in (14):

(14) he song sang her give > he song sang her-for > he sang song her-for

In this derivation we observe, first, grammaticalization, and second, analogical change moving the direct object to the right of the verb (cf. however the derivation in (7) representing another logical possibility). We of course expect her-for to change to for-her in accordance with the newly developing SVO syntax. However, since Givón is correct to point out that Proto-Bantu did not serialize verbs (though an earlier ancestor may very well have involved serial verbs), the grammaticalization of verbs to postpositions could not have caused the change of SOV to SVO in Bantu--where, recall from the preceding section, the whole thing is presumed to have started. We must therefore conclude that grammaticalization plays little if any role in the word order changes discussed in the first part of Givón's paper.

3.4. Afterthought

The fourth proposed explanation for word order change receives considerable support from Niger-Congo. According to this view, violations of a strict SOV word order occur in all such languages to meet the needs of speakers in natural discourse. An example was given from Standard German relative clauses in section 2.4. Consider now some facts from Kru, first from noun + noun conjunction, and second from relative clause formation.[3]

As seen in (15), the basic word order in Kru is SVO:

(15) ɔ́ tɛ̀ kɔ̀   'he bought rice'
     he buy rice

However, there are a number of situations where an SOV order is found.
First, as seen in (16),

(16) a. ɔ́ mú kɔ̀ tɛ̀ mù   'he will (go) buy rice [today]'
        he FUT rice buy go

     b. ɔ́ sé kɔ̀ tɛ̀   'he didn't buy rice'
        he NEG rice buy

there are certain modality markers which require that the main verb be
last in the sentence. In (16a) we observe that the future marker $\underline{mú}$
appearing after the subject, which derives historically from the verb
'to go', forces two verbs to appear at the end, namely $\underline{tɛ̀}$ 'to buy' and
$\underline{mú}$ 'to go'. In (16b), the negative marker $\underline{sé}$ sends 'to buy' also the
end. Both of these constructions are explained if we assume the origi-
nal verbal status of both the FUT and NEG markers.[4] These sentences
therefore reconstruct as SV_1OV_2, where V_1 was an intransitive verb. The
resemblance of this reconstruction to present-day Ịjọ (Williamson 1965)
is obvious.

A second source of present-day SOV word order in Kru is in subjunctive clauses, which are introduced by the markers in (17):

(17) béɛ̀ 'that I...'   bàè 'that we...'

     bèɛ̀ 'that you...'   bàé 'that you (pl.)...'

     bɔ̀é 'that he...'   bìí 'that they...'

Thus, the word order is SOV in the subjunctive clause in (18):

(18) ɔ́ jlâ bɔ̀é kɔ̀ tɛ̀   'he wants to buy rice'
     he wants that-he rice buy

Although the history is not clear to me at this moment, it seems likely
that there was a verb in the subjunctive marker and that the markers in
(17) represent a fusion of three different morphemes, as in (19):

(19) bV + PRON + VERB

The reconstructed verb in (19) has of course become some kind of a modal, which like the future and negative markers sends the main verb to the end. At least some evidence for this reconstruction is observed in (20),

(20)   bɔ́   tḛ̀   kɔ̀   'let him buy rice!'
       let-him buy rice

where this verbal element is apparently missing--and the result is an SVO word order.

Turning now to the question of word order change, we note in (21) that conjoined direct object nouns in negative constructions both precede the final verb:

(21)   ɔ́ sé súa táḭ kɔ̀ tḛ̀   'he did not buy fish and rice'
       he NEG fish and rice buy

While (21) is the normal construction, a sentence such as (22) is possible,

(22)   ɔ́ sé súa tḛ̀, táḭ kɔ̀   'he did not buy fish... and rice'
       he NEG fish buy and rice

but only if there is a pause where I have placed the comma. What such an utterance would mean is that the speaker had completed the simple sentence, and then remembered that he wanted to say that the person had not bought rice either. And so, just as in the German relative clause in (10) above, new information can be added after a verb-final clause, but only with special intonational features.

We might at this point ask what kind of information is likely to be forgotten by a speaker in verb-final utterances. Among the likely candidates are adverbs and adverbial phrases, prepositional phrases, conjoined nouns, relative clauses and oblique cases (e.g., dative and benefactive, also agentive in languages with passive constructions). This list is not exhaustive, nor does it represent any hierarchy (which probably can be uncovered with further study). But what all of these candidates have in common is that they are likely to be new information, and hence tend to come later in an utterance--and ultimately can appear in the form of an afterthought, strung after the rest of the sentence.[5] The one candidate we are ruling out is single (i.e., non-conjoined) direct objects. In an utterance such as 'he NOT rice buy', one is not likely to forget 'rice' and say 'he NOT buy'. Notice also that pronoun direct objects would be even less likely to be postposed, since one is not likely to forget 'him' in 'he NOT him see', where the definiteness of pronouns attests to their topical (old information) character.[6] Of course, even noun and pronoun direct objects eventually postpose to yield a consistent SVO language. But in speaking of the likelihood that something may appear as an afterthought, we must not only consider the dichotomy between old vs. new information, but also the relative prominence of new information.

If what I am saying is correct, there should be languages somewhere in Niger-Congo which exhibit intermediate word orders in their basic sentences (i.e., without the intonational phenomena found in Kru). I suggest that the typical word order found in Mande, as outlined in (23),

(23) Subj + Dir Obj + Verb + Everything else

provides evidence for my position. Givón has provided an extensive list, based on Welmers, of the kinds of things found after the verb in Kpelle, a Southwestern Mande language spoken in Liberia (cf. Welmers 1964). These include locative, instrumental, manner, benefactive and dative phrases. An example of a post-verbal dative phrase is reproduced in (24):

(24) è sɛŋ-kâu tèe ˋkâloŋ-pɔ́   'he sent the money to the chief'
      he money sent chief to

Givón points out that case markers are postpositional in Kpelle (reminiscent of an older strict SOV order) and are derived from nouns. The postposition 'to' in (24) is derived from the noun pɔ́ still used in modern Kpelle with the meaning 'presence'. Thus, (24) once meant 'he sent the money chief's presence'. If these postpositions were derived from verbs, then we would have an example of word order change based solely on grammaticalization, as in the hypothetical example in (14) above. However, the fact that these postpositions come from nouns poses a problem for grammaticalization (of verbs) as the cause of word order change in Mande, since the extended Li and Thompson model (see footnote 2) cannot explain why 'chief-to', coming from 'chief's presence', occurs after the main verb 'sent' and not before it.

There is good evidence that datives once preceded the verb. First, as reported in Welmers (1964), certain adverbs can occur with greater freedom than either the direct object or other complements. He gives the two equivalent word orders in (25):

(25) a. sumo è wɛ́ɛ wúru tèe   "Sumo cut sticks yesterday'
          Sumo he yest.sticks cut

      b. sumo è wúru tèe wɛ́ɛ
          Sumo he sticks cut yest.

The older order is preserved in (25a), while the newer order in (25b) corresponds to the general word order pattern given in (23). I suggest that the reason why complements and adverbial modifiers have moved out to the right of the verb is precisely the same reason why Kru is currently moving out conjoined direct object nouns in negative constructions.

As a direct parallel to the Kru situation, consider the order of conjoined nominals in Kpelle. Welmers (1968) reports, as seen in (26),

(26) kwà ǹya kú lì   'he and I went' (lit. we including him went)
      we him we went

that if both nominals are pronouns, they both occur before the verb. Similarly, if one of the nominals is a noun and the other a pronoun, they both precede the verb, as in (27):

(27) kwà ǹɛnîî tí kú lì   'that woman and I went' (lit. we includ-
      we woman that we went   ing that woman went)

However, if both are nouns, the second nominal goes to the right of the verb, as seen in (28):

(28) a. surɔ́ŋ feerɛ lì, `tà ńɛnî feerɛ   'two men and two women came'
          men two came they women two

      b. ŋá surɔ́ŋ feerɛ kàa, `tà ńɛnî feerɛ   'I saw two men and two
          I men two saw they women two   women'

In (28a) the conjoined nouns are subject of the verb 'to go', while in (28b) the conjoined nouns are direct objects of the verb 'to see'. In both cases the second noun appears _after_ the verb. Such a situation was possible with a pause between the verb and the second noun in Kru, only

if the second noun was originally forgotten by the speaker. I see no
other way to explain the word orders in (28) except by an extension of
what is now on-going in Kru. Since we are not dealing with falling
case markers--or with topicalization--the model presented by Vennemann
does not seem applicable. There has, however, been somewhat of a
grammaticalization, since the marker 'and' clearly comes from a conjunctive pronoun meaning 'they' (or 'with them'). Notice that Welmers
places a comma between the verb and the second conjunct. It is likely
that the postverbal conjunction + noun was once of an appositional
nature. That is, (28b) could have once been better glossed as 'I saw
two men, [with] them [there were] two women'.

In this interpretation the afterthought quality of the postposed
conjoined nominal becomes clear. It seems likely that the reconstructed order of elements is as in (29):

(29) I two men and two women saw

However, working hand in hand with the principle of afterthought is
another principle, which can be stated roughly as follows: in an SOV
language, there is a tendency to keep the direct object head noun as
close to the verb as possible. In a sentence involving a lot of postnominal modifiers and other incidentals, there will always be a tendency to move non-essentials (likely to be afterthoughts) to a post-
verbial position. Evidence for this claim comes from relative clause
formation in Kru. From the two sentences in (30),

(30) a. ɔ́ dí kɔ̀ nǎ   'he ate the rice'
          he ate rice DEF

      b. jú nǎ tɛ̀̃ kɔ̀   'the child bought rice'
          child DEF bought rice

a relative construction can be formed as in (31):

(31) ɔ́ dí kɔ̀ jú nǎ tɛ̀̃ à nǎ   'he ate the rice that
      he ate rice child DEF bought REL DEF   the child bought'

The word order in relative clauses is SVO (though this is not clear
from this particular example). Relative clauses involve an a relative
marker after the verb (something which Givón sees as a remnant of SOV
word order), as well as a definite marker at the end of the clause.

What is of interest in the study of word order is the negative of the
main clause of (31), which is presented in (32):

(32) ɔ́ sɛ́ kɔ̀ jú nǎ tɛ̃̀ à nǎ dí   'he didn't eat the
    he NEG rice child DEF bought REL DEF ate   rice that the child
                                      bought'

As already seen in the negative construction in simplex sentences (cf.
(16b) above), the negative marker sɛ́ comes after the subject, and the
main verb is "transported" to the end of the sentence. In (32) there
is a relative clause intervening between the negative marker and the
main verb dí 'to eat'. Given what I have shown to be the case concerning conjoined nominals, it is not surprising to find that when the
speaker has uttered a negative sentence such as in (33),

(33) ɔ́ sɛ́ kɔ̀ nǎ dí   'he didn't eat the rice'
    he NEG rice DEF ate

where the verb comes last, and then wants to add further information in
the form of a relative clause, this is possible with a pause, indicating a break in intonation, as in (34):

(34) ɔ́ sɛ́ kɔ̀ nǎ dí, jú nǎ tɛ̃̀ à nǎ
    he NEG rice DEF ate child DEF bought REL DEF

'he did not eat the rice... that the child bought'

Sentences (32) and (34) differ then only in that the speaker has
planned ahead in (32) (the normal situation), whereas he has not
planned ahead in (34). While I see afterthought as providing the original impetus for (34), the postverbal relative clause may gradually
come to be accepted even in well-thought-out prose. In English, where
the two comparable word orders in (35) are found,

(35) a. a student who wanted to see you came by

      b. a student came by who wanted to see you

(35b) does not necessarily mean that the speaker forgot to plan the
whole sentence in advance.[7]

    Kru becomes more interesting when we try to construct relative
clauses within relative clauses, as seen in (36):

(36) ɔ́ dí kɔ̀ jú ní jé á nǎ   tɛ̀   à nǎ
     he ate rice boy I saw REL DEF bought REL DEF

     'he ate the rice that the boy I saw bought'

The most common way of negating the sentence in (36) is seen in (37):

(37) ɔ́ sé kɔ̀ nǎ dí jú ní jé á nǎ   tɛ̀   à nǎ
     he NEG rice DEF ate child I saw REL DEF bought REL DEF

     'he didn't eat the rice that the boy I saw bought'

In this example it is observed that the verb dí 'to eat' appears in
the main clause with the two relative clauses after it. When asked if
this sentence would be acceptable with dí in utterance-final position,
i.e., as in (38),

(38) ɔ́ sé kɔ̀ nǎ jú ní jé á nǎ   tɛ̀   à nǎ dí
     he NEG rice DEF child I saw REL DEF bought REL DEF ate

     'he didn't eat the rice that the boy I saw bought'

the informant volunteered the information that this was the "real Kru"
which his father spoke. In other words, we appear to have caught a
change in progress. Most Kru speakers would probably feel that in (38)
the verb has been left off too long. While (32) is preferable to (34)
(indeed the sentence in (34) requires a pause and gives the impression
of the relative clause being an afterthought), (37), with the verb in
the main clause is preferable to (38)--where, notice, there is no pause
required between the main verb and the relative clause complex. With
time we can expect (other things being equal) for (34) to become preferable to (32). On the other hand, it may happen that Kru speakers will
completely give up the SOV word order in negative constructions. That
is, we may look forward to a future SVO construction as given in (39):

(39) ɔ́ sé dí kɔ̀ jú nǎ   tɛ̀   à nǎ
     he NEG ate rice child DEF bought REL DEF

     'he didn't eat the rice that the child bought'

This word order is doubly good since it 1) brings the auxiliary and
verb together; and 2) brings the noun and relative clause together. As
Theo Vennemann has pointed out to me (personal communication), this

eventual syntactic change conforms with Behagel's First Law, as discussed in Vennemann (1973c).

3.5. Word Order Changes in Noun Phrases

I should like to conclude this section with a brief discussion of
word order changes within noun phrases. While I have shown in section
3.1 that these changes are subject to diffusion by contact, an internal
cause of the change from Mod-N to N-Mod (where Mod can stand for a number of noun modifiers and complements, e.g., possessives, relative
clauses, etc.) was not given. In particular, one might ask why languages with SOV order tend to have Mod-N, and why languages with SVO
order tend to have N-mod--and finally, why Mod-N changes to N-Mod once
an SOV language becomes SVO.

The intuitive answer is that this represents some kind of analogy.
Since Lehmann (1973a) has argued that what is important is the relationship between the object and the verb (OV vs. VO), we can say that O is
to V as Mod is to N. Givón (1971, 1974) has claimed that the syntactic
order of sentences creeps into the noun phrase via nominalization.
Since John lions tames, with SOV order, can become nominalized as lion-
tamer, where the Mod-N order mirrors the SOV sentential order, when SOV
changes to SVO, i.e., John tames lions, we might expect new nominalizations to eventually follow this modified word order, i.e., tamer-lion.
Other changes (e.g., my yams to yams my) are seen to proceed by analogy.

Evidence from West Africa suggests that this view of the role of
nominalization is inadequate. Rather, the same notion of afterthought
seems to be at work in noun phrases as well as in verbal clauses. As
noted in section 3.1 above (see in particular the examples in (13)),
Nupe and Gwari, the major representatives of the Niger-Kaduna branch of
Kwa, have opposite word orders in their noun phrases. In Gwari the
proto order Mod-N is maintained, while Nupe has changed it (along with
its neighbors to the South) to N-Mod, to conform with SVO syntax.
Examples are given in (40):

(40) Nupe   ēyé ētsū   'eye of chief'

      Gwari ōsū ōwyé   'chief's eye'

There is good reason to believe (as was asserted above) that Gwari maintains the proto word order. First, as pointed out by Westermann (1927),

there are a number of lexicalized compounds in Nupe which exhibit the
old Mod-N order, as seen in (41):

(41) ēyā zǔmà   'hull' (lit. boat-back)

     èwò kpātsǔ   'neck of a garment' (lit. garment-neck)

Although Nupe now has N-poss, these compounds were by virtue of their
being lexicalized not subject to the change from poss-N to N-poss discussed in section 3.1. Second, in both Nupe and Gwari there is a productive process of nominalization which is effected by changing the
order of the direct object and the verb, as in (42) from Nupe:

(42) ší ēčī   'buy yams!'

     ēčī-ší   'yam-buying'

Although structurally 'yam-buying' is mod-N (more specifically, poss-N),
when ordinary possessives (genitives) were subjected to the word order
change (so that my yams became yams my), nominalizations were exempted.
The fact that this process, which also exists in Akan and Ewe (indicating the former SOV nature of these languages), is maintained in Nupe
(which has otherwise moved on to N-Mod in accordance with its advanced
SVO status), suggests that Givón's model of SOV syntax creeping into the
noun phrase via nominalization is incorrect--at least for Kwa. In Nupe,
it is nominalization alone which has not shifted from Mod-N to N-Mod.
There must, therefore, be another cause, whether analogy or whatever,
for this change.

That nominalizations such as in (42) should resist the word order
change is not surprising. After all, if ēčī-ší 'yam-buying' were to
change to ší-ēčī, there would be no way to tell a true verb plus object
(as in the imperative 'buy yams!') from a nominalization.[8] True possessives (as well as demonstratives, relative clauses, etc.) could
change their word order without any resulting confusion.

Westermann (1927) provides a structural cause for the change of
poss-N to N-poss in Gǔ, the dialect of Ewe which exhibits Eastern Kwa
characteristics. The following stages are posited:

(43) my-boat > boat my-thing > boat my-own > boat-my

We start with the possessive pronoun preceding the possessed noun boat.

In the first change the noun <u>thing</u> typically comes to be used for emphatic support, as in various West African languages. In the second
change 'thing' has become grammaticalized, perhaps ceasing to be phonetically identical with the independent noun it derives from. It gradually becomes a pronoun of sorts. This stage is sometimes glossed 'boat
that-of-mine' (giving the impression of an appositive), or simply 'boat
mine', since the pronominal part typically can stand alone in the meaning of 'mine'. Finally, we drop the 'own' part and now have a simple
possessive pronoun <u>after</u> the noun.

As already mentioned, many West African languages have a morpheme
which comes between the noun and its possessor (see Welmers 1963). In
Igbo and Nupe, for instance, as seen respectively in (43a) and (43b),

(43) a. ụ́gbọ̣ 'm̄   b. ēyā ´ mǐˋ   'my boat'

    ụ́gbọ̣ ŋ̀kè m̄   ēyā nyá mǐˋ   'my (own) boat'

ŋ̀kè and nyá both mean 'thing' and are used for emphasis. The Nupe case
is particularly instructive since nyá 'own' derives from the noun ēnyā
'thing' (with mid-mid tone) followed by an associative (or genitive)
high tone, which is also seen in 'my boat' in Nupe in (43b). Nupe differs from Gũ, however, in that the intermediate order is 'boat thing-my'
rather than 'boat my-thing'. This suggests either that 'thing' came to
be used after Nupe had already become N-poss, or else that the intermediate 'boat my-thing' switched to 'boat thing-my', just as 'my-boat'
switches to 'boat-my'. What this latter reconstruction would mean is
that speakers were still aware of the noun-ness of 'thing' when the
switch took place--which, recall, we attributed to contact (presumably
from Yoruba) in section 3.1. In other words, the derivation in (43)
remains at this point merely an attractive, but unsupported hypothesis.

There is, however, more to be said about such appositionals. In
particular, while morphemes such as ŋ̀kè in Igbo and nyá in Nupe can be
used in a contrastive sense (i.e., my <u>own</u> yams--not yours), the fact
that ŋ̀kè m̄ and nyá mǐˋ (both meaning 'mine') can stand alone is significant. This means that should the possession of yams be left out, it
can be added on later, as in a two-word reply to a question, or as we
shall see, after a final verb. In order to see how this might work, let
us turn to a different construction, this time with data from Gwari. As

pointed out in Hyman and Magaji (1970), there are a number of tense/
aspect markers which require the word order in (44):

(44) Subj + TM + Dir Obj + Verb + Everything else

This word order in Gwari, which is reminiscent both of the role of
tense/aspect markers (TM) in Kru and the general syntactic order in
Mande (see (23) above), is illustrated in the following example:

(45) wó kú àshnamá àbà gyǐ   'he has eaten two yams'
     he PAST yams two eat

In this sentence àshnamá àbà 'two yams', the direct object, comes between the completive marker kú (which comes from a verb 'to take'), and
the main verb gyǐ 'to eat'. Just as Nupe has an intensifier nyá which
can occur between a noun and its possessor, Gwari can place an intensifier ōgnú 'unit' between a noun and a numeral, e.g., àshnamá àbà 'two
yams' or àshnamá ōgnú àbà 'yams units-two'. The only possible nuance
between these two phrases is that the second emphasizes the fact that
there were two units of yams, while the first simply communicates 'two
yams worth' (cf. sūlè àbà 'two shillings' vs. sūlè ōgnú àbà 'two shil-
ling pieces'). What is interesting is that the normal word order for an
ōgnú construction parallel to (45) is that seen in (46):

(46) wó kú àshnamá gyǐ ōgnú àbà   'he has eaten two yams'
     he PAST yams eat units two

This sentence looks very much like an apposition, 'he has eaten yams...
two of them', something which would be likely to function as an afterthought. Thus, I would like to propose that the ability of ōgnú àbà
to be postposed after the main verb in (46) is directly tied to the
autonomy of this phrase (meaning 'two units', i.e., 'two of them'), just
as the ability of 'my thing' to postpose is seen from the autonomy of
the Nupe phrase nyá mǐˋ 'mine'.

In conclusion, we can hypothesize that afterthought is an important element in changes in the noun phrase as well as in the sentence
at large. The reason why it hits the sentence first is because of the
magnitude of the problem of afterthought--i.e., the units which can
serve as afterthoughts are simply larger in scope, more likely to be
forgotten. Thus, if afterthought is to lead to a rearrangement of the
syntactic units, it will take place historically first in the change

from SOV to SVO, and then in the change from Mod-N and N-Mod, as was
seen in the two separate syntactic waves which hit Kwa territory (section 3.1).

4.0 The Development of "Serialization"

Much of the historical picture portrayed by Givón (1974) centers
around the role verb serialization <u>potentially</u> plays in changes of word
order, particularly in the change from SVO to SOV. I have already suggested that grammaticalization of a serial verb does not contribute to
an understanding of the SOV to SVO change in Niger-Congo. However, I
feel that a reply to Givón's treatment of serialization is both necessary and called for.

4.1. The Nature of Serialization

I have already shown that contact plays an important role in the
diffusion of syntactic change. This applies to the change from SOV to
SVO and from Mod-N to N-Mod. In this section I should like to claim
that it also applies to the syntactic development of serialization.
However, before launching into this very complex situation, it is worthwhile to consider exactly what is meant by serialization or "serial
verbs". The term generally refers to verbs which occur in sequence, but
which are not overtly marked for coordination or subordination with respect to each other. Some of the major references in African languages
are Stahlke (1970), Hyman (1971), Bamgboṣe (1972, 1973), Awobuluyi
(1973) and Lord (1973). An example of verb serialization is given from
Nupe in (47):

(47) Mūsā lá èbī bā nākã̀   'Musa cut the meat with a knife'
      Musa take knife cut meat (lit. Musa took knife cut meat)

Sentences such as (48), on the other hand,

(48) Mūsā lá èbī čī bā nākã̀   'Musa took the knife and (then)
      Musa take knife and cut meat   cut the meat'

are not considered to have serialization, since there is an overt mark
of conjunction (čī 'and then').

In Hyman (1971) I pointed out that serialized verbs derive historically from a consecutive type of coordination, citing as evidence the
fact that certain West African languages (e.g., Igbo and Feʔfeʔ-Bamileke)

have verbs with overt consecutive markers in exactly those constructions
where Nupe and other languages have a serialized verb. Thus, corresponding to the Nupe sentence in (47) is the Feʔfeʔ sentence in (49):

(49) a la lãh piɛ ncwēe mbaɑ   'he cut the meat with a knife'
      he PAST take knife and-cut meat

The nasal prefix of ncwēe is the mark of consecutivization (see Hyman
1971).

Givón prefers to give a semantic definition to serialization, a
term which he uses whenever the content of two verbs is seen to be one
event or action. This usually means that one of the verbs will not
appear in its literal sense, i.e., will become grammaticalized. Thus,
what is important to Givón in (47) and (49) is the fact that the verb
'to take' is not being used in its literal physical sense. That this is
the case is seen from the sentence in (50),

(50) a la lãh piɛ ndãh   ncwēe mbaɑ
      he PAST take knife and-take and-cut meat

'he took the knife and cut meat with it'

where a second occurrence of the verb 'to take' appears in its literal
sense (note that l becomes d after n in ndãh 'and take', which is frequently simplified to nãh). In fact, in all of the languages in which
'to take' is used in an instrumental sense, it is better glossed as 'to
use'. Thus, (49) can be glossed 'he used a knife to cut the meat' and
(50) can be glossed 'he took a knife and used (it) to cut the meat'.

Givón's observation is that the semantic shift from 'to take' to
'to use' precedes the morphological adjustment which is bound to follow.
While this semantic shift is reflected in the strict ∅ marking of the
second verb in the Nupe sentence in (47),[9] Feʔfeʔ still keeps the consecutive nasal prefix on ncwēe 'and cut'. However, using a strictly
semantic criterion by itself obscures the syntactic distinctness of
these languages, and devoids the notion of serialization of any significance as a typological feature. Givón sees the rise of serialization as a response to the loss of case markings on nouns, in our case,
the one which marks instrumentality on nouns via suffixation. It is
clear that an African language (or any language for that matter) which

has neither a case marker nor a preposition meaning 'with' will have to
devise some way to express the notion of instrumentality (to take just
one of the several situations where serialization is often observed--
cf. Hyman 1971, Givón 1974). However, I don't think it is so remark-
able that they do so by means of the verb 'to take' in West Africa.
Assuming that every language has a verb meaning roughly 'to take' and a
verb meaning 'to cut', it is hard to imagine any language where (51)
cannot be used in an instrumental sense:

(51) take the knife and cut the meat!

While (51) can be used to express either one or two events, (52) can
only be used to express two separate events:

(52) take the knife and cut the meat with it!

Of course there may be an understood 'with it' in (51), in which case
it is probably best seen as expressing two actions. What is noteworthy
in West Africa is that so many languages have dropped the 'with it', and
not that so many languages can use 'take' in a special way. In fact,
some of Givón's statements about serialization apply equally well to
English--in which case English becomes a serializing language and the
distinction between serializing and not serializing becomes trivial, if
not nonexistent.

In Hyman (1971) I suggested that the consecutive naturally lends
itself to "semantic serialization" (i.e., two verbs acting together to
describe one event, à la Givón), because of the resultative nature of
the construction. A sentence such as in (53),

(53) he went to the market and bought yams

is normally construed as indicated two connected actions, where the
second results from the first, which it follows temporally. This resultative relationship, which will be the natural one which a listener will
assign to such a sentence, is further seen in (54),

(54) he took the knife and sang a song

where one will seek a resultative relationship between the knife-taking
and the song-singing. Only after having exhausted this possibility,
will the temporal relationship be assigned. One might imagine, for
instance, that the person in (54) had to first take the knife as a

prerequisite for singing, either as the result of having been ordered to do so--or perhaps the knife was necessary for the performance. Of course, languages frequently provide the means for conjoining sentences in a non-resultative way. Thus, the sentences in (55),

(55) a. he went to the market and also bought yams

b. he took the knife and also sang a song

not only disassociate the two actions from any resultative relationship, but also say nothing about their relative chronology. Naturally, it is the consecutive/resultative conjunction in (53) and (54) which gives rise to serialization, not the kind of loose conjunction seen in these last examples.

4.2. Serialization as an Areal Phenomenon

For the purposes of this section, let us go along with Givón and assume that serialization occurs in a language when two verbs either must be or are usually used to express a single event, i.e., let us accept for the moment the semantic definition, rather than a morphosyn-tactic one. I should like to suggest that serialization (e.g., the use of 'to take' in an instrumental sense) is restricted areally, just as we saw to be the case with poss-N vs. N-poss. Givón points out that serialization is frequently encountered in West Africa. However, with-in this vast area there are important exceptions. Fe?fe?, for example, while using 'to take' in the sense of 'to use', as was seen in (49), also has a preposition mà 'with' which can be used instead, as in (56):

(56) à lá cwée mbáα mά piε   'he cut the meat with a knife'
      he PAST cut meat with knife

In addition, closely related in a group just outside Bamileke is Babanke,[10] where the normal way to express the idea in (56) is as in (57):

(57) γə̄ tə́ˆ tɛ̀n ɲàm nə̀ fə̀ɲì   'he cut the meat with a knife'
      he PAST cut meat with knife

The Babanke sentence in (58),

(58) γə̄ tə́ˆ lyə̀ fə̀ɲì ə̀tɛ̀n ɲàm (nə̀ fə̀wɛ́n'fə́)
      he PAST take knife and-cut meat   with it

      'he took the knife and cut the meat (with it)'

is equivalent to the English gloss given, not to the instrumental gloss given in previous examples. The same set of facts cover 'to take' in what Givón calls an "associative" sense. While Nupe and Fe?fe?-Bamileke use serialized and consecutivized versions of 'to come', as in (59a) and (59b), respectively,

(59) a. ū lá èbī bě   'he brought a knife'
          he take knife come   (lit. he took knife come)

      b. à là láh pìɛ nsá̃?
          he PAST take knife and-come

Babanke (which is, recall, in the same Bantoid group as Bamileke) has the corresponding sentence in (60):

(60) γə̄ tá̂ˇ vè nə̀ fə́ɲì   'he brought a knife'
      he PAST come with knife   (lit. he came with a knife)

The sentence in (61), which involves the verb 'to take',

(61) γə̄ tá̂ˇ lyὰ fə́ɲì   ə̀vè   (nə̀ fə̀wέn'fə́)
      he PAST take knife and-come with it

      'he took the knife and came (with it)'

is not likely to be used in the sense of 'brought'. That is, its meaning is exactly that of the English gloss.

These data suggest that Givón's statement that serialization occurs in "Semi-Bantu" (i.e., non-Bantu Bantoid in Greenberg's classification) is overgeneralized.

Givón has already noted several languages where serialization does not occur--e.g., it is almost totally lacking in Mande. Within Kwa, where most of the serialization phenomena have been reported, Kru stands out as lacking the 'take' construction found to the East of it. In addition, Gwari, located in Northern Nigeria, does not use serialization for this purpose. In instrumental and associative constructions, the preposition ò̩ ... ī is used:

(62) a. wó kú ābû cè̩ ò̩bè̩ ī   'he has cut meat with a knife'
          he PAST meat cut knife with

      b. wó kú ɓě ò̩bè̩ ī   'he has brought a knife'
          he PAST come knife with   (lit. he has come with a knife)

Thus, it seems best to treat serialization of this type as a wave hitting most of Kwa (except the extreme West, i.e., Kru, and the extreme North, i.e., Gwari), as well as parts of other sub-branches of Niger-Congo. It should be clear from a comparison of non-serializing Gwari with its close relative and serializing language, Nupe, that serialization will probably not turn out to be a useful clue in historical reconstruction.[11]

There is, however, one interesting note which should be mentioned in this regard. Ịjọ, as reported by Williamson (1965), is a serializing language which is SOV. All of the other serializing languages are SVO. There are two ways to explain this. First, serializing first hit all of these languages, and then the SOV to SVO wave hit all of these languages except Ịjọ; or, second, the SOV to SVO wave hit all of these languages except Ịjọ, and then the serialization wave hit all of these languages including Ịjọ. Because of the complication mentioned in footnote (11), I am unable to determine which is an older innovation, SOV to SVO or serialization. If, however, the second historical account is correct, then Givón's claim that serialization is disfavored by SOV languages (or is perceptually complex) is somewhat weakened. The anomalous Ịjọ case could be entirely attributed to historical wave effects, and not to the naturalness or unnaturalness of serializing with an SOV syntax. At the very least we can say that the claimed complexity of serialization in SOV languages was not great enough to prevent its introduction by contact into Ịjọ. I should point out that serialization does occur in SOV languages, e.g., Lahu (Matisoff 1973) and Japanese (Masayoshi Shibatani, personal communication). It just doesn't occur in too many African SOV languages, because the only SOV language in the serialization belt is Ịjọ. And there it occurs.

5. Summary and Conclusion

The conclusion of the foregoing sections is that the change from SOV to SVO in Niger-Congo was activated by afterthought and diffused by contact. Admittedly, the concept of afterthought remains somewhat unrigorous at this point, and it probably covers a number of more or less related phenomena. What ties these phenomena together as a cause of word order change is the fact that speakers may find it necessary to append additional information after completing the basic sentence with the inherited SOV syntax. In so doing, a certain point is reached at which a restructuring of the syntactic order takes place, yielding a preferred syntax with the verb no longer final--and ultimately, a standardized syntax with the verb second. It may even be the case that similar afterthought phenomena may give rise to VSO and VOS word orders, as when in French one hears the utterance <u>il a mangé le pain, Jean</u> 'he ate the bread, John'. Whether this rightward dislocation process is used for contrast, disambiguation, or simply for the addition of forgotten information, its role in syntactic change must be recognized.

<u>NOTES</u>

1. Research on this paper was supported in part by a Postdoctoral
Fellowship from the Miller Institute for Basic Research in Science,
University of California, Berkeley. I would like to thank Wallace
Chafe, Charles Fillmore, Talmy Givón, Charles Li, Theo Vennemann and
Karl Zimmer for discussing various aspects of this paper with me.

2. Li and Thompson talk only about the change from SVO to SOV as being
caused by grammaticalization, though my discussion of grammaticalization
providing the impetus for a change from SOV to SVO is exactly parallel.

3. The Kru data are based on two quarters informant work in Los
Angeles, which was jointly conducted with Baruch Elimelech and Seyon
Jackson.

4. Steve Luckau has informed me (personal communication) that sé 'not'
derives historically from a verb 'to lie, tell a falsehood', which probably was intransitive.

5. Saeed Ali has informed me (personal communication) that virtually
the same grammatical clauses appear as afterthoughts after the verb in
Sanskrit. See Gonda (1959), Ali (1974).

6. Vennemann (1973a) sees the conservativeness of pronouns as the result of the fact that case markings on pronouns remain longer than case
markings on nouns (e.g., English he vs. him). One additional thing to
consider in Bantu is the fact that direct object pronouns are wedged
between tense/aspect markers and the verb stem and therefore are frozen
in that position, so to speak (cf. Givón 1971).

7. I ignore here potential nuances which may have originally been associated with restricted vs. non-restricted relative clauses, e.g., non-
restricted relative clauses may once have been (and may still be) more
likely to postpose than restricted relative clauses.

8. The associative high tone found in such constructions has long
been lost in nominalizations in Niger-Kaduna (cf. lion-tamer, not *lions'-
tamer).

9. The one change that occurs on the second verb in series in Niger-
Kaduna is that a high tone verb becomes a rising tone, as if there were
a preceding "floating" low tone in the underlying structure (cf. the

example in (59a), where bé 'to come' has an underlying high tone, but a rising tone as the second of two verbs in series).

10. The Babanke data is based on informant work in Berkeley, which was jointly conducted with Joseph Ntiangsi, Jean-Marie Hombert and Annie Hawkinson.

11. There is one problem here, namely, Gwari uses the verbs lá/kú 'to take' as completive markers, e.g., example (62a) literally means 'he take meat cut knife with', where the take shows the same syntactic properties as the take in Nupe and Fe?fe?, but has the meaning of completion. It is possible that Gwari (and to a certain extent Nupe, though I cannot go into this here) has modified the take + verb construction semantically, and that it too had serialization of the instrumental and associative type at one time.

REFERENCES

Ali, Saeed. 1974. "Society for the preservation of SOV languages". Ms. UCLA.

Awobuluyi, Qladele. 1973. "The modifying serial construction: a critique". Studies in African Linguistics 4.87-111.

Bamgboṣe, Ayọ. 1972. "On serial verbs and verbal status". To appear in Journal of West African Languages.

Bamgboṣe, Ayọ. 1973. "The modifying serial construction: a reply". Studies in African Linguistics 4.207-217.

Bartsch, Renate and Theo Vennemann. 1972. Semantic Structures: a study in the relation between semantics and syntax. (Athenäum-Skripten Linguistik, No. 9). Frankfurt am Main: Athenäum.

Givón, Talmy. 1971. "Historical syntax and synchronic morphology: an archeologist's field trip". In Papers from the Seventh Regional Meeting, University of Chicago: Chicago Linguistic Society.

Givón, Talmy. 1974. "Serial verbs and syntactic change: Niger-Congo". In this volume.

Gonda, J. 1959. "On amplified sentences and similar structure in the Veda." In Four Studies in the Language of the Veda, 7-70. Mouton, The Hague.

Greenberg, Joseph H. 1966. "Some universals of grammar with particular reference to the order of meaningful elements". In Universals of Language (J. Greenberg, ed.), 73-113. Cambridge, Mass.: M.I.T. Press.

Hyman, Larry M. 1971. "Consecutivization in Feʔfeʔ". Journal of African Languages 10.29-43.

Hyman, Larry M. and Daniel J. Magaji. 1970. Essentials of Gwari Grammar. (Occasional Publication No. 27, Institute of African Studies). Ibadan: Ibadan University Press.

Lehmann, Winfred P. 1972a. "On the rise of SOV patterns in New High German". In Grammatik, Kybernetik, Kommunikation (Festschrift für Alfred Hoppe) (K. Schweisthal, ed.), 19-24. Bonn: Dümmler.

Lehmann, Winfred P. 1972b. "Proto-Germanic Syntax". In Toward a Grammar of Proto-Germanic (F. van Coetsem and H. Kufner, eds.), 239-268. Tübingen: Max Niemeyer.

Lehmann, Winfred P. 1973a. "A structural principle of language and its implications". Language 49.47-66.

Lehmann, Winfred P. 1973b. Historical Linguistics: An Introduction. Second Edition. New York: Holt, Rinehart and Winston.

Li, Charles N. and Sandra A. Thompson. 1973. "Historical change of word order: a case study of Chinese and its implications". Paper presented at First International Conference on Historical Linguistics. Edinburgh, September 1973.

Lord, Carol. 1973. "Serial verbs in transition". Studies in African Linguistics 4.269-296.

Matisoff, James A. 1973. The Grammar of Lahu. (University of California Publications in Linguistics 75). Berkeley: University of California Press.

Pike, Kenneth L. 1967. "Grammar as wave". Monograph Series on Languages and Linguistics 20 (E. Blansitt, ed.), 1-14. Also in Kenneth L. Pike Selected Writings (R. Brend, ed.), 231-241. The Hague: Mouton. 1972.

Pike, Kenneth L. 1970. Tagmemic and Matrix Linguistics Applied to Selected African Languages. Oklahoma: Summer Institute of Linguistics.

Stahlke, Herbert. 1970. "Serial verbs". Studies in African Linguistics 1.60-99.

Vennemann, Theo. 1972. "Analogy in generative grammar: the origin of word order". Paper read at the International Congress of Linguists, August-September 1972.

Vennemann, Theo. 1973a. "Explanation in syntax". In Syntax and Semantics Vol. II (J. Kimball, ed.), 1-50. New York: Seminar Press.

Vennemann, Theo. 1973b. "Language type and word order". Paper read at the Symposium on Typology, Prague, August 14-17, 1973. Reproduced by Linguistic Agency, University at Trier.

Vennemann, Theo. 1973c. "Topics, subjects, and word order: from SXV to SVX via TVS". Presented at First International Congress of Historical Linguistics, Edinburgh, September 1973.

Welmers, William E. 1963. "Associative a and ka in Niger-Congo". Language 39.432-447.

Welmers, William E. 1964. "The syntax of emphasis in Kpelle". Journal of West African Languages 1.13-26.

Welmers, William E. 1969. "The morphology of Kpelle nominals". Journal of African Languages 8.73-101.

Westermann, Diedrich. 1927. "Das Nupe im Nigerien". Mitteilungen des Seminars für Orientalische Sprachen 30.173-207.

Williamson, Kay. 1965. A Grammar of the Kolokuma Dialect of Ijọ. (West African Language Monographs 2). Cambridge: University Press.

A DISCUSSION OF COMPOUND AND WORD ORDER

by

Winfred P. Lehmann

The current interest in general principles of syntactic change indicates that this topic is no longer premature, as suggested by the last
great linguist in the direct Humboldtian tradition, Ernst Lewy. In his
1930 review of Wackernagel's impressive lectures on syntax, Lewy dis-
missed an attempt of Wackernagel's to propose a universal of change with
the words: "We'll still have to wait a bit before we set up general
(universal) laws of language development" (Lewy 1961:243, translation
mine). About the same time Hermann Hirt wrote his plaintive critique of
syntactic studies in which he lamented that syntacticians didn't know
what to do with the series of facts they assembled (1934:vi). We assume
that we do know what to do with them, and that the time has come to set
up universal laws of language development, if cautiously.

   If so, we should state our procedures and abide by them. Hirt
stated his, but though his proposals have some merit they do not touch
on the central problems. For Hirt there were two ways of dealing with
syntax. One was philological investigation; this aims at grammars having
observational and descriptive adequacy. The other was comparative study.
By comparative study Hirt limited himself to one of the two kinds of comparison so excellently characterized by Meillet (1967). Hirt used the
kind of comparison which leads to "historical information" rather than to
"universal laws" (Meillet 1967:13). In this way Hirt hoped to arrive at
an "understanding of syntactic phenomena" (1934:viii); but his success
was limited. We seek an understanding of syntactic phenomena by prac-
ticing comparison to determine universal laws, combining such comparison
with the philological study and historical comparison practiced by Hirt.
In doing so we want to avoid errors that may have kept Hirt and the
earlier syntacticians he criticized, such as Delbrück, Brugmann and
Wackernagel, from providing an understanding of syntax (1934:vi-vii).
This examination of the position of nominal elements of verbs is designed
to illustrate some of the procedures we must observe.

   In studies concerning universals of language we generally start from
an examination of data and then ask questions regarding the data. For
example, in dealing with compounds we may determine that a language, for
example Proto-Indo-European, has few, or no copulative (dvandva) compounds;
and then we may ask why. Similarly, if a language has many synthetic and
possessive (bahuvrihi) compounds we may ask for the bases of these. But
we should also be able to ask why specific syntactic constructions are

not present in a language. Why for example does Hittite have virtually
no compounds? Why doesn't English have synthetic compounds like those
in Proto-Indo-European and Vedic, for example, 'honey-drink' as an adjective? An answer to this last question has been proposed (Lehmann
1969). The previous question, and others like it, remain to be discussed.
I would like especially to move towards answers to questions like that
about the reason for the absence of compounds in Hittite.

In dealing with such questions we must examine the data in accordance
with a model of language, and in accordance with specific principles that
have been observed regarding linguistic structures. Moreover, we must
recognize that languages are historical products.

The data on compounds in late Proto-Indo-European are clear. They
have been assembled through concentrated work by some of the outstanding
linguists of the past century. We assume that Proto-Indo-European compounds consist to about 60% of synthetics, 30% of possessives; the remainder we disregard here (Risch 1944-49). Synthetics are made up of a
nominal and a verbal element in OV order, e.g. Vedic madhu-pa 'drinking
honey'; possessives are made up of two nominal elements, e.g. madhu-varna
'having honey color'. Both kinds of compounds agree in structure with
our expectations in an OV language. The synthetics have OV order of their
elements; the possessives have the modifying element preceding the element
modified. Both kinds correspond in further formal characteristics with
other syntactic constructions in the language, most strikingly in the
accent placement of bahuvrihis and in their correspondence with the Proto-
Indo-European pattern of expressing possession.

The compounds found in late Proto-Indo-European then illustrate a
situation we can explain in part. As indicated above, we can account for
their structure by assuming a generative model of language, and by posit-
ing a language with OV order. But we cannot account for the presence of
compounds in late Proto-Indo-European unless we examine other languages,
among them the early Indo-European dialects.

The compounds in the dialects most widely used for Indo-European
studies, Vedic Sanskrit and Classical Greek, can also be readily interpreted and explained. In their later phases both dialects have propor-
tionately fewer compounds of each of the Proto-Indo-European kinds,
introducing in addition the adjective : noun kind of compound which is
still predominant in Modern English. Thus in Classical Sanskrit we find

compounds like madhu-druma, literally, 'honey-tree (used of the mango)'.
An apparently comparable compound in the Rigveda, madhu-jihva 'honey +
tongue', does not simply characterize the second nominal element as
'sweet' but rather carries the meaning of possession--'one who has sweet-
ness on the tongue, speaking pleasantly'. Similar examples of the shift
in relationship from possessive to descriptive might be cited from
Classical Greek, and from most of the early Indo-European dialects.
Whether having the initial element madhu-, or another nominal element,
the predominant kind of compound in later Indo-European dialects consists
of a modifier : modified pattern, as in Old Norse miǫðrann, Old Russian
meduša 'meadhall', Old English mil-dēaw 'honey-dew > mildew', New English
honey-child, and the like. In the dialects the synthetics disappear as
productive compounds; the possessives are used in restricted spheres. We
would like to be able to explain why the dialects have developed in this
way.

Before we undertake to seek an answer it may be useful to review the
situation in Hittite. Though Hittite contains a very small number of
compounds, in comparison with Vedic Sanskrit or Homeric Greek the process
of compounding is almost non-existent. In trying to account for this
situation we must recall that our knowledge of Hittite is recent, and
fragmentary; further, to use contemporary terminology Hittite has been
characterized as extensively creolized. But since other creoles have
compounds, the lack of compounding in Hittite requires a different explanation. I suggest that such an explanation can be given by means of a
hypothesis of Solveig Pflueger's: compounds with a relationship between
nominal and verbal element are possible only in a language with a predicate node. That is, such compounds are productive only when O's and V's
are contiguous in the underlying syntactic string. Constraints resulting
from the hypothesis would apply to languages like Hittite, in which the
position of the O with regard to the V is not definite, and also to VSO
languages. Insular Celtic, which became VSO after Celtic was introduced
into Britain, gradually abandoned even modifying compounds like the name
Moridunum 'Sea-Fort' of Roman times in favor of phrases like Coed Mawr
'Wood-Big' (Jackson 1953:225). For Hittite however the situation differs
from that of Insular Celtic inasmuch as Hittite maintained its verb-final
clause structure.

We account for the lack of productive compounding of nominal and verbal elements in Hittite because there is no OV predicate. When verbs are accompanied by objects, subjects and other syntactic elements, these are not strictly ordered. Accordingly we must characterize Hittite as a language which has originated from an OV language, but has given up the node from which OV would be derived. This detail is important for the understanding of Hittite.

Even more important is the observation that we can explain compounds and other syntactic patterning of a language by analyzing it in accordance with a framework. Further, I would like to propose as a general working procedure that any hypothesis of syntactic change must be framed in accordance with a strict framework. The impressive paper of Li and Thompson (1973) needs supplementing in this way; if indeed we assume that serializing verbs provided the mechanism for change from a VO to an OV structure we must generate them in accordance with a specific framework. The working procedure proposed above must be observed in dealing with any hypothesis of change in syntax. For only by observing it can we make progress in dealing with the question which may be the most pressing in historical linguistics at present: identifying the events and structures resulting when a language undergoes syntactic change.

It is clear that very few languages can be characterized as consistent, whether OV or VO. While we eagerly seek examples of consistent languages, we take warning from two of the languages attested earliest: Akkadian and Sumerian. As an Afro-Asiatic language Akkadian should be VSO. Sumerian is verb final. But the materials which have come down to us indicate that as early as 2000 B.C., and probably earlier, neither was consistent. Akkadian is not consistently VSO, nor is Sumerian consistently OV.

The reasons for departures from a consistent structure are those any historical linguist is prepared for: mutual influence, or in the troublesome but established linguistic term, borrowing; and internal modification. The regulated syntactic patterns in a language virtually assure marked constructions, which might be called counter-patterns. If these come to be predominant, under circumstances that would have to be identified for any given language, syntactic change may result from internal modification. Other influences resulting in shifting patterns within the language have been a focus of recent research (Li-Thompson, Vennemann, Givón and others). Any such proposed influences must be rigorously examined.

The processes of syntactic change, and the influences proposed for it, must be determined by observing what happens to languages in transition. Although we have scarcely begun to deal with this question it may not be premature to indicate that we must approach it with careful attention to various linguistic structures and to a well-considered theory of language. It is quite likely that we will find different developments when a language changes from OV to VO structure from those in which a VO language becomes OV, or an SVO language becomes VSO. Since I am primarily concerned with Proto-Indo-European, I deal here with characteristics of a language in transition from an OV to a VO structure.

When a language is undergoing syntactic change, some of its characteristics must be modified before others. English, as well as Chinese, Niger-Congo, and many others provide examples. Which constructions change first? Generative phonologists have proposed that low level rules do, that changes are introduced near the "end" of a grammar. Clearly this assumption does not apply to syntactic change. Li, Thompson and Tai have made it clear that the order of O and V changed in Chinese while other constructions determined by rules "later" in the grammar, such as that for modifier and noun, remain unchanged. Similarly Givón on Niger-Congo. We find therefore that syntactic change may be carried out first on early rules, and only subsequently on late rules.

How does this change take place? Some syntactic changes may be ascribed to borrowing, others to internal modifications, in accordance with statements made by many linguists in the past. Unlike our predecessors, however, we now have linguistic evidence which we can interpret within a rigorous framework or theory of language. When we examine languages within such a framework we find that in some languages discrepancies exist between the characteristic patterns expected in a given language; these discrepancies exist in such a way that the verb : object order accords with expectations, but noun modifying orders may not. In French and Spanish, for example, the verb : object order is highly consistent; so in general is the noun : adjective order, but a small group of adjectives, those among the most frequent, precede nouns. Noting such phenomena, as well as similar patterning in other languages, we may be reasonably sure of the conclusion that the verb : object order is somehow prior and the modifying order subsequent to it. German provides evidence for other constructions with which to support this conclusion (Lehmann 1971). As a working principle then we assume that the adoption of a specific verb : object order in a language entails the modification of other syntactic characteristics, such as noun modifier order. We also assume that morphological and phonological modifications are entailed, but these are not of interest to me here (Lehmann 1972). Such a series of assumptions is certainly more attractive in an explanation of syntactic change than is the assumption of analogy between unlike constructions, especially when no attention is given to a syntactic framework (Givón SVSC 41-3).

Moreover, this series of assumptions accords with a generative approach to syntax. A generative approach permits us to account for many features associated with noun modifying constructions in English, starting with the derivation of relative clauses through embedding, and then the derivation of genitival modifiers and of adjectival modifiers from relative constructions. Similar support for such a derivation has been provided on the basis of data in other languages, as in Dixon's of two Australian languages (1969). On the basis of such observations we hold that when an OV language becomes VO, embedded modifying sentences are placed after nouns in the commonly known relative clauses, and also adjectives and genitives; though the changes may take place over a long period of time. The changes in modifiers accordingly entail a massive disruption.

One result of such disruption may well be the development of constructions, such as nominal compounds of the kind called synthetics in Proto-Indo-European. Rather than a relative clause, a compound consisting of a noun with a verbal element may result from the embedded sentence, as in Vedic compounds such as madhu-pá and many others. Support for such an explanation for the production of synthetic compounds may be provided by citing examples of their occurrences.

Of the five occurrences of madhu-pá in the Rigveda, the two found in Archaic hymns may serve to illustrate how synthetics were used. Used adjectivally, RV 8.22.17, the synthetic modifies a noun, as it does in three other of its five occurrences.

ā	no	áśvāvad	aśvina	vartír
hither	to-us	horse-bringing	O Aśvins	trip
		acc. sg. nt.	nom. du.	acc. sg. nt.

yāsiṣṭam	madhupātamā	narā
you-travel-to-make	O-most-mead-drinking	heroes
2 du. aor. imper.	voc. du.	voc. du.

gómad	dasrā	híraṇyavat
cattle-bringing	assisting-with-wonders	gold-bringing
acc. sg. nt.	voc. du.	acc. sg. nt.

'Travel hither to us to make a horse, cattle, and gold bringing
trip, O heroes who drink the most honey, you assisting with
wonders!'

In the other Archaic passage, RV 1.180.2, madhu-pá is used independently
as a vocative.

svásā	yád	vāṃ	viśvagūrtī	bhárāti
sister	when	you	all-praised	she-will-bring
nom. sg. f.			voc. du.	3 sg. subj. pres.

vā́jāyeṭṭe		madhupāv	iṣé	ca
for-food-asks-for		O-honey-drinkers	for-nourishing-drink	and
dat. sg. m. 3 sg. pres.		voc. du.	dat. sg. f.	

'When the sister will bring you, who are praised by all, and
(the singer) calls on you, who drink honey, for food and drink.'

All of these occurrences can be accounted for as results of embedding.

These patterns of use for synthetics led Jacobi to label the verbal
element of synthetics a participle (1897). To distinguish them from the
participles of the dialects he terms them "relative participles", considering them constructions of the Ursprache (1897:21). Jacobi accordingly in his important monograph clearly recognized the position of synthetic compounds at the time of late Proto-Indo-European and the early
dialects, accounting for them in a remarkably prescient analysis. As
indicated above, he pointed out that synthetic compounds corresponded to
relative clauses. He also noted that relative clauses were infrequent
in late Proto-Indo-European, and that only Indo-Iranian, Greek and
Phrygian use yo- as basis for the relative pronoun. Moreover, even as
late as Sanskrit and Homeric Greek, relative clauses are restricted in
use; in Sanskrit for example they occurred only at the beginning or end
of the principal clause according to Jacobi. Unfortunately his interpretation and his insights were disregarded; the standard handbooks

propose for Proto-Indo-European relative clauses like those in the classical languages, with forms derived from yo- as the relative markers. We can account for this unhappy lapse among Indo-Europeanists by noting that little was known about syntactic change, and that historical change was measured purely by surface forms, with little regard for universal or typological criteria. Today much of the requisite theory and the basic data are clear, even though many details remain to be described.

Proto-Indo-European was an OV language. By late Proto-Indo-European the language was changing towards a VO structure. I have indicated this course of development elsewhere (1972). Other scholars, for example Carol Raman, have accounted admirably for particular constructions in accordance with this point of view. But there still is reluctance to conceive of the trend of development of Proto-Indo-European in this way. We will best overcome the reluctance by assembling data on syntactic development from other language families, as in the papers by Li and Thompson on Chinese and Givón on Niger-Congo. We also need to enlarge our understanding of the changes in syntactic constructions when languages change from an OV to a VO structure, or conversely from VO to OV. This paper is designed primarily to direct attention to compounding patterns and the inferences we can draw from them.

A further syntactic pattern of late Proto-Indo-European and the early dialects can also be understood from the changing structure: the widely developing infinitival constructions. On them too the data are well-known; for a brief survey see Brugmann 1904:351-3, 603-6. The various Indo-European dialects have infinitives which are nominal forms of verbs, with the forms of infinitives varying from dialect to dialect. The Sanskrit infinitive is made with an accusative ending: -tum; in the Vedas the most wide-spread endings are dative. The more commonly used Greek and Latin infinitives have locative endings; the Germanic infinitive an accusative, though with a different ending from that of Sanskrit. These morphological facts alone would indicate that infinitival constructions are late in Indo-European.

Infinitival constructions have provided various problems, of which I will deal with only one: the placing of such infinitives after the finite verb. This position has been taken by some scholars as evidence that Proto-Indo-European was VO rather than OV. Although the topic is far too extensive for less than monographic treatment, I would like to

point out a few essentials. The morphologically simplest of the approximately 700 infinitives in the Rigveda are dative forms in -e, as in the
following example.

RV 9.23.2   rucé   jananta   sū́ryam
                for-shining   they-created   sun
                inf. dat.   3 pl. imperf.   acc. sg. m.
                'They created the sun for shining.'

With this infinitive we may compare the dative noun in RV 9.105.5.

sákheva   sákhye   náryo   rucé   bhava
friend-like   to-friend manly for-light esteem   be
nom.sg.m.ptc. dat.sg.m.   nom.sg. m.   dat.sg.f./2 sg.imper.
'Add to esteem like a manly friend to his friend.'

The dative of <u>ruc</u> in this Archaic hymn, RV 9.105.5, is equivalent in form
to the infinitive from <u>ruc-</u> in the chronologically younger hymn 9.23.
Both can be understood as datives of purpose. The dative ending on verb
stems comes to have its distinctive use, and to be accompanied by other
noun forms, as is well-known from the later Indo-European dialects, including English.

    By the time of Homer, and even in Vedic, the infinitive was often
placed after the principal verb, as in RV 1.52.8.

ádhārayo   divy   ā́   sū́ryaṃ   dr̥śé
you-placed   in-heaven   in   sun   for-seeing
2 sg. impf.   loc. sg.   acc. sg.
'You placed the sun in the sky so that (we) could see.'

Infinitive patterns like this abound in Homer, as in Odyssey 1.33.

eks   hēméōn   gár   phasi   kák'   émmenai
out-of   us   for   they-say   evil   be
'For they say that evil comes from us.'

The nominal forms from verbs came in this way to be used in separate
clauses, in the various uses that are well-known.

    Without discussing the Indo-European developments further we may
note that a similar situation is found in Niger-Congo with regard to the
position of case-forms, as pointed out by Givón for Kpelle. The accusative is most conservative as opposed to the other cases in maintaining

the SOV order; locatives, instrumentals, datives and other cases follow the verb, as in the examples cited by Givón (SVSC 8-9). Apparently in the shift to VO structure, these case-forms, which reflect a less direct relationship to the V than does the O, abandon the old sequence first. Whether as nouns, or as infinitives, the Indo-European datives come to follow the principal verb, and in this way assist in the disruption of the OV pattern. The postposed infinitives of Homer and even the Rigveda, as well as those of the later dialects, must accordingly be interpreted as constructions to be expected of a language shifting from OV to VO order.

If the interpretations presented above are correct, synthetic compounds represent maintenance of the OV pattern. Infinitival constructions on the other hand represent a departure from an OV towards a VO structure. Such a departure may be compared with others, for example, the development of postposed relative constructions, of constructions derived from them, and the development of postposed subordinate clauses. Indo-Europeanists must concern themselves with determining these in detail for each of the dialects.

General linguists need to determine the diverse kinds of syntactic changes and their implications. Proto-Indo-European illustrates phenomena occurring upon a change from OV to VO structure. Chinese illustrates change from VO to OV structure. Such changes may be interrupted, as was true for Old Norse, late Classical Sanskrit, Tocharian and presumably many languages which have not yet been studied for their syntactic modifications. We are at the beginnings of our understanding of syntactic change, and hence of the changes which languages undergo in their central structure. The results of improved understanding of such changes scarcely need to be pointed out in detail. Besides interpreting much more fully the history of individual languages and language families, students of historical syntax will contribute highly significant information about language and its structure by determining the modification of constructions in syntactic change.

References

Brugmann, Karl. 1904. Kurze vergleichende Grammatik der indogermanischen
Sprachen. Strassburg: Trübner.

Dixon, R. M. W. 1969. Relative clauses and possessive phrases in two
Australian languages. Language 45.35-44.

Givón, Talmy. Serial verbs and syntactic change: Niger-Congo. Paper prepared for Conference on Word Order and Word Order Change. Santa
Barbara. January 1974.

Hirt, Hermann. 1931-34. Handbuch des Urgermanischen. I-III. Heidelberg: Winter.

Jackson, Kenneth. 1953. Language and history in early Britain. Edinburgh: University Press.

Jacobi, Hermann. 1897. Compositum und Nebensatz. Bonn: Cohen.

Lehmann, W. P. 1969. Proto-Indo-European compounds in relation to other
Proto-Indo-European syntactic patterns. Acta Linguistica Hafniensia
12.1-20.

-------------. 1970. The Nordic languages: lasting linguistic contribu-
tions of the past, pp. 286-305 of The Nordic languages and modern
linguistics, ed. Hreinn Benediktsson. Reykjavík: Vísindafélag
Íslendinga.

-------------. 1971. On the rise of SOV patterns in New High German,
pp. 19-24 of Grammatik Kybernetik Kommunikation, ed. K.G.Schweisthal.
Bonn: Dümmler.

-------------. 1972. Contemporary linguistics and Indo-European studies.
PMLA 87.976-93.

-------------. 1973. A structural principle of language and its implications. Language 49.47-66.

Lewy, Ernst. 1961. Kleine Schriften. Berlin: Akademie.

Li, Charles N. and Sandra A. Thompson. 1973. Historical change of word
order: A case study in Chinese and its implications. (Unpublished
paper.)

Meillet, Antoine. 1967. The comparative method in historical linguistics.
Trans. from the French by Gordon B. Ford, Jr. Paris: Champion.

Raman, Carol F. 1973. The Old Hittite relative construction. Austin:
The University of Texas dissertation.

Risch, Ernst. 1944-49. Griechische Determinativ-Komposita. Indogermanische Forschungen 59.1-61, 245-94.

Tai, James H-Y. 1973. Chinese as a SOV language. pp. 659-71 of Papers from the Ninth Regional Meeting. Chicago: Chicago Linguistic Society.

Vennemann, Theo. Topics, Subjects, and Word Order: From SVX to SXV via TVX. Paper presented at the First International Congress of Historical Linguistics. Edinburgh. September 1973.

Wackernagel, Jacob. 1926-28. Vorlesungen über Syntax. I-II. 2nd ed. Basel: Birkhäuser.

THE SEMANTIC FUNCTION OF WORD ORDER: A CASE STUDY IN MANDARIN *

by

Charles N. Li and Sandra A. Thompson

*We are grateful to the following people for valuable discussion in the preparation of this paper: Chi Te-lee, Talmy Givón, Robert Hetzron, Marie-Claude Jorland, Robert Kirsner, Edith Moravcsik, Arthur Schwartz, James H-Y. Tai, McMillan Thompson, and Eric Zee. None of them, of course, is responsible for the form our remarks take here.

0. Introduction

It has been observed by a number of scholars that word order in Mandarin Chinese plays a role in distinguishing definite from indefinite nouns.[1] The interaction between the word order of sentence construction and the definite/indefinite property of nominals is nothing startling. In many languages, for instance, the unmarked or the preferred word order of certain constructions tends to place the definite noun before the indefinite noun. This type of inter-play between word order and definite/indefinite nouns has been discussed by a number of linguists. Kuno (1971), arguing on the basis of evidence collected from both OV and VO languages, stated that the indefinite subject noun following the locative is the unmarked word order for existential sentences. Clark (1970), on the other hand, showed that the definite subject noun of a locative sentence usually occurs before the locative phrase. Givón (personal communication) notes that in the absence of morphological markers for definiteness in Rwanda and Luganda, a definite object noun must be placed at the initial position of a negative sentence, whereas an indefinite object noun remains in the post-verbal position. Underhill (1972) pointed out that in Turkish, while the subject normally is in sentence initial position, an indefinite subject is placed after a definite object or a definite location noun. These cases of correlation between word order and definite/indefinite nouns are not surprising in view of the fact that a widespread tendency in discourse strategy among languages is to place old information, hence, definite nominals, before new information, hence indefinite nominals.[2] What is significant about the Mandarin Chinese case is the systematic aspect of the correlation. In the absence of morphological markers, word order has taken on the function of denoting the definite/indefinite property of nominals. This semantic function of word order is not confined to just certain syntactic constructions, but appears to be a general grammatical strategy of the language.

In this paper, we will describe the semantic function of word order with respect to definiteness in Mandarin Chinese. Evidence will be presented to demonstrate that definite nouns, whether subject or object, tend to be placed before the verb, whereas indefinite nouns tend to follow the verb. We will then point out that this function of word order in Chinese was developed in the past millenium and that, as a relatively new grammatical device, it is in conflict with the shift from SVO to SOV--a diachronic process presently in action (see Li & Thompson [1973a], [1973c]). Our analysis will indicate that this conflict is most likely to be resolved in favor of the shift to SOV word order.

1. Definiteness and Word Order

1.1 Previous Scholarship

Let us briefly examine the observations of three scholars mentioned in footnote (1): J. Mullie, F. Li, and Y.R. Chao.

Mullie (1932) makes the following two generalizations:

1) A subject already known by reason of the circumstances in which the speakers happen to be ... must be placed before the verb, because it is determinate. (Underlining Mullie's)

    (1) Bīng   lái   -dào   le[3]
           soldiers come arrive asp.

    The soldiers have arrived.

    (2) Zéi   pǎo   le
           thief run asp.

    The thief has run away.

2) Whenever the indetermination of the subject of intransitive verbs is expressed in English by the indefinite article, by the absence of an article, or by the partitive demonstrative there, the subject is placed after the verb in Chinese.

    (3) Lái   le   bīng
           come asp. soldiers

    There came soldiers.

    (4) Pǎo   le   zéi
           run asp. thief

    There escaped a thief.

Some further examples are provided by him to make the distinction clear:

(5) a. Sǐ   rén   le
      die   person asp.

      <u>A</u> man has died.

   b. Rén   sǐ   le
      person die   asp.

      <u>The</u> man is dead.

(6) a. Kāi   le   shēng-kou
      loose asp.   animal

      <u>An</u> animal is loosed.

   b. Shēng-kou   kāi   le
      animal   loose asp.

      <u>The</u> animal is loosed.

Mullie's term "indeterminate" corresponds to our usage "indefinite". The concept definite/indefinite can be thought of as referring to a "registry" established in a discourse. A nominal is considered definite if its referent has already been established in the registry at the time of the utterance. Thus, the speaker presupposes the hearer's knowledge of the referent of a definite noun phrase. A definite noun, in our usage, corresponds approximately to "known information". An indefinite noun, on the other hand, is new to the registry of discourse. The speaker does not presuppose the hearer's knowledge of its referent. Hence, an indefinite noun represents "new information". These terms "known" and "new" correspond to a certain extent to the terms "theme" and "rheme", respectively, which were first introduced in the writings of the Prague School. (For discussion of these latter terms, see Li [1971] as well as Firbas [1964], [1965], [1966] and references cited in these works.)

Mullie's observations indicate that intransitive sentences with subjects morphologically unmarked for definiteness have two word orders: SV and VS. The former, with a pre-verbal subject, correlates with the definite interpretation of the nominal; the latter, with a post-verbal subject, correlates with the indefinite interpretation of the nominal.[4]

When we turn to sentences with a transitive verb, it becomes obvious that Mullie's observations should be part of a broader generalization. Let us first examine some data. The following word order patterns, among others, can be found in colloquial Mandarin:

(7) a. N V N

b. N N V[5]

Examples of (7a), the "SVO" pattern, include the following:

(8) Zhāng-sān   dǎ-pò   chuānghu   le
     Zhang-san   hit-be broken window   asp.

Zhang-san broke a window.

(9) Zhāng-sān   chī-wán   le   fàn   le
     Zhang-san   eat-finish   asp.   food   asp.

Zhang-san has finished eating.

Examples of (7b), the verb-final pattern, are usually described as constructions transformationally derived by rules fronting the direct object of the SVO sentence: "topicalized" sentences, BA sentences, and BEI sentences. The generalizations concerning the semantic function of word order reached in this study, however, cast serious doubt on the adequacy of deriving these verb-final sentences from the SVO sentence. We deal with this problem in a separate work (see Li & Thompson [forthcoming]).

"Topicalized" sentences

(10) Shū,   háizi   mǎi   le
      book   child   buy   asp.

As for the book, the child bought it.

(11) Háizi,   shū   mǎi   le
      child   book   buy   asp.

The child bought the book.

BA sentence

   (12) Háizi   bǎ   shū   mǎi   le
         child   obj. marker   book   buy   asp.

   What the child did to the book was buy it.

BEI sentence

   (13) Shū   bèi   háizi   mǎi   le
        book   agent marker   child   buy   asp.

   The book was bought by {the / a} child.

These examples, with the exception of (13) (the noun after bèi), clearly illustrate that morphologically unmarked nouns placed after the verb in a transitive sentence are interpreted as indefinite, whereas those placed before the verb are interpreted as definite.

Li (1971), quoting Chao (1968), sums this up as follows:

"Unlike English, Chinese surface structure does not require that some NP precede the verb. Consequently, even when there is only one NP in the underlying proposition, this NP may freely occur either before or after the verb. As a reflection of this freedom, Chinese shows a very high correlation between theme-rheme function and pre- and post-verbal position.

"To a great extent, theme-rheme coincides with the definite-indefinite distinction. Chao, who treats a sentence-initial NP as 'subject' and any post-verbal NP as 'object', explains the relation between word order and definite-indefinite in terms of information:

'the subject is likely to represent the known while the predicate introduces something unknown... Thus there is a very strong tendency for the subject to have a definite reference and the object to have an indefinite reference (Chao, 1968, p. 76)'.

(Li, 1971, p. 157)

"Although Chao does not explicitly name the verb as the demarcation between definite and indefinite reference, remarks such as the following indicate that position relative to the verb is the crucial factor:

'It is, however, not so much the subject or object function
that goes with definite or indefinite reference as position
in an earlier or later part of the sentence that makes the
difference. Thus, by the use of the pretransitive BA an
object is moved farther ahead and is made more suggestive of
a definite reference (Chao, 1968, p. 76f)'.
(Li, 1971, p. 165)"

We have quoted Li so extensively here partly because she incorporates Chao's remarks on this topic, but more importantly because she
provides the best statement in the extant literature regarding the correlation between definiteness and word order in Chinese.

The observations on the interplay between word order and definite-
ness/indefiniteness quoted and discussed in the preceding paragraphs
came from three sources. They converge on the generalization that

Tendency A

Nouns preceding the verb tend to be definite, while those
following the verb tend to be indefinite.

While this generalization is correct, it needs some further refinement.[6]

1.2 Refinements

We have indicated that the correlations between the word order of
sentences and the definite/indefinite property of nominals are more
complex than what has been stated. To a large extent, the complexity
is a consequence of the conflict between these correlations and the
diachronic process of word order change which Mandarin Chinese is currently undergoing. It is our opinion that the phenomenon--the interaction between synchrony and diachrony--represented here by this conflict, is not a rarity in languages. On the contrary, the interaction
between synchrony and diachrony seems to be wide-spread, as it is well
attested in phonology. However, in syntax, the identification of a
diachronic process in action is difficult, and this difficulty may
explain the lack of attention given to this important linguistic phenomenon. Yet synchronic heterogeneity is often the result of different rates of grammatical change among the members of a syntactic class,
and synchronic complexity may be caused by the interference of a separate and distinct diachronic shift. We will describe the nature of the

conflict between the semantic function of word order and the word order change in Mandarin Chinese in the next section. In the following discussion, we will attempt to present the details of the correlation between word order and definiteness/indefiniteness and suggest why the correlation is best described as a tendency.

1.2.1 The post-verbal noun

The generalization given at the end of Section 1, Tendency A, was stated in terms of morphologically unmarked nouns. In present-day Mandarin, there are no definite articles, but there are the demonstratives zhèi- 'this' and nèi- 'that'. Although a post-verbal noun unmarked for definiteness is interpreted as indefinite, a noun marked with one of these demonstratives, which signals definiteness, may occur in post-verbal position in an NVN sentence. For example,

(14) Háizi   dǎ-pò   le   nèige   chuānghu
     child   hit-be broken   asp.   that   window

     The child broke that window.

In addition, proper nouns and personal pronouns, which are inherently definite, can occur in this position.

(15) Tā   dǎ   le   Zhāng-sān   le
     he   beat asp.   Zhang-san   asp.

     He has beaten Zhang-san.

(16) Tā   dǎ   le   wǒ   le
     he   beat asp.   I   asp.

     He has beaten me.

Thus, a definite noun may occur in post-verbal position in an NVN structure if it is morphologically or inherently definite.

There are also cases of morphologically unmarked nouns in post-verbal position in such sentences, which may be interpreted as definite because of the context.[7] Here are some examples for which the natural context makes an indefinite interpretation extremely unlikely.

(17) Nǐ   gěi   wǒ   kànkan   háizi
     you   for   me   watch   child

     Look after the {child / children} for me.

(18) Qǐng nǐ tuōxia xiézi
     please you take off shoes

Please take off <u>your</u> shoes.

(19) Qǐng nǐ guān mén
     please you close door

Please close <u>the</u> door.

(20) Wǒ wàng le yàushi le
     I   forget asp. key   asp.

I forgot the key(s).

Whereas we have translated the post-verbal nouns in sentences (21)-(24) as definite in English, it is important to note the difference between the "definiteness" of these nouns, on the one hand, and the definiteness of those nouns whose referents have <u>already</u> been mentioned in the previous <u>discourse</u>, on the other hand. In the latter case, the referents are pre-established <u>linguistically</u>; they have <u>antecedents</u>. They are, to borrow an excellent term that S. Kuno has been using consistently,[8] <u>anaphoric nouns</u>. In the former case, the nouns are not anaphoric. Their referents have not been mentioned in previous <u>discourse</u>. Nevertheless they represent known information because their referents are known to the speaker and the hearer through <u>extralinguistic</u> channels. Thus, (18) can, in fact, be the very first utterance in a conversation, if one imagines the situation in which the speaker living in a Japanese style house is addressing the delivery boy who has just arrived. The object noun, <u>xiézi</u> 'shoes', uttered in this context is clearly <u>non-anaphoric</u>. But it is known information in the sense that its referent has already been established in the discourse registry of both the speaker and the hearer through visual perception. In English, a nominal that is known information, whether it is known because it has been pre-established <u>linguistically</u> in the discourse or known because it has been established <u>extra-linguistically</u>, always has the same surface manifestation--it takes on the definite article. Mandarin Chinese, however, has different syntactic reflexes in terms of word order for the two types of known information. A post-verbal object noun morphologically unmarked for definiteness can only

be definite in the non-anaphoric or extra-linguistic sense. (22) is
extremely unnatural as an answer to the question (21):

Question: (21) Yàoshi   ne?
                key   question particle

               What about the key(s)?

Answer: (22) Wǒ   wàng   le   yàoshi   le
               I   forget asp. key

               I forgot the key(s).

The unacceptability of (22) as an answer to (21) is due to the
fact that in this situation, the morphologically unmarked object noun,
yàoshi 'key' is forced to be anaphoric. The acceptable answers to (21)
are

(23) a. Yàoshi,   wǒ   wàng   le
          key(s),   I   forget asp.

      b. Wǒ   bǎ   yàoshi   wàng   le
          I   ba   key   forget asp.

          I forgot the key(s).

      c. Wǒ   wàng   le
          I   forget asp.

Thus, the word order in Mandarin Chinese serves to signal the
subtle semantic distinction between the anaphoric definite noun whose
referent is pre-established linguistically by means of an antecedent in
the previous discourse and the non-anaphoric definite noun whose referent is established extra-linguistically.

In view of the facts presented above, we modify Tendency A with
the following refinement:

Refinement 1

    The noun in post-verbal position will be interpreted as
    indefinite unless it is morphologically or inherently or
    non-anaphorically definite.

1.2.2 Initial position

Tendency A was seen to be weakly manifested in post-verbal position, due to the fact that definite nouns can occur there under special
conditions. In sentence-initial position, however, the opposite situation is true; the sentence initial noun <u>must</u> be interpreted as definite
even if it is marked with the numeral yi- 'one', which appears to be
acquiring a new function as an indefinite determiner in certain
contexts.

In all of the example sentences given so far, the initial noun is
interpreted as definite. Some of these examples, with morphologically
unmarked nouns, are repeated here for convenience.

(24) Bīng   lái-dào   le
      soldiers come arrive asp.

      The soldiers have arrived.

(25) Zéi   pǎo   le
      thief run   asp.

      The thief has run away.

(26) Rén   sǐ   le
      person die   asp.

      The man is dead.

(27) Shēng-kou   kāi   le
      animal   loose   asp.

      The animal is loosed.

(28) Shū,   háizi   mǎi   le
      book   child   buy   asp.

      As for the book, the child bought it.

(29) Háizi, shū   mǎi   le
      child   book   buy   asp.

      The child bought the book.

(30) Háizi   bǎ   shū   mǎi   le
      child   obj. marker   book   buy   asp.

      What the child did to the book was buy it.

It has been claimed above that even nouns marked with yi- 'one' will be interpreted as definite in the initial position. The claim, however, is not as self-evident as that involving the unmarked nouns. There are four types of sentences with initial nouns marked by yi- 'one':

A. Generic

Although a sentence such as (31) sounds very strange, (32) is much more natural.

(31) * Yí-ge   rén   shuì-jiào
      one-class.person   sleep

A person sleeps.

(32) Yí-ge   rén   shuì-jiào-de   shíhòu, chángcháng
     one-class.person sleep subord. marker/time,   often

         zuò   mèng
         make   dream

When a person sleeps, he often dreams.

The reason for the acceptability of (32) is that it is easy to assign the initial noun a generic interpretation. Generic noun phrases should be considered a type of known information because they are established in the permanent registry of discourse. Hence, semantically, generic nouns are definite nouns insofar as they represent known information.

B. A member of a definite set

A sentence-initial noun phrase beginning with yi- can occur with a meaning "one of the N's". Again, we regard this as a type of definite noun phrase: the set referred to is known information, even though the particular member may not be. For example, in a discussion about a peasants' meeting, we might find a sentence such as

(33) Yí-ge   nóngfu shuō, "Wǒ xiǎng-chū yí-ge
     one class. peasant say   I think-out one-class.

        bànfǎ le"
        way   asp.

One of the peasants said, "I've thought of a way".

C. Elliptical sentences

(34) Yí-ge   rén   dǎ-pò   le   neìge chuānghu
one-class. person hit-be broken asp. that   window

Such a sentence as this one is acceptable to some native speakers as an elliptical form of

(35) Tā yí-ge   rén   dǎ-pò   le   neìge chuānghu
he one-class. person hit-be broken asp. that   window

He broke that window by himself.

Assuming that for such speakers, tā 'he' can be deleted, it is clear that the yíge ren 'one person' in (34) is not indefinite.

A similar elliptical example would be a sentence such as:

(36) Yí-zhī   jiǎo bèi   chē   yā-duàn   le
one-class. foot agent marker car press-break asp.

[My/His] foot was broken by $\{\substack{a \\ the}\}$ car.

A sentence of this type can only be understood as an elliptical form of a fuller sentence beginning with a "possessor" noun:

(37) $\left\{\begin{array}{l}\text{Wǒ} \\ \text{I} \\ \text{Tā} \\ \text{he}\end{array}\right\}$ yí-zhī   jiǎo bèi   chē   yā-duàn   le
one-class. foot agent marker car press-break asp.

My/His foot was broken by $\{\substack{a \\ the}\}$ car.

D. "Each"

(38) Yí-ge   rén   chī yí-kǒu
one-class.person eat one mouth(ful)

Each person gets one mouthful.

In sentences of this type there is a correlation between the two yí-'s; the interpretation of the subject in such cases corresponds to that of a noun phrase containing "each" in English. The Mandarin morpheme meǐ 'each' could be added at the beginning of the sentence with no discernable change in meaning. According to our definition of definiteness/ indefiniteness in Section 1, a noun modified by the quantifier "each"

is not definite because the referent of such a noun is not pre-established. On the other hand, the noun modified by "each" is also distinct from the true indefinite noun modified by "a". Whereas the
referent of the "each" noun itself is not pre-established, the set to
which the "each" noun belongs must be old information. Such a restriction does not apply to the true indefinite noun modified by "a". Hence
the "each" noun, yí-ge rén 'each person', in (38) must belong to a set
of people that is already known to the hearer and the speaker. But
this is not the case for "a person" in (39):

(39) A person ate a mouthful of cake.

In view of this semantic distinction between "a person" and "each person", we will refer to the latter as un unspecified member of a definite
set rather than an indefinite noun.

The above facts can be summarized as Refinement 2:

Refinement 2

A sentence-initial noun must be interpreted as definite,
and may not be interpreted as indefinite even if it is
preceded by the numeral yi- 'one'.

Mandarin does have a way of allowing the subject of a transitive
sentence to be indefinite. Interestingly enough, the strategy is consonant with both Tendency A and Refinement 2 which was given just
above. An indefinite subject in Mandarin must be preceded by the
existential verb yǒu 'exist'. Sentences (40) and (41) illustrate this
phenomenon.

(40) Yǒu   yíge rén   dǎ-pò   nèige chuānghu le
      exist one   person hit-be broken that window asp.

      A person broke that window.

(41) Yǒu   rén   dǎ-pò   nèige chuānghu le
      exist person hit-be broken that window asp.

      Someone broke that window.

The yǒu sentences conform to Tendency A, which predicts that the indefinite noun will be after a verb since the verb yǒu is introduced for
just this purpose. Such sentences also conform to Refinement 2, which

disallows an indefinite noun in sentence-initial position, because the indefinite noun is forced out of this position by the existential verb yǒu.

Sentence-initial position, then, is reserved for definite nouns. We will return to this point again.

1.2.3 BEI Sentences

In Section 1 above, with (13) as an illustration, we pointed out that BEI sentences constitute a class of exceptions to Tendency A. We repeat (13) here for convenience.

(13) Shū   bèi   háizi mǎi le
     book agent marker child buy asp.

The book was bought by {the / a} child.

The noun following the agent marker bèi in a BEI sentence may be marked with a demonstrative zhèi- 'this' or nèi- 'that', as well as the numeral yi-. If unmarked for definitiveness, it may be interpreted as either definite or indefinite. We give here an example of each of these possibilities.

(42) Fàn   bèi   zhèi tiaó gǒu chi-diào le
     food agent marker this class. dog eat-down asp.

The food was eaten by this dog.

(43) Fàn   bèi   nèi-tiaó gǒu chī-diào le
     food agent marker that-class. dog eat-down asp.

The food was eaten by that dog.

(44) Fàn   bèi   háizi chī-diào le
     food agent marker child eat-down asp.

The food was eaten by {a / the} child.

(45) Wǒ bèi   yí-ge   rén   mà   le   yí-dùn
     I agent marker one-class. person scold asp. one-class.

I was scolded by a (certain) person.

This evidence suggests Refinement 3.

Refinement 3

The noun following bei, although pre-verbal, is immune to Tendency A.

The immunity of the bèi noun does not seem to hold for the noun following bǎ, the "object marker". It has often been observed that the noun following bǎ must be interpreted as definite, even if marked with a numeral.[9] We give here a few examples.

(46) Háizi bǎ   fàn   chī-diào le
     child obj. marker food eat-down asp.

The child ate the food.

(47) Mao bǎ   yī-tiáo yú chī-diào le
     cat obj. marker one-class. fish eat-down asp.

The cat ate one of the fish.

(48) Tā bǎ   yī-běn shū mǎi-cuò le
     he obj. marker one-class. book buy-wrong asp.

He failed to buy the book he was supposed to buy.

(or)

He bought the wrong book.

The freedom of interpretation of the post-bèi noun, then, is not matched by the post-bǎ noun. What might be the reason for this? According to Wang Li (1959), the Mandarin passive construction, using bèi or one of its variants, has been heavily influenced by Western languages, particularly English. One of the obvious ways in which this influence is felt is in translation: a passive sentence in the target language will often be used to translate a passive in the source language. Under this Western influence, not only has the use of passive sentences increased dramatically in the last several decades in both writing and speech, but an earlier semantic restriction on the occurrence of the construction has now been dropped. Until the beginning of this century, the passive could only be used with verbs having a "negative" meaning, so that, for example, dǎ 'beat' could occur in passive sentences, but chēngzàn 'praise' could not. The dropping of this requirement naturally allows the construction to be used with a wider range of verbs than had been possible previously, contributing to its

spread. It is possible, then, that the fact that the Mandarin passive
has been influenced by Western languages where there is no restriction
on the definiteness of the agent, may account for the relaxation of
Tendency A for nouns after bèi.

1.2.4 Prepositional phrases

Most prepositional phrases in modern Mandarin are pre-verbal,
occurring after the subject.[10] There are only two prepositions (gěi
'to, for' and zài 'at') which can occur in both pre- and post-verbal
position. The nouns following all of these prepositions seem to be
immune to Tendency A. In the case of those prepositional phrases which
must precede the verb, it is clear that word order could not be a factor in distinguishing definite and indefinite nouns, since no contrast
exists. It is, of course, the possibility of occurring in either pre-
or post-verbal position which allows the definite/indefinite distinction
to be made in the case of those nouns traditionally described as subjects and objects. In the case of the two prepositions for which a
contrast in position is possible, this positional contrast seems to
signal quite another semantic distinction. For example, compare the
pre- and post-verbal gěi phrases below:

(49) Tā gěi wǒ mài le chēzi le
     he for me sell asp. car asp.

     He sold a car for me.

(50) Tā mài gěi wǒ chēzi le
     he sell to me car asp.

     He sold a car to me.

The positional contrast with gěi signals a distinction between 'benefactive' and 'dative'. The distinction is, however, slightly more complicated. There are some well-known examples with pre-verbal gěi
phrases which allow both the benefactive and the dative readings. For
instance,

(51) Qǐng nǐ gěi wǒ dǎ diànhuà
     please you to/for me make phone call

     Please call me on the phone.
     Please make a phone call for me.

(52) Qǐng   nǐ   gěi   wǒ   xiě   xìn
    please you   to/for me   write letter

Please write a letter to me.
Please write a letter for me.

However, the sentences are no longer ambiguous when the prepositional
phrase gei wo 'to/for me' is placed after the verb, as in (53) and (54):

(53) Qǐng   nǐ   dǎ   diànhuà   gěi wǒ
    please you   make phone call to   me

Please call me on the phone.

(54) Qǐng   nǐ   xiě   xìn   gěi wǒ
    please you   write letter to   me

Please write a letter to me.

Now there may well be a semantic basis with respect to the verb for the
fact that (51) and (52) are ambiguous while (49), for example, is not.
However, what is significant here is that the restrictions [pre-verbal
gěi phrase: benefactive], [post-verbal gěi phrase: dative] is relaxed
for the pre-verbal case only, but not for the post-verbal case in these
examples. This is not surprising in view of the word order shift from
SVO to SOV currently in action in Mandarin Chinese. If the word order
shift is to continue, the meaning of the pre-verbal gěi phrase must be
broadened to include the meaning for the post-verbal gěi phrase, so
that the post-verbal alternate (SVO) may be eliminated in time.

In the case of zài 'at', the pre- and post-verbal occurrences
involve several different semantic distinctions, none of which is related to the definiteness or indefiniteness of the nominal following it.
For some verbs, a sentence with a pre-verbal zài phrase differs from
one with a post-verbal zài phrase only in terms of the question it
answers. Thus, (55) might answer the question "What is Zhang-san doing
on the floor?":

(55) Zhāng-sān   zài   dì-shang   shuì
    Zhang-san   at   floor-on   sleep

Zhang-san is sleeping on the floor.

182

(56), on the other hand, could answer the question "Where is Zhang-san sleeping?":

(56) Zhāng-sān shuì zài dì-shang
     Zhang-san sleep at floor-on

Zhang-san is sleeping on the floor.

With some motion verbs, however, the post-verbal zài phrase becomes directional, whereas the pre-verbal zài phrase remains strictly locational. Compare (57) and (58):

(57) Zhāng-sān tiào zài zhuōzi-shang
     Zhang-san jump at table -on

Zhang-san jumped onto the table.

(58) Zhāng-sān zài zhuōzi-shang tiào
     Zhang-san at table -on jump

Zhang-san is jumping (up and down) on the table.

We will not pursue this aspect of the prepositional phrases any further here since it is beyond the scope of this study. The point is that the pre-verbal position and the post-verbal position do signal semantic distinctions for some prepositional phrases, but these distinctions are unrelated to the definite/indefinite contrast which is the theme of this study. Hence, we propose

Refinement 4

Nouns in prepositional phrases are immune to Tendency A.[11]

It is obvious from the preceding data and discussion that Refinement 4 is not an accident. For the vast majority of prepositional phrases, the positional contrast does not exist, rendering the definite/indefinite contrast impossible. In the case of gěi and zài, the positional contrast is already being utilized, as it were, for other semantic distinctions, leaving no room for the definite/indefinite contrast. It is to be noted that several diachronic processes related to the word order change play a significant role in causing gěi and zài to behave differently from the other prepositions. These diachronic processes concern the different rate of change from verbs to prepositions, the collapse of certain serial verb constructions in the creation of a new word order, and the elimination of the post-verbal prepositional phrase. (See Li & Thompson, [1973a], [1973b], [1973c].) It is sufficient to point out here that gĕi and zài are two of the few prepositions that still retain their full verbal status just as they did at the ancient stage of the language when the present-day Mandarin prepositions were mostly verbs. Their occurrence in the post-verbal positions, the proper position of prepositional phrases in archaic Chinese, is a manifestation of their conservative characteristics.

Before leaving the subject of prepositional phrases, we would like to mention one particular property of zài ('at') phrases which further supports Tendency A. Locative phrases with zài 'at' can occur in sentence-initial position with intransitive verbs. In sentence-initial position (only), the preposition zài 'at' can be deleted. Sentences (59) and (60) are examples of this frequently used construction:

    (59) (Zài) qiáng-shang guà-zhe   yí-fu   huà
          (at)   wall-on   hang-asp. one-classifier painting

    A painting is hanging on the wall.

    (60) (Zài) tóu-shang   méng-le   yí-kuai   bù
          (at)   head-on   cover-asp. one-classifier cloth

    A piece of cloth covered the head.

Now, Refinement 2, which concerns sentence-initial nouns, predicts a definite interpretation for the locative nouns if zài 'at' is deleted. Interestingly enough, however, a definite interpretation is the only one possible even if the zài 'at' is present. Sentence (59), for example, cannot mean

    (61) A painting is hanging on a wall.

Further, the post-verbal noun in such sentences must be indefinite, just as in Mullie's sentences (3), (4), and (5) cited at the beginning of this paper, repeated here:

    (3)   Lái le   bīng
          come asp. soldiers

          There came soldiers.

(4) Pǎo   le   zéi
    run   asp. thief

    There escaped a thief.

(5) Sǐ   rén   le
    die person asp.

    A man has died.

Thus, although Refinement 4 holds for prepositional nouns, stating
that they are immune to Tendency A, an unmarked noun in a locative
prepositional phrase in sentence-initial position must be interpreted
as definite.

1.3 Summary

Let us summarize the four ways in which Tendency A must be
refined:

Refinement 1

The noun in post-verbal position will be interpreted as
indefinite unless it is morphologically or inherently or
non-anaphorically definite.

Refinement 2

A sentence-initial noun must be interpreted as definite,
and may not be interpreted as indefinite even if it is
preceded by the numeral yi- 'one'.

Refinement 3

The noun following bèi, although pre-verbal, is immune to
Tendency A.

Refinement 4

Nouns in prepositional phrases are immune to Tendency A.

Given these refinements, it is clear why Tendency A must be expressed as a tendency, just as Chao put it in the quote cited above.
There is by no means a strict correlation between the definite interpretation of a noun and its position relative to the verb. The tendency in this direction, however, is much too strong to be ignored in
a grammatical description of the language. Our conclusion can be
stated as follows: word order in Mandarin plays a significant and

systematic role in distinguishing definite from indefinite nouns, although it is not the only means by which definite and indefinite nouns may be distinguished from each other.

2.   Synchrony versus diachrony

In an earlier paper, Historical Change of Word Order: A Case Study in Chinese and Its Implications, we documented and proposed an explanation for the word order change from SVO to SOV that has been in action for nearly two millenia in Chinese grammar. This process can be described as Tendency B:

Tendency B

Mandarin is presently undergoing a word order shift from SVO to SOV.

A puzzling aspect of this historical process is its duration. Why is it taking so long for Mandarin to undergo a word order change from SVO to SOV? This becomes all the more disconcerting in view of the fact that SVO remains the unmarked word order in present-day Mandarin.[12] The semantic function of word order for denoting the definiteness/ indefiniteness of the nominals in a sentence may provide a clue to the understanding of this prolonged diachronic process. Word order in archaic and ancient Chinese was strictly SVO until the emergence of the bǎ-construction in 8th century A.D. Except for topicalization, the SVO word order of archaic and ancient Chinese appears to have been rigid. In other words, word order did not bear the semantic function of ex- pressing the definiteness/indefiniteness of sentence nominals in the days of archaic and ancient Chinese. This is obvious from the texts available to us. For example, in an essay written by Hán Yù of the Tang dynasty (800 A.D.), the first sentence is

(62)   Yuè   rì Yù zài   bài[13]
       month day Yu again pay-his-respect

On a certain day of a certain month, Yu again pays his respects.

where the sentence-initial nominal, yuè rì 'month day' is indefinite. Or we may take as an example the famous Confucius saying in The Analects:

(63) Sān   rén   xíng,   bì   yǒu   wǒ   shī
     three   people   walk,   must   have   my   teacher

If there are three people walking, there must be a
teacher for me.

where the subject nominal <u>sān rén</u> 'three people' in the sentence-
initial position is clearly indefinite.

Since the use of word order for denoting definiteness/indefinite-
ness seems to have begun no earlier than Middle Chinese, its historical
origin is certainly later than the beginning of the word order change.
The two correlations between word order and definiteness/indefiniteness
that we have observed in Section 1 are: pre-verbal--definiteness,
post-verbal--indefiniteness. The focal point of these correlations is
the verb. Consequently, if the word order change to SOV is completed,
these correlations can no longer exist. Thus, the use of word order
to mark the definiteness or indefiniteness of nouns, which is a synchronic phenomenon, may have impeded the process of word order change.
In other words, there is a conflict between the two word order tendencies discussed above: Tendency A and Tendency B.

In the light of the two opposing forces in Chinese grammar, we
can perhaps understand why some of the complexities discussed in Section 1 exist in synchronic Chinese grammar. We have pointed out in
our study of co-verbs in Chinese that a diachronic process concomitant
with the change in word order is the shift of certain verbs to prepositions (Li & Thompson [1973b]). At the present stage of the language,
there is a group of co-verbs which, on the whole, have the syntactic
properties of prepositions. But certain verbal characteristics are
preserved among them, some retaining more verbal characteristics than
the others because of the differential rate of change from verbs to
prepositions in different lexical items. The result is a lack of homo-
geneity among the syntactic properties of the co-verbs. In synchronic
grammar, such non-homogeneity means descriptive complexity; this synchronic complexity is often caused by diachronic processes in action.
Since we have isolated a diachronic process conflicting with a synchronic phenomenon in modern Mandarin Chinese, the correlation between
word order and definiteness/indefiniteness, and the word order change

from SVO to SOV, it is not surprising that the synchronic nature of
the word orders in Mandarin is highly complex.

Considering the two opposing trends of word order in present-day
Mandarin, we may become speculative and ask whether one will prevail,
and if so, which one. Will word order change proceed toward SOV, or
will word order become more diverse, to enhance its function for denoting the definiteness and the indefiniteness of nouns? It should be
clear that logically these are not the only options. We are assuming
that an observed diachronic tendency in a language has a certain
"momentum", which in effect pushes the language in a specific direction.
Thus, we are assuming that each of the two tendencies discussed above
is pushing the language to achieve a certain conclusion; in this case
the end points are incompatible. It is conceivable that this assumption is wrong. Such a case would suggest that there need be no conflict at all, that the language might exist in its present state with
regard to word order for hundreds of years. However, a survey of the
changes which have been occurring as well as the empirical facts concerning the directions in which these changes are leading, seems to
forecast unmistakably that the shift to SOV is the stronger tendency
and that it will continue to push the language to an SOV state. What
is the evidence which might suggest that this will happen?

First of all, the proliferation of the bǎ-construction (allowing
SOV sentence order) during the past three centuries is extensive. For
example, in a 17th century version of the novel, Water Margin, one finds
the following type of sentence:

(64)   S   +   V   +   O   +   V
        Wáng-pó   shōushi   fáng-lǐ   gānjing   le
        Wang-po   arrange   house-inside clean   asp.

Wang-po cleaned up the house.

In present-day Mandarin Chinese (64) is no longer grammatical. Super-
ficially its word order, SVOV, appears to be identical with that of the
serial verb construction in modern Chinese. However, the object
nominal, fáng-lǐ 'house-inside = the inside of the house', is also the
subject of the second verb. This type of serial verb construction has
already been phased out in modern Mandarin. It has been replaced by an

SOV <u>bǎ</u>-sentence:

    (65) Wáng-pó bǎ fáng-lǐ   shōushi - gānjìng le
           Wang-po ba house-inside arrange - clean   asp.

           Wang-po cleaned up the house.

In fact, not only is the <u>bǎ</u> construction becoming more widespread, but
it appears to be more frequently used with indefinite nouns; that is,
sentences such as the following are increasing:

    (66) Tā bǎ   yí-ge   háizi dǎ   le   yí-dun
           he obj. marker one-class. child hit asp. one-classifier

           He spanked a child once over.

    (67) Wǒ bǎ   yí-jian shìqing wàng   le
           I obj. marker one-class. matter forget asp.

           I forgot something.

The increase of this type of <u>bǎ</u>-sentences, which is an SOV sentence
type with an indefinite <u>bǎ</u> noun, follows logically from the fact that
SOV is becoming more and more preferred to SVO. The gradual ascendency
of the SOV word order can be seen as one side of a phenomenon whose
other side is the gradual demise of the SVO word order. This phenomenon is accompanied by the rise of compound verbs. If the SVO sentences
are gradually being eliminated, Tendency A must become weaker. The
occurrence of <u>bǎ</u>-sentences with an indefinite <u>bǎ</u> noun signifies precisely that.[14]

    The second piece of evidence in support of the prevailing word
order change is the gradual development of the definite and indefinite
articles in present-day Mandarin. M.C. Jorland (personal communication) has pointed out that in relative clauses, the demonstrative
article, <u>nèi</u>- 'that' and the numeral <u>yi</u>- 'one' may serve as the definite and the indefinite articles respectively. For example,

    (68) Wǒ diū le   de   yí - běn   shū...
           I lost asp. relative clause marker one-classifier book

           A book I lost...

(69) Wǒ diū le   de   nèi - běn   shū...
     I lost asp. relative clause marker that- classifier book
     The book I lost...

Finally, in support of our speculation that the word order shift
will prevail, we would like to draw attention to one aspect of the function of word order in distinguishing definite from indefinite nouns.
Recall that of all the statements we have been able to make concerning
this function of word order, only one was inviolate and exceptionless:
that was Refinement 2:

> A sentence-initial noun must be interpreted as definite,
> and may not be interpreted as indefinite even if it is
> preceded by the numeral yi- 'one'.

Notice that this is the only statement concerning the relationship between word order and definiteness which does not refer to the relative
positions of nouns to the verb. It is not surprising, then, that sentence-
initial position should be the position least weakened in its ability to
signal definiteness, since it is the position least affected by the shift
from SVO to SOV.

3. Conclusion

We have shown that word order plays a significant role in Mandarin
in signaling the contrast definite/indefinite for nouns, allowing, in
fact, some very subtle distinctions to be made, such as that between
anaphoric and non-anaphoric definiteness. Bearing in mind that Mandarin
is in the process of shifting its favored word order from SVO to SOV
(see Li and Thompson [1973a], [1973b], [1973c]), we have argued that
progress toward the conclusion of this word order shift has been impeded
by the rise of the use of word order to signal definiteness. The evidence presented in this paper, however, points towards the "relentless-
ness" of the process of shifting to an SOV order, and suggests that it
will be carried through. To whatever extent the SOV order does become
the favored order, the ability of position relative to the verb to signal definiteness is thereby weakened.

We hope, of course, to have provided some insights into the structure of Mandarin, and to have shown that explanations can be given for

certain previously unrelated phenomena in the grammar of this language. More broadly, we also hope to have demonstrated the importance of considering the interplay among various general tendencies at work, both diachronic and synchronic, in seeking explanations for the observed facts in a language.

NOTES

1. See especially Mullie (1932) pp. 161-169, Chao (1968) pp. 76-78, Li (1971) 156-167.

2. There may be certain languages which manifest a tendency in just the opposite direction, by consistently placing old information after new information. L. A. Reid (personal communication) has pointed out that not only are there dozens of VOS languages in the Phillipine islands but the word order of Proto-Austronesian was probably VOS. We should be cautious, however, in advancing claims about the placement of old and new information for these languages, since (i) it is known that most of these languages have VSO and other alternative word orders that are widely used and (ii) it is not clear what is meant by 'subject' when Reid and other grammarians who have worked on these languages use the term. But the fact that VOS is the unmarked word order and that it is stable (assuming that Proto-Austronesian is VOS and that the VOS word order of Ilokano, Tagalog, etc., is the order retained from the Proto stage) certainly increases the probability that they would tend to place old information after new information.

3. We have transcribed Mullie's examples into the Pin-yin romanization, which will be used throughout this paper. We have also provided literal glosses. The free translations are Mullie's.

4. A similar point is made in Teng (1972).

5. For the time being we are excluding prepositional phrases from consideration. They will be taken up below.

6. It should be pointed out here that we are not concerned in this paper with generic nouns, which can occur either before or after the verb. Since generic nouns are a type of definite noun, it should be noted that its occurrence in the post-verbal position may be construed as a weakening of the tendency: post-verbal---indefinite.

> (i) Méiguì   shì   hóngde
>   rose   be   red   =
>   Roses are red.

7. A similar point is made in Li (1971), p. 166.

(ii) Wǒ xǐhuän méiguì
      I   like   rose =
      I like roses.

8. See, for example, Kuno (1971) and (1972). However, a further distinction among the anaphoric nouns should be noted: the linguistic antecedent of an anaphoric noun may be described as either <u>direct</u> or <u>indirect</u>. An antecedent is direct if it actually occurs in the discourse. 'A vase' in the following narrative serves as a direct antecedent of 'the vase'.

I presented <u>a vase</u> to my teacher. <u>The vase</u> was blue.

An antecedent is indirect if it is not present as a morpheme but its presence can be inferred from the linguistic context. Thus, in the following narrative, 'the favors' is an anaphoric noun with an indirect antecedent.

John was a heartless man. I got a job for him, found him a
place to live, listened to his problems, cheered him up, etc.
But <u>the favors</u> I did for him were all forgotten.

As a general rule, we have observed that only abstract nouns but not concrete nouns may have an indirect antecedent.

9. There are exceptions to this generalization. We will discuss this problem in Section 2. The point to notice here is that for a <u>beì</u> noun, there seems to be no restriction on definiteness, whereas for a <u>bǎ</u> noun there is such a restriction, although exceptions to it can be found.

10. The correlation between the pre-verbal position of prepositional phrases and the shift from SVO to SOV which Mandarin is presently undergoing is discussed in Li and Thompson (1973a), (1973c).

11. The object marker <u>bǎ</u>, when considered a preposition, is an exception to this generalization, as was pointed out in 1.2.3.

12. One might well ask, "How long do such changes usually take?" Susan Fischer (this volume) shows that for American Sign Language, a word order change has taken place in less than a century. Talmy Givón (personal communication) has estimated that the word order change from SOV to SVO in some Niger-Congo languages took approximately three hundred years.

13. The essay is entitled, 獲丫諤釦目柱畀 , by Hán yù, 韓愈.

14. Two explanations for the occurrence of bǎ with nouns preceded by yi- 'one' have been proposed in the recent literature. Li (1971) suggests they signal an indefinite noun phrase. Teng (1972) proposes that such noun phrases introduced by yi- should be viewed as specific (his term is 'actual', following Frei [1956]). Although we are not ready to propose a complete account of these sentences ourselves, we are even less ready to accept either of these suggestions, since examples can be found in which the bǎ noun is preceded by yi- and is neither definite nor specific. The following two examples are both taken from Lee Pao-Chen's textbook Read About China:

(i) [Nàrde cíqi zuò-de fēichang hǎo.] Cháng
    There china make-nom. extremely good Often

    yǒushíhòu yào jīngguo qīshí duō rén - de
    sometimes will pass seventy more person - poss.

    shǒu cái néng bǎ yí-jiàn cíqi zuò-hǎo. (p. 8)
    hand then can object marker one-class. china make-ready =

    [The china which is made there is extremely good.] Often
    it must pass through the hands of more than seventy people
    before one piece of china is finished.

(ii) Zheìxie sùhuà dōu shì yòng buduōde zì, jiù
     these sayings all are use not many word just

     bǎ yí-ge dàoli huóshi yí-ge lǐxiǎng
     obj. marker one-class. principle or one-class. ideal

     shuōde hěn qīngchu ...
     express very clearly =

     These sayings all use very few words, but express clearly a
     principle or an ideal...

REFERENCES

Chao, Yuen Ren (1968). A Grammar of Spoken Chinese. Berkeley and Los Angeles: University of California Press.

Clark, Eve V. (1970). "Locationals: a study of the relations between 'existential', 'locative' and 'possessive' constructions", Working Papers on Language Universals, Committee on Linguistics, Stanford University.

Firbas, J. (1964). "On Defining the Theme in Functional Sentence Analysis", Travaux Linguistiques de Prague 1:267-280.

---------- (1965). "A Note on Transition Proper in Functional Sentence Analysis", Philologica Pragensia 8:170-176.

---------- (1966). "Non-Thematic Subjects in Contemporary English", Travaux Linguistiques de Prague 2:239-256.

Frei, Henri (1956). "The ergative construction in Chinese: theory of Pekinese pa", Gengo Kenkyu 31:22-50, 32:83-115.

Kuno, Susumu (1971). "The Position of Locatives in Existential Sentences", Linguistic Inquiry, 2.333-78.

----------- (1972). "Functional Sentence Perspective: A Case Study from Japanese and English", Linguistic Inquiry 3:269-320.

Lee, Pao-ch'en (1958). Read About China. Institute of Far Eastern Languages, Yale University, New Haven, Connecticut.

Li, Charles N. and Sandra A. Thompson (1973a). "Historical Change of Word Order: A Case Study of Chinese and Its Implications". Paper presented at the First International Conference on Historical Linguistics, September 2-7, 1973, University of Edinburgh. To appear in Selected Papers from the First International Conference on Historical Linguistics.

------------------- (1973b). "Co-verbs in Mandarin Chinese: Verbs or Prepositions?", presented at the Sixth International Conference on Sino-Tibetan Language and Linguistic Studies, October 19-22, 1973, University of California, La Jolla. To appear in proceedings from the conference.

------------------- (1973c). "An Explanation of Word Order Change: SVO → SOV", to appear in Foundations of Language.

------------------- (forthcoming). "The Issue of Word Order in a Synchronic Grammar". Paper presented at the Fourth Annual California Linguistics Association Conference, May 3-5, 1974, University of Southern California, Los Angeles.

Li, Frances C. (1971). Case and Communicative Function in the Use of BA in Mandarin. Unpublished Ph.D. dissertation, Cornell University. Available from University Microfilms, Ann Arbor, Michigan.

Mullie, Joseph (1932). The Structural Principles of the Chinese Language, Vol. 1, Peiping: The Bureau of Engraving and Printing.

Teng, Shou-hsin (1972). "An Analysis of Definite and Indefinite", paper presented at the LSA Summer Meeting, Chapel Hill.

Underhill, R. (1972). "Turkish Participles", Linguistic Inquiry 3.87-100.

Wang Li (1959). Zhōngguó Xiàndai Yǔfǎ [Contemporary Chinese Grammar]. Peking: Zhōng-huá Shū-Jú.

ON SOME FACTORS THAT AFFECT AND EFFECT WORD ORDER

by

Susan Steele

<u>0.0</u> Grammatical elements have played a peripheral, if supportive, role in considerations of word order and word order change. The positions of grammatical elements have been used to support the typing of languages (e.g. prefixation is evidence of a verb initial language; suffixation, of a verb final language) or as evidence of change in the order of subject, verb, and object relative to one another (e.g. if a language evidences a number of characteristics which indicate it could be typed a verb final, but also has a few verb prefixes to mark tense or aspect, these prefixes may be taken as indication of the older verb initial character of the language.) This paper suggests a reconsideration of assigning this role to grammatical elements. A cross-linguistic survey of the position of grammatical modal elements reveals that they are ordered with respect to the other elements of a sentence in a regular fashion. The question such a finding poses about the reason--a question which is answered only in part by appeals to language typology and on which diachrony has no obvious bearing--immediately removes grammatical elements from the periphery.

The first part of this paper considers the positional tendencies of modal elements. Modal elements cross-linguistically occur in three sentential positions--first position, second position, and final position--but most commonly they occur in sentential second position. The second and third parts of the paper argue that this pattern finds explanation in the interaction of two language-general forces--the attraction of the verb for certain elements (including, but not exclusive to, modal elements) and the attraction for these same elements to sentence initial position. The last part of the paper returns to the implications of these attraction forces for a theory of word order and word order change.

<u>0.1</u> For my purposes, the class of modal elements is defined semantically as elements that mark one or more of the following notions: possibility or the related notion of permission, probability or the related notion of obligation, certainty or the related notion of requirement.[1] Consider the modals in the following English sentences, for example.

1. a. You may know what I am talking about but I am not convinced.

   b. You may leave when you have finished your exam.

2. a. Mary should be hitting John with a rabbit right now; she does so every afternoon at 3 and it is 3 now.

   b. Mary should hit John with a rabbit; he won't learn to mind his manners any other way.

3. a. Dick's fly must be open; no one is listening to what he is saying.

   b. Dick must open his fly if he wants to be comfortable after eating his daily 16 ounce steak.

May in (1a) indicates possibility; may in (1b) indicates the granting of permission. Should in (2a) indicates probability; should in (2b) indicates an avoidable obligation--Mary may choose not to hit John with a rabbit. Must in (3a) indicates certainty; must in (3b) indicates a requirement, a requirement in this case dictated by physical limitations. It was not assumed that modal elements in languages other than English would be ambiguous;[2] rather any element which indicates at least one of the six notions above was considered modal in character.

0.2 The class of modal elements, within this semantic class, is restricted syntactically on two counts. First, as the beginning of this section indicated, the positional tendencies of grammatical elements only will be considered.[3] Second, the class of grammatical elements is itself restricted to those elements which are defined to occur in a single sentential position. For example, in Kapampangan, one modal element--siguru--is most commonly a sentence initial element (or in second position if some element is topicalized around it):[4]

4. siguru mwa - iya   'It's probable that he is angry.'
   MODAL angry - SM   (Kapampangan)

but it doesn't necessarily occur in either position.

5. i wan masaya - iya siguru   'John seems to be happy.'

    John happy - SM MODAL   (Kapampangan)

The restriction to modal elements which occur in a single sentential position effectively eliminates adverbial elements from consideration here since adverbial elements generally have some freedom of position. Consider English:

6. a. Probably Mary knows her job better than John knows his.

    b. Mary probably knows her job better than John knows his.

    c. Mary knows her job better than John knows his probably.

Given the (at least potential) freedom of the class of adverbial elements, whatever was defined as adverbial in the grammatical description of a language has been excluded, regardless of whether the data of the particular language indicated that the particular element could occur in more than one sentential position.[5]

1.0 This part of the paper presents the data. The language sample from which the data is drawn contains the 44 languages listed in Table 1 below. For two good reasons, it is reasonable to expect that whatever tendencies this sample exhibits will be indicative of universal tendencies. First, as a perusal of Table 1 will indicate, many of the world's language groups are to be found in the sample. Second, these 44 languages were drawn from a still larger sample and the tendencies they exhibit are representative of it.[6]

TABLE 1[7]

A. Genetic groups represents

Indo-European	Austronesian
English	Indonesian
Albanian	Kapampangan
Marathi	Oceanic
Ural-Altaic	Nguna
E. Ostyak	Rarotongan
Khalka	Ulithian
Korean	Wolio

Afro-Asiatic
   Tera
Andean-Equatorial
   Quechua
Congo-Kordofanian
   Diola-Fogny
   Yoruba
   Swazi
   Gbaya
   Lunda (Luvale)
Austro-Asiatic
   Chrau
Azteco-Tanoan
   Luisẽno
Sino-Tibetan
   Thai
   Mandarin
   Burmese
   Lahu
   Garo
Vietnamese
   Vietnamese
Dravidian
   Tamil

Indo-Pacific
   Awa
Australian
   Aranda
   Walbiri
   Gunwinjgu
Eskimo-Aleut
   Alaskan Eskimo
Na-Dene
   Navajo
Algonkian-Mosan
   Fox
   Snohomish
   Squamish
Hokan-Siouan
   Washo
   Kashaya Pomo
   Mojave
   Wichita
Penutian
   Sahaptin
   Maidu
   Achi

B. Genetic Groups unrepresented

Japanese
Caucasian
Paleosiberian
Nilo-Saharan
Khoisan

Yuki
Macro-Otomanguean
Macro-Chibchan
Ge-Pano-Carib

Information about modal elements in these languages is drawn for the most part from written accounts,[8] ranging widely in their theoretical framework, but other sources have also provided information-- other linguists' field notes (Mojave, Navajo, Eskimo),[9] linguists who are native speakers of some language other than English (Korean),[10] native informants (Luiseño, Kapampangan, Thai, Sahaptin, Indonesian.)[11] There are undoubtedly holes in my information; for example, when I began reading grammars and collecting data it wasn't clear how modals were to be defined, much less where I should look for them. I expect, however, that the holes are random; inclusion of the information which the holes represent should not significantly alter the positional tendencies to be discussed.

The positional patterning of modal elements becomes evident when considered in the light of language classifications. But before I consider both the classifications and the patterns they reveal, let me present the necessary background data on modal elements.

<u>1.1</u> The majority of languages in the sample have modals the position of which within a clause is in some fashion dependent on the main verb; I will refer to this class as TYPE A. However, there is a strong counter-tendency for the position of modal elements to be defined by certain sentential positions solely; I will refer to this as TYPE B.[12]

I. TYPE A	32	(Tamil, Korean, Eskimo, Lahu, Navajo, Kashaya, Pomo, Fox, Wolio, Majave, Quechua, Khalka, Washo, Burmese, Mandarin, Swazi, Lunda, Thai, Vietnamese, Albanian, Diola-Fogny, English, Gbaya, Indonesian, Kapampangan, Snohomish, Ulithian, Chrau, Yoruba, Nguna, Rarotongan, Marathi, Tera)
TYPE B	9	(Achi, E. Ostyak, Gunwinjgu, Garo, Aranda, Walbiri, Squamish, Sahaptin, Luiseño)
Languages of both TYPE A and TYPE B	3	(Maidu, Wichita, Awa)

In the three languages which combine both types, some modals are dependent on a verb and some modals are defined as occurring in certain sentential positions. In Maidu, for example, one modal is an affix to the verb:

7. wóno - b - y - h̰es   /wónobyhes/
   die - modal - POSSIBILITY - person marking
            suffix

      'We all might die.'
         (Maidu; Shipley, 49)

and another modal is a sentential second position element.

8. /hṵ́kojnum   ʔáj   syʔyj   mym   májdym   nìkí
                    DUBITATIVE
   héskym   ma   jắkk̰en/

      'I suppose that man is still my friend.'
         (Maidu; Shipley, 54)

Maidu, Wichita, and Awa are included in both the discussion of TYPE
A languages and the discussion of TYPE B languages below.

The distinction between TYPE A and TYPE B languages corresponds
roughly to the two types of grammatical (but not adverbial) modal
elements. Modals may be verbal elements--either auxiliaries to a
verb or affixes on a verb--or less verb-dependent elements like
clitics or particles. As an example of the former, some Kapampangan
modals are auxiliary verbs.

9. dapat - iya - ng mandiluq   'He should bathe.'
   SHOULD - SM   bathe   (Kapampangan)

As an example of the latter, Gunwinjgu modals are particles:

10. gunubewa   bininj gabirini   gured   'Maybe there are some
    MODAL   people they-are-camp   people in camp.'
                       sitting

                                    (Gunwinjgu; Oates, 92)

The correlation is not absolute, however, because the division between the two syntactic classes is not absolute. There are a few
languages where a modal which is dependent on a verb in some fashion
is also defined as a clitic/particle (Chrau, Rarotongan, Nguna).
On the other hand, it is not clear that some clitic/particle-like
elements should not be considered auxiliaries. In Luiseño and

Walbiri, modals occur in certain sentential position; the same
position is defined to include clitic pronouns and tense markings.
In Sahaptin, modals occur in a certain sentential position; the same
position is defined to include clitic pronouns. Among the languages
of the sample there is the following division between two syntactic
classes:

II. Verbal elements   36   (Eskimo, Korean, Awa, Maidu,
Wichita, Lahu, Navajo, Kashaya
Pomo, Tamil, Fox, Wolio,
Mojave, Quechua, Khalka, Washo,
Burmese, Mandarin, Swazi,
Lunda, Thai, Vietnamese,
Albanian, Diola-Fogny, English,
Gbaya, Indonesian, Kapampangan,
Snohomish, Ulithian, Yoruba,
Walbiri, Luiseño, Squamish,
Sahaptin, Marathi, Tera)

Particles/clitics   11   (Achi, E. Ostyak, Gunwinjgu,
Garo, Aranda, Maidu, Wichita,
Awa, Chrau, Nguna, Rarotongan)

(III) below joins (I) and (II):

III. Verbal elements   Particles/clitics
     TYPE A   32   TYPE A   3
     TYPE B   4   TYPE B   8

Modal elements in TYPE A languages--modals which are dependent
on the main verb in the clause--may either precede or follow the main
verb. English modal auxiliaries precede the verb. In Tamil, modal
elements follow the verb.

11.   ceruppe kaRatti-vacci-TTu   kooyil - ukk - ulle pooka-laam
         1   2   3   4   5   6   7   8   9
       'After having taken off (and put aside) one's shoes, one
         4   2   3   1
       may go into the temple.'
       9   8 7/6   5

                        (Tamil; Schiffman)

IV below charts the position of the modal element relative to the verb in TYPE A languages.

IV. Preceding verb   19 (Tera, Chrau, Vietnamese, Swazi, Thai, Albanian, English, Diola-Fogny, Gbaya, Lunda, Yoruba, Nguna, Indonesian, Snohomish, Kapampangan, Ulithian, Wolio, Mandarin, Wichita)

Following verb   16 (Mojave, Quechua, Khalka, Eskimo, Korean, Tamil, Lahu, Navajo, K. Pomo, Washo, Burmese, Marathi, Maidu, Awa, Fox, Rarotongan)

In TYPE B languages, languages where modals are dependent on certain sentential positions, there are three possible modal positions. The modal may occur sentence finally, sentence initially, or in sentential second position.

V. Sentence final   1   (Garo)

Sentence initial   4   (Achi, Gunwinjgu, Awa, Squamish)

Second position   7   (Luiseño, Sahaptin, Aranda, Walbiri, E. Ostyak, Maidu, Wichita)

In Garo, "...[modals] are most frequently used at the very end of a sentence, or even of an utterance...." (Burling, 35)

12. sok - ba - gen - kon   '(he) will probably come."
     V - direction of - future -   (Garo)
                        MODAL
           speaker   'dubitative'

In Gunwinjgu, modals are in sentence initial position most generally.

13. mandi   gunmaln   garolgan 'Maybe the spirit will
     MAYBE   spirit   he-will-get-up rise.'[13]

(Gunwinjgu; Oates, 111)

The most common position for modals which are positioned in certain
sentential positions is, as the chart illustrates, sentential second
position. Modal elements in Luiseño and Walbiri illustrate the
dominant tendency.

14. noo - xu - n - po pukwaa - n   'I could run.'
     I - MODAL - SM - incomplete run - future   (Luiseño)

15. kanta - ngu - tjapaka kuyu ngani 'A woman might be
     woman - transitive - MODAL meat eat eating meat if she
                                          is allowed to.'
                                          (Walbiri; Reece, 1962)

The dominant tendencies of the two language types may then be
summed up as follows:[14]

VI.   TYPE A   TYPE B

        V + MODAL   #X + Modal.......#

        Modal   V   # Modal.........#

                                  X......X + Modal #

1.2.0 I have discussed the tendency for modals to be dependent on
the main verb and the tendency for modals to occur in certain sentential positions. I turn now to the discussion of the two tendencies
in terms of two classifications of languages; first, in terms of surface word orders and second, in terms of a more abstract classification of languages. As a preliminary I will consider how the language
sample is organized by these two classifications.

1.2.1.1 The languages discussed in this language sample distribute
among three unmarked word orders--SVO, VSO, SOV--in the following
way:

VII.   S V O   17   (Chrau, Vietnamese, Swazi, Thai, Albanian,
                     Diola-Fogny, English, Gbaya, Tera, Lunda,
                     Yoruba, Nguna, Indonesian, Snohomish,
                     Wichita, Mandarin, Sahaptin)

       V S O   7   (Squamish, Fox, Rarotongan, Kapampangan,[15]
                     Wolio, Achi, Ulithian)

       S O V   20   (Gunwinjgu, Aranda, Luiseño, Walbiri, E.
                   Ostyak, Garo, Mojave, Quechua, Khalka,
                   Korean, Tamil, Lahu, Navajo, Kashaya Pomo,
                   Washo, Burmese, Marathi, Maidu, Awa, Eskimo)

Many of the languages allow other word orders. VSO languages in particular generally allow an alternate surface word order SVO. An alternation of another sort is that some of the languages--SOV languages generally--have what appears to be a rather free word order. The identification of a language as one of the three types above excludes what may be alternate word orders regardless of the reason for the alternation; a language is identified as a particular type by its <u>unmarked</u> word order.

<u>1.2.1.2</u> The more abstract classification divides languages into two classes--verb initial languages and verb final languages.[16] The 44 languages in the sample are divisible into 22 verb initial languages and 22 verb final languages as follows:

VIII. Verb initial   (Chrau, Vietnamese, Swazi, Thai,
                          Albanian, Diola-Fogny, English,
                          Gbaya, Tera, Lunda, Yoruba, Nguna,
                          Indonesian, Snohomish, Kapampangan,
                          Ulithian, Wolio, Achi, Fox, Rarotongan,
                          Sahaptin, Squamish)

          Verb final   (Gunwinjgu, Aranda, Luiseño, Walbiri,
                          E. Ostyak, Garo, Mojave, Quechua,
                          Khalka, Eskimo, Korean, Tamil, Lahu,
                          Navajo, Kashaya Pomo, Washo, Burmese,
                          Marathi, Mandarin, Awa, Maidu, Wichita)

To classify a language as either verb initial or verb final, I have considered primarily:

(1) Whether the language has (a) prepositions or (b) postpositions.

(2) Whether the genitive order of the language is (a) possessed possessor or (b) possessor possessed.

(3) Whether inflection and derivation are (a) prefixing or (b) suffixing.

(4) Whether, in the unmarked order, the verb (a) precedes the object or (b) follows it.

(5) Whether, if it could be ascertained, a relative clause (a) follows a head noun or (b) precedes it.

The first possibility in each of these five pairs characterizes verb initial languages; the second, verb final languages. The classificatory nature of these characteristics has been noted before. Consider five of Greenberg's language universals and the implications that can be drawn from them.

Universal 2. "In languages with prepositions, the genitive almost always follows the governing noun, while in languages with post-positions it almost always precedes." (110)

Universal 3. "Languages with dominant VSO order are always prepositional." (110)

Universal 4. "With overwhelmingly greater than chance frequency, languages with normal SOV order are postpositional." (110)

Univeral 24. "If the relative expression precedes the noun either as the only construction or as an alternative construction, either the language is postpositional or the adjective precedes the noun or both." (112)

Universal 27. "If a language is exclusively suffixing, it is postpositional; if it is exclusively prefixing, it is prepositional." (112)

Greenberg's universals provide two clusters of characteristics--the same two which I used to classify languages as either verb initial or verb final. Languages with the order SOV (object preceding the verb) have postpositions. Postpositions imply that a language has the genitive order:

possessor possessed

that it has inflectional and derivational <u>suffixes</u>, and that the relative clause may <u>precede</u> the head noun. Languages with the order VSO (object following the verb) have prepositions. Prepositions imply that a language has the genitive order:

possessed possessor

that it has inflectional and derivational <u>prefixes</u>, and that the relative clause does <u>not precede</u> the head noun.

The particular set of characteristics which I have chosen as classificatory is obviously not an exhaustive list of the differences between verb initial languages and verb final languages,[17] but other differences were not usable as tests on a regular basis. Either they weren't mentioned in the descriptions of the language, or the test was too weak to predict language type.

Consider Luiseño and Kapampangan in terms of criteria 1-5. In the unmarked surface word orders of Luiseño, the object precedes the verb.

16. čaam - čapo   pupuuk - i he ə i - n   'We will open the
    we - clitic door - object open -   door.'
    future
         S   O   V   (Luiseño)

Luiseño has two postpositions.[18]

17. tooṣax - tal   'with the rabbit'
    rabbit - with   (Luiseño)

Causatives, as an example of the suffixing nature of Luiseño, are verb suffixes.

18. a. mariya - up wultu - q   'Mary is angry.'
       Mary - clitic angry - present   (Luiseño)

Although relative clauses generally follow the head noun, they may precede it.

19. ?awaal [po ?oy waxaam ko?imokwiš] takwaya - q
    dog relative you yesterday bit   dead - present
            pronoun (object)
    'The dog that bit you yesterday is dead.' (Luiseño)

In Kapampangan, the unmarked surface word order is V(erb) O(bject).

20. sinipa - ne - ng wan ing bola kang maria
    kick - SM   John   ball   Mary
    V   S   O
    'John kicked the ball to Maria.' (Kapampangan)
Kapampangan has prepositions.

21. ke - ng bale   'in a house'
    prep   house   (Kapampangan)
Causatives, as an example of the prefixing nature of Kapampangan,
are verb prefixes.

22. a. tuknang - ke   'He stopped.'
       stop - SM   (Kapampangan)

    b. pepa - tuknan - ke   'I made him stop.'
       CAUS - stop - SM   (Kapampangan)
Relative clauses must follow the head noun.

23. ita - ng babai - ing [ikit - mu] malaguq - iya
    that   girl   saw - SM pretty - SM
                               you   she
    'The girl you saw is pretty.' (Kapampangan)

Luiseño and Kapampangan differ systematically on all criteria.
The characteristics of Kapampangan considered here are those of a
verb initial language; the characteristics of Luiseño considered here
are those of a verb final language.

The neat clustering which Luiseño and Kapampangan illustrate is
not necessarily characteristic of all languages. In some languages
there are what appear to be random aberrations. For example, Baure,
an Arawakan language, is verb initial according to criteria 2-4, but
it also has postpositions. More systematically, there are cross-
linguistic regularities in the depatures from some of the five criteria, regularities which suggest that other factors may impinge on
word order. For example, in two languages in the sample (Wichita and
Mandarin), languages which otherwise exhibit primarily verb final
characteristics,[19] the surface order is SVO. Greenberg notes that VO
order is dominant over OV order; that is, OV order occurs only under

specified conditions, while VO order is not subject to such limitations. (Greenberg 97) Thus, the expected OV order of verb final
languages conflicts with the dominance of VO order.

Given that there are factors which affect the expected order of
elements, languages can still be classified as verb initial or verb
final by the clustering of characteristics into one or the other set,
and if the importance of certain characteristics is weighted relative
to others, the clustering of characteristics as evidence of the language's type can be further refined. For example, Greenberg claims
that prepositions are dominant over postpositions; that is, prepositions occur unless some other condition exists to require post-
positions. (Greenberg, 98) In the languages I examined, post-
positions are most obviously evident in languages with OV order.[20]
I abstracted from this fact the hypothesis that the appearance of
postpositions is good indication of the verb final character of the
language. In languages like Mandarin and Wichita, the appearance of
postpositions thus takes precedence over the fact that the verb precedes the object; the presence of postpositions in conjunction with
criteria 2, 3 and 5 classifies these languages as verb final.[21]

The division of the language sample into 22 verb initial and 22
verb final languages mentioned at the beginning of this section is
based on these considerations. I turn now to a discussion of what
the orders SOV, SVO, and VSO mean for the position of modals, and
then to the discussion of what the verb initial/verb final classification reveals about the regularities of these positional tendencies.

1.2.2.1 Given that modals may either precede or follow a verb if they
are dependent on it, and given the unmarked surface word orders SOV,
VSO, SVO, there are the following surface word orders in TYPE A languages, languages where modals are dependent on the main verb for
their position within the clause:

IX.   S Modal VO   16   (Chrau, Vietnamese, Swazi, Thai,
                                Albanian, English, Diola-Fogny,
                                Gbaya, Lunda, Yoruba, Nguna, Indo-
                                nesian, Snohomish, Wichita, Mandarin,
                                Tera)

```
S O V Modal      14    (Mojave, Quechua, Khalka, Korean,
                        Tamil, Lahu, Navajo, Washo, Burmese,
                        Eskimo, Marathi, Kashaya Pomo)

Modal V S O       3    (Kapampangan, Ulithian, Wolio)

V Modal S O       2    (Fox, Rarotongan)
```

VSO languages have two possible orders.

```
Modal V S O

V Modal SO
```

SVO and SOV TYPE A languages are more restricted. The only word order for SVO languages is

```
S Modal V O
```

and the only word order for SOV languages is

```
S O V Modal
```

There are thus two gaps in the patterns. Both

```
* S V Modal O
```

and   * S O Modal V

are conceivable word orders, but neither occurs in this language sample.

Given that modals may occur in three sentential positions, and given the unmarked surface word orders above, there are the following surface word orders for languages of TYPE B:

```
X.    First Position Modal

      Modal S O V      2    (Gunwinjgu, Awa)

      Modal V S O      2    (Achi, Squamish)

      Second Position Modal

      S Modal O V      5    (Luiseño, E. Ostyak, Maidu, Aranda,
                             Walbiri)

      S Modal V O      2    (Wichita, Sahaptin)
```

214

    Final Position Modal

    S O V Modal   1 (Garo)

The chart above doesn't include one possibility which does occur as an apparently unmarked alternative order in Squamish and Sahaptin.

    V Modal S O

In Squamish, the modal is either sentence initial or the verb may precede it.

    Modal V S O

    V Modal S O

In Sahaptin the modal is generally in second position; either the subject or the verb generally precede it.

    S Modal V O

    V Modal S O

There are three gaps in the surface order pattern of TYPE B languages. Three orders could occur and do not.

    * Modal S V O

    * V S O Modal

    * S V O Modal

1.2.2.2 Examining the TYPE A and TYPE B patterns above in conjunction with one another illuminates a tendency for modal elements to occur in sentential second position. The data arrangement suggests that modals are more likely to be in sentence initial or sentential second position than in sentence final position and, further, that sentential second position is more important for modals than sentence initial position.

The word orders which could occur and do not, point to the tendency away from final position. Given the three surface word orders, the tendency of modal elements to occur either dependent on the main verb or in one of the three sentential positions makes the following surface orders logically possible.

XI. S O V Modal   * V S O Modal   * S V O Modal

    Modal S O V   Modal V S O   * Modal S V O

    S Modal O V   V Modal S O   S Modal V O

    * S O Modal V   * S V Modal O

But only the unstarred orders above occur.

XII. S O V Modal

    Modal S O V   Modal V S O

    S Modal O V   V Modal S O   S Modal V O

The possibilities which do not occur tend to be those cases where
modals would appear in other than sentence initial position or
sentential second position.

XIII.   * V S O Modal   * S V O Modal

                                     * Modal S V O

    * S O Modal V   * S V Modal O

These gaps are good indication of a tendency for modals to occur
toward the beginning of a sentence.

    Further indication of the tendency away from final position is
found by considering the surface positions of modal elements when
the tendency for the modal to occur in certain sentential positions
allows a different word order than the tendency for the modal to be
dependent on the verb. There are four surface word orders where the
two tendencies are in agreement.

XIV. S O V Modal

           Modal V S O

           V Modal S O   S Modal V O

In the order S O V Modal a modal can be either dependent on the verb
or positioned sentence finally; in the order Modal V S O a modal can
be either dependent on the verb or positioned sentence initially; in
the orders V Modal S O and S Modal V O a modal can be either dependent

on the verb or positioned in sentential second position. There are
two surface word orders which could not be produced by the tendency
of the modal to be dependent on the verb; in these the modal is in
either sentence initial position or sentential second position.

Modal S O V

S Modal O V

Finally, if we restate the surface orders that occur, with some
indication of where TYPE A and TYPE B languages cluster, the importance of sentence initial position and sentential second position for
modals as opposed to sentence final position is illustrated again.
I restate the orders below with the number of TYPE A and TYPE B languages in each. Maidu, Awa, and Wichita are included twice, once
for the modal elements that are positioned by sentential position
alone, once for the modal elements that are dependent on the verb.
Squamish and Sahaptin are also included twice, once for each of the
sentential positions in which a modal element may occur, as discussed
above.

XV.

	A B		A B		A B
S O V Modal	14 - 1				
Modal S O V	0 - 2	Modal V S O	3 - 2		
S Modal O V	0 - 5	V Modal S O	2 - 2	S Modal V O	16 - 2

Modal elements in TYPE B languages occur primarily in either sentence
initial position or sentential second position. And in the majority
of these languages for the modal to be at the beginning of the sentence requires that it be non-contiguous to the verb.

XVI. Verb final, Modal at beginning   7   (Gunwinjgu, Awa,
                                             Luiseño, E. Ostyak,
                                             Maidu, Aranda, Walbiri)

    Verb at beginning, Modal at   4   (Achi, Squamish,
    beginning   Sahaptin, Wichita)

    Verb final, Modal final   1   (Garo)

In seven languages (of the nine TYPE B languages and the three languages that have some TYPE B modals) the modal is at the beginning of the sentence and the verb is at the end. In the rest, the modal and the verb are either both at the beginning or both at the end.

Assuming then that there is a tendency for modals to occur toward the beginning of a sentence, it is also clear that within that tendency there is a stronger tendency toward second position than toward initial position. First, in both TYPE A and TYPE B languages where modals occur at the beginning of the sentence (that is, with the exclusion of S O V Modal languages), the dominant position for modals is in sentential second position. Given the exclusion, the most common word order in TYPE A languages is:

S Modal V O

Given the exclusion--indeed, even without it--the second position tendency in TYPE B languages is obvious. The most common word order is:

S Modal O V

And modals occur in second position in two of the five remaining possibilities. (See Chart XV)

V Modal S O

S Modal V O

More importantly, while for each of the three surface word orders there is a dominant modal position which is different from that of each of the other orders, the only position for modals in SVO languages converges with a strong secondary tendency in VSO and SOV languages for modals to be in sentential second position. I restate Chart XV with out the division into TYPE A and TYPE B languages. Again, Awa, Maidu, Wichita, Sahaptin, and Squamish are included twice.

XVII. S O V Modal   15

    Modal S O V   2   Modal V S O   5

    S Modal O V   5   V Modal S O   4   S Modal V O   18

The only position for modals in SVO languages, regardless of whether
the language is TYPE A or TYPE B, is in sentential second position.
The dominant position for modals in S O V languages is in sentence
final position; the dominant position for modals in V S O languages
is in sentence initial position. But there is a strong secondary
tendency in each for modals to occur in second position.

1.2.2.3 In summary, the most common word orders for TYPE A languages are:

    S Modal V O

    S O V Modal

    Modal V S O

In TYPE B languages modals tend to occur in second position. The
conjunction of the two types suggests that modal elements tend to
occur toward the beginning of a sentence rather than at the end and
that the beginning of the sentence is defined most often as second
position.

1.2.3 In this section I will reconsider the positions of modal
elements in terms of the verb initial/verb final classification.
With this second classification, the importance of the beginning of
the sentence for modal elements is thrown into sharper relief.

The 22 verb initial and 22 verb final languages distribute
between TYPE A and TYPE B in the following fashion:

XVIII.	Verb Initial	Verb Final
TYPE A	19	13
TYPE B	3 (Sahaptin, Achi, Squamish)	6 (E. Ostyak, Aranda, Walbiri, Garo, Luiseño, Gunwinjgu)
COMBINATION	0	3 (Awa, Maidu, Wichita)

Kapampangan is an example of a verb initial TYPE A language.

24. dapat - iya - ng mandiluq   'He should bathe."

    SHOULD - SM   bathe   (Kapampangan)

Mojave is an example of a verb final TYPE A lanauge.

25. ? - a?we - p ə sum   'I've got to do it.'

    ISM - do -   MODAL   (Mojave; Munro field notes)

Sahaptin is an example of a verb initial TYPE B language.

26. x̣tu - x̣ac i-wa   'He certainly must be strong.'

    strong-MODAL he-is   (Sahaptin; M. Jacobs, 130)

Walbiri is an example of a verb final TYPE B language.

27. kanta - ngu - tjapaka kuyu ngani

    woman - transitive MODAL meat eat

               S

    'A woman might be eating meat if she is allowed to.'

    (Walbiri; Reece, 162)

Maidu is an example of a verb final language which has modals which are dependent on a verb (TYPE A) and modals which are positioned sententially (TYPE B):

28. wóno - b - y - hes̩ /wónobyhes/

    die - modal - POSSIBILITY - person

        suffix   marking

    'We all might die.' (Maidu; Shipley, 49)

29. /húkojnum ?áj sy?ýj mym májdym níkĭ heskym ma jáaken/

            DUBITATIVE

    'I suppose that man is still my friend.' (Maidu; Shipley 54)

XVIII above makes clear that TYPE B languages tend to be verb final. While in the majority of both verb initial and verb final languages modal elements are dependent on a verb (TYPE A), the number of languages where the modal element is dependent on a certain sentential position (TYPE B) is proportionally greater in verb final languages than in verb initial languages. In six of the 22 verb final languages, modals occur in a certain sentential position; in three

of the remaining 16 languages, at least some modals are defined
to occur in certain sentential position. Therefore, in a total of
nine of the 22 verb final languages, a discussion of modal elements
need not make reference to dependence on the verb, but only to the
importance of certain sentential positions. In only three of the
22 verb initial languages is that the case.

That the preponderance of TYPE B languages should be verb final
languages is indication of the tendency for modal elements to occur
at the beginning of the sentence. For a language to be both TYPE A
and verb final would generally force a modal to occur away from the
beginning of the sentence, most often in sentence final position.
XIX charts the position of modal elements relative to the verb in
TYPE A languages.

XIX.   Verb initial

Preceding   17   (Chrau, Vietnamese, Swazi, Thai,
                                    Albanian, Diola-Fogny, English,
                                    Gbaya, Tera, Lunda, Yoruba,
                                    Nguna, Indonesian, Snohomish,
                                    Kapampangan, Ulithian, Wolio)

Following   2   (Fox, Rarotongan

Verb final

Preceding   2   (Mandarin, Wichita)

Folowing   14   (Mojave, Quechua, Khalka, Eskimo,
                                    Korean, Tamil, Lahu, Navajo,
                                    Kashaya, Pomo, Washo, Burmese,
                                    Marathi, Awa, Maidu)

Consider the Mojave sentence in (25) as an example of the dominant
tendency in TYPE A verb final languages. Of course, it was noted
above (see Chart V) that modal elements in TYPE B languages can
occur in one of three sentential positions and that one of these is
sentence final position. The position of modal elements in TYPE B
languages distributes between verb initial and verb final languages
in the following fashion:

XX. TYPE B		Verb initial	Verb final
Sentence initial	2	(Achi, Squamish)[22]	2 (Gunwinjgu, Awa)
Sentence final	0		1 (Garo)
Second position	1	(Sahaptin)	6 (Luiseño, Maidu, Walbiri, Aranda, E. Ostyak, Wichita)

Sentence initial and sentential second positions are general to both verb initial and verb final languages; furthermore, they are the only positions for modals in verb initial languages and the dominant positions for modals in verb final lanauges. One language works against the tendency to first and second positions in TYPE B languages-- Garo, a verb final language. We must allow the possibility that sentence final position is important, at least for verb final languages, but the relative weakness of the tendency to this position correlates with the fact that TYPE B languages tend to be verb final.

1.3 In this section I have discussed the position of modal elements both in terms of surface word orders and in terms of the division between verb initial languages and verb final languages. I have shown that languages can be classified into one of two types on the basis of how the modal is positioned. I have shown that the surface word orders for TYPE A languages tend to be:

S O V Modal

S Modal V O

Modal V S O

and that modals tend to be in sentential second position in the surface word order of TYPE B languages. I have shown that, while modals may be either positioned by the sentence or dependent on a verb, they tend to occur in certain sentential positions. Finally, I have shown that the distinction between TYPE A and TYPE B languages is not random, but that TYPE B languages are more likely to be verb final languages than verb initial languages. The next section discusses two language general forces as a possible explanation of these regularities.

222

<u>2.0</u> Two theories about grammatical modals have commonly been enter-
tained. One argues that modals are grammatical forms and are therefore generated in deep structure in the position in which they appear
on the surface, dominated by the category symbol <u>Modal</u>. The other
argues that modals show similarities to main verbs and are therefore
derived by the same rules that derive other main verbs. Neither
theory explains the positional tendencies presented in Section 1,
although bits and pieces can be captured very neatly by one theory
or the other. Neither theory has of course been considered in terms
of its predictions for the cross-linguistic positional tendencies
of grammatical modal elements. The point of contention and acrimony
has been whether the similarities of modals to main verbs are to be
stressed and some process of grammaticization assumed, or whether the
non-main-verb nature of modals is to be stressed and the similarities
to main verbs ignored. It is hardly a moot question, but the intri-
cacies of it are far beyond the scope of this paper. I will assume
at the outset a third alternative, an alternative based on the following:

a. Modals, at the level of semantic representative, are
    abstract higher predicates.

b. The non-main-verb nature of modals is a function of their
    being modals.

The argument behind (a) depends on the positional regularities that
have been discussed. Since there are such cross-linguistic regularities to the class of modal elements on the surface, it is
possible that the class has a more abstract regularity, an underlying regularity. Because of similarities to verbs,[23] this regularity may be due to the abstract higher predicate nature of modal
elements. Because they are not main verbs, however, they will not
necessarily be derived like regular main verbs in all respects.

The argument for (b) depends on the semantic coherence of the
class of modal elements. Since the grammatical modal elements considered here are a coherent semantic class (i.e., they are defined
by the semantic parameters suggested at the beginning of this paper),

it is possible to argue that the semantics of the class requires--
or at least strongly recommends-grammaticization. Consider in this
context Langacker's (1972) discussion of what he calls "objective
content." "Roughly speaking, the objective content of a sentence
is the basic situation which the sentence described and which the
remainder of the sentence takes a position on. For example, the
proposition Peter finish represents the objective content of (61)
and Ralph bite Betsy is the objective content of (62).

(61) Could Peter perhaps have finished?

(62) I say to you that Ralph most certainly did not bite
Betsy." (25) He argues that modals--and certain other elements--
represent non-objective content and that there is a tendency for
objective content to surface in a prominent position. Therefore,
higher predicates which specify non-objective content tend not to
be more prominent in surface structure than the objective content
of the sentence. In other words, modals tend to be grammaticized.

I turn then to the factors that affect and effect the position
of modal elements. I will argue that the position of modal elements
in the surface structure of a sentence is a function of two factors
cross-linguistically.

1. There are certain unmarked surface positions for modal
    elements. In verb initial languages, this is sentence
    initial position; in verb final languages, sentence final
    position.

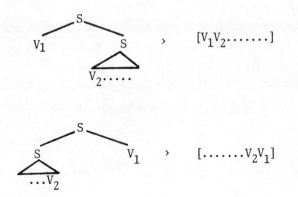

2. The unmarked positions are acted upon by two tendencies--
the tendency for certain elements (including, but not
exclusive to, modal elements) to be attracted to the
verb and the tendency for these same elements to be
positioned initially.

2.1 Section I noted that modal elements tend cross-linguistically
to precede the verb in verb initial language and to allow it in
verb final languages; this tendency is not necessarily a function of
the grammaticized higher predicate's dependency on the main verb.
As Chart XV above illustrates, modals in verb initial languages tend
to occur sentence initially, even when they are not dependent on the
main verb; in fact, assuming obligatory subjectivalization in SVO
languages and topicalization in those TYPE B VSO languages where
the modal follows the verb, modals are exclusively sentence initial
elements in verb initial languages. Modals may occur sentence
finally in verb final languages, even when they are not dependent on
the main verb.

That modals should tend as a class to positions at either end
of a sentence finds explanation in their scope relationship to the
sentence. Modal elements are sentential in scope. This hypothesis
is supported by the brief semantic definition of modal elements given
at the beginning of this paper, as well as by Langacker's (1972)
definition of the term "non-objective content" and the inclusion of
modals within that definition. My very brief semantic definition of
modals suggested that modals indicate the possibility of the
situation described in the sentence. Epistemic modals (those modal
elements that indicate possibility, probability, or certainty) do
so directly; root modals (those modal elements that indicate permission, weak obligation, or requirement) do so indirectly--it is
infelicitous for example, to allow someone to do something the
possibility of which is precluded in advance. According to Langacker's definition of "non-objective content", modals are excluded
from objective content, are considered non-objective content. "Very
roughly we can say that the objective content of a sentence resides

in the deep structure nominals and predicates together with their grammatical relations as specified by phrase structure rules. Negation, auxiliary verbs, and complementizers (including those pertaining to illocutionary force--e.g. the Q and IMP of Katz and Postal 1964) would be excluded, since they are neither nominals nor syntactic predicates." (Langacker 1972, 29) He defines the non-objective content as specifying the location along various parameters of the situation which the objective content describes; that is, the non-objective content specifies something about the sentence.

If modal elements are sentential in scope, it is to be expected that they would exhibit a regular relationship to the sentence on the basis of the following hypothesis, a hypothesis which is generally accepted by members of at least two of the major linguistic factions--interpretivism and generative semantics:

Surface position reflects semantic scope.

Illustrations of the hypothesis abound. To take one, Lakoff (1969) argues that a quantifier which precedes another quantifier on the surface is generally higher in the semantic structure of the sentence, unless the second quantifier commands the first asymmetrically. The relative order of certain grammatical elements provides yet another example; this particular issue is complicated by other factors, so I consider simply one specific case that is somewhat representative and relatively straightforward. In Classical Aztec, negatives occur generally in sentence initial position. (See (34) and (35) below) This means that negatives will precede modals as a rule.

30. amo wel   iš - namik - ko   'It was impossible to
     NEG possible face - meet - come to   look directly at it.'
                                    (Classical Aztec; Garibay, 134)

However, there is one construction, apparently frozen and therefore possibly older, which indicates that negation could follow a modal when the modal included the negative within its scope.

226

31. maa - k - a?mo   ni - miki tee - teoo - e?
    let - be - NEG   I - die redup - god - vocative

'Let it be that I not die, gods'

'Don't let it be that I die, gods'

(Classical Aztec; Garibay, 135)

If modals are sentential in scope, then, given the relationship
of surface position and semantic scope, it is to be expected that
they will appear regularly in certain sentential positions. Assuming
(as I have) that modals are higher predicates underlyingly, these
positions are predictable from the typology of the language. Modals
should occur initially in verb initial languages (with some change
due to subject placement) and finally in verb final languages. From
a tree like:

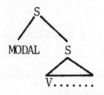

we would expect the surface order:

   # Modal V........#

Subject placement could move the subject around the modal, allowing
for the possibility of:

   # S Modal V.......#

From a tree like:

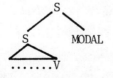

we would expect the surface order:

   #............V Modal#

As discussed in Section 1, these positions are indeed

the most common; others do exist. I turn then to Hypothesis 2 and the factors that act on the missionary positions.

2.2.0 The first part of the discussion of Hypothesis 2 will provide some evidence that the tendency we have seen for modals to occur either dependent on the verb or in certain sentential positions, primarily the beginning of the sentence, is not an isolated phenomenon. In the second part of this section, I will consider what might be reasons for either tendency.

2.2.1 The class of elements that acts like modals includes past tense markers, negatives, quotatives, and topic. I consider, of course, only grammatical tense, negatives, and quotatives.[24]

Past tense markers occur most commonly within the verb phrase--generally affixed to the first or the last element--but there are a few languages with both this sort of past tense marker and some other form of past marker which is in sentential second position.[25]

XXI.[26]   TYPE A

Languages where past tense is dependent on the verb

25 (Achi, Squamish, Ulithian, Lunda, English, Vietnamese, Rarotongan, Yoruba, Sahaptin, Gunwinjgu, Aranda, E. Ostyak, Garo, Quechua, Khalka, Burmese, Korean, Kashaya, Pomo, Tamil, Washo, Awa, Mojave, Navajo, Wichita)

COMBINATION

Languages with past tense of both TYPE A and TYPE B

3 (Luiseño, Maidu, Walbiri)

Negatives[27] and quotatives are similar to both past tense markers and modals. In most languages negatives are verbal particles of some sort; in English, for instance, the negative occurs

after the first element in the verb complex, regardless of whether
it is the verb that is negated or the sentence.

32. He didn't walk, he ran.

33. My brother didn't walk to the store; my sister ran to
the post office.

In another set of languages, negatives are sentence initial elements,
regardless of the scope of negation--Classical Aztec, for example.

34. amo olino   in   tona - tiw   'The sun does not
    NEG move   article   sun   move.'
                                  (Classical Aztec;
                                  Garibay 135)

35. aw amo on - nešti - kakta   in   se   ƛaakaƛ
    and NEG direction-stand out-was article one person
    'And not one person stood out.'
    (Classical Aztec; Garibay, 131)

36. John is said to be leaving.

In many languages, quotatives are grammaticized. (37) is an example
of the Luiseño quotative.

37. xwaan - kun hellilut   'John is said to be going
    John - QUOT going-to-sing   to sing.'
                             (Luiseño)

kun in Luiseño can be diachronically related to a proto Uto-Aztecan
verb, but it is not a regular verb form in Luiseño synchronically.
Luiseño illustrates that quotatives may be second position elements.
They may also be verb affixes; Kashaya Pomo has a complex set of
elements which suffix to the verb and indicate the information source
for the sentence.

    Finally, topic may be positioned sentence initially or, less
commonly, sentence finally; topic may also be positioned around the
verb. The term topic, used somewhat roughly here, includes both
topicalization and dislocation. In English, topicalization is the
movement of an element to sentence initial position, preceding the
subject.

38. Ant poison Harry likes on his salad.

In Kapampangan, a topicalized element is moved to sentence initial position, immediately preceding the predicate.

39. a. sinipa - ne i wan ing bola kang maria
         kick - SM   John   ball   Maria
         'John kicked the ball to Maria.'

     b. i wan sinipa - ne ing bola kang maria
         John   kick - SM   ball   Maria
         'It's John who kicked the ball to Maria.'

                                        (Kapampangan)

In Japanese, the subject will be initial generally, since the language has an SOV surface word order, but if the subject is also the topic it is marked as such.

40. John - wa ano - hon - o kat-ta
     John - topic that-book-object buy
     'John bought that book.'
     (Japanese, Kuroda, 2-1)

On the other hand, if the object is the topic it may precede the subject.

41. ano - hon - wa John - ga kat - ta
     that - book - topic John-subject buy
     (Japanese; Kuroda, 2-1)

There is a weak counter-tendency to sentence final position for topicalized elements. In English, dislocation is, very roughly, the copying of an element in sentence initial or sentence final position.

42. a. Ant poison, Harry likes it on his salad.

     b. Harry likes it on his salad, ant poison.

In Chinook, Wichita, and Algonquin, what appears to be a topic NP may be either sentence initial or sentence final. But generally, if a language allows a topicalized element to be in sentence final position, it also allows it to be in sentence initial position. So, in English, Chinook, Wichita, and Algonquin, topicalization may be indicated either by a sentence final element or by a sentence initial element. But, in Kapampangan and Japanese, sentence initial position alone is the position of the topicalized element.[28]

Topic may also be attracted to the verb.[29] Below is an example from Turkish:

43. a. ressam geçen hafta Bebek'te bize resimlerini gösterdi
artist last week Bebek-at us pictures-his showed
'The artist showed us his pictures last week at Bebek.'

   b. geçen hafta Bebek'te bize resimlerini RESSAM gösterdi
'It was the artist who showed us his pictures last
week at Bebek.'

   c. ressam Bebek'te bize resimlerini GEÇEN HAFTA gösterdi
'It was last week that the artist showed us his pictures at Bebek.'

   d. ressam geçen hafta bize resimlerini BEBEK'TE gösterdi
'It was at Bebek that the artist showed us his pic-
tures last week."
(Turkish; Lewis, 24-1)

Past tense, negatives, quotatives, topic, and modal elements exhibit slightly different tendencies within the possibilities of being dependent on the main verb or being positioned solely by sentential position. In terms of their division between the two possibilities the five semantic types are distributed in the following fashion:

Mostly sentential	Topic
Mostly on verb	Negatives, quotatives, modals
Almost all on verb	Past tense

A comparison of Chart I and Chart XXI will suffice to show the difference in these terms between past tense markers and modal elements. In the attraction of the topic to the verb, Turkish is rare; far more common is what Japanese, Kapampangan, and English

illustrate--the occurrence of topic in sentence initial position.
The claim that negatives and quotatives are mostly indicated by some
sort of element which is dependent on the verb will have to be taken
on faith. I do not claim by the above chart that negatives, quotatives, and modals show exactly the same distribution, but simply that
the three of them fall between tense and topic in terms of their
division between the two possibilites. Even with this modification,
it is significant that the entire class of elements exhibits the
split that was discussed in some detail for modal elements, significant because past tense, negatives, quotatives, and topic are included, along with modal elements, in Langacker's (1972) definition
of those elements that mark non-objective content; that is, all
mark the location along various dimensions of the situation specified
by the objective content.[30]

"It is perhaps easier to say what is excluded from the
objective content of a sentence. The illocutionary force of
a sentence is excluded, as are specifications of tense. Negation is excluded together with such notions as topic, focus,
and emphasis. Honorifics would not be part of the objective
content, and neither would indications of speaker doubt, esti-
mations of reality or veracity, or markers of affective reaction. In short, the objective content of a sentence specifies
a situation which the sentence is to deal with, and the remainder of the sentence--what I will call the non-objective
content--specifies the location of this situation along various
dimensions...."(25-6)[31]

I have discussed modality in these terms. Regardless of the
details of the analysis, there is general agreement that tense is
sentential in scope. In generative semantics, tense has been
analyzed as a higher predicate whose scope includes the entire sentence. Interpretivists would probably agree that the scope of
tense is the entire sentence. And Chafe (1970) argues "....that
any unit like past which is added semantically to a verb is added
simultaneously to the entire sentence which is built around that

verb...." (97) There is no doubt that negation may be sentential
in scope. I loosely defined quotatives above as indicating the information source for the sentence. Topic specifies what the sentence
is about.

Modal elements are not alone, then, in that they may be dependent on the main verb in the sentence or be positioned solely by
sentential position; other elements with sentential scope have
similar possibilities. I turn now to what might be reasons for the
dependency of such elements on the main verb.

2.2.2.1 The dependency of elements on the main verb finds its explanation is the centrality of the verb to the sentence. A first
bit of evidence, with the incorporation of an object noun in the
verb, the verb and the predicate, a term used here in its traditional sense, may be equivalent. In Gunwinjgu, for example, the object
noun may be incorporated in the verb by placing the object noun between verb affixes and the verb itself.

    44. ŋa - boy - maŋ   'I will gather antheap.'
         SM - Nobj. - V   (Gunwinjgu; Oates, 55)
         I - antheap - gather

Second, with the specification of both subject and object on the
verb, the verb and the sentence may be equivalent. In Kapampangan,
for example, both subject and object may be attached to the verb as
clitic pronouns.

    45. dimdam - mu - ku   'I heard you.'
         hear - you - I

Finally, Lehmann (1972) reports that psychologists (e.g.
Gazzaniga) have done experiments which suggest that verbs are more
definitely based in the language producing center of the brain than
are nouns: "...only the hemisphere with a specialized speech center
can process verbs. Accordingly it is difficult to avoid the conclusion that the distinctive part of man's system of communication is
the verb." (270) Distinctiveness to human communication does not
automatically entail centrality to the sentence, but it does lend

considerable plausibility to the view that the verb is central.

The centrality of the verb creates the potential that elements which include the entire sentence within their scope will be specified on the verb as opposed, say, to the direct object; that is, the elements of non-objective content considered above are potential candidates for being attracted to the verb.

Assuming that the centrality of the verb explains the attraction of modal elements to the verb, there is still to consider where modal elements occur relative to the verb and why they occur there. As Chart XIX indicated, modal elements tend to follow the verb, if they are dependent on it, in verb final languages and to precede the verb, if they are dependent on it, in verb initial languages.

The missionary position of modals in verb initial languages is sentence initial position, immediately preceding the verb.

Modal V S O

The missionary position of modals in verb final languages is sentence final position, immediately following the verb.

S O V Modal

The attraction to the verb maintains these patterns. The possibility that other elements--like topic--may have other unmarked positions is another question. The important point for my purposes is that modal elements, when they are attracted to the main verb, will tend to precede it in verb initial languages and to follow it in verb final languages.

2.2.2.2 I have argued that modal elements may be attracted to the verb and, when they are, their position relative to the verb maintains to a large extent the missionary positions. Given that elements like modals may attract to the verb, there is some explanation of the fact that modals in some languages will be dependent on the verb and in others will be positioned solely by sentential position. If, for some reason, the modal element is not attracted to the verb, it will be positioned sentence initially in verb

initial languages and sentence finally in verb final languages.
However, the centrality of the verb in combination with the prediction of certain unmarked sentential positions--sentence initial
for verb initial languages and sentence final for verb final lan-
guages--is not enough to predict the data. As Section 1 showed,
modals tend toward the beginning of the sentence even in verb final
languages. The beginning of the sentence is not defined necessarily
as sentence initial position, but rather more commonly as sentential
second position. For the time being, let me assume that second position is predictable from the importance of first position and discuss them both as the tendency to sentence initial position. The
other four elements which were considered in terms of a division
between being dependent on the verb and occurring in certain sentential positions show the same tendency to sentence initial position. All tend to occur at the beginning of the sentence rather
than at the end. Topic, it was noted, is much less commonly found
sentence finally than sentence initially. Past tense, as Chart XXI
indicated, occurs in second position in those languages where it is
specified to occur separate from the verb. The sentential position
tendency of quotatives is exhibited by Luiseño; quotatives which are
not dependent on the verb tend to occur in sentential second position. Finally, there are a number of languages--Classical Aztec,
for instance (See (34) and (35))--where negation is a sentence
initial element; I am not aware of a language where negatives that
are not attached to the main verb occur in sentence final position.[32]

The fact that past tense, modals, quotatives, negatives and
topic tend to the beginning of the sentence would not be especially
noteworthy if there were other sentential positions which were
specified with the same regularity. There is no rule in the language sample with which I am familiar that states, for instance, that
the quotative is the third element from the beginning of the sentence, or that the negative must be in the middle. Since it is the
beginning of the sentence which all these elements hold in common,
it would appear that some primary importance attaches to it. It is
the beginning of the sentence that pulls elements out of their

unmarked sentence final position in verb final languages.

I hypothesize that the importance of sentence initial position
is related to a strategy that psychologists have called "primacy".
By this strategy the first element in a series is perceived to be
the most important; in sentential terms, the first element in the
sentence is perceived to be the frame for the elements which follow.
Evidence abounds throughout language that some kind of dominance is
associated with an element which precedes another element. "Precedes" is one of the primacy relations introduced by Langacker
(1969) for pronominalization and argued for by G. Lakoff (1969)
to explain some of the data on English quantification. Furthermore,
there are indications that certain importance attaches to preceding
as opposed to following. First, even though there should be an
equal likelihood cross-linguistically of the orders VO and OV,
Greenberg (1966) suggests that the dominant order is for the verb
to precede the object. Second, Tranel (1972) reports that phonological processes can apply iteratively from left to right or from
right to left. He notes, however, that the number of rules that
apply from left to right considerably outweighs the numbers that
apply from right to left. If we expand to sentence initial and
sentence final positions the conclusion that preceding and following are not equivalent but rather that preceding is dominant, sentence initial position should be a more important position than sentence final position. The semantic elements that I have been discussing indicate how the objective content of the sentence is to be
interpreted--possible or probable, derived from somebody else, past
or present. It is not all all surprising, then, that these elements
would tend to be specified at the beginning of the sentence rather
than anywhere else, if first position is the frame position for the
sentence.

The suggestion that first position is a frame is buttressed by
an experiment reported by Boomer (1965). Boomer examined the places
of hesitation in a sentence with the hypothesis that "....hesitations
in spontaneous speech occur at points where decisions and choices
are being made." (159) He found that in only one position in the

sentence are the number of hesitations greater than chance and that position is immediately following the initial position in the sentence. His conclusion was that hesitation "...in...clauses are most likely to occur <u>after</u> [his italics] at least a preliminary decision has been made concerning its structure...." (168) The preliminary decision is represented by the word in initial position. Therefore:

> "The initial word in a....clause sets certain constraints for the structure of what is to follow. The selection of a first word has in greater or lesser degree committed the speaker to a particular construction or at least a set of alternative constructions, and has also foreclosed the possibility of other constructions." (168)

2.2.2.3 I have argued that the centrality of the verb and the importance of first position can operate on the missionary positions of modals--and other elements. The first can make the modal dependent on the main verb in the sentence; the second can position the modal in sentence initial position. It is possible that these two tendencies are not two unrelated sentential forces, that they are intimately connected. Langacker (1969) argues that "precede" is one of two structural relations--primary relations; the second is "command".

> "We may distinguish between two kinds of structural relations that are represented in a P-marker. For one thing, a P-marker represents a set of dominance relations (e.g. S dominates NP; NP dominates N; VP dominates V; S dominates VP). In addition, a P-marker represents a linear ordering of constitituents. We have defined a primacy relation in terms of each of these two dimensions of tree structure; the command relations pertains to the former, and the precedes relation pertains to the latter." (169)

The two forces under consideration here--the importance of first position and the centrality of the verb--correspond to the notions "precede" and "command" respectively. The importance of first position pertains to the linear order of constituents; modals, for example, can precede the sentence, come in S-initial position. The attraction of the main verb allows indication of the underlying relationship between the grammaticized predicate and the main verb. The position of this grammaticized predicate relative to the main verb as predicted by language typology retains the relative to the main verb as predicted by language typology retains the relative underlying height of the two predicates. Perhaps, then, there is some notion like primacy relation which subsumes the attraction of sentence initial position and the attraction of the verb.

The interaction of these two gives some explanation of one of the more puzzling facts about modals noted in Section One. TYPE B languages, languages where modals are positioned solely by sentential position, tend also to be verb final languages. The two attractions are non-contradictory for verb initial languages. By the strategy which makes first position important, modals will be in sentence initial position, their unmarked position in any case.

Modal V S O

By the attraction of the main verb--an attraction that has a directionality based on the typology of the languages--modals will precede and be dependent on the main verb in the sentence, sentence initial position.

Modal V S O

In verb final languages, by verb attraction, modals will follow the main verb in sentence final position, the unmarked position for modals in verb final language in any case.

S O V Modal

But--by the importance of first position, modals will be positioned in sentence initial position--out of their unmarked position and non-contiguous to the main verb in the sentence.

Modal S O V

There is a conflict which is resolved in favor of verb attractions

in some verb final languages and in favor of first position in
others.

Since each of the "non-objective content" elements--past
tense, topic, negatives, quotatives, and modal elements--has its
own cross-linguistic pattern of attraction to either the verb or
first position, the interaction of the two, their strength relative
to one another, cannot be specified for the entire class. How these
differences are to be effected I leave to some other time.

2.2.3 Let me repeat Hypothesis 2:

> The unmarked positions are acted upon by two tendencies--the
> tendency for certain elements (including, but not exclusive
> to, modal elements) to be attracted to the verb and the ten-
> dency for these same elements to be positioned initially.

I have argued that the centrality of the verb attracts elements to
it and the importance of sentence initial position is captured by
the notion of "primacy". I have suggested that the two tendencies
are relatable much as the notions "command" and "precede" are.

The arguments for the attraction of the verb and for the importance of sentence initial position are substantial. The weakest
part of this section is the discussion of the relation between the
two language-general tendencies. While the notion precede is intimately involved with the importance of sentence initial position,
there are difficulties in relating the notion command to the
attraction of the verb. Regardless of whether the two tendencies
I argued for here can be related in some manner--and I think it
important that they be--I take the attraction of the verb and the
importance of sentence initial position as well-justified hypotheses about what affects word order.

3.0 At a number of points I have assumed that the tendency of
modals, specifically, to sentential second position is a function
of the importance of first position. I turn now to a very brief
consideration of this claim. The hypotheses are: (1) of all the
elements (topic, negative, past tense, quotatives, and modal

elements) that may be attracted by sentence initial position, the
attraction for topic is the strongest; (2) topic may solidify in
sentence initial position, thus forcing all of the other elements to
sentential second position.[33]

We have already seen that topic shows less tendency cross-linguistically to attract to the main verb than any of the other elements. The force of the attraction of sentence initial position for
topic is more than primacy; it is, in addition, the fact that sentence initial position is assocated with old information, and
topic, alone of the non-objective content elements specifies old
information. Chafe (1973) argues that in sentence initial position
is found old information. Boomer's experiment, referred to earlier,
would suggest that sentence initial position is associated with
old information; preliminary decisions about the sentence might more
easily be based on old, as opposed to new, information. It is surely
not unrelated that a factive interpretation is forced on sentence
initial that complements which are not factive if they follow the
matrix verb. (Kiparsky & Kiparsky, 1970)

46. a. That Tricia messed up her hair was reported by UPI.
    b. UPI reported that Tricia messed up her hair.

In indirect support, Hetzron (in this volume) argues that the end of
a sentence tends to be associated with new information. The connection of topic with old information can only be suggested here, but the
claim is based on the fact that a topicalized NP in many languages
must be definite. Consider English and Albanian as examples. In
English a topicalized NP must be definite.[34]

47. a. The dog, John poisoned it.
   *b. A dog, John poisoned it.

The Albanian data is slightly more complicated. A verb with a
definite object is marked with an object marker. Sentences like this
allow dislocation.

48. a. e - due genin - tem   'I like my dog.'
          OM - like dog - my

    b.   genin - tem   e - dua   'My dog, I like it.'

         dog - my OM - like   (Albanian)

Sentences with an indefinite object do not require that the verb
be marked with an object marker.

   49. përzuna   nje gen   'I chase a dog away.'

        chased: away a dog   (Albanian)

But sentences like (49) do not allow topicalization:

   50. *nje gen perzuna   'A dog, I chased away.'

                          (Albanian)

unless the verb is marked with the object marker, and even then the
sentences are questionable.

   51. ?nje   gen   e-përzuna   'A dog, I chased it away.'

                          (Albanian)

The question of definite and indefinite of course requires much more
inquiry. I merely suggest that definiteness implies prior information
of some sort; and that definiteness is, therefore, intimately connected with old information. If first position does tend to be connected
with old information, if topic and modal elements both tend to first
position because of "primacy", and if topic is more closely connected
with the notion of old information than modal elements are, the battle
for first position is weighted in favor of topic.

The hypothesis that topic can solidify in sentence initial position is no different from the (possibly more substantial) hypothesis
that the relationship of morphemes within a word or within a phrase
can be changed through reanalysis. The reanalysis of nouns as prepositions or postpositions is one example of this sort of change.
Givon (1971) argues for the reconstruction of certain prepositions
in English and Bantu as nouns and suggests that the reinterpretation
of these nouns as prepositions is the result of a change in constituency relationships.

   52. (30) [noun [of noun]$_{mod}$] np > [[noun-of]$_{prep}$noun] np

The solidification of topic can be one of two types: Topic may
simply solidify (as illustrated in those languages with second posi-

tion modals where something other than a subject may precede the
modal). In the

    V Modal S O

languages and in some of the

    S Modal O V

languages where word order is rather free, like Luiseño, the obligatory occurrence of topic in sentence initial position has shifted
the modal back to second position. Topic may solidify to subject
(as illustrated in those languages with second position modals where
the subject must precede the modal). In most of the

    S Modal V O

languages and in the

    S Modal O V

languages without free word order, topic has been reinterpreted as
the subject.

Luiseño (S Modal O V) and Sahaptin (S Modal V O, V Modal S O)
are examples of the first. In both there is evidence that it is the
development of obligatory topicalization that has forced modals to
sentential second position. Modal elements may be initial in either,
under certain conditions peculiar to each. In the apodosis of a conditional sentence in Luiseño, the clitic complex which includes modality and 'if' is necessarily initial.

> 53. tee-xu-n-po   noo   hunwut-i   tiiwun   pi   noo   ya?anin
>   if - modal-I-incomplete I bear-object see and I run:away
>   (future)   (future)
>   'I might see a bear and I will run away.'
>   'If I see a bear, I will run away.'

In Sahaptin dependent clauses, the clitic complex which includes
modality is necessarily initial, after dependent clause marking.
These first position modals are surely remnants of the non-solidified
topic stage; it is not possible to topicalize in clauses where first
position is obligatorily filled by some other element--either the

marker that corresponds to English 'if' or a dependent clause marker.

Inquiry into the second type would, of course, require an exhaustive examination of the relationship between subject and topic, but there is evidence that topic may solidify to subject rather than conversely. Gruber (1967b) suggests that child language acquisition data argues for the development of subject from topic. Kuroda (1965) suggests for Japanese that "...the logical subjects of sentences, which are represented by wa-phrases, are always at the same time the syntactic subjects (but not vice versa, since sentences may not have logical subject.)" (2-28) [Read this sentence as: It is possible that sentences will not have logical subjects.]

The number of languages with verb initial characteristics and an SVO surface word order should be some further indication of the possibility for topic to become subject, if, of course, we assume that these languages are underlying VSO. Somewhat more concretely, consider what might force reanalysis of topic as subject. Kapampangan is a VSO languages with an SVO alternate order by topicalization.

54. a. sinipa - ne i wan ing bola kang maria
         kick - SM John   ball   Maria
         'John kicked the ball to Maria.'

     b. i wan sinipa - ne ing bola kang maria
         'It's John who kicked the ball to Maria.'
         (Kapampangan)

There are other forces which act to produce an SVO order in this language and these may lead to the loss of the topic function of preceding the verb, a circumstance which in turn could lead to a change in word order. For example, when the subject of the embedded sentence is raised to object position in the embedding sentence, the subject of the embedding sentence is moved to sentence initial position, but is not topicalized.

55. i wan buri - ne - ng bumasa - ng libru i maria
     John wants - SM   read   book   Mary
     'John wants Mary to read a book.'

The topic function of preceding the verb overlaps with other forces causing an NP to precede the verb. The situation is ripe for re-analysis.

In conclusion, it is not at all improbable that topic may solidify in sentence initial position.

4.0 This paper began with an examination of the positional tendencies of modal elements and concluded with the hypothesis of two language general strategies that explain--I use the term advisedly--these tendencies. The hypothesis of the existence of these strategies is well-founded; the possible existence of such strategies suggests certain additions to theories of word order and word order change. First, as we have seen, these strategies may be in conflict. The tendency of grammatical elements to attract to the verb conflicts in verb final languages with the attraction of sentence initial position. The multi-purpose importance of first position forces grammatical elements--and verbs--out of first position and topic (developing to subject) in. If the order of elements is, at least in part, a function of strategies which may conflict, word order change may be the result of ever-changing resolutions of conflicts. Second, since grammaticized elements tend to certain positions, their positions do not necessarily reflect pre-grammatication word order. Rather the strength of the tendency of grammaticized elements to certain positions may in itself effect changes in word order.

The obvious next steps are to provide more, and more substantial support for what I have suggested and, assuming the suggestions are valid, to discover what other strategies exist to affect and effect the order of elements.

<u>NOTES</u>

*Research for this paper was supported in part by a grant from the Society of Sigma xi.

1. This definition is necessarily rough, since a more complete one would require a paper at least as long as this one. Although other parameters are necessary to a complete definition of modality--as, for example, how the speaker is part of modality--these six notions are a basic outline. Excluded from modality according to my definition are quotatives and elements that indicate irrealis or realis. Quotatives do not mark possibility, probability, or certainty or the related notions directly or as their primary function. Markers of irrealis and realis indicate that the situations which the sentence describes are unreal or real respectively; they do not indicate how close it approximates either.

2. Modals in at least some other languages are ambiguous, however. In Thai, for example, one modal indicates either an avoidable obligation or a probability, much like English <u>should</u>.

> khǎw khuan tii mǎa kong khǎw
> he SHOULD hit dog his
> 'He should hit his dog.

> khǎw khuan cà? tua yày maak
> he SHOULD big
> 'He is supposed to be really big.'
> 'He should be really big.

Interestingly enough, when modals in other languages are ambiguous, they seem to be ambiguous between the same modal concepts that English modals are. (See Steele (1973b))

3. Given that I restricted consideration to grammatical modal elements, it is not possible to draw any conclusions about their universality as opposed to main verbs which are modal in force. However, it should be noted that finding grammatical modals was no problem. Almost every language that I examined has them in one form or another, and I expect those grammars which do not

note them have avoided discussing them.

4. Example sentences taken from sources other than my own notes use the transcription of the author. Classical Aztec is an exception; the sentences were originally written in a Spanish orthography. The example taken from my notes--and the Classical Aztec examples--are in a regular phonemic transcription, except for these conventions: /ng/ is written for /ŋ /; long vowels are written as two vowels, e.g. /ee/ for /e:/.

5. Some languages had to be excluded from consideration totally because of this restriction. For example, the descriptions I found of Egyptian Arabic called modals adverbial elements. Even though I could find no evidence that these elements could occur anywhere but sentence initial position, I did not include Egyptian Arabic in the language sample.

6. Other languages examined include: Tagalog, Akkadian, Serbo-Croatian, Egyptian Arabic, Khasi, Sonsoral-Tobi, Bobangi, Cayuvava, Itonama, Nimboran, Madurese, Quiche, Acooli, Lapp, Kashmiri, Kannada, Haida, Tonkawa, Tunica, Shasta, Chukchee, Dakota, Hupa, Konkow, Japanese, Crow, S.E. Pomo, Tarascan, Coos, Guaraní, Yokuts, Classical Aztec, Papago, Baure, Nez Perce, Sango.

7. The language classification is based in large part on the "Languages of the World" series published by Anthropological Linguistics, although some revisions based on opinions of these people familiar with any particular group have been made. There is a disagreement and confusion everywhere on the subject of the classifications, even among people who know the languages involved, so the language sample attempts also to represent major divisions within the genetic groups, divisions which are slightly less in dispute, e.g. Hokan-Siouan is less well-established; Hokan is represented by Mojave, Washo, and Pomo; Siouan, by Wichita. In the genetic groups which are more readily agreed upon, e.g. IndoEuropean, I tried also to include languages from different divisions, e.g. IndoEuropean is represented by Albanian, English and Marathi, Ross Clark, Nancy Frishberg and

I spent a few weeks in the spring of 1972 working out the rough classification which Table I represents.

8.   Although I believe that a study of this sort, a study which is based on a representative language sample is potentially more solidly based than one which is more restricted, I have no delusions that the number of languages with which I have had contact immunizes me from mistakes. There are many points at which I could have misinterpreted data. First, since I couldn't have an intimate knowledge of all the languages involved, I had to base my study in large part on other people's descriptions. Second, I had to make sense of grammars written from various theoretical viewpoints and with varying degrees of competence. Third, I had to wend my way through a sometimes bewildering proliferation of terminology. What one person calls a particle, another will call an affix and a third will invent a name for. The term _modal_ itself subsumes an almost magically expanding and contracting set. Fourth, for a number of reasons--the fact that writers of grammars tend not to make generalization of the sort I was looking for, the fact that grammars (at least older grammars) are often written with little discussion of syntax, and the problem that occasionally the grammar offered a description that didn't fit the data--generally _I_ had to make the generalization about certain patterns, especially the tendency of modals to occur in a certain position in a particular language. These problems are potentially serious. That it became easier for me to find information eases my concern. That any misinterpretation I made has to be random should destory some objections that might arise. Finally, the fact that I found a pattern, regularities, should serve to dispel many of the remaining doubts.

9.   Pamela Munro is the expert on Mojave; Suzette Elgin and Alec Bamford, on Navajo; and Brooke Hill and Coral Bergman on Alaskan Eskimo. I also consulted Ove Lorentz on Lapp, but did not include Lapp in the final sample.

10. Charles Lee spent time explaining some facets of Korean to me.

11. Much thanks is due to the patience of Mrs. Villiana Hyde
    (Luiseño), Edgardo Gomez (Kapampangan), Chanida Chanyapate
    (Thai), Mrs. Hazel Miller (Sahaptin), and Vonny Lorentz
    (Indonesian). I also worked with Sadik Berisha (Albanian)
    and Marina Dos Santos (Guaraní) briefly, although Guaraní is
    not included in the final sample.

12. Whether the modals of Albanian and Thai are grammatical elements
    is a question. In Thai, it is difficult to tell whether the
    modal is a main verb or an auxiliary due to the lack of verbal
    inflection. I based my decision on the fact that tense markers
    occur in a different position relative to modals than they do
    with demonstrably main verbs. Some Albanian modals occur in a
    construction--what Newmark (1957) calls the "conjunctive" con-
    struction--that is like an English verb and infinitive con-
    struction.

    duhet   të - skoim   'We should go."
    MODAL   conjunctive-verb
    (3rd sg. subject agreement)   (1st pl. subject agreement)
                    (Albanian)

    të appears to be parallel to English to. If what follows the
    modal in sentences like this one is a complement, it may be
    possible to argue that the modal is a main verb. However, New-
    mark notes that this construction is extremely limited, occurring
    only with modals and with the element that indicates progressive.
    I assume, therefore, that the modal is not a main verb.

13. Oates says that modals precede the verb, but examples like
    (13) indicate that modals precede the noun subject as well.
    Quite likely, Oates' claim is based on the fact that most sen-
    tences contain only a verb since both object and subject may
    appear as pronominal clitics to the verb. In such a sentence,
    it will of course appear that the modal immediately precedes the
    verb.

14. Chart VI includes specification of affixation of the modal element, a topic which is in itself very interesting, although not essential to the positional tendencies considered here. Briefly and with overgeneralization, a modal which is described as following another element--either verb or some other element-- is suffixed to it; a modal which is described as preceding another element--either verb or some other element--is unaffixed.

15. I include Kapampangan as VSO, although it often has a VOS word order.

16. I'm not going to argue for the validity of this position. I realize it has not gained any uniform acceptance, although there have been interesting arguments in its behalf--McCawley (1970) for instance. There are regularities which such a division points up and that is good argument for its inclusion here.

17. Others which have been suggested are the direction of gapping, the position of adjectives relative to a head noun, and the position of the conjunction.

18. The question of how to distinguish between postpositions and case will be carefully avoided.

19. Tai (1973) argues that Mandarin is a verb final language.

20.

	Postpositions	Prepositions
Languages with VO order	2 (Mandarin, Wichita)	18 (Kapampangan, Thai, Indonesian, English, Chrau, Ulithian, Nguna, Gbaya, Lunda, Squamish, Achi, Swazi, Diola-Fogny, Wolio, Khasi, Snohomish, Acooli, Albanian)
Languages with OV order	16 (Quechua, Khalka Balti, Walbiri, Lapp, E. Ostyak, Aranda, Garo, Burmese, Luiseño, Korean, Navajo, Kashaya, Pomo, Tamil, Washo, Maidu)	

21. This assumption does not represent Greenberg's position.

22. Modals in Squamish can be in sentential second position, but the most common position seems to be in sentence initial position, that is, they occur with the auxiliary in sentence initial position.

23. In many languages, modals are marked to agree with the subject of the sentence like main verbs, and they occur with verb forms that resemble the verbs of complements.

24. Not all negatives nor all quotatives are grammatical elements, of course. In Yuman languages, the negative is reported to be a regular verb form. If sentences like:

    John is said to be leaving.

    are considered to contain a quotative, some quotatives are regular main verbs. In that most negatives and most quotatives are grammatical elements, they do not appear to be like modals. Unlike quotatives, modals, and negatives, past tense, is, as far as I know, always grammatical; it does not occur as a main verb form. The main verb source of tense is often transparent, though. Verbs meaning 'be' and 'have' are regularly involved in marking past tense. Ultan (1972) notes that future markings are often derived from verbs which express direction, like 'go' and 'come'.

25. I include English here as TYPE A, even though past tense does tend to be a second position element in English sentences.

26. The language sample for tense (27 languages) is a subset of the language sample for modals (44 languages). For the remaining 17 languages, either I have no information about past tense markers or past tense is unmarked.

27. Sentential negation, not constituent negation, is the phenomenon under consideration.

28. There is some importance which attaches to a subject NP in sentence final position in Kapampangan, something closer to focus.

250

29. It isn't clear that the attraction of topic to the verb should
be considered exactly the same phenomenon as the attraction of
the other elements to the verb, but, on the other hand, it isn't
clear that it shouldn't be.

30. Clitic pronouns are often second position elements, a fact
which does not destroy the sentential scope argument, but
which suggests that pragmatic factors are involved in the importance of the beginning of the sentence.

31. I have excluded causatives from this discussion because they
do not exhibit the tendency to be positioned by sentential
position alone that the other elements mentioned do. I have
not discussed aspect either, but (See Steele (1973b)) there is
a real question about what are the divisions between aspect and
tense, and aspect and modality--and of course between tense and
modality.

32. While I am not convinced that negatives are to be generated at
the most abstract level within the same clause as the objective
content, Klima's (1964) argument for English that a negative is
generated at the beginning of the sentence and then moved to
whatever element it negates is a beautiful insight into the
tendency of negatives toward sentence initial position.

33. Negatives appear to be less subject to being moved to second
position from initial position than the other elements considered here.

34. This statement might demand some slight revision, to the claim
that a topicalized NP must be specific.

Bibliography

Anceaux, J. C. 1965. The Nimboran Language. The Netherlands, Martinus, Nijhoff.

-----. 1952. The Wolio Language. The Netherlands, H. L. Smits.

Antinucci, Francesco and Dominico Parisi. 1971. "On English Modals," Papers from the Seventh Regional Meeting of the Chicago Linguistic Society, p. 38-39.

Aoki, Haruo. 1970. Nez Perce Grammar. University of California Publications in Linguistics 62. Berkeley, University of California Press.

Bach, Emmon, and Robert T. Harms (eds.) 1968. Universals in Linguistic Theory. New York, Holt, Rinehart, and Winston.

Bangbose, Ayo, 1966. A Grammar of Yoruba. Great Britain, Cambridge University Press.

Baptista, Priscilla and Ruth Wallin. 1967. "Baure." Bolivian Indian Grammars I. Esther Lavina Matteson (ed.). SIL Publications 16, University of Oklahoma. p. 27-84.

Bascom, Burton W. Jr. 1965. Proto-Tepiman. University of Washington dissertation.

Bever, T. G. and D. T. Langendoen. 1971. "A Dynamic Model of Evolution of Language." Linguistic Inquiry II:4, p. 443-463.

Bills, Garland D., Bernardo Vallejo C., and Rudolph C. Troike. 1969. An Introduction to Spoken Bolivian Quechua. Austin, University of Texas Press.

Binnick, Robert I. 1967. "Semantic and Syntactic Classes of Verbs." Manuscript.

-----. 1971. "Will and Be Going To." Papers from the Seventh Regional Meeting of the Chicago Linguistic Society, p. 40-52.

-----. 1972. "Will and Be Going To II." Papers from the Eighth Regional Meeting of the Chicago Linguistic Society.

252

Bloomfield, Leonard. 1917. <u>Tagalog Texts with Grammatical Analysis</u>. Studies in Language and Literature III, May-November 2-4. Urbana, University of Illinois Press.

Boas, Franz (ed.). 1969. <u>Handbook of American Indian Languages</u>, Volume I and II. The Netherlands, Anthropological Publications, Oosterhout N.B.

Boomer, D. S. 1968. "Hesitation and Grammatical Encoding." <u>Language</u>. R. C. Oldfield and J. C. Marshall (eds.). Baltimore, Penguin Books.

Boyd, J. and J. P. Thorne. 1969. "The Semantics of Modal Verbs." <u>Journal of Linguistics</u> 5:1, p. 57-74.

Brown, Roger and Camile Hanlon. 1968. "Derivational Complexity and the Order of Acquisition in Child Speech." Manuscript for the 1968 Carnegie-Mellon Symposium on Cognitive Psychology.

Browne, Wales. 1967. "On the Problem of Enclitic Placement in Serbo-Croatian." Manuscript.

Burgess, Dora and David Fox. 1965. "Quiche." <u>Languages of Guatemala</u>. Marvin K. Mayers (ed.). The Hague, Mouton. p. 49-87.

Burling, Robbins. 1961. <u>A Garo Grammar</u>. Poona, Deccan College Monograph Series: 25.

Buse, J. E. 1963. "The Structure of the Rarotongan Verbal Piece." <u>Bulletin of the School of Oriental and African Studies</u>, 26, p. 152-160.

Calbert, Joseph P. 1971. "Modality and Case Grammar." <u>Working Papers in Linguistics</u> 10. Charles Fillmore (ed.). Ohio State University, p. 85-132.

Camp, Elizabeth and Millicent Liccardi. 1967. "Itonama." <u>Bolivian Indian Grammars</u> II. Esther Lavina Matteson (ed.). SIL Publications 16, University of Oklahoma, p. 257-352.

Canger, Una Rasmussen. 1969. <u>Analysis in Outline of Mam, a Mayan Language</u>. University of California at Berkeley dissertation.

Canonge, Elliot. 1958. Comanche Texts, Summer Institute of
    Linguistics.

Capell, A. 1967. "The Analysis of Complex Verbal Forms." Pacific
    Linguistics Series A, Occasional Papers II, p. 43-73.

-----. 1969. Grammar and Vocabulary of the Language of Sonsoral-
    Tobi. Oceania Linguistic Monographs 12, University of Sydney.

Chafe, Wallace L. 1973. "Language and Memory." Language 49:2,
    p. 261-281.

-----. 1970. Meaning and the Structure of Language. Chicago,
    University of Chicago Press.

Chapin, Paul G. 1973. "Quasi-Modals." Journal of Linguistics
    9:1, p. 1-10.

Chomsky, Noam. 1965. Aspects of the Theory of Syntax. Cambridge,
    MIT Press.

-----. 1970. "Some Empirical Issues in the Theory of Transforma-
    tional Grammar." Manuscript.

-----. 1964. "A Transformational Approach to Syntax." The
    Structure of Language. Jerry A. Fodor and Jerrold J. Katz
    (eds.). Englewood Cliffs, Prentice-Hall. p. 211-245.

Closs, Elizabeth. 1965. "Diachronic Syntax and Generative Grammar."
    Language, 41:2, p. 402-415.

Crazzalara, J. P. 1955. A Study of the Acooli Language. Oxford
    University Press.

De Molina, Fray Alonso. 1571. Vocabulario en Lengua Castellana y
    Mexicana. Facsimile edition: Ediciones Culture Hispanica,
    Madric. 1944.

Durbin, Marshall, 1971. "Identifying Semantic Foci in Lexical Items."
    Papers from the Seventh Regional Meeting of the Chicago Lin-
    guistic Society. p. 350-359.

Ehrman, Madeline. 1966. The Meanings of the Modals in Present-day
    American English. The Hague, Mouton.

Fillmore, Charles. 1971. "Toward a Theory of Deixis." Working Papers in Linguistics 3:4. University of Hawaii. p. 219-243.

Forman, Michael. 1971a. Kapampangan Dictionary. Honolulu, University of Hawaii Press.

-----. 1971b. Kapampangan Grammar Notes. Honolulu, University of Hawaii Press.

Fraser, Bruce. 1973. "On Accounting for Illocutionary Forces." A Festschrift for Morris Halle. S. Anderson and P. Kiparsky (eds.). New York, Holt, Rinehart, and Winston, p. 287-307.

-----. 1969. "A Reply to 'On Declarative Sentences'." Indiana University mimeo.

-----. 1971. "Sentences and Illucutionary Forces." Language Research Reports 4.

Gamal-Eldin, Saad M. 1967. A Syntactic Study of Egyptian Colloquial Arabic. Janua Linguarum, studia memoriae. The Hague, Mouton.

Garibay, K., Angel Maria. 1970. Llave del Nahautl. Mexico, Editorial Porrua.

Givón, Talmy. 1971. "Historical Syntax and Synchronic Morphology: An Archaeologist's Field Trip." Papers from the Seventh Regional Meeting of the Chicago Linguistic Society. p. 304-315.

Golla, Victor Karl. 1970. Hupa Grammar. University of California at Berkeley dissertation.

Gorbet, Larry. 1973. "The Isthmus of Anaphor (and Idiomaticity)." Stanford Occasional Papers 3. James Paul Gee et al. (eds.). p. 25-34.

Grimes, Joseph. 1964. Huichol Syntax. Janua linguarum, series practica, no. 11. The Nague, Mouton.

Grosu, Alexander. 1971. "On Perceptual and Grammatical Constraints." Papers from the Seventh Regional Meeting of the Chicago Linguistic Society. p. 416-427.

Greenberg, Joseph H. 1956. "The Measurement of Linguistic Diversity." Language 32:1, p. 109-115.

-----. 1963. "Some Universals of Grammar with Particular Reference to the Order of Meaningful Elements." Universals of Language. Joseph Greenberg (ed.). Cambridge, MIT Press.

Gruber, Jeffrey S. 1967a. "Correlations between the Syntactic Construction of the Child and of the Adult." Manuscript.

-----. 1967b. Functions of the Lexicon in Formal Descriptive Grammars. System Development Corp. Technical Memorandum.

-----. 1969. "Topicalization in Child Language." Modern Studies in English. David Reibel and Sanford Schane (eds.). Englewood Cliffs, Prentice-Hall. p. 422-447.

Gulya, Janos. 1966. Eastern Ostyak Chrestomathy. Indiana University Uralic and Altaic Series, Volume 51.

Hale, Kenneth, 1973. "Gaps in Grammar and Culture." Manuscript.

-----. Undated. "A Note on Subject-Object Inversion in Navajo." Manuscript.

-----. 1969a. "Papago /či-m/." IJAL 35:2, p. 203-212.

-----. 1969b. "Papago /čɨm/." Manuscript.

-----. 1973. "Person Marking in Walbiri." A Festschrift for Morris Halle. Stephen R. Anderson and Paul Kiparsky (eds.). New York, Holt Rinehart, and Winston. p. 308-344.

Hill, Kenneth. 1967. A Grammar of the Serrano Language. UCLA dissertation.

Hofmann, T. R. 1966. "Past Tense Replacement and the Modal System." The Computation Laboratory of Harvard University Mathematical Linguistics and Automatic Translation Report No. NSF 17.

Horn, Laurence. 1972a. "Modality and Quantification." Chapter 3 of untitles UCLA dissertation.

-----. 1972b. "Scalarity and Negation." Chapter 2 of untitled UCLA dissertation.

Horton, A. E. 1949. A Grammar of Luvale. Johannesburg, Witwatersrand University Press.

Huang, Shuan-Fan. 1969. "On the Syntax and Semantics of English
Modals." Working Papers in Linguistics 3, Ohio State
University. p. 159-180.

Hyde, Villiana. 1971. An Introduction to the Luiseño Language.
Ronald Langacker (ed.). Morongo Indian Reservation, Malki
Museum Press.

Inoue, Masako. 1972. "Some Observations on Japanese Complement
Constructions." Manuscript.

Jackendoff, Ray S. 1969. "An Interpretive Theory of Negation."
Foundations of Language 5:2, p, 218-241.

-----. 1971a. "Modal Structure in Semantic Representation."
Linguistic Inquiry II:4, p. 479-515.

-----. 1972. Semantic Interpretation in Generative Grammar.
Cambridge, MIT Press, Studies in Linguistics Series.

-----. 1971b. "On Some Questionable Arguments about Quantifiers
and Negation." Language 47:2, p. 282-297.

-----. 1968. "Speculations on Presentences and Determiners."
Indiana University mimeo.

Jacobs, Melville. 1931. Northern Sahaptin Grammar. University of
Washington Publications in Anthropology Volume 4, p. 87-291.

Jacobs, Roderick A. 1972. Syntactic Change: A Cupan (Uto-Aztecan)
Case Study. University of California at San Diego dissertation.

Jacobsen, William Horton. 1964. A Grammar of the Washo Language.
University of California at Berkeley dissertation.

Jaiswal, Mahesh Prasad. 1962. A Linguistic Study of Bendeli.
Leiden, E. J. Brill.

Jenkins, Lyle, 1972a. "On English Modals." from Modality in English
Syntax. MIT dissertation.

-----. 1972b. "Will-Deletion." Papers from the Eighth Regional Meeting of the Chicago Linguistic Society. Paul Peranteau et al. (eds.). p. 173-182.

Karttunen, Lauri. 1971. "Implicative Verbs." Language 47:2, p. 340-358.

Kayne, Richard. 1969. The Transformation Cycle in French Syntax. MIT dissertation.

Key, Harold H. 1967. Morphology of Cayuvava. The Hague, Mouton.

Kiparsky, Paul. 1968. "Tense and Mood in Indo-European Syntax." Foundations of Language 4:1, p. 30-57.

-----, and Carol Kiparsky. 1970. "Fact." Progress in Linguistics. Manfred Bierwisch and Karl Erich Heidolph (eds.). The Hague, Mouton, p. 143-173.

Klima, Edward. 1964. "Negation in English." The Structure of Language. Jerry A. Fodor and Jerrold J. Katz (eds.). Englewood Cliffs, Prentice-Hall. p. 246-323.

Koutsoudas, Andreas. 1971. "The Strict Order Fallacy." Indiana University mimeo.

Kraft, Charles H. 1963. A Study of Hausa Syntax, Volume I, Structure. Hartford Seminary Foundation.

-----, and Salisu Abubaker. 1965. An Introduction to Spoken Hausa. African Studies Center, Michigan State University.

Kuipers, Aert H. 1967. The Squamish Language. Janua linguarum, series practica LXXIII. The Hague, Mouton.

Kuroda, S. Y. 1965. "Wa." Chapter 2, MIT dissertation.

Lakoff, George. 1970a. "Adverbs and Modal Operators." Manuscript.

-----. 1966. "Deep and Surface Grammar." Manuscript.

-----. 1969. "On Derivational Constraints." Papers from the Fifth Regional Meeting of the Chicago Linguistic Society. Robert I. Binnick et al. (eds.). p. 117-139.

-----. "On Generative Semantics." Semantics--an Interdisciplinary Reader in Philosophy, Linguistics, Anthropology and Psychology. London, Cambridge University Press, p. 232-296.

-----. 1972. "Hedges: A Study in Meaning Criteria and the Logic of Fuzzy Concepts." Papers from the Eighth Regional Meeting of the Chicago Linguistic Society. Paul Peranteau et al. (eds.). p. 183-228.

-----. 1970b. Irregularity in Syntax. New York, Holt, Rinehart, and Winston.

-----. 1970c. "Linguistics and Natural Logic." Studies in Generative Semantics 1. Phonetics Laboratory, University of Michigan.

-----, and J. R. Ross. 1968. "Is Deep Structure Necessary?" Indiana University mimeo.

Lakoff, Robin. 1971a. "Language in Context." Manuscript.

-----. 1971b. "Passive Resistance." Papers from the Seventh Regional Meeting of the Chicago Linguistic Society. p. 149-162.

-----. 1972. "The Pragmatics of Modality." Papers from the Eighth Regional Meeting of the Chicago Linguistic Society. p. 149-162.

Lamb, Sydney. 1958. Mono Grammar. University of California at Berkeley dissertation.

Langacker, Ronald. 1972. "Movement Rules in Functional Perspective." Manuscript.

-----. 1973. "Predicate Raising: Some Uto-Aztecan Evidence." Issues in Linguistics, Papers in Honor of Henry and Renée Kahane. Braj. B. Kachru et al. (eds.). Urbana, University of Illinois Press. p. 468-491.

-----. 1969. "Pronominalization and the Chain of Command." Modern Studies in English. David Reibel and Sanford Schane (eds.). Englewood Cliffs, Prentice-Hall. p. 160-186.

-----. 1972. "Review of Chafe: Meaning and the Structure of Language." Language 48:1, p. 134-160.

Langendoen, D. Terence. 1970. "The 'Can't Seem to' Construction."
Linguistic Inquiry 1:1, p. 25-36.

Law, Harold M. 1966. Obligatory Construction of Isthmus Nahaut
Grammar. Janua linguarum, studia memoriae. The Hague, Mouton.

Lebrun, Yvan. 1964. "Can and May, a Problem of Multiple Meaning."
Proceedings of the 9th International Congress of Linguists.
The Hague, Mouton. p. 552-555.

Lee, P. Gregory. 1969. "Do from Occur." Working Papers in Linguistics 3, Ohio State University. p. 1-21.

Lehmann, W. P. 1972. "Converging Theories in Linguistics." Language
48:2, p. 266-275.

-----. 1973. "A Structural Principle of Language and its Implications."
Language 49:1, p. 47-66.

Lenneberg, Eric. 1967. Biological Foundations of Language. New York,
John Wiley and Sons.

Lewis, G. 1967. Turkish Grammar. Oxford University Press.

Li, Fang-Kuei. 1946. "Chipewyan." Linguistic Structures of Native
America. Cornelia Osgood (ed.). Viking Fund Publications in
Anthropology 6, New York. p. 398-423.

Li, Ying-che. 1970. Abstract Investigation of Case in Chinese
Grammar. University of Michigan dissertation.

Lindenfeld, Jacqueline. 1969. A Transformational Grammar of Yaqui.
UCLA dissertation.

Lindsay, W. M. 1963. The Latin Language. New York, Hofner Publishing
Company.

Long, Ralph B. 1966. "Imperative and Subjunctive in Contemporary
English." American Speech 41:3, p. 199-210.

Loving, Richard and Howard McKaughan. 1964. "Awa Verbs Part I: The
Internal Structure of Independent Verbs." Verb Studies in Five
New Guinea Languages. Benjamin F. Elson (ed.). SIL. p. 1-30.

Lowie, Robert H. 1960a. Crow Texts. Berkeley, University of
    California Press.

Lyons, John. 1968. Introduction to Theoretical Linguistics. Cam-
    bridge University Press.

McCawley, James. 1970. "English as a VSO Language." Language.
    46:2, p. 286-299.

-----. 1971. "Tense and Time Reference in English." Studies in
    Linguistic Semantics. Charles Fillmore and D. Terence Langen-
    doen (eds.). New York, Holt, Rinehart, and Winston.

McLendon, Sally Virginia. 1966. The Eastern Pomo Language. Univer-
    sity of California at Berkeley dissertation.

Malcolm, D. Mck. 1966. A New Zulu Manual. Revised by D. N. Bang.
    Johannesburg, Longmans Southern Africa Ltd.

Mason, John Alden. 1950. The Language of the Papago of Arizona.
    Pennsylvania Museum Monographs.

Master, Alfred. 1964. A Grammar of Old Marathi. Oxford, Clarendon
    Press.

Matisoff, James Alan. 1967. A Grammar of the Lahu Language.
    University of California at Berkeley dissertation.

Meskill, Robert Hugh. 1970. A Transformational Analysis of
    Turkic Syntax. Studia memoriae, series practica 59. The
    Hague, Mouton.

Mirikitani, Leatrice T. 1972. Kapampangan Syntax. Oceanic Lin-
    guistics Special Publication 10, University of Hawaii Press.

Mitchell, Lawrence. 1972. "Old English as an SVO Language:
    Evidence from the Auxiliary." Papers in Linguistics 5:2,
    p. 183-202.

Mitchell, T. F. 1956. Introduction to Colloquial Egyptian Arabic.
    New York.

261

Morgan, Jerry L. 1969. "On the Treatment of Presuppositions in Transformational Grammar." Papers from the Fifth Regional Meeting of the Chicago Linguistic Society, p. 167-177.

Moshinsky, Julius Barry. 1970. Southeastern Pomo Grammar. University of California at Berkeley dissertation.

Muraki, Masatake. 1972. "Intransitive Analysis of Root Modals." Studies in English Literature. The English Literary Society of Japan. p. 109-127.

Newman, Paul. 1970. A Grammar of Tera. University of California Publications in Linguistics 57. Berkeley, University of California Press.

Newman, Stanley. 1944. Yokuts Language of California. Viking Fund Publications in Anthropology 2, New York.

Newmark, Leonard. 1957. Structural Grammar of Albanian. Indiana University Research Center in Anthropology, Folklore and Linguistics 4. Bloomington, Indiana University Press.

Newmeyer, Frederick. 1970. "The Root Modal: Can it be Transitive?" Studies Presented to Robert Lees by H is Students. J. M. Sadock and A. Vanek (eds.). Edmonton, Linguistic Research Inc.

Oates, Lynette Francis. 1964. A Tentative Description of the Gunwinjgu Language. Oceania Linguistic Monographs 10, University of Sydney.

Ogawa, Kunihiko. 1971. A Generative Transformational Study of Tunica Syntax. University of Utah Master's thesis.

O'Kell, John. 1969. A Reference Grammar of Colloquial Burmese, Volume I and II. London, Oxford University Press.

Osborn, Henry and William A. Smalley. 1949. "Formulae for Comanche Stem and Word Formation." IJAL 15:2, p. 93-99.

262

Osgood, Cornelius (ed.). 1946. Linguistic Structures of Native America. Viking Fund Publications in Anthropology 6, New York.

Oswalt, Robert. 1961. Kashaya Grammar. University of California at Berkeley dissertation.

-----. 1964. Kashaya Texts. University of California Publications in Linguistics 36. Berkeley, University of California Press.

Ott, Willis G. and Rebecca H. Ott. 1967. "Ignaciano." Bolivian Indian Grammars I. Esther Lavina Matteson (ed.). SIL Publications 16, University of Oklahoma. p. 85-137.

Perlmutter, David M. 1968. Deep and Surface Structure Constraints in Syntax. MIT dissertation.

-----. 1970. "The Two Verbs Begin." Readings in English Transformational Grammar. Roderick Jacobs and Peter Rosenbaum (eds.). Waltham, Ginn and Company. p. 107-119.

Poppe, Nicholas. 1960. Buriat Grammar. Indiana University Uralic and Alaic Series 2. The Hague, Mouton.

Postal, Paul. 1970. "On the Surface Verb 'Remind'." Linguistic Inquiry I:1, p. 37-120.

Pulte, William. 1973. "A Note on Gapping." Linguistic Inquiry IV:1, p. 100-101.

Rabel, Lili. 1961. Khasi, A Language of Assam. Louisiana State University Studies 10, Louisiana State University Press.

Ramstedt, G. J. 1968. Korean Grammar. The Netherlands. Oosterhout N. B.

Read, A. F. C. 1934. Balti Grammar. The Royal Asiatic Society.

Reece, Reverend Laurie L. S. C. E. 1970. Grammar of the Walbiri Language of Central Australia. Oceania Linguistics Monograph 13, University of Sydney.

Reighard, John. 1971. "Some Observations on Syntactic Change in Verbs." Papers from the Seventh Regional Meeting of the Chicago Linguistic Society . p. 511-518.

Reiner, Erica. 1966. A Linguistic Analysis of Akkadian. Janua linguarum, series practica XXI. The Hague, Mouton.

Saxton, Dean and Lucille Saxton. 1969. Dictionary. (Papago and Pima to English; English to Papago and Pima). Tucson, University of Arizona Press.

Schiffman, Harold F. 1969. A Transformational Grammar of the Tamil Aspectual System. University of Washington Studies in Linguistics and Language Learning, Volume VII.

Schutz, Albert J. 1969. Nguna Grammar. Oceanic Linguistics Special Publication 5, University of Hawaii Press.

Schwartz, Arthur. 1971. "General Aspects of Relative Clause Formation." Stanford University Working Papers on Language Universals 6. p. 139-170.

-----. 1972. "The VP-Constituent of SVO Languages." Stanford University Working Papers on Language Universals 8. p. 21-53.

Seiler, Hansjakob. 1971. "Abstract Structures for Moods in Greek." Language 47:1, p. 79-90.

Shaw, Mary and Helen Neuenswander. 1965. "Achi." Languages of Guatemala. Marvin K. Mayers (ed.). The Hague, Mouton. p. 15-49.

Shipley, William F. 1964. Maidu Grammar. University of California Publications in Linguistics 41. Berkeley, University of California Press.

Silver, Shirley King. 1966. The Shasta Language. University of California at Berkeley dissertation.

Sohn, H. 1969. An Outline of Ulithian Grammar. University of Hawaii dissertation.

Spenst, Henry, Ila J. Spenst, Betsy H. Wrisley, and Grace E. Sherman. 1967. "Quechua." Bolivian Indian Grammars II. Esther Lavina Matteson (ed.). SIL Publications 16, University of Oklahoma. p. 27-97.

Stevens, Alan M. 1968. Madurese Phonology and Morphology. American Oriental Series Volume 52. New Haven, American Oriental Society.

Rescher, Nicholas. 1967. "Temporal Modalities in Arabic Logic." Foundations of Language 7:3, p. 305-336.

Rood, D. S. 1971. "Agent and Object in Wichita." Lingua 28:1, p. 100-107.

-----. 1970. Wichita Grammar: A Generative Semantic Sketch. University of California at Berkeley dissertation.

Ross, J. R. 1972. "Act." Semantics of Natural Language. Donald Davidson and Gilbert Harman (eds.). Dordrecht, D. Reidel. p. 70-126.

-----. 1969. "Adjectives as Noun Phrases." Modern Studies in English. D. Reibel and S. Schane (eds.). Englewood Cliffs, Prentice-Hall. p. 352-360.

-----. 1969. "Auxiliaries as Main Verbs." Studies in Philosophical Linguistics Series 1, Evanston, Illinois, Great Expectations Publications.

-----. 1970. "On Declarative Sentences." Readings in English Transformational Grammar. Roderick Jacobs and Peter Rosenbaum (eds.). Waltham, Ginn and Company. p. 222-272.

-----. 1971. "Gapping and Order of Constituents." Recent Developments in Linguistics. M. Bierwisch and K. Heidolph (eds.). The Hague, Mouton. p. 249-259.

Sadock, J. 1969. "Super-Hypersentences." Papers in Linguistics. 1:1, p. 1-15.

Samarin, William. 1966. The Gbaya Language. University of California Publications in Linguistics, 44. Berkeley, University of
California Press.

-----. 1967. A Grammar of Sango. Janua linguarum, studia memoriae,
series practica XXXVIII. The Hague, Mouton.

Sanders, Gerald. 1970. "Invarient Ordering." Indiana University
mimeo.

Sapir, Edward. 1930. The Southern Paiute Language. (Parts 1-3).
American Academy of Arts and Sciences, Proceedings.

Sapir, J. David. 1965. A Grammar of Diola-Fogny: A Language
Spoken in Bosse-Cosa-mance Region of Senegal. Cambridge
University Press.

Steele, Susan. 1973a. "Is it Possible?" Paper presented at
1973 LSA.

-----. 1973b. The Positional Tendencies of Modal Elements and
Their Theoretical Implications. UCSD dissertation.

Street, J. C. 1963. Khalka Structure. Indiana University Uralic
and Altaic Series Volume 24. Indiana University Publications.

Strehlow, T. G. H. 1945. Aranda Phonetics and Grammar. Oceania
Linguistics Monographs 7, University of Sydney.

Tai, James H-Y. 1973. "Chinese as an SOV Language." Papers from
the Ninth Regional Meeting of the Chicago Linguistics Society.
Claudia Coruna et al. (eds.). p. 655-671.

Taylor, Allan Ross. 1969. A Grammar of Blackfoot. University of
California at Berkeley dissertation.

Thomas, David Dunton. 1967. Chrau Grammar, A Mon-Khmer Language
of Vietnam. University of Pennsylvania dissertation.

Thompson, Laurence Cassius. 1965. A Vietnamese Grammar. University of Washington Press.

266

Thord-Gray, I. 1955. Tarahumara-English, English-Tarahumara Dictionary and Introduction to Tarahumara Grammar. University of Miami Press.

Tranel, Bernard. 1972. "The Case of Optional Schwa Deletion in French: Some Theoretical Implications." Manuscript.

Traugott, E. C. 1972a. A History of the English Language. New York, Holt, Rinehart and Winston.

-----. 1972b. "On the Notion 'Restructuring' in Historical Syntax." Manuscript.

-----. 1969a. "Simplification vs. Elaboration in Syntactic Change." Manuscript.

-----. 1969b. "Toward a Grammar of Syntactic Change." Lingua 23, p. 1-27.

T'sou, Benjamin Ka-Yin. 1971. Studies in the Phylogenesis of Questions and Diachronic Syntax. University of California at Berkeley dissertation.

Twaddell, W. F. 1960. The English Verb Auxiliary. Providence, Brown University Press.

Tyler, Stephen. Undated. "A Summary of Koya Grammar." Manuscript.

Ultan, Russell. 1967. Konkow Grammar. University of California at Berkeley dissertation.

-----. 1972. "The Nature of Future Tenses." Stanford University Working Papers on Language Universals 8. p. 55-100.

Vanek, Anthony. 1967. "The Tense Auxiliary Verb in Czech." Manuscript.

Verhaar, John W. M. (ed.). 1967. The Verb "Be" and Its Synonyms Parts 1-5. Foundations of Language Supplementary Series. Dordrecht. D. Reidel.

Visser, F. Th. 1969. An Historical Syntax of the English Language, Volume III. Leiden, E. J. Brill.

Voegelin, C. F. 1935. Tübatulabal Grammar. University of California Publication in American Archaeology 34. p. 55-189.

-----, and F. M. Voegelin. 1969. "Hopi /?as/." IJAL 35:2, p. 192-202.

-----, F. M. Voegelin and Kenneth Hale. 1962. Typological and Comparative Grammar of Uto Aztecan I (Phonology). Indiana University Publications in Anthropology and Linguistics, Memoir 17. Supplement to IJAL 28:1.

Wali, Kashi. 1972. "Negation Dependent Idioms and the Structure of Marathi Modals." Papers in Linguistics 5:3, p. 382-401.

Wares, Alan Campbell. 1968. A Comparative Study of Yuman Consonantism. The Hague, Mouton.

Wheeler, Alva Lee. 1971. Grammar of the Siona Language, Colombia, South America. University of California at Berkeley dissertation.

Whitehead, John. 1899. Grammar and Dictionary of the Bobangi Language. London, Baptist Missionary Society.

Wierzbicka, Anna. 1967. "Negation--A Study in Deep Grammar." Manuscript.

Winter, Werner. Forthcoming. "Switch Reference in Yuman Languages." Hokan Studies. M. Langdon and S. Silver (eds.). The Hague, Mouton.

Wurm, S. A. 1964. "Motu and Police Motu, a Study in Typological Contrasts." Papers in New Guinea Linguistics 2, p. 19-36.

Ziervogel, D. 1952. A Grammar of Swazi. Johannesburg, Witwatersrand University Press.

Zipf, George Kingsley. 1935. The Psycho-Biology of Language. Cambridge, MIT Press.

Zwicky, Arnold M. Jr. 1968. "Naturalness Arguments in Syntax."
Papers from the Fourth Regional Meeting of the Chicago
Linguistic Society.

AN EXPLANATION OF DRIFT*

by

Theo Vennemann

* An earlier version of this paper was presented at the University
of Leiden, February 1973. I am grateful to Jan Kooij for arranging
that meeting. Further versions were presented in a seminar at
UCLA and at the conference from which the present volume derives.
I have to thank the participants of all three occasions for much
useful discussion of the views presented here. If the present
version leaves much to be desired, it would be worse had it not
been for those discussions.

1. Drift: E. Sapir 1921.

That languages change is common knowledge among linguists. It is
not common knowledge among linguists that the course of change is to a
large extent predictable. Yet such predictability can be inferred from
the very nature of linguistic change--this is, in a nutshell, the
startling idea of the famous seventh chapter of E. Sapir's book
Language: an introduction to the study of speech (1921). If all individual deviations from a linguistic norm were of equal status, equally
probable to be accepted by the speech community and to become a new
norm, they would cancel each other out so that a linguistic norm would
not change or would only vascillate insignificantly in a way that reflects the variation among individual speakers. Since linguistic norms
neither remain unchanged nor change back and forth but change in certain directions, and fairly rapidly so, it cannot be the case that
individual deviations from the norm have equal status. Rather, certain
deviations, or certain types of deviations, must be favored over
others, must be more readily produced and must definitely more readily
be accepted. Since such cumulative favorization occurs, at least for
the most part, without conscious awareness on the side of the language
users, it must be rooted in general psychological tendencies. If we
can identify these tendencies, we can predict the future course of a
language, the direction of its "drift". We can "prophesy".

Sapir's main example is the gradual replacement of whom by who in
sentences such as Who(m) did you see?: "It is safe to prophesy that
within a couple of hundred years from to-day not even the most learned
jurist will be saying 'Whom did you see?' By that time the 'whom' will
be ... delightfully archaic ... No logical or historical argument will
avail to save this hapless 'whom'." (156)

Sapir offers four immediate reasons for this development. First,
who/whom does not belong to the class of personal pronouns where the
difference between subject and object case is made (I/me, he/him, she/
her, we/us, they/them--but also you/you, it/it); rather, it belongs to
the class of interrogative and relative pronouns (which, what, that)
where the difference is not made. Second, as an interrogative pronoun,
it is associated further with "a group of interrogative adverbs--where,
when, how--all of which are invariable and generally emphatic. I

believe it is safe to infer that there is a rather strong feeling in
English that the interrogative pronoun or adverb, typically an emphatic
element in the sentence, should be invariable." (159) Third, the contrast between the subject and object forms of the personal pronouns (I/
me, etc.) is in English associated with a difference of position: I
see the man but The man sees me. Who and whom, however, both occur
only in clause-initial position, if we disregard the rare echo questions such as Did I see whom? Finally--a point which I reproduce here
only for the sake of completeness--the combination whom did is phonetically "clumsy". (160)

Sapir goes on to relate "the particular drifts involved in the use
of whom" to "larger tendencies at work in the language" of which they
are only "symptoms", viz. to the following "three drifts of major
importance", each of which "has operated for centuries, ... is at work
in other parts of our linguistic mechanism [and] is almost certain to
continue for centuries, possibly millenia." (163) These major drifts
are the following--I number them (S1) - (S3):

(S1) "the familiar tendency to level the distinction between the sub-
      jective and objective [the subject and object cases], itself but
      a late chapter in the steady reduction of the old Indo-European
      system of syntactic cases" (163),

(S2) "the tendency to fixed position in the sentence, determined by
      the syntactic relation of the word" (166),

(S3) "the drift toward the invariable word" (168).

Sapir offers a straightforward explanation for (S1): "The distinction
between the nominative and accusative was nibbled away by phonetic
processes and morphological levelings until only certain pronouns retained distinctive subjective and objective forms." (164) The phonetic
processes referred to are themselves but manifestations of yet another
drift, a "phonetic drift" (181) of the Germanic languages, viz. "the
old drift toward reducing final syllables, a rhythmic consequence of
the strong Germanic stress on the first syllable." (175)

For (S2) Sapir gives the obvious explanation: the stabilization
of word order is a consequence of the loss of morphological case marking. "As the inflected forms of English became scantier, as the

syntactic relations were more and more inadequately expressed by the
forms of the words themselves, position in the sentence gradually took
over functions originally foreign to it." (166)

While Sapir thus states repeatedly that the primary causal connection between (S1)--loss of case morphology--and (S2)--stabilization of
word order--is such that (S2) is a consequence of (S1), he also suggests that there is a secondary causal connection in the opposite
direction: As position in the sentence has developed as the main signal of syntactic relations, "the case system ... has been steadily
weakening in psychological respects" (164), so that remnants of the
morphological subject-object case distinction have lost their contrastive value and have become redundant functions of position in the
sentence:

Are the subjective value of he and the objective value of him entirely,
or even mainly, dependent on the difference of form? I doubt it. ...
At least part of the case feeling in he and him is to be credited to
their position before or after the verb. May it not be, then, that he
and him, we and us, are not so much subjective and objective forms as
pre-verbal and post-verbal forms? (166-7) True, the phonetic disparity
between I and me, he and him, we and us, has been too great for any
serious possibility of form leveling. It does not follow that the case
distinction as such is still vital. One of the most insidious peculiarities of a linguistic drift is that where it cannot destroy what
lies in its way it renders it innocuous by washing the old significance
out of it. It turns its very enemies to its own uses. (166)

Sapir gives a first example of (S3), the drift toward the invariable word, when he discusses the loss of morphological case marking.
Clearly the leveling of subject and object forms reduces variation in
the word. Also the old morphological genitive has in part been replaced
by a prepositional phrase containing the preposition of and the "invariable word"--another drift which Sapir discusses (165) and which I give
a separate number for later reference:

(S4) "a strong drift towards the restriction of the inflected pos-
       sessive forms to animate nouns and pronouns." (165)

To that extent, then, Sapir has shown that (S3), the drift toward the invariable word, is a consequence of (S1), the loss of case marking. Clearly, therefore, Sapir considered his "three drifts of major importance" as related. This is once again apparent from the following remark: "The drift toward the abolition of most case distinctions and the correlative drift toward position as an all-important grammatical method are accompanied, in a sense dominated, by ... the drift toward the invariable word." (168) What is less clear to me is why Sapir says that the third drift is in a sense dominant, rather than merely a consequence of the other two. He seems to attribute a certain mystical quality to the English lexicon when he says, "English words crave spaces between them, they do not like to huddle in clusters of slightly divergent centers of meaning, each edging a little away from the rest." (169) Here we have reached a point, it seems, where Sapir's understanding of drift ended. He could not see in his days that the nature of the overall drift of the English language is such that suffixation as a means of derivational word formation is necessarily doomed in general and that, in the transitional absence of a substitute method (other than word composition), the invariable word with "a simple, unnuanced correspondence between idea and word, as invariable as may be" (169) is simply all that is left.

In summarizing this section on Sapir's concept of drift, let us note what he has achieved but also what he left undiscussed, either because he failed to recognize its relation to the topic or because he could not explain it. Sapir explains certain past and present morphological, syntactic, and lexical changes of English by revealing that they are consequences of certain major psychological tendencies of speakers of this language--which he calls "drifts". Since such tendencies remain alive over long periods of time, he feels safe to predict certain further, similar changes for the future of English and points out that these predictions are already in part becoming true in the English of lower-class speakers, the "folk". He shows, furthermore, that the three major drifts--loss of case marking, stabilization of word order, and the drift toward the invariable word--are, at least to a large extent, causally related to each other and are, ultimately, consequences of yet another drift of English, the "phonetic drift" of the Germanic languages toward reduction and loss of final syllables,

itself a consequence of the word-initial stress accent of these languages. This seems to me a considerable achievement, a big step in the
development of a theory of grammar change.

One should also, however, note how much Sapir has either not seen
or kept to himself. From our present viewpoint, more than half a century later, the omissions look almost as large and surprising as the
accomplishment. First, Sapir limits his discussion to English. Yet
similar changes occur in many other languages. It is not, therefore,
clear whether drifts are language-specific or whether, or to what extent or under what conditions, they are universal, viz. automatic consequences of the interaction of, on the one hand, a particular linguistic structure and, on the other, the linguistic organization of the
human mind, species-specific but independent of any particular language.

Second, Sapir does not note that the stabilized word order is a
particular one, the Subject-Verb-Object (SVO) order, while the dominant
word order of an older period of the language, some five thousand years
ago, had demonstrably been Subject-Object-Verb (SVO), as Sapir must
have known from his own experience with ancient Indo-European languages
and from the writings of earlier authors (cf. Lehmann 1972a,b for evidence and references). Thus, Sapir does not consider that English has
been subject to another major drift, the gradual change from an SOV to
an SVO language, and the same question arises, viz. whether this drift
is language-specific or somehow universal. We will see later that this
drift is again causally related to the other three, so that Sapir's
picture of the major tendencies in the development of English syntax
remains incomplete in a rather conspicuous way.

Third, the question of language-specificness or universality also
arises for the relation between morphological, syntactic, and lexical
drifts on the one hand and phonetic drifts on the other. While in the
case on hand, and, we can extrapolate, in all suffixing languages with
a drift of final syllable reduction, the relation between phonetic
change and syntactic change is an obvious one, Sapir would probably
have abstained from making a general statement on this relation simply
because he was skeptical about the general cause and course of phonetic
change: "We do not yet understand the primary cause or causes of the
slow drift in phonetics." (183) "The explanation of primary dialectic

differences is still to seek." (149) However, he also says: "I believe
that such influences [of the morpho-syntactic structure of a language
on its phonetic development, just like vice versa] may be demonstrated
and that they deserve far more careful study than they have received."
(184) "There are likely to be fundamental relations between them
[phonetics and grammar] and their respective histories that we do not
yet fully grasp." (184) I believe that in certain important respects
our understanding of phonological change has progressed in recent years
so that more confident statements about the relation between phonetics
and syntax are now justified than in Sapir's days. I return to this
question later.

2. On the Development of the Structural Use of Word-Order in Modern English: Ch.C. Fries 1940.

While Sapir identifies his three major drifts, as well as particular aspects of them, in an impressionistic way, by using a few
examples and appealing to common knowledge of English-speaking linguists, Fries bases certain aspects of Sapir's second drift, (S2), the
stabilization of word order in English, on statistical data. Surpris-
ingly, he does not seem to recognize a connection between his work and
Sapir's, even though he cites his book for a different point (207); and
he does not use the word "drift". It could not be more obvious, however, that his study does belong under this heading; therefore, I will
treat it here anyway. I number his drifts (F1) - (F6):

(F1) the increasing tendency to place the accusative-object after
the verb (201).

This drift is immediately apparent from the following percentages.

	c. 1000	c. 1200	c. 1300	c. 1400	c. 1500
Acc-obj: after verb	47.5%	46.3%	60-%	85.7%	98.13%

(F2) the increasing tendency to place the dative-object after the
verb (202).

		Old English (900 - 1000)	Early Middle English (c. 1200)
	Nouns	72.4%	77.0%
Dat-obj. after verb	Pronouns	51.3%	57.0%
	Both together	56.6%	60.6%

Fries does not provide percentages for later dates, but a comparison with Contemporary English indicates that the development must have been similar to that of the accusative-object.

(F3)   the increasing tendency to place the (non-prepositional) dative-object before the accusative-object (202-3).

		Old English (900 - 1000)
	Nouns	64.0%
Dat-obj. before acc-obj.	Pronouns	82.8%
	Both together	76.6%

Fries does not provide percentages for later dates but remarks: "The materials examined for Early Middle English (c. 1200) show ... practically the same pattern of the position of the [non-prepositional] dative-object in relation to the accusative-object as do the materials for Old English." (202)   "The general situation at approximately the middle of the 15th Century seems to have been as follows. ... Accusative- and [non-prepositional] dative-objects are distinguished by the fact that the dative-object, when present, precedes the accusative-object." (202-3)   Drift (F3) is thus quite safely established.

Fries notes yet another drift relating to the verb position, without, however, giving statistics for it:

(F4)   the increasing tendency to place the subject before the verb (203).

Fries says: "The position before the verb, cleared of the presence of formally distinct accusative- and dative-objects, becomes in itself the distinguishing feature of the form class of nominative expressions." (203)   The evidence he gives is perhaps even more persuasive than percentages would be: Constructions with so-called impersonal verbs, such as like, need, want, which in Older English were normally arranged as

Dative-Verb-Subject, are, as case inflection is lost, re-interpreted as ordinary Subject-Verb-Object constructions: Hem nedede no help → They needed no help; and the same holds for passive constructions with Dative-Verb-Subject arrangement: Me waes gegiefan an boc → I was given a book.

(F5) the increasing tendency to place the non-prepositional genitive modifier before the headnoun (205).

	c. 900	c. 1000	c. 1100	c. 1200	c. 1250
Gen. before noun	52.4%	69.1%	77.4%	87.4%	99.1%

(F6) the increasing tendency to use the prepositional (periphrastic, analytic) genitive with of rather than the non-prepositional (flexional, synthetic) genitive as a noun modifier (206). The prepositional genitive is always placed immediately after its headnoun (206).

	c. 900	c. 1000	c. 1100	c. 1200	c. 1250	c. 1300
Post-positive flexional genitive	47.5%	30.5%	22.2%	11.8%	0.6%	0.0%
Pre-positive flexional genitive	52.0%	68.5%	76.6%	81.9%	68.9%	15.6%
Pre-positional genitive	0.5%	1.0%	1.2%	6.3%	31.4%	84.5%

All of this is very valuable information to which we will have to return. Beyond the statistics and examples--which are taken from the works of his students--Fries offers one very insightful generalization: "In Present-day Standard English the pressure of position is such that all word groups tend to modify the word immediately preceding." (206) No explanation is given for this pressure; the individual statistics as well as the generalization remain entirely at the level of observation. Therefore, in regard to the development of linguistics as a

theoretical discipline, Fries' work represents a regression from the
advanced position of Sapir.

3.   Another Look at Drift: Lakoff 1972.

In this paper, a considerable number of additional drift phenomena
is brought into the discussion. Moreover, the investigation of drift
is given a new dimension by relating it to comparative and typological
linguistic studies. In this way, a connection is established between
the study of drift on the one hand and the theory of grammar--rather
than merely the grammar of English--on the other.

Lakoff begins by presenting "a list of some changes...that occur in
many or all of the Indo-European languages, clearly not as a result of
one being influenced by another." (174) I number the changes (L1) - (L6).

(L1) "The obligatory use of anaphoric, nonemphatic, subject pronouns."

(L2) "The use of articles, definite and indefinite."

(L3) "The use of prepositions instead of case endings." (174)

(L4) "The development of periphrastic causatives, inchoatives, etc."

(L5) "The development of periphrastic auxiliaries."

(L6) "The development of adverbs and comparatives." (175)

In the following paragraphs I will summarize some of the illustrative
comments Lakoff makes on the individual drifts. I will omit most of
her extensive theoretical discussion because it deals with the technical treatment of the affected structures in the particular model of
grammar she is working with, the "generative semantics" variety of transformational grammar, and adds nothing toward an explanation of the phenomena, as she points out repeatedly.

Ad (L1): The use of anaphoric nonemphatic, subject pronouns is a
"feature [which] is absent in most of the older Indo-European languages,
but present in probably a majority of the modern ones. Even in those
in which it is not now obligatory, the tendency toward the use of these
pronouns is stronger now than it was in the past. (Compare Spanish and
Latin in this respect.)" (174) "They are mandatory in English, French,
and German, but not in Spanish or Latin." (180) Lakoff assumes that
Latin has an obligatory rule of anaphoric unstressed subject pronoun

deletion which is optional for some dialects of Spanish and discarded in French. She calls this "simplification for a purpose: The loss of a rule allows another independent segment to exist in the superficial structure of the language." (182) Thus, the purpose is segmentalization, but it remains unclear, here as well as in the other cases of drift, what the purpose of segmentalization is.

Ad (L2): "In the earliest stages of most languages of this family, there were no articles ... In some of the languages only the definite article developed; in others, both. In one or two, like Russian, neither has developed. But the trend is to a system containing both a definite and an indefinite article." (174) Lakoff points out that in the Romance languages and in English, the definite article derives historically from a demonstrative, and the indefinite article from the numeral 'one'. (174, 182-4) She also points out that in Romance the definite article developed much earlier than the indefinite article. (183) She notes further that in the model of grammar she is working with, the definite article and the indefinite article are derived in different ways from their respective "underlying sources". Therefore, "it is not surprising that these two changes should occur independently of each other. They involve different processes, although both are the result of the tendency to segmentalize." (184) What would be interesting to know in this case is not only the "purpose" (I would prefer to say, the cause) of this segmentalization but also why the definite article arose earlier than the indefinite article in Romance.

Ad (L3): "The older IE languages expressed grammatical relationships in nouns through the use of case endings ... Later languages have tended to develop, instead, an invariable independent noun without endings (except for plural) and a set of prepositions, also morphologically independent, to fulfill the functions previously performed by case endings." (174) "The change can be considered as one in favor of segmentation." (185) Since Lakoff denies a causal relation between phonological change and the loss of case endings, we must again ask for the causes of this instance of segmentalization. We must ask further why the functions of the endings (to the extent that they are not taken care of by word order stabilization) are taken over by prepositions rather than by postpositions.

<u>Ad (L4)</u>: "In the early languages, particularly Greek and Sanskrit, there were special endings that could be added to most verbs to give causative, inchoative, frequentative, or other meanings. These suffixes were generally productive. Within the history of the ancient languages, we can trace the loss of these productive processes. ... To replace them there arose a group of independent verbs already in the language, which came to be used to carry the meanings formerly carried by the special endings; they took as complements the verbs that formerly had the suffixes added to them. In the modern languages, this is the usual way of forming expressions of this type." (175) Lakoff notes in particular that the mode of constructing causative verbs changed earlier for transitive verbs than for intransitive verbs. (187) No explanation is offered for this particular observation, and the only explanation for the gradual replacement of lexical complex verb formation that Lakoff offers is "a growing tendency toward segmentalization" which "in this part of the grammar is definitely the result of changes in the lexicon itself: the loss of markings on verbs." (188) But, of course, this tendency and this change in the lexicon need explanations themselves. In addition, one would like to know why the <u>postposed</u> complex verb formation affixes are replaced by <u>preposed</u> full verbs, compare Sanskrit <u>vid-</u> 'know' + <u>-aya-</u> (causative affix) → <u>vedaya-</u> 'cause to know, inform' (* <u>ayaved</u>) but English <u>know</u> + <u>cause</u> → <u>cause to know</u> (*<u>to know cause</u>).

<u>Ad (L5)</u>: "In the older languages, the tenses were expressed almost exclusively as endings on verbs, not as morphologically independent elements. There is a tendency...for these endings to be replaced by independent verbs, generally verbs that also occur independently. Thus, compare Latin <u>amāvi</u> with Spanish <u>he amado</u>; Latin <u>amābo</u> with English <u>I will love</u>." (175)

This, then, is another change that "goes from synthetic to analytic" (190) and leads to greater segmentation (191), and there the problem rests.

<u>Ad (L6)</u>: In Spanish (and similarly in the other Romance languages), deadjectival adverb formation went from the suffixation of unanalyzable <u>-e</u> or <u>-iter</u> (e.g., <u>rapidus</u> 'rapid', <u>rapide</u> 'rapidly') to the construction of an adverbial noun phrase in the ablative case, using the noun

m̄ens 'mind' (e.g., rapidā mente 'in a rapid manner, rapidly') and further to suffixation of this same mente as an unanalyzed invariable
suffix (e.g., rápidamente). "Modern speakers feel this form is a synthetic one, but it was not synthetic originally." (175-6) With this,
the change "has already been discussed in sufficient detail." (191)

    "Similarly [?], the comparative ending in various Indo-European
languages is becoming less used, or is practically obsolete. In Romance, the -yo- comparative of Latin is gone completely except for a
few irregular forms; in English, more is appearing in environments
where previously only -er was found." (176) While use of plūs or magis
'more' occurred in Latin only in a few exceptional cases, "these two
adverbs are used in Italian, French, and Spanish (as piu, plus, and más)
as the only means of forming the comparative." (191) In English there
appears to be a trend ... away from -er, -est comparative and superla-
tive endings toward more, most. All adjectives can be used with more
and most; those of more than two syllables cannot take -er, -est, and
those of two syllables now seem more and more to prefer the analytic
form." (191-2)

    Spanish adverb formation in an earlier period [not in a later
period, however] and the comparative formation of various Indo-European
languages are thus further examples of the trend from synthetic to analytic construction methods. More cannot be said because unfortunately
"we must wait for synchronic transformational theory to provide acceptable deep structures and derivations for both adverbs and comparatives."
(192)

    The common feature of all six drifts (L1) - (L6) is, thus, that
they "go from synthetic to analytic" or toward greater "segmentation".
Under this aspect, they "constitute a single phenomenon." (178) This
trend is also called by Lakoff a "metacondition on the way the grammar
of a language as a whole can change." (178)

    This "metacondition" causes great concern to Lakoff. "I do not at
present see any way of characterizing this metacondition formally. Nor
can I imagine how it could be considered as part of a synchronic description of a language: I cannot imagine how it could have been learned
by a speaker, if it is part of his linguistic knowledge at all. ...

Other things, too, remain unclear. I have no idea why this metacondition exists. ... It is also not clear what sort of thing this metacondition is." (179) "It is not at all clear where this metacondition
exists: neither as part of a grammar nor as a universal condition on
the forms of grammars." (192)

This metacondition cannot be universal because "languages outside
the Indo-European family [are] still highly synthetic" and "in other
language families... the drift seems to be operating in the other direction, toward greater syntheticity" (179), while still others "swing back
and forth from one to the other. Further, since there is this great
discrepancy among languages as to the direction of drift, it seems unlikely that one can assume any psychological motivation for languages
to work toward one state or the other. So drift acts as a sort of linguistic pendulum--but why should language have such a pendulum built in?
It appears not to be accidental, but a very real part of human linguistic
ability." (180) Since at this point the quotations become contradictory--
"seems unlikely ... any psychological motivation" but "a very real part
of human linguistic ability" only four lines apart, I will quote no more
passages about the metacondition. The following Lakoff quotations will
help us return to the solid ground of scientific research: "No explanation of the facts will be offered; it should be noted that there is no
mechanism within the present theory of transformational grammar that
would allow an explanation." (173) "We are so far from understanding
why drift exists." (180)

Lakoff concludes her paper by saying: "Either another explanation
[than which ? T.V.] must be postulated, which seems unlikely [!], or we
must accept the idea that in order to understand syntactic change we
must come to a fuller understanding of synchronically oriented syntactic theory." (192) I should like to add: or both.

Lakoff's paper is valuable and goes beyond Sapir's discussion in
that it points out that certain drifts may be shared by several languages, at least of a given family. In all other respects it represents
a regression from Sapir's advanced position. Where Sapir strives for
and offers sober scientific explanations, Lakoff merely restates the
problems by relating them to an unexplained "metacondition". To add but
one example: Where Sapir in the most explicit way characterizes the

loss of inflections as a consequence of phonetic change (cf. the quotations in section 1 earlier), Lakoff writes:

It has often been noted that the loss of cases coincides roughly in time with the phonologically governed loss of endings in the form of falling-together of vowels and loss of final consonants, leading to a lack of distinctiveness among case endings. There has been discussion in the past [Where? T.V.] as to how to interpret the interaction of these changes, one purely syntactic, the other purely phonological. The question is usually raised [By whom? T.V.], Which came first? Did the loss of distinctiveness in endings force the Romans to abandon their beloved case system? Or, conversely, did the decline and fall of the case system and consequent growth of prepositions enable the decadent Romans to slough off the endings, which were so hard to pronounce? These arguments are as ridiculous as they sound. Clearly, the two changes took place simultaneously; neither was caused by the other. Rather, each depended on the other. The phonological changes could not have occurred, with preservation of intelligibility, unless prepositions had developed beyond their functions in Classical Latin; and the syntactic changes in the case system would not have flourished had not changes in the phonology rendered them essential. (185-6)

That the two kinds of changes depend on each other is quite obvious (and was also explicitly said by Sapir). But to deny that a causal relation exists between the two (in an article addressed to Sapir's theory, yet without mentioning his specific hypothesis on this point--or calling it "ridiculous" by way of implication), is a surprising step. Why should prepositions ever develop in a language with a fully functional system of case markers, so as to render the case markers redundant and invite phonetic change to step in and take them away? Phonetic change leading to reduction and loss is always going on, in all languages at all times, and cannot in the long run be stopped. Therefore, a language with case endings can never exist for an indefinitely long time without losing them and therefore has to develop other means to take over the functions of the endings. But prepositions are not always around in a language; in fact there normally isn't a single preposition around in a language with a fully functional system of case endings. So the original impulse toward the phonological weakening of case endings cannot ever come from the existence of prepositions in the system.

Of course, one must also ask: If neither change is caused by the other, what causes the whole development? What sets it in motion? The evasion of this simple question of causation (as well as of Sapir's simple answer) and the appeal to an unexplained "metacondition" as the common cause of both phonetic change and the use of prepositions is surprising indeed. (Lakoff does not explicitly invoke this "sort of thing" in this connection, but I assume that this is what she meant to have done, because even the invocation of this peculiar cause is preferable to the assumption that certain developments in the physical universe just happen, repeatedly and simultaneously, without any cause at all.) But if there is such a simple and immediately plausible hypothesis--why not use it? Phonetic change wears off endings; the result is a word without endings, the "invariable word". Why anyone should want it to be the other way around and assume that the development of the invariable word causes the loss of endings and correlative phonetic change is not clear to me.

After giving a lengthy quotation from Sapir's "drift" chapter (154 middle - 155 middle), Lakoff writes:

Sapir's point here is clear: that language moves in certain directions, despite the randomness of individual variations in language learning. This direction is not discoverable from inspection of the synchronic language itself, but only from looking at the historical changes in the syntax over a period of time. He gives three examples of drifts, as he calls them, within the history of English. I would prefer to call all his examples subclasses of my (1c) above [i.e., (L3) here, T.V.], rather than separate and isolated drifts. Moreover, judging from his terminology (he speaks of drifts in the plural), Sapir would consider the types of changes that I am discussing independently motivated and not necessarily related; while my point in discussing them is that they are, in fact, all part of the same phenomenon. ... His three drifts are: the loss of case endings, the stabilization of word order, and the rise of the invariable word. (177)

This is an astonishing interpretation. Sapir says (and Lakoff quotes it): "This direction may be inferred, in the main, from the past history of the language." (Sapir 155, Lakoff 177) But his analysis of the tendencies in the English pronominal case system is synchronic. Why interpret him as saying that "this direction is not discoverable from inspection of the synchronic language itself, but only from looking at the historical changes in the syntax over a period of time"? Can one really hope to defend the view that Sapir's three drifts are "subclasses of my (1c) above", i.e., "the use of prepositions instead of case endings"? Can one really say that "Sapir ... fails ... to propose any generalization as to why all these things happen or whether they are connected" (178) and impute that he would have called his three drifts "separate and isolated"? It is true that Sapir uses the word "drift" in the plural to refer to certain aspects of drift and to individual drift phenomena--even though in the passages quoted by Lakoff only the singular occurs, five times, in locutions such as "Language ... has a drift", "The linguistic drift has direction" (Sapir 150, 155, Lakoff 176, 177); should one really judge from this terminology that "Sapir would consider the types of changes that I am discussing independently motivated and not necessarily related"? These are amazing misrepresentations of Sapir's straightforward and insightful original account of drift.

4. Syntactic Universals and Linguistic Reconstruction: Greenberg 1966 and Lehmann 1972.

Neither Greenberg (1966) nor Lehmann (1971, 1972a,b,c, 1973) employs the term "drift" or makes reference to Sapir 1921. Yet the phenomena they investigate are closely related to drift, and the work they have done has contributed so much to the explanation of drift as a universal phenomenon in section 5 that a separate section is justified. Since I have characterized and analyzed these works in considerable detail elsewhere (Vennemann 1972, 1973a,d), I will simply list here what can be learned from both works in conjunction, and at the same time limit the list to what contributes toward an explanation of the drift phenomena (S1) - (S4), (F1) - (F6), (L1) - (L6).

The syntactic constructions of a language are not independent of each other but are all statistically correlated to the relative position

of the verb, V, and its complement, the most prominent representative
of which is the nominal direct object, O. If the dominant arrangement
in a language is verb before object, it is called a VO language; if
the dominant arrangement is object before verb, an OV language. The
correlations of statistical preference are as follows:

(GL 1) Genitive attributes tend to precede their headnouns in OV lan-
        guages, but to follow them in VO languages.

(GL 2) OV languages tend to have only postpositions, VO languages only
        prepositions.

(GL 3) Main verbs tend to precede auxiliaries in OV languages, but to
        follow them in VO languages.

(GL 4) Standards of comparison tend to precede comparative adjectives
        in OV languages, but to follow them in VO languages.

(GL 5) Subjects tend to precede objects in declarative sentences.

(GL 6) OV languages "almost always" have case systems. (Greenberg
        universal 41)

Lehmann suggests a causal connection of the kind that when a language,
for whatsoever reason, strengthens a particular arrangement of V and O,
certain ones of the other patterns may follow course according to the
listed correlations. Why this should be so, i.e., what the reasons for
the causal relation are, remains unclear. Also, no reason is given why
a language should ever change the basic arrangement of V and O (except
for the suggestion that contact with languages of the opposite arrangement may have some influences in certain cases). Greenberg makes no
suggestion whatsoever concerning possible reasons for his universals.
Nevertheless, it is apparent that we have here all the bricks we need.
All it takes now is some explanatory cement to build a theoretical
framework which will accommodate drift as a natural occupant.

5.   The Universality of Drift: Natural Generative Grammar.
      Steps have been taken recently to develop a framework in which
cooccurrence universals such as (GL1) - (GL4) of the preceding section
appear as automatic consequences of the most fundamental assumptions.
There is no need to repeat those assumptions here because a sufficient

number of publications in which they are laid down and justified have
appeared in print (Bartsch 1972, Bartsch and Vennemann 1972, 1973,
Vennemann 1973a), and others will appear (Vennemann 1971, 1972, 1973b-d).
I will here merely mention those aspects of the theory that are needed
for an explanation of the individual drifts mentioned, and of drift in
general.

(1) Languages tend to serialize operator-operand hierarchies unidi-
     rectionally:

     Principle of natural serialization.

$$\{\{\text{Operator}\}(\{\text{Operand}\})\} \Rightarrow \begin{cases} [\text{Operator}[\text{Operand}]] \text{ in XV languages} \\ \\ [[\text{Operand}] \text{ Operator}] \text{ in VX languages} \end{cases}$$

Those Greenberg universals which involve Operator-Operand relationships
(or relationships between specifier and specified, or déterminant and
déterminé, in other terminologies), in particular those discussed by
Lehmann, are applications of the principle of natural serialization;
cf. (GL1-4) in section 4 above. The history of the word order syntax
of each language can be understood to a large extent as a development
toward consistent implementation of this principle; Fries noticed this
for English, cf. the final quotation in section 2 above.

(2) Languages tend to place topical material early in sentences
     (Behaghel's Second Law, cf. Behaghel 1923:4).

Since the subject case is the principal case for expressing topical
terms, this 'law' is at the root of the apparent fact that a large majority of languages have the subject early in the sentence, i.e., are
either SXV or SVX languages (Greenberg 1966:77); cf. (GL5) in section 4
above. [I write "X" for the verb complement where Greenberg and
Lehmann use the more specialized "O".]

(3) Languages with uniform, conspicuous, and dependable Subject-Object
     marking of a substantive nature (i.e., with a device which makes
     it clear for every sentence containing both S and O which one is
     which, independently of the order in which they appear) tend to be
     XV languages; languages without such an S-O morphology tend to be
     VX languages. [Cf. (GL6) in section 4 above.]

This is a generalization of Greenberg universal 41 which says, "If in a language the verb follows both the nominal subject and nominal object as the dominant order, the language almost always has a case system" (Greenberg 1966:96). Reasons for formulating (3) as above, and discussion intended to explain this correlation between S-O morphology and basic word order, may be found in Vennemann 1973a,c.

(4) If an XV language loses its substantive S-O marking system [of the kind characterized in (3)], it changes to VX.

I have wrestled with this problem in Vennemann 1973a,b,c. I agree with the criticism proposed by several (among them Larry Hyman here at this conference) that an essential step is lacking in my explanation as proposed so far: I have not shown in those papers how speakers actually go about organizing their sentences in a VX arrangement, where earlier the arrangement was XV. Hyman himself proposes that the grammaticalization of afterthought patterns is the mechanism by which this happens. This seems to me to be an excellent idea. However, I would like to point out that where I tried to give reasons but did not pinpoint the mechanism, Hyman proposes a mechanism but misses the essential part of the explanation: Since consistent XV languages such as Japanese make very sparing use of "afterthought" syntax, how do we explain that in some XV languages "afterthought" syntax becomes so important that it changes the type of the language to VX?

I have addressed myself to this question in Vennemann 1974. I cannot repeat here the lengthy discussion given there but will only summarize the essential aspects of that discussion. In a consistent XV language, complement clauses precede their head nouns and verbs, relative clauses precede their head nouns, and adverbial clauses precede their head verbs [cf. (1)]. Louis Goldstein (UCLA) has pointed out to me in discussions and in an unpublished paper that if case markings are lost from noun phrases in this kind of syntax, then the resulting patterns conflict with the basic clause recognition strategy (in the sense of Bever and Langendoen 1972), which is that every NP V_I pattern (with an intransitive verb) and every NP NP V_T pattern (with a transitive verb) constitutes a clause. Also one receives unmarked sequences of up to four noun phrases followed by two verbs, where the relation of the noun phrases to their respective verbs can be tackled

only after the complex sentence is completed, and even then only with
difficulty. (Cf. constructions in German such as <u>weil Hans Maria Peter
Paul vorzustellen bat</u> 'because John asked Mary to introduce Peter to
Paul').

But the problems are worse than that. In relative clauses with
transitive verbs, it may become systematically unclear whether the noun
phrase in the relative clause is subject or object of that verb. This
may result in an interpretation where such noun phrases are always
interpreted as objects (I owe this suggestion to Katsue Akiba, UCLA),
which deprives the language of a significant type of relative construction, viz. that in which the head noun is object to the relative clause
verb. (Cf. also German preposed relative constructions, which are
limited in precisely this fashion.)

But the problem is still worse. Kuno (1974) has pointed out that
because of perceptual difficulties inherent in center-embedding, a consistent verb-final language tends to place subordinate clauses, and
noun phrases with subordinate clauses, at the beginning of the sentence.
Consider now sentences with the patterns $(Rel)NP_{Subj}$ NP_{Obj} V and
$(Rel)NP_{Obj}$ NP_{Subj} V. Loss of case marking results in a uniform pattern
$(Rel)NP$ NP V, for which it is systematically unclear whether it represents the basic SOV pattern or a pattern with a preposed object.

My proposal in Vennemann 1974 is that it is these kinds of ambiguities and perceptual difficulties which cause speakers of an SXV
language with an eroding case system increasingly to rely on devices
that are to a greater or lesser extent available in, though not typical
for, an SXV language, viz. the passive, demonstratives, etc., and
especially the intonational integration of postposed clarificational
sentences into the main sentence. The assumption that subordinate
clauses following the main verb originate from postposed clarificational sentences accounts for the following facts in the most direct
fashion:

(a) The subordinators are morphologically related to deictic or
anaphoric pronouns and adverbs, because a reference is made to something mentioned in, or implicit in, the main clause.

(b) The subordinator occurs at the beginning of the subordinate clause, because referential constituents are normally placed sentence-initially.

(c) Complement, relative, and adverbial clauses follow their head constituents in VX languages, because as they tend to be reunited with their heads according to Behaghel's First Law (or Bartsch's principle of natural constituent structure, cf. Vennemann 1973a,c), they will naturally remain in a position following them.

(d) The perceptual difficulties connected with center-embedding (Kuno 1974) will prevent that subordinate clauses are pulled back before the verb of the main clause for reunification with their head constituents (although this may occur to some extent, as in German); instead, the head constituent will be pulled to a position following the verb of the main clause (unless, of course, it is itself the verb of the main clause).

(e) As the language is now VX for clausal constituents but still XV for sub-clausal constituents, it is inconsistent in its word order type; the principle of natural serialization [cf. (1)] now exerts pressure on the sub-clausal constituents to fall in line with the clausal constituents: the looser their connection to the main verb, the greater their chances of occurrence in postposed clarificational position, which explains hierarchies of VX-iness such as clauses > adverbs > noun-phrases > pronouns, observed for African languages by Givón and Hyman and for German by several authors (cf. Vennemann 1974 for references).

(f) The reorganization of the noun phrase lags behind that of the complex verb (except for relative clauses and adverbial attributes) because the main processes for complex noun phrase construction are nominalization (Givón 1971, 1974) and attributive clause reduction.

(g) As the main clause develops toward VX under the pressure of the natural serialization principle, the subordinate clause may retain the XV pattern because the forces at work in the main clause are not equally strong in the subordinate clause, there being less subordination in subordinate clauses than in main clauses; eventually the word order of subordinate clauses is changed on the analogy of that of main clauses, because the principle of natural serialization disfavors mirror image serialization, and the main declarative sentence represents the basic word order of a language. (The mechanism by which this analogy is carried out is simply the replacement of subordinate clauses by main clauses under subordinating intonation; i.e., essentially the same process by which postposed sentences came to be subordinate clauses in the first round of VX-ing.)

Finally, the change from SXV to SVX just outlined explains the following point (5): Since topical material tends to come early in the sentence, while the process sketched here moves primarily large, non-topical constituents, there will be a stage when the verb comes to stand between all topics and all non-topical constituents.

(5) The change of an SXV language into an SVX language goes via TVX, i.e., a stage during which the basic word order is that in which the finite verb immediately follows the topic or topics (T).

(6) If at any stage in its development from XV to VX a language re-builds a substantive system of S-O marking [of the kind charac-terized in (3)], it will develop back to XV (Vennemann 1973a,c).

Specific examples of languages developing new substantive S-O marking are given in Li and Thompson 1973, 1974, Vennemann 1973c, Givón 1974. From what little material I have seen concerning this problem it seems to me that S-O morphology on O develops first as a device for topical object marking (or 'definite object' marking), which may subsequently generalize into object case marking; further that S-O morphology on S, if it does not develop in a similar fashion, arises from adpositional agent marking in passive constructions through resubjectivization (in the course of which ergative systems evolve, for which cf. Comrie 1973); and that S-O morphology on V develops as a voice distinction, viz. active vs. passive. An S-O morphology may, of course, also be replen-ished by analogical extension; the history of the Russian case system shows several instances of this process, but none of them has led to the rebuilding of a system sufficient to revert the ongoing development from XV to VX.

(7) The dominant types of phonological change are neutralizing and reductive. The long-range overall effect of phonological change is neutralization and reduction.

Linguists not very familiar with the nature of phonological change tend to have difficulties accepting this generalization. They are, therefore, skeptical about the following application of (7).

(8) Every morphological system is destroyed in time by phonological change.

Those linguists will point to cases where otherwise general phonological changes were suspended to preserve a grammatical distinction, as e.g. the suspension of the Greek change s → h → ∅ / V_V in precisely those sigmatic future forms in which application of the change would have created homophony with the present (cf. Anttila 1972:98f). But even conceding the occasional neutralization of a grammatical distinction through phonological change, those linguists may deny the relevance of the following specific conclusion, pointing to the ubiquity of ambiguity in language.

(9) As a substantive S-O marking system is eroded by phonological change, word order syntax must react to compensate for the ambiguities and perceptual complexities arising in a consistent verb-final language.

I would like to answer such objections to (7), (8), and (9) in the following way.

Ad (7): I have given a condensed statement of my view of this matter in Vennemann 1973c. The relevant paragraph is this:

Phonological change is always operative, in all languages at all times. A few types of phonological change lead to maximization of contrast; e.g., diphthongizations, Spanish [s ṣ š] to [θ ṣ x]; a few types make items longer, e.g., bisegmentalization, as in [t$^\ell$] to [kl], anaptyxis, and epenthesis. The dominant types of phonological change are reductive: their result is leveling and loss, e.g., assimilation, consonant gradation, consonant loss, syncope, apocope, monophthongization, coarticulation of consonants, haplology. Some types of phonological change are compromises between reductive tendencies and the need for contrast: push chains, dissimilation, metathesis. The net result of phonological change, given long periods of time, is phonological reduction. To put it bluntly, words become shorter by phonological change, not longer (cf. Indo-European languages, Chinese); where they seem to become

longer, the mechanism is non-phonological: borrowing, analogy, compounding, degeneration of full words into affixes. Reductive change is
the dominant type of phonological change.

Try yourself, or ask any linguist, and for every case of phonological
differentiation or word lengthening he remembers he can cite a hundred
examples of neutralization and reduction. The overall effect of phonological change is the monosyllabic word of CV structure. Chinese, if
we discount new combinatorial word formations, and the Germanic portion
of the English vocabulary are telling examples of this universal phonological trend. (Cf. also Lüdtke 1970:47: "Lautenwicklung ist stetige
Reduktion." Lüdtke presents striking examples and statistics.)

Ad (8): Traditional grammarians have considered it as commonplace
that phonological change renders morphological systems dysfunctional.
I quote only one example:

In the history of Sanskrit, "consonant groups were drastically reduced
... With a few exceptions (e.g., nom. sg. úrk from úrj 'vitality') not
more than one consonant may stand at the end of a word, however many
were there to begin with. This had serious results in some aspects of
the morphology, and led to some grammatical innovations. Thus the terminations are lost in the case of the second and third persons singular
of the root and s-aorists, and the s of the s-aorist suffers the same
fate in these persons when preceded by a consonant, so that the formations lose their grammatical clarity. On account of this the root
aorist comes to be abandoned in Classical Sanskrit except in the case
of roots in long ā, and new extended formations are provided in the
case of the s-aorist (ánaiṣīt for ánais)." (Burrow 1955:99; emphasis
added)

Examples of the abandoned root aorists are

    2. á-kar   <*á-kar-s

    3. á-kar   <*á-kar-t

cf. 2. á-bhū-s

    3. á-bhū-t

for the original terminations. Examples of the remodeled sigmatic aorists are:

2. á-naiṣ-ī-s for *á-nais <*á-nai-s-s

3. á-naiṣ-ī-t for (á)-nais <*(á)-nai-s-t

(The roots are k̥r 'make', bhū 'be', nī 'lead'.) Such comments, and
such examples, could easily be produced in abundance.

Ad (9): While it is true that ambiguities and occasional perceptual difficulties are not uncommon in languages, those resulting from
the neutralization of substantive S-O distinctions are of a particularly
damaging nature. Much human communication is about interactions between
human beings, and there is accordingly a large number of verbs which
allow both human subjects and human objects; e.g., love, kiss, anger,
invite, ask, call, scold, hit, kill, etc. It is essential that it is
always clear what the relation of all noun phrases to their respective
verbs is in any sentence, whether simplex or complex; and the context
does not always make this clear either.

Linguists doubtful of the correctness of this entire approach to
the XV → VX change, viz.

| Phonological change | = => | Loss of morphology | = => | Compensating change of word order |

will point to languages such as Russian, Finnish, Old English, and
Modern German and claim that those are languages that are basically VX
even though they have S-O morphology. I believe, however, that those
languages do not have the kind of S-O morphology that warrants XV
structure: their S-O morphologies are non-uniform and not dependable.
Fries says, "In a count covering more than 2000 instances, less than
ten per cent of the Old English forms which are syntactically nominative
or accusative lack the distinctive case endings" (1940:200). But even
if most of the remaining instances could be shown to be unambiguous
because of the semantics of the verb and the noun phrases involved, or
the context, the remaining instances would still be too numerous. The
S-O morphology is not dependable. It is also non-uniform; as a matter
of fact, it consists of a plethora of formally unrelated devices depending on basic category, number, gender, person, largely arbitrary stem-

class membership, and even total idiosyncrasy. It is furthermore largely inconspicuous in that it often consists in subtle changes, such as a vowel ablaut in an unstressed syllable subject to causal reduction. Sapir had in my opinion the correct view of such a situation when he said that throughout the history of English "the case system ... has been steadily weakening in psychological respects" (1921:176). Surely learners and speakers of a language do not wait until the last trace of a case marking is lost before they realize that something is going wrong in their language. Adult speakers notice ambiguities, if not spontaneously then as soon as someone asks "Who did?" They will avoid constructions most or all of the time if they run them into difficulties some of the time, and rely on constructions that guarantee success. Children learning Old English, and much earlier stages of the language as well, must have found it hard to believe that what they were exposed to was supposed to be a case system; small wonder that they increasingly mistook a different structural device of their language to be the real marker, viz. word order.

Let us now, in concluding this paper, see how, and to what extent, explanations of the individual drifts discussed in the earlier sections of this paper follow from the assumptions summarized in the present one. [I already commented on (GL1-6) of section 4, so that only (S1-4) of section 1, (F1-6) of section 2, and (L1-6) of section 3 require discussion.]

Ad (S1), i.e., "the familiar tendency to level the distinction between subjective and objective".

Sapir's explanation--neutralizing and reductive phonological change--is valid. It need not be restricted to the English, or even Germanic-- development but is generally applicable, cf. (7) and (8) of the present section.

Ad (S2), "the tendency to fixed position in the sentence determined by the syntactic relation of the word".

Sapir's explanation--as a compensating measure--is valid. Point (4) above [cf. also (9)] explains even more, viz. that most conspicuous drift which Sapir left undiscussed:

(D1) The drift of English toward VX order.

Both (S2) and (D1) are furthermore recognized as universal phenomena of languages with imperfect S-O morphology, rather than language-specific drifts of English. The same is true of (S3).

Ad (S3), "the drift toward the invariable word".

The change from XV to VX is universally accompanied by a change from agglutination to flexion to isolation. The explanation follows from (1) and (7): In a consistent XV language, prefixes are operators on their stems, and stems are operators on their suffixes:

```
| Prefix        Stem  |      Suffix
|_____|
|    X          V                   |
|_____|
     X                  V
```

This arrangement is contrary to the principle of natural serialization in a VX language. New productive patterns will be of the opposite arrangement, and the old patterns will fall victim to phonological reduction and/or to oblivion. Of course, the period of isolation is merely one of transition: the stage is set for a new system of agglutination, prepositive if it develops in the VX stage, postpositive after a change to XV.

Ad (S4), "a strong drift towards the restriction of the inflected possessive forms to animate nouns and pronouns".

This should be viewed together with (F5) and (F6):

Ad (F5), the increasing tendency to place the non-prepositional genitive before the headnoun.

Ad (F6), the increasing tendency to use the postpositive-prepositional of-genitive rather than the prepositive-flexional genitive.

The genitive-attribute pattern consistent with VX order is postpositive-prepositional, i.e., the of-genitive, according to the principle of natural serialization. The prepositive-flexional genitive lingers for awhile where it is most commonly topical, i.e., with animate nouns and pronouns: animate beings, especially human beings, are more likely to be topical than inanimate ones, given the totality of human interests. (Cf. also Kirsner 1973.) Topicality favors early position in the sentence, cf. Behaghel's Second Law, (2); note the analogous situation with proclitic object pronouns in Romance languages.

Ad (F1) and (F2), the increasing tendency to place the accusative-object and the dative-object after the verb.

These are special applications of (D1), the drift toward VX order.

Ad (F3), the increasing tendency to place the (non-prepositional) dative-object before the accusative-object.

The basic order of Verb, Direct Object, and Indirect Object in consistent languages is IDV or VDI, according to the principle of natural serialization. Shifting to VX order changes IDV to the inconsistent VDI. A new prepositional $_p$I develops, serialized as VD$_p$I, in conformity with the principle. ID order lingers for awhile, most commonly used for topical I, in accordance with Behaghel's Second Law.

Ad (F4), the increasing tendency to place the subject before the verb.

This is the development from TVX to SVX, cf. (5).

Ad (L1), "the use of anaphoric, non-emphatic, subject pronouns".

Subject agreement for person and number (and possibly generally) derives from subject pronouns by cliticization (as Vs in VS languages, as sV in SV languages). Since s develops from S-pronouns, S-pronouns are not used except for comment or contrast ("emphasis"). As s is rendered non-dependable by phonological change, cf. (8), once-"emphatic" S-pronouns become obligatory in topical function (and as such unstressed) to avoid ambiguity.

Ad (L2), "the use of articles, definite and indefinite".

Definiteness is closely related to topicality: most topical terms containing a common noun as head are definite. Definite articles develop from demonstratives; the semantic relatedness of demonstratives and definiteness is quite transparent. Consistent XV languages do not have articles. In TVX languages, demonstratives are increasingly used in topical noun phrases, because they preserve S-O distinctions longer than nouns; it is thus clear from the beginning of a sentence whether a topical NP is S or O. This non-deictic but rather anaphoric use of the demonstrative is the birth of the definite article, whose functions may

subsequently change so that it becomes increasingly useful as an S-O
marker even in non-topical functions. Being inherently unstressed, the
definite article has but a short life. A consistent VX language does
not have articles. A part of one such tragedy is illustrated in the
following data from Zurich German (Moulton 1971:939-940). The nominative and accusative forms of the Middle High German definite article
were der, den, daz, die, and diu. We consider only die [diə] and diu
[dü]. The forms coalesced into [di] "by regular phonetic change".
Syncope yielded [d], but this [d] is subject to immediate further modification, with the following result:

Noun	Definite NP	
füəss	pfüəss	'feet', 'the feet'
muətər	pmuətər	'(the) mother'
xind	kxind	'(the) children'
sax	tsax	'(the) thing'
hand	thand	'(the) hand'
ōrə	tōrə	'(the) ears'
bæi	pæi	'(the) legs'
dörffər	törffər	'(the) villages'
gass	kass	'(the) street'
pošt	pošt	'(the) mail'
tišš	tišš	'(the) tables'
ksets	ksets	'(the) laws'

The [d] assimilates to the place of articulation of an initial consonant. With a lax stop it combines into a tense stop. Before segments
other than oral stops it retains its identity as a stop, but is tense
[I should think on the analogy with the tensing characteristic for
initial lax stops]. But note the incipient tragedy: there is no trace
of this article where the noun begins with a tense stop.

There are many languages with a definite article that do not have
an indefinite article. (Icelandic, Greek; the English indefinite
article is zero in the plural.) There are very few languages with only
an indefinite article. If we assume that the use of the numeral 'one'
is originally complementary to that of the anaphoric-demonstrative, we
can explain its rarity and relative timing from its limited usefulness

for S-O marking: it occurs most commonly in the comment and thus late in the sentence, compared to topical noun phrases. This is obviously a vague suggestion. Comparative work on this problem is much needed.

Ad (L3), "the use of prepositions instead of case endings".

The only point still requiring comment is the use of prepositions rather than postpositions. This follows from the principle of natural serialization:

$$\underline{\text{Prep} \quad \text{NP}} \qquad \underline{\text{NP} \quad \text{Postp}}$$
$$\;\;\text{V} \qquad \text{X} \qquad\qquad \text{X} \qquad \text{V}$$

Only prepositions are consistent with VX order.

Ad (L4) and (L5), "the development of periphrastic causatives, inchoa-tives, etc." and "of periphrastic auxiliaries".

One of the two points still requiring comment is not noted in Lakoff 1972, viz. the prepositive, rather than postpositive, development of the helping verbs. This too follows from the principle of natural serialization:

$$\underline{\text{Helping Verb} \quad \text{Main Verb}} \quad \underline{\text{Main Verb} \quad \text{Helping Verb}}$$
$$\quad\;\; \text{V} \qquad\qquad \text{X} \qquad\qquad \text{X} \qquad\qquad \text{V}$$

Only prepositive helping verbs are consistent with VX order. The second point is the observation that the change occurs earlier for transitive than intransitive verbs. The greater the number of noun phrases that have to be related to a verb (a causative of a transitive verb is a three-place relation), the greater the chances for ambiguity or perceptual confusion when case distinctions become blurred. The alternative construction with a verb meaning 'cause' and a complement clause will therefore be favored earlier as a replacement for causatives from transitive verbs than for causatives from intransitive verbs, but never the other way around.

Ad (L6), "The development of adverbs and comparatives".

The development of adverbs with postpositive -mente is, together with the postpositive future and conditional morphology from forms of habēre 'have', the last creation of XV character of a language well on its way to XV:

rapidā mente		cantāre habeō
X V	X V

This development took place because the respective forms had not
changed their order yet because they stood in a close nexus, but it
actually constitutes an exception to the general drift of the language--
a fact which Lakoff could not appreciate because she lacked a theoretical framework in which to analyze such observations.

However, the development of comparative constructions is again a
true exemplification of the drift from XV to VX. The only point still
requiring comment is the order change:

$$Adj + ER > MORE + Adj$$

More generally:

NP_{Case} +	Adj + ER	>	MORE + Adj	+	THAN + Standard
X V	X V		V X		V X
X	V		V		X

Only the newly developing comparison constructions are consistent with
VX order.

It is clear, then, that we need no unexplained metacondition to
explain drift. Sapir was moving in the right direction when he established causal relationships among his individual drifts and viewed
phonological change as the ultimate cause of drift. We are now, half
a century after Sapir's exposition of the problem, in a position to
make deeper and more comprehensive generalizations about the nature of
phonological and syntactic change. This enables us to say that given
the inevitability of neutralizing and reductive phonological change,
and given the various, often conflicting demands of pragmatics and
semantics on grammatical structure, drift is inescapable, and its course
predictable. If we kindly excuse Sapir's occasional lapses into mystical diction, such as that about English words "craving spaces between
them", we find ourselves in the most fundamental agreement with Sapir,
continuing--and continuing to succeed in--his scientific approach to

"the study of speech": a refusal to accept descriptions as explanations, a quest for causal explanations even of the most mystifying
properties of language.

REFERENCES

Anttila, Raimo A. 1972. An introduction to historical and comparative linguistics. New York: Macmillan.

Bartsch, Renate. 1972. Adverbialsemantik: die Konstitution logisch-semantischer Repräsentationen von Adverbialkonstruktionen. Frankfurt am Main: Athenäum.

Bartsch, Renate, and Theo Vennemann. 1972. Semantic structures: a study in the relation between semantics and syntax. Frankfurt am Main: Athenäum.

---. 1973. Sprachtheorie. Lexikon der germanistischen Linguistik, ed. by Hans P. Althaus et al., 34-55. Tübingen: Max Niemeyer.

Behaghel, Otto. 1923-32. Deutsche Syntax: eine geschichtliche Darstellung. 4 vol.'s. Volume 4: Wortstellung, Periodenbau. Heidelberg: Carl Winter.

Bever, Thomas G., and D. Terence Langendoen. 1972. The interaction of speech perception and grammatical structure in the evolution of language. Linguistic change and generative theory, ed. by Robert P. Stockwell and Ronald K.S. Macaulay, 34-95. Bloomington: Indiana University Press.

Burrow, T. 1955. The Sanskrit language. London: Faber and Faber.

Comrie, Bernard. 1973. The ergative: variations on a theme. Lingua 32. 239-253.

Fries, Charles C. 1940. On the development of the structural use of word-order in Modern English. Language 16. 199-208.

Givón, Talmy. 1971. Historical syntax and synchronic morphology: an archaeologist's field trip. Papers from the 7th Regional Meeting, Chicago Linguistic Society, 394-415.

---. 1974. Serial verbs and syntactic change: Niger-Congo. This conference.

Greenberg, Joseph H. 1966 [1962]. Some universals of grammar with particular reference to the order of meaningful elements.

Universals of language, ed. by Joseph H. Greenberg, 2nd ed., 73-113. Cambridge (Mass.): M.I.T. Press.

Kirsner, Robert S. 1973. Natural focus and agentive interpretation: on the semantics of Dutch expletive er. Stanford occasional papers in linguistics, 3:101-113.

Kuno, Susumo. 1974. The position of relative clauses and conjunctions. Linguistic Inquiry 5. 117-136.

Lakoff, Robin. 1972. Another look at drift. Linguistic change and generative theory, ed. by Robert P. Stockwell and Ronald S.K. Macaulay, 172-198. Bloomington: Indiana University Press.

Lehmann, Winfred P. 1971. On the rise of SOV patterns in New High German. Grammatik, Kybernetik, Kommunikation (Festschrift Alfred Hoppe), ed. by K.G. Schweisthal, 19-24. Bonn: Dümmler.

---. 1972a. Proto-Germanic syntax. Toward a grammar of Proto-Germanic, ed. by Frans van Coetsem and Herbert L. Kufner, 239-268. Tübingen: Max Niemeyer.

---. 1972b. Contemporary linguistics and Indo European studies. PMLA 87. 976-993.

---. 1972c. Converging theories in linguistics. Language 48. 266-275.

---. 1973. A structural principle of language and its implications. Language 49. 47-66.

Li, Charles N., and Sandra A. Thompson. 1973. Historical change of word order: a case study in Chinese and its implications. Paper read at the First International Conference on Historical Linguistics, Edinburgh, Sept. 1973. Forthcoming in the Proceedings.

---. 1974. The semantic function of word order. This conference.

Lüdtke, Helmut. 1970. Sprache als kybernetisches System. Bibliotheca Phonetica 9. 34-50. Basel: Karger.

Moulton, William G. 1971. Review in Language 47. 938-943.

Sapir, Edward. 1921. Language: an introduction to the study of speech. New York: Harcourt, Brace and Company. Now Harvest Book HB 7.

Vennemann, Theo. 1971. Natural generative phonology. Paper read at the Annual Meeting of the Linguistic Society of America, St. Louis, Mo., Dec. 1971.

---. 1972. Analogy in generative grammar: the origin of word order. Paper read at the XIth International Congress of Linguists, Bologna, August-September 1972. Forthcoming in the Proceedings.

---. 1973a. Explanation in syntax. Syntax and semantics II, ed. by John Kimball, 1-50. New York: Seminar Press.

---. 1973b. Language type and word order. Paper read at the Symposium on Typology, Prague, August 1973. Forthcoming in the Proceedings.

---. 1973c. Topics, subjects, and word order: from SXV to SVX via TVX. Paper read at the First International Conference on Historical Linguistics, Edinburgh, September 1973. Forthcoming in the Proceedings.

---. 1973d. Theoretical word order studies: results and problems. Paper read at the annual meeting of the LSA, San Diego, December 1973. Forthcoming in Papiere zur Linguistik 7, 1974.

---. 1974. Exbraciation as a mechanism of word order change. MS.

ORDER IN BASE STRUCTURES*

by

Emmon Bach

* I wish to thank Stanley Peters and Barbara Hall Partee for helpful
discussion of a number of points in the paper. Naturally, all
blunders are my own.

1.   Introduction

There has been considerable discussion in the last several years
about the ordering of elements in the 'deeper' structures underlying
sentences of natural languages. My purpose here is to clarify some
hypotheses relating to this putative left-to-right orientation of base
structures, to assess the evidence in favor of the hypothesis that
these structures are ordered in the usual sense, and to point toward
the kind of further research which must be carried out in order to refute or further bolster this hypothesis. The question is particularly
relevant to hypotheses about universal grammar, especially the various
claims that have been advanced about a universal base.

Underlying many of our arguments is the following general principle: Linguistic theory must make the strongest claims compatible with
the facts. A hypothesis, $\underline{A}$, is stronger than another, $\underline{B}$, if $\underline{A}$ implies
but is not implied by $\underline{B}$. Looked at in another way, $\underline{A}$ rules out more
possible states of affairs within the domain of its application than $\underline{B}$.
Consider, for example, the question whether the phonological features
in underlying representations are related in some direct way by means
of phonological rules to the features in phonetic representations of
sentences. To answer this question in the affirmative is to embrace a
hypothesis which is stronger than one which allows but does not require
such a direct relation (since a statement $\underline{p}$ always implies the disjunc-
tion $\underline{p}$ or $\underline{q}$, no matter what $\underline{q}$ is). Similarly, a theory of syntax which
claimed that deep representations are always identical to surface rep-
resentations would be a stronger hypothesis than one in which they
could be distinct. We find that the facts support the stronger hypothesis in the first of these situations (the phonological case) but not
in the second (the syntactic one), where overwhelming evidence is in
favor of the weaker hypothesis.

A second general remark has to do with various interpretations of
the nature of 'universal grammar.' On the one hand, universal grammar
is sometimes taken to be simply the set of statements in linguistic
theory about the grammars of individual languages. On the other hand,
universal grammar is sometimes meant as literally part of each individual grammar. Restricting our attention to the base, a theory of the
latter sort would be, for instance, a version of the universal base

hypothesis which claimed that the base rules of every language were exactly the same, while a theory of the former sort would be one which merely placed certain restrictions on the base components of individual grammars. In this case, since the former type of theory includes the latter as one possibility ('The base rules of any language are ...') we see that the universal base hypothesis is a stronger hypothesis than some version of a less specific metatheory about all grammars.

It seems to me that the distinction between these two views of universal grammar is sometimes glossed over. Suppose we wish to support the universal base hypothesis but find overwhelming evidence of different deep orders in two languages. Two moves are then possible: we might say that deep structures are unordered and that language-particular ordering rules produce one or another order for the two languages. But we can also change the hypothesis to some such form as this: The base rules of every language conform to the following schemata: 'S' on the left of the arrow; 'NP''VP' on the right' and so on. This metagrammar would then delimit all the grammars constructible according to the specifications, but each grammar would be one with the usual left-to-right orientation in the base structures ('S → NP + VP', ...; 'S → VP + NP', ...; ...). In this instance the two hypotheses do not stand in any relation on the scale of weak to strong. What we have done is to weaken our original hypothesis about the universal base in two directions. In fact, our two new hypotheses are mutually contradictory. Under the first, 'set-system' hypotheses we claim that for no language will we find evidence that the base structures are ordered; under the second, that for no language will we find evidence that they are unordered.

These last two claims are empirical claims, but it cannot be emphasized too strongly that the evidence we seek must perforce be very indirect. Just like other theoretical constructs in linguistic theory and in the theories about individual languages (e.g., phonemes) base structures cannot be directly observed or intuited. Moreover the observations and predictions which provide evidence for or against notions about base structures are never derivable from those notions alone but rather from a complex set of hypotheses about language in general and the individual language in which the evidence is sought.

The best that we can do in attempting to refute some notion about base structures is to make explicit the other premises entering into the deduction and to provide as much independent evidence for the correctness of these latter premises as possible.

It is not always clear just what is intended in the various suggestions and comments having to do with 'unordered' base structures. In so far as those suggestions remain vague one could simply ignore them until such time as they have been made precise and some evidence offered in their support. I shall instead take another course and examine a number of possible interpretations (noting where one or another of these possibilities seems to agree with some published work). Before looking at points of dispute let us consider some points of agreement. Every linguistic theory must, I would assume, include the requirement that a grammar of a language not only specify what the sentences of the language are but provide one or more structural descriptions for each of the sentences of the language. Just what these structural descriptions are like and how many of them there are is determined by the nature of the theory, especially the system of 'levels,' 'components,' 'strata' etc. which is claimed by the theory to be necessary and sufficient for a grammar of a natural language. Further, it would be generally agreed that the set of structural descriptions assigned by a grammar to each sentence includes a representation of the categories and relationships of the sentence (in approximately its phonetic form) that are given by labeled tree-diagrams, labeled bracketings, or some equivalent notation. Finally, we are concerned only with theories which are in agreement that the structural description of every sentence in the non-phonological component(s) of the grammar must provide some other representation which will in general differ from its 'surface-structure' representation of constituency assignments and relationships. The question with which we are concerned is the nature of these underlying representations or as I shall call them 'base-structures' of sentences.

A surface-structure is representable by a labeled tree-diagram. Such a diagram expresses three kinds of relationships: relations of dominance and constituent type (labeling) ('the string x is a constituent of type A in the sentence with the phrase-marker P') and a "left-to-right" ordering corresponding roughly to the order in time of the parts of the utterance represented. One theory of grammar (call it 'standard transformational grammar,' although a number of distinguishable theories are in agreement on this point) makes the claim that the underlying representations are of exactly the same sort: 'deep structures' of sentences are formally the same kind of objects as surface structures. The claim is embodied not only in this theory's conception of the operation of the base rules but in the formal specification of the nature and operation of transformations. Thus a claim to the contrary entails not only a change in the theory of the base but also a change in the theory of transformations either by way of a complete revision of the type of formal operations corresponding to transformations or by a provision of some new type of rule which can operate in some order-free way in addition to transformations of the usual sort. Part of the argument presented below will be a demonstration that theories of the standard transformational sort which incorporate what I shall call the Ordered Base Hypothesis are stronger theories than some theories which include a version of the Unordered Base Hypothesis (other things being equal).

2. Theories of the Base

Let us now consider in more detail some possible interpretations that could be given to the claim that base structures do not include in their definition a specification of a left-to-right ordering for their elements and constituents.

In standard transformational theory the base consists of a set of context-free branching rules (plus possibly feature redundancy rules and a lexicon, neither of which is immediately relevant here). The rules are used to construct a set of possible deep phrase markers which express not only the dominance and labeling relations holding among the subparts of the phrase-marker but also a left-to-right ordering relation. Thus given a rule '$A \rightarrow B_1 B_2 \ldots B_n$' we construct a part of a phrase marker representable as '$[_A B_1 B_2 \ldots B_n]$' or in the familiar form of a tree-diagram

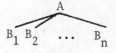

Suppose we replace such a system by one in which only the dominance
relations are expressed. Such a system is then one in which for all A,
x, y [$_A$ x] is equivalent to [$_A$ y] (where A immediately dominates x, y)
just in case x and y contain exactly the same elements (regardless of
order). Such a system has been suggested by Shaumjan and has been
called by Chomsky and perhaps others a 'set-system'. There are, however, two possibilities when we ask about the objects generated by a
system of this sort. On the one hand, we may think of the elements
dominated directly by a given category symbol as constituting simply a
set of elements. The entire operation of the base rules then gives us
objects which are simply stratified sets of elements: the entire
marker is a set S consisting of, say, two elements, NP and VP, NP and
VP in turn are sets of elements, node labels, and so on. Immediate
constituency is then the relation of set-membership and we may define
the derivative notion of constituency (if we need it) as follows: x is
a constituent of A with respect to a marker P if there are elements
y_1, y_2, ..., y_n (n > 1) such that y_1 = x, y_n = A and for y_i (i < n) y_i
is a member of y_i + 1 (a different system, but I believe ultimately
equivalent for linguistic purposes, might utilize set inclusion rather
than membership). Let us call such a system an L-system ('L' for
lattice).

On the other hand, we might think of the system as generating at
each point strings of elements but in such a fashion that from a rule
'A → B_1 B_2 ... B_n' any permutations of the B_i would follow from the
application of the rule. Such a system would directly generate ordered
phrase markers in the usual sense. It would be equivalent to a grammar
in which the following condition is met: 'R is a rule of the grammar
if and only if every rule which is just like R except that the elements
on the right are arranged in a different order from that of R is also
in the grammar.' Thus 'A: B C' (to use an obvious notation) would
stand for the ordinary rules 'A → B + C' 'A → C + B'. Let us call
such a system an M-system ('M' for mobile).[1]

The last consideration suggests yet another possibility. Suppose
rather than changing the nature of the grammar, we introduce in connection with the evaluation metric on grammars an abbreviatory convention
(like currently used parentheses, braces, and so on) to express the

fact that all permutations are permitted. Then the system would be just like that sketched except that 'A: X' would be an abbreviatory notation which might or might not be used, but if used would make the grammar more highly valued in the metric. This conception incorporates the claim that the abbreviation of two or more rules differing only by the order in which the elements occur on the right of the arrow (and exhausting the set of such rearrangements) expressed a linguistically significant generalization about base structures. Let us call such a system a G-system ('G' for generalization).

One of the main reasons for interest in systems with unordered base structures, I take it, has been the phenomenon of free word order. Indeed, a kind of Whorfian effect can be noted in that linguists who have favored such systems have been those working in languages which are generally considered to exhibit free word order (Shaumjan and Soboleva for Russian, Staal for Sanskrit). But as has been noted by several writers, none of the above systems account directly for free word order, since the constituents will be grouped according to the dominance relations expressed by the rules and only those orders conforming to this grouping will be generated by the rules. Thus an M-system with the two rules 'S: NP, VP', 'VP: V, NP' will yield only the four permutations (marking the NP's to distinguish them): NP^1 V NP^2, NP^2 V NP^1, V NP^2 NP^1, NP^1 NP^2 V: no arrangement in which two constituents are separated by a constituent of another construction will be generated (Hall 1964, Staal 1967). This fact suggests yet another interpretation of an order-free base. Suppose we interpret the rules to be such as to provide sets for which dominance relations hold but add the stipulation that any permutation of the elements in the whole set dominated by S is generated by the system. This is obviously the same as a system consisting of a set of context free rules and a 'scrambling' rule which rearranges the terminal strings of the CF grammar into arbitrary orders. Let us call such a system an S-system ('S' for scrambling).

All the systems considered so far share the property that the structures generated are assumed to behave in a uniform manner with respect to the simple ordering of a left-to-right sequence. It is conceivable that there could be systems also in which the base order is a partial ordering. Fillmore's remark about the question of ordering in his case system (1968) might be interpreted in this way. His Proposition consists of a Verb followed by one or more case categories which may or may not be ordered with respect to each other. If the V constituent always precedes the case categories, then we have a partial ordering in place of the usual (simple) linear ordering of elements. Most of the remarks below apply to this possibility also and I will discuss the partially ordered system only where special comments are necessary.

We need now to consider the internal relations among these attempts to explicate the notion of unordered base structures. In particular, how are they related in terms of the strength of their claims about language. One system stands out from the others as incorporating notions of order not directly in the formalism of base structures and rules but in the abbreviatory devices made available for use in a simplicity metric which translates generality of grammars into length of grammars: what I have dubbed the G-system. It stipulates that a grammar in which a number of base rules can be abbreviated into a schema standing for all and only the rules constructed out of permutations of the right-hand elements is to be more highly valued than one in which this is not the case. Of course, such a system does not at all fall within the class of systems in which the base structures are unordered. It is worthwhile, however, to remind ourselves that evidence as to lack of order in the form of rules might conceivably be reflected in the notational system made available for evaluating grammars rather than in our hypotheses about the structures acted upon by the rules. This point will be taken up again below in connection with rules of a transformational sort. In connection with the base rules it would seem that we can dismiss this idea rather quickly.

There are two kinds of evidence that might be used to support the idea that an abbreviatory convention reflects a true linguistic generalization: psycholinguistic and historical. Note that in order to demonstrate the linguistic significance of the particular convention we are considering we would need not only to show that the creation of structures occurring in all possible orders came about through a process of generalization but that this result was a function specifically

of the base rules. No evidence either from language development in the
individual or from historical change is available, to my knowledge, for
this idea. What evidence there is bears only on the question of ordering per se (not ordering in the base) and it points in the other
direction, that is, against the idea of generalizations of this kind in
general and a fortiori against such generalization with respect to base
rules.

A child is exposed to a highly fortuitous and incomplete sample of
the language he eventually learns. One set of speculations about how
his relatively rapid learning takes place is based on the idea that he
constructs the most highly valued grammar compatible with the data (in
successive approximations). For instance, if we can believe the formulation of the English Auxiliary rule developed in transformational
grammars (first in Chomsky 1957),

   1. Aux → Tense (Modal) (Perfect) (Progressive)

and if we hold that the parenthesis abbreviation expresses a linguistically significant generalization we would expect the child to learn the
rule by projecting from even an incomplete set of sentences none of
which contained a complete expansion of the form could have been running
or the like. That is, given sentences with sequences like runs, has
run, is running, can run, and can be running the child will generalize
to (1) (cf. Chomsky 1965:42-44). I am aware of no studies which show
that children generalize in this way in the direction of 'free word
order'. In fact, a study by Gvozdev (cited by Slobin 1966:133-135) of
Russian children showed that even given primary data from a language
with presumably free word order the word order of the children's language was 'quite inflexible' (and in some instances did not even conform to the dominant order of the model language, as when the children
created subject-object-verb sentences where Russian has a dominant SVO
pattern). There is apparent counterevidence to my claim in two further
studies. Gruber (1967) discusses a stage in the development of one
child where the characteristic sentence form was that of a 'topic' plus
'comment' but occurring in either order (milk all gone, all gone milk),
while Klima and Bellugi (1966) present data on negatives which at one
stage take either the form Nucleus+Neg or Neg+Nucleus (No play that,
Wear mitten no). Even if we assume that these sentences result from a

generalization of some kind there is no reason to think that this would
have to be explained on the basis of a generalization with respect to
base structures. On the contrary, I believe that these are facts about
particular bipartite constructions (topic-comment and negation) and not
about generalizations of the order of deep structures. There are two
reasons for this conclusion: first, there is no evidence either in
Gruber's data or in Klima and Bellugi's that such generalizations are
made for other constructions. Klima and Bellugi's data on questions
from the same period show complete agreement on the front position of
the interrogative word and in neither sets of data are there any
examples of dislocations of, say, determiners and nouns (we have there's
the man and fire truck there in Gruber's study but not *man the there
or the like). Further, in adult language topic-comment sentences typically occur in either order (the hotel, where is it? or Where is it, the
hotel? or colloquial Japanese Hoteru wa doko desu ka? Doko desu ka,
hoteru wa?) but the topicalized noun phrase can correspond to just
about any noun phrase in the deep structure (I saw it yesterday, the
hotel) so that no explanation can be forthcoming from a generalization
about the order of deep constituents. Along the same line of argument,
when we consider second language learning, experience in the language
classroom suggests that generalizations (and hence mistakes) about
order of constituents do not take place. No teacher has to take pains
to drill his students to prevent them from rearranging the constituents
of the sentences in the target language spontaneously (as opposed to
carry-over of specific patterns of order from the first language).

As several writers have noted (Bach and Harms 1972, Kiparsky 1968)
evidence from historical change can be used to support the idea that an
abbreviatory convention reflects significant generalizations. Such
arguments rest on the assumption that a dominant force in historical
change is rule simplification. To support the straw man we are trying
to burn up here we would need to find frequent cases where languages
changed by adopting base rules that could be abbreviated by our convention. Although there are plenty of examples of languages changing
their word order characteristics (compare German, English, Russian, and
Modern Persian, for example), there is no evidence whatsoever of a
change of the sort that would be required here. In sum, I see no reason

at all to think that a G-system would have any linguistic relevance at all. (It should be noted that the notion of an evaluation metric is incomparably more vague and speculative in connection with syntactic questions than in phonology.)

Recall that the M-system is a system in which the base rules obey the restriction that a rule $\underline{R} = \underline{A} \rightarrow \underline{B}_1 \ \underline{B}_2 \ldots \underline{B}_n$ is in the set of rules if and only if every rule (of the $\underline{n}$!) rules that are just like $\underline{R}$ (except for the permutations of the $\underline{B}_i$ is in the grammar. Like the G-system just discussed the M-system does not fall into the class of grammars with unordered base structures. Both systems differ from the other systems we will consider in that the latter entail, while these systems do not, that elsewhere in the grammar rules or statements specify the linear order of the elements of sentences. With no further stipulations about other parts of the grammar, it is apparent that the systems with unordered base structures make weaker assumptions about the class of possible grammars (and languages). We can see this by asking in what way two languages could differ under the two sets of hypotheses. In the systems with ordering rules and transformations (that all systems must have transformations in the usual sense--that is, with linear arrays in their structure indices--is an assumption that will be supported below), two languages could differ in their transformations and in their ordering rules (and in the relationships, e.g., ordering of rules) among these two types of rules), whereas in one of the other systems they could not since there would be no ordering rules.

Turning to the system of base phrase markers we have then three systems in which these involve a left-to-right ordering: the structures of standard transformational grammars, those of an M-system, those of a G-system. Since the type of marker is the same in all three, the systems differ only in the sets of markers available in each. The G-system and the system of an STG are completely equivalent in the sets of allowed base markers, the only difference being in the evaluation metric applied to the grammars. We have just seen that there is not a shred of evidence to support such an addition to the evaluation metric. Hence, we can confine our attention to STG's.

As it stands, present linguistic theory allows that every system of rules available under an M-system could be a base system of rules available under standard transformational theory. Consider a putative relation among sentences, noun-phrases and verb-phrases. All of the following sets of rules could occur in grammars of natural languages under present theory:

1. S → NP VP

2. S → VP NP

3. S → NP VP

   S → VP NP

Under the M-system no grammar with 1 or 2 alone would be admissible but all grammars would have to have 3 (if any). Thus, the M-system makes stronger assumptions about language than does ordinary transformational theory (facts of this sort were pointed out to me by Gerald Sanders). Of course, this defect--if it is a defect--can be remedied in an indefinite number of ways, only one of which is provided by an M-system. One could, for instance, specifically disallow grammars with subsets of rules like those in 3. Then it would be case that languages could differ as between pairs of rules like 1 and 2 (but not as between either and 3).

[Excursus: the systems of STG and the M-system are grammars in the formal sense. Before looking at the systems with truly unordered base-structures, we might briefly look at the systems considered so far from the mathematical point of view. Both M-systems and ordinary base systems are context-free grammars. We have just seen that the sets of strings generated by M-systems from a proper subset of the context-free languages: There is for example no M-grammar for the language $L_1 = \{ x \mid x = a^n b^n \}$.[3] Suppose we ask the question: What class of languages do we get from grammars with context-free rules and an operation freely permuting the elements of the terminal strings. That is, given $\underline{L}$ a context-free language, define L' as the set $\{ x \mid = y$ in L, x is a permutation of y $\}$. Obviously, L' is a context sensitive language. But L' is not necessarily context free. Let L be the context-free (in fact regular) language $\{ x \mid x = (abc)^n, n=1, 2,... \}$. Intersect L' (the set of all permutations of $\underline{a}$, $\underline{b}$, $\underline{c}$ such that the number of $\underline{a}$'s $\underline{b}$'s and $\underline{c}$'s is equal) with $L'' = \{ x \mid x = a^n b^m n^i$ $mni \neq 0 \}$.

L'' is regular, but the intersection of L'' and L' is not context free. Therefore, L' is not context free.]

The systems considered so far remain within the broad framework of transformational theory as it has developed in the last decades. We depart from this framework when we turn to systems in which the objects generated by the 'base' are order-free in some way. I have argued above that such systems make weaker claims about language than do systems with ordered base structures. It is easy to concoct an indefinite number of hypotheses about order-free systems which are incomparable to those with ordered base systems with respect to strength of claims and an indefinite number of systems which make stronger claims than do ordinary transformational grammars. The difficulty is that most writers who have proposed order-free base systems have not been specific about the exact nature of these systems and the constraints they wish to place on them (and the remainder of their grammars!). Shaumjan has made the most elaborate scheme for a grammar with order-free structural representations at some level, but it is still not clear to me how actual word order is to be specified for one language or another or whether the system would differ essentially from what I have called an M-system here together with a notation for certain (or all?) transformational operations or relations with 'unordered' structure indices. In any case Shaumjan's model is embedded in a framework that is so different from that of transformational grammar that it can only be compared as a whole rather than on this specific feature. Lamb's stratificational system is supposed to contain a level of representation in which the relations between elements is not representable in the form of a phrase-marker (Gleason 1964) but as of the date of writing the exact nature of this 'sememic' stratum remains unknown. Of those writers who remain roughly within the framework of transformational grammar (Lyons 1966, Steal 1967) statements in the direction of unordered base structures are very vague and can be interpreted as pointing toward M-systems rather than true unordered base systems. I shall deal with some more clearly articulated hypotheses below.

With these qualifications in mind we can proceed to compare the two remaining systems. Of these, the L-system makes stronger claims than the S-system, largely by default. In an L-system we obtain a deep representation of the dominance relations among the elements of a sentence. Such a representation is just like a tree except that no order is defined among the elements directly dominated by a given node. An S-system, on the other hand, must differ from such a system in some completely unknown way. Without some specific suggestions about the system, then, it remains weaker than an L-system: to say that the base is some system or other is not even a hypothesis, and hence by default makes weaker claims about language than does any hypothesis which does make such claims.

Even weaker than the more or less definite systems we have considered (i.e., all but the S-system) would be a theory based on a partial ordering of elements (without again any further stipulations). To see this it is necessary only to consider that the set of possible base structures of an L-system would be a proper subset of the set of possible base structures under a system with partial ordering. Weakest of all would be a mixed theory of general grammar which allowed languages to differ with respect to the type of base structures posited. Summing up then we have the following hierarchy from weak to strong:

Mixed systems

Partial ordering

(S-system?)

L-systems

Standard TG base   G-system

M-systems

3. Arguments for Unordered Base Structures

Let's look now at some arguments that have been or might be advanced for the view that base structures are unordered, noting at each point whether the arguments support the weaker or stronger versions of this thesis that have been laid out above. The arguments can be divided into those which are purely a priori and those which attempt to show some empirical support for the idea. As I have noted at several points already, some stipulations about constraints on the rest of the grammar are necessary before we can even tell if the proposals have any empirical content. For example, let us imagine a hypothesis that the base structures are produced by rules of an L-system but that particular orders are introduced by a set of rules that precede any transformations. If these rules are constrained by the requirement that no constituents of the unordered structure be made discontinuous by these pretransformational rules, then it is difficult to see how any empirical evidence could bear on the choice of this system as against an ordinary base system with ordered structures.

3.1 Arguments a priori. In his intervention after Chomsky's presentation of 'The logical basis of linguistic theory' at the Ninth International Congress, Shaumjan stated:

> ...the IC model cannot do without spatial considerations confining it to the level of observation. What I have in mind is the linearity of elements. The IC model does not permit of the rearrangement of symbols bound by the relation of concatenation. Although the transformation model permits the rearrangement of symbols, it is not free of spatial considerations which in the nature of things pertain to the observation level.
>
> In view of all this a more general question suggests itself: is it possible to build up a model completely free of spatial considerations [,] which are in principle incompatible with the explanatory level?' He then goes on to describe his own 'applicational generative' model 'based upon the operation of setting up domination relations among the elements irrespective of their arrangement in the flow of speech ... As it is necessary to divest the model of any spatial considerations, I introduce the concepts of linear and metrical distribution,' etc. [my italics]. (Proceedings 980 f.)

Shaumjan's argument is at best an assertion offered without support, at middle an a priori argument, at worst a case of bad reasoning. In the first interpretation it can be taken as a claim for the correctness of a particular theory of grammar for which empirical evidence can be found. I will assess such evidence in a moment. As an a priori argument it can be connected with Shaumjan's general views on the nature of science, the so-called 'two-level' view of science, where a distinction is drawn between 'genotypic' and 'phenotypic' concepts, the former being (as I understand it) theoretical constructs not immediately available to observation, the latter referring directly to observables (see Shaumjan 1964 in the same volume), Shaumjan apparently connects these ideas with Chomsky's distinction between 'observational' and 'explanatory' adequacy.[4] The linearity of the surface form of sentences is claimed to be phenotypic (pertaining to the 'observation level'). Even if we grant this much it is necessary to add another premise to justify the conclusion italicized above, namely that no meaning can be given to the linearity of the structures set up on the genotypic level. But this second premise is quite false. Even if we agree that the underlying structures belong to the genotypic level and the surface representations of sentences in phonetic form belong to the phenotypic level, it is perfectly possible to have genotypic structure with an (abstract) order related by 'rules of correspondence' to the phenotypic ordering of phones (e.g., a homomorphism or just the relations that obtain in a transformational grammar, where there is such a homomorphism unless some specific rule has changed the underlying order).

Actually, Shaumjan claims that his argument is not a priori (in Shaumjan 1964), that certain theoretical difficulties of empirical linguistics are cleared up by adopting the two-level view. The two-level view is then an empirical hypothesis about science and the results of linguistics count as evidence for this metatheory. But no support is offered for this assertion. The theoretical difficulties cited are illustrated by the problem of discontinuous morphemes (or constituents). Shaumjan's examples here are particularly infelicitous, for they happen to involve a situation where there is some evidence for a particular underlying (abstract) order which differs from that of the surface elements. He notes that in an English sequence like have taken the underlying constituents are actually S, HAVE + EN, and TAKE, which are then realized as above with the discontinuous sequence have and the participial element suffixed to the verb take. As is well known, Chomsky (1957) proposed an explanation for some peculiarities of English verbal constructions (chiefly involving the use of do as a carrier for unattached affixes) by setting up an underlying order conforming to the constituency with the suffix EN (among others) preceding the element with which it is introduced (HAVE). Rules of question formation and negative placement taken in conjunction with an affix-hopping transformation and a rule of DO-support serve to give the actual surface forms. The explanation depends crucially on a difference in order between the underlying and the surface structures. No other explanation of these facts has been offered and Shaumjan gives none. Thus if the 'two-

level' theory of linguistic structure forces us to abandon this explanation, the example must count as evidence against that theory. But as
I have indicated, I do not believe that the necessity for an order-free
underlying structure follows at all from this view of the nature of
science. If it does and if the facts count against this assumption (as
in this case they seem to), too bad for the two-level theory.

In discussing Shaumjan's views, Chomsky (1965: 124-126) correctly
denies the assumption that 'set-systems' are more abstract than concatenation systems. I have been unable to find any documentation for the
following argument although it seems to underlie much discussion of
questions like those touched on here, so I shall simply set it up as a
straw argument. Linguistic research of the last decades has shown that
the underlying structures of sentences are much more 'abstract' than
was supposed in previous theories of language. These more abstract
theories are superior to the earlier ones. If a little abstractness is
a good thing, a whole lot must be even better. But this is absurd.
Even if Chomsky were wrong, and given some reasonable interpretation of
'abstractness' it could be shown that set-systems were more abstract
than concatenation systems, so what? By this sort of reasoning we can
argue that five-hundred-pound football players are better than two-
hundred-pound ones, or that children should drink a hundred gallons of
milk a day. If set systems are more abstract than concatenation systems because they involve only dominance relations while the latter
involve not only dominance relations but also ordering relations and
are thereby superior, then best of all would be a system in which deep
structures were just sets of elements with not even dominance relations
(I owe this example to Larry Martin). Or again, why should set-systems
be superior to systems in which only ordering relations obtained but
no dominance relations?

Among the arguments a priori are those in which it is flatly stated that underlying structures do not exhibit a simple ordering relation. Thus, H.A. Gleason, Jr. (1964) writes about the sememic stratum
of language 'It cannot be dominated, as is the phonemics, by a general
and necessary linearity.' This is apparently felt to be so self-
evident that no justification or evidence is offered. Once again, I
believe, there is an underlying assumption that no meaning can be

attributed to an ordering of elements except for the ordering in time
of the physical signal. But this assertion is, as we have noted, false
in that a perfectly clear meaning can be given to such an ordering.
The assumption is further vitiated by the consideration that even the
ordering of elements in phonological representations (or even phonetic
representations) is 'abstract', that is, does not correspond directly
to the temporal order of cues in the physical signal. To pick just one
of numerous examples, David DeCamp (personal communication) has reported that spectrographic evidence shows that the difference between
utterances like 'Catch 'em' and 'Catch 'im' (both pronounced with a
syllabic [m]) is present only in the formant structure of the vowel of
'catch'.

3.2 Empirical evidence. What empirical evidence could be offered for
the view that deep structures are unordered, or that one of our other
hypotheses above were correct? None of the arguments that I have seen
or that I have been able to imagine seems to have much force.

3.2.1 Arguments from surface order. Let us grant for the sake of the
argument that there really are languages with 'free word order' (some
interpretations of this notion are discussed in Bach 1964:108-112),
letting this mean, for the moment, that for any sentence x which is in
the language all the permutations of the elements of x are also sentences in the language and furthermore are similar enough in cognitive content that we could attribute to all of them the same base structure.
Presumably, this would be the strongest case for order-free base
structures.

Let us note first that some additional conditions must be met and
assumptions added before we can draw any conclusions about order in base
structures. Suppose I am interested in constructing a theory about the
basic structure of physical substances. I observe that substances fall
into several fairly clear cut classes with respect to their physical
characteristics: there are substances like gasoline, water, syrup
which are runny (in varying degrees, flow downhill, remain in open con-
tainers, etc.), substances like carbon dioxide, helium, nitrogen which
are airy, fill closed spaces, etc., others like wood, lead, rubber
which just sit there more or less, tend to retain or regain their shape,
etc. On the basis of these observations alone I cannot conclude

anything about the underlying structure of matter. What I need to do
is construct a theory from which I can derive predictions and statements related to these observations. I might, for instance, guess that
there are three types of basic 'substance': runny, airy, and sessile.
But I might also guess that one of these types of substance was basic
and the other derived, or that none were basic and that the underlying
structure was quite different from any of these. Exactly the same situation prevails here. From surface characteristics of one language we
cannot conclude anything directly about the underlying structures.
Moreover, faced with languages with fixed order and languages with free
order we might guess that the underlying structures differ with respect
to ordering characteristics (an example of the 'mixed' hypothesis we
have seen above to be the weakest conceivable). Looking for a stronger
hypothesis, we might guess that base structures in all languages are
the same in this respect. But there is no reason a priori why we should
choose either the free type or the fixed type as basic. In either case
or if we derive both from some other type of structure we have to show
cause for our decision by looking at the consequences of each view and
considering evidence that would refute one or the other hypothesis.

One principle that might be appealed to is the idea that underlying structures are just like surface structures unless we can show a
reason why they should not be. This would lead to a mixed hypothesis.
But note that it does not lead to the assumption of order-free base
structures even for free word-order languages. This is so because
every surface structure does have an order. What we would need would
be something like an M-system in which all orders of elements would be
produced directly in the base and identity of base structure were defined
in an order-free way. Thus, 'base structure of S with analysis D' might
be defined as a class of structures meeting a condition of identity of
dominance relations and meeting the condition on terminal elements that
the structures contain the same terminal elements related in the same
way up to order. But even if we could make reasonably precise not only
the nature of the underlying structures and their grammar but the
remaining parts of the grammar as well--and it is easy to underestimate
the magnitude of such a task--it would still be necessary to show why

such a hypothesis were to be preferred over some other hypothesis that would allow us to explain the same facts.

Assuming a stronger theory in which it is claimed that base structures are the same sort of beast for all languages, there are two possibilities. Either all base structures are unordered and particular languages have ordering rules which produce fixed orders or all languages have ordered base structures and particular languages have reordering rules of some kind that produce free word order. There is no a priori reason why one or the other should be true. If we could show that even for free word order situations a particular order must be assigned before certain rules can operate correctly and then the free word order must result by further operations of some kind, we would have a strong argument against order-free base structures. For presumably the order-free hypothesis is supposed to explain free word order. But in this case we would need also certain reordering rules to explain free word order. Then Occam's razor would shave away and we would have to ask if the reordering rules were not sufficient. There are a number of such cases that will be considered below. The order-free base hypothesis must claim that no such situations will be found, and the lack of such would constitute negative evidence in favor of that hypothesis.

3.2.2 Explanatory power. So far, I have made the tacit assumption that the categories of the base and the dominance relations among them are completely independent of our hypotheses about ordering in base structures. This assumption is false. Consider the base structure representation of sentence pairs like John killed Bill and Bill killed John. All languages express such differences in surface structures, whether by word order as in English, or by case marking or some such device. It has been argued (Kuroda 1967, Jackendoff 1972) that some meaning differences may result from transformations but the cases considered were those in which the differences in meaning did not touch the basic grammatical relations of the sentence. In all the theories we are considering here sentences like those cited must differ in basic underlying structure. It follows that in such theories with unordered base structures the difference between John killed Bill and Bill killed John must be expressed in some order-free way in the base. The differ-

328

ence could be expressed in terms of different categories (like <u>Subject</u> and <u>Object</u>) or case-like markings (Fillmore 1968)[5] or by means of some difference in the configuration of dominance relations, for instance (using wavy lines for L-structures):

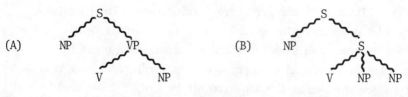

(A)   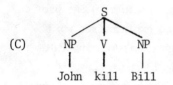   (B)

In a theory with ordered base structures, on the other hand, such differences could also exist, but (without further stipulations) the difference could be given merely by a difference in order

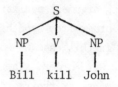

(C)

S				S		
NP	V	NP		NP	V	NP
John	kill	Bill		Bill	kill	John

To the extent that structures like those given in (A) and (B) or categories like those of Fillmore's case-grammar have been found to be correct and those under (C) incorrect we have confirming evidence for the hypothesis of order-free base structures. This constitutes the strongest evidence that I know of for the theories of unordered base structures and a point at which standard theory is especially weak.

Note that the particular choices given above do not follow at all from the Unordered Base Hypothesis. That is, there might be according to this hypothesis a base category Nucleus (say) comprising what we ordinarily consider the Subject and its Verb with the Object outside of it. On the other hand, Chomsky's suggestions about universal relational categories like Subject and Object (which he defines in an order-free way in terms of dominance relations) exclude some such analyses. Moreover, they are claimed to be not ad hoc machinery to get us out of the weakness mentioned above (if it is a weakness) but necessary for independent reasons, namely the proper operation of universal projection rules in the semantic component. Even if Chomsky's definitions lead in the right direction here, however, they do not seem to be very helpful in determining possible deep structure orders (Bach 1974).

In any case, it would seem that the tangle of problems touched on here (types of deep structure relations, existence and nature of an interpretive semantics) must be pursued in some detail if one wished to support a particular hypothesis about unordered or ordered base structures.

3.2.3 <u>Arguments from arbitrariness of deep order</u>. Suppose that a language has a number of related constructions which differ in the order of the constituents involved (it doesn't matter whether they are optional stylistic variants or instances of different constructions even with quite different meanings like English questions and non-questions or obligatory variants like German subordinate and insubordinate clauses). The ordered base hypothesis makes the strongest claim possible about such situations: there will always be evidence that one order should be basic and the other derived (if they are transformationally related at all). (Cf. Chomsky 1965:124-126)[6] If this turns out to be the case, the unordered base hypothesis is on shaky ground since it can only explain this by a special assumption, for instance, by claiming that the rules which introduce a left-to-right order precede all other rules (in which case it is unclear whether the hypothesis makes any substantive claims at all, as we have noted). Hence, it is important to look at cases where it seems that imposing a particular order in the base structures is completely arbitrary. We shall consider a number of cases below, where it will turn out that there is good reason for considering one order basic.

Suppose we find instances where the assumption of an underlying order leads to arbitrary decisions. Which of the various hypotheses we have distinguished above would this support? Apparently all of them, that is, even the strongest would be compatible with this state of affairs. For to explain the fact that of two orders A and B it would be arbitrary to consider either as derived from the other, we can say that both are present in the base as easily as we can say that neither is present in the base.

3.2.4 <u>Arguments from missing generalizations</u>. The following argument is due to Gerald Sanders. In Japanese, modifiers of nouns precede the nouns that they modify, if complements of verbs are considered to be modifiers of the verbs we can also say that modifiers of verbs precede

verbs. There appears to be no way within current theory to express the
generalization that modifiers precede modified elements. Similarly in
English, determiners as well as attributive adjectives (for the most
part) precede the nouns that they modify. There is now no way to express this generalization. Looked at in another way, if English had
the normal rules for adjective placement etc. and also the rule 'NP →
Noun + Det' its grammar would be just as simple as it is at present.
On the other hand, given appropriate machinery we might be able to state
a single rule about the placement of these elements before the noun.
Presumably such machinery would be available in a grammar in which unordered structures were determined in the base and then certain ordering
rules operated in the other parts of the grammar. Or again, consider
the so-called output conditions on the order of elements that have been
claimed by Ross (1967) and Perlmutter (1968) and others to be necessary
in a grammar. If we can arrange things so that these structures are
unordered and the order of output conditions is stated actually as a
rule we would be able to account for such facts easily. On the other
hand, if it turns out that some order-dependent rules must precede operation of the output conditions (or on the other hypothesis ordering
rules) then we would have strong evidence against the notion of order-
free structures since we would be doing the same job twice. Some evidence on just this point will be considered below. Any arguments about
missing generalizations presupposes that in the view being defended
there is some machinery to capture the generalization. I know of no
such machinery in this case (i.e., for ordering rules about 'modifiers'
and 'heads' etc.) and therefore will leave the defense of this idea to
those who are proposing such machinery.[7] It should be noted, however,
that to say that a certain generalization is not captured by a grammar
or a theory is not to say that some rule must be posited to capture it.

3.2.5 Sanders' invariant ordering hypothesis. By far the most precise
hypothesis about unordered base structures (at least that I am aware
of) is due to Gerald Sanders (1969, 1970): Sanders proposes the following scheme: the underlying structures of every grammar are unordered.
All ordering rules follow all other transformational rules (regrouping,
deletion, etc.). No rules can reorder constituents once their order
has been established. It is evident that this hypothesis is stronger

than any of the other order-free hypotheses we have considered. I do not know whether it is stronger than the theory of STG.[8]

This _invariant ordering hypothesis_ could be falsified if we could find a situation in which we find it necessary to specify one order of elements and then derive a different order from the first. I shall take up a number of situations of this sort in the next section. For now, let us just look at a typical situation in order to see what is involved. In Amharic, there is a definite determiner suffix (-u, -wa respectively for masculine and feminine nouns). This determiner is suffixed to nouns that have no adjective modifiers, but if there is a string of adjectives, it is suffixed to the first adjective:

1. betu   'the house'

2. tillik'u bet   'the big house'

3. tillik'u k'ə yy bet   'the big red house'

A standard kind of analysis might go like this. Assume that noun phrases have an intermediate or underlying structure like this:

(Det) (Adj^n) Noun

Then a reordering rule might suffix the article to the next lexical item (like the affix-hopping rule of English). Under the invariant ordering hypothesis, this account is ruled out. It is obviously possible to specify the two different orderings of these constituents independently from lattice structures. The only question is which of the two is to be preferred on grounds of generality or the like.

4. Against Unordered Base Structures

In this section I will try to undermine the notion that base structures are unordered. The arguments are of two kinds. First, I will discuss a number of facts which seem to best explicable on the basis of rules or constraints that are applicable to intermediate structures that differ in their order from surface structures. In this way, I will be giving arguments against invariant ordering, which appears to be the strongest extant version of the unordered base hypothesis. To the extent that we can push the need for ordering back toward the base we will be supporting the idea that order is needed in the base structures themselves. (A theory in which base structures are unordered and in which the ordering rules apply before transformations is obviously completely equivalent to the standard theory.) Then, I will take up some general arguments for the idea that base structures are ordered.

4.1.1 Metathesis. The simplest examples of reordering rules come from phonology and I will say little about them except to point them out. It is well known that metathesis occurs as a phonological process. Surely, no one would argue that the underlying phonological representations of formatives are unordered. But if they are ordered and if metathesis is a possible phonological rule, the invariant ordering hypothesis must make the peculiar claim that reorderings are allowed in phonology, where they are the exception and not the rule, but disallowed in syntax, where they are the rule rather than the exception.[9]

4.1.2 Pronouns and antecedents. Order plays a crucial role in all theories of pronoun-antecedent relationships, whether transformational (Ross 1967, Langacker 1969) or interpretive (Jackendoff 1972). The relevant constraints that must apply at some point in the derivation of sentences with pronouns and antecedents is that a pronoun may not both precede and command its antecedent. I don't know of any fully satisfactory theory of pronouns but I believe that there are facts which are best explained by the assumption that this constraint must apply at some point prior to surface structure and to structures that are not in their terminal order. Consider the sentence

    1. That Mary loves John is obvious to him.

This is a perfectly good sentence on the interpretation that the underlined items are stipulated coreferents. Similarly for (2):

    2. It is obvious to John that Mary loves him.

Not so with (3):

    3. *It is obvious to him that Mary loves John.

Now, consider sentences in which on a standard account some movement rule has applied to structures like (3):

    4. *John, it's obvious to him that Mary loves.

    5. *It's John that it's obvious to him that Mary loves.

6. *Who is it obvious to him that Mary loves?

It seems to me that these sentences are bad because their intermediate structures are bad ((3) for (4) and (5), a parallel source for (6)). (Cf. Postal 1972;fn.24) The obvious explanation for the ungrammaticality of (3) is the violation of the precedence-command constraint. But this condition is not violated in (4)-(6). The explanation thus depends crucially on a reordering of ordered structures. Another example of the same situation occurs with sentences of the sort discussed by Postal (1971:198):

*Cruel to Harry though he expects me to be, I will still help him.

Again, the ungrammaticality (on the intended reading) of this sentence seems to derive from the ungrammaticality of its source:

*Though he expects me to be cruel to Harry, ...

It is difficult to see how a theory with invariant ordering could explain these examples.

4.1.3 Postal's global constraint on pronominalization. Postal (1972) discusses a class of sentences in which a wh-phrase cannot be interpreted as antecedent to a pronoun, even though the wh stands to the left of the pronoun:

1. *To which actress's mother did the columnist report her victory? (= Postal's (25a))

Postal argues that such facts can only be explained on the basis of a constraint involving left-to-right ordering both before and after the application of the interrogative movement rule. If his account is correct, then it is necessary to have reordering rules. That these examples cannot be assimilated to the type discussed in the last section is shown by the fact that such sentences are perfectly grammatical if the movement does not take place:

2. Which columnist reported her victory to which actress's mother? (24a)[10]

4.1.4 Stress facts. Bresnan (1971) has shown that a wide variety of intonational facts of English can be explained on the assumption that the stress rules apply within the syntactic cycle. Among other things,

her hypothesis accounts for the difference in placement of main stress
and high pitch on examples like these:

                       /

1.   What has Helen written?

              /

2.   What books has Helen written?

But this account depends crucially on the application of the stress
rules to examples like (1) and (2) <u>before</u> the interrogative has been
shifted to the front of the sentence. Of course, the stress rules
themselves depend crucially on both the constituency and the ordering
of the phrases in question.

This situation seems to be quite general for languages that have
syntactically determined stress and intonation systems. In German, for
example, which shows differences in order between subordinate and insubordinate clauses, the stress relations remain the same among the
various constituents:

                   /

3.   Peter schrieb ein Buch.

                         /

4.   Ich weiss, dass Peter ein Buch schrieb.

Whether we believe that (3) or (4) represents more closely the underlying order of elements in German, we will want a uniform set of stress
rules to apply before the alternate order is established, and the most
general statement of the stress rules requires a linear ordering of
constituents. Similarly, Yehiel Hayon (in an unpublished paper) has
shown that the facts of Modern Hebrew stress can best be explained by
assuming that the stress rules apply to a specific ordering of constituents before the application of the rules that yield the relatively
free surface orders of Hebrew sentences.

4.1.5 <u>Chinese as an SOV language</u>. In a recent paper (with the same
title as this section), James Tai (1973) has shown that a wide variety
of facts in Chinese support the hypothesis that the underlying order
is verb-final and that the surface order is derived by an NP postposing
rule. Although Tai does not directly address the question whether the
facts could not also be accounted for by assuming an underlying order-

free structure, some of the facts he cites directly bear on the question of reordering. For example, with the sole exception of relative clauses, Chinese has no backwards pronominalization. Tai argues that the best explanation for this fact is that the relative clause follows its head in underlying structure (as argued in Bach 1965 and also Bach 1974), that pronominalization is always forward (from "left' to 'right') and that the order of relative clauses before their heads is derived by a (universal) relative clause preposing rule.[11]

4.1.6 <u>Order dependence of universal rules.</u> It is well known that languages cluster into relatively few order types with an interdependence of ordering characteristics (Greenberg 1963 and related work, Bach 1974, Chapter 11). Within a standard theory with ordered underlying structures, we can account for such facts by the assumption that certain universal transformations or transformation schemata are available and that the occurrence of a certain type of order allows the application of a certain universal rule (Bach 1971). For example, the relative clause preposing rule mentioned in the last section appears to depend on the verb-final character of the relative clause. Obviously, a theory with order-free structures and linearization rules can capture such facts by stating interdependencies among the ordering rules. What we need to do is examine the alternative accounts of such facts. To do this in detail would take far too much space and time, and indeed most of the work for such comparison has not been done. I would like to suggest that this area is one in which the most important testing of the several hypotheses we are considering here must be carried out. To see what is involved, let us look at one type of structure-dependent rule, Extraposition.

I propose that Extraposition is a universal rule or rule schema, which postposes a clause and which requires the presence of a clause-initial complementizer for its applicability. Postal (1974) has shown that sentences like (1) do not arise by Extraposition:

1. It's fun swimming.

Extraposition in English thus occurs with <u>For-to</u> and <u>that</u> complementizer's only. I claim it is no accident that it is just the two clause-initial complementizers which allow Extraposition. Typological support for this hypothesis comes from the fact that languages like Japanese, with clause-final complementizers, never seem to allow extraposition, while languages like Hindi do allow it (both being verb-final languages). In Turkish, it is just those clauses that have clause-initial complementizers (ki) that can extrapose. Kuno (1974) has shown that there is a functional reason for this fact and for the connection between complementizer fact position and the verb-final, verb-initial dichotomy. Languages seem to avoid or prohibit constructions in which nesting or self-embedding occurs in such a way that there is a string of subordinating particles (complementizers, prepositions). We can see a reflex of this prohibition in the unacceptability of sentences like (2):

2. That that he said those words is inconceivable is false.

We can give a straightforward account for this fact simply by assuming that the structure index of the universal extraposition rule includes a specification of the clause-initial complementizer. The claim made by such a theory is perfectly clear, we can falsify the theory by showing that some language has an extraposition rule which does not meet this condition. In an order-free theory facts like this must be accounted for by stating an implication between two ordering rules. So far, then there does not seem to be any way to choose between the two accounts.

But now consider how we would account for these facts within a grammar with unordered structures and ordering rules. Since Extraposition affects not just order but also dominance relations, it must be a regrouping rule ordered before any order has been defined on the structures. Since it occurs only with structures containing complementizers that will eventually be preposed, we must constrain this rule to operate only on clauses containing these items. But now it is just an accidental fact that these very same complementizers must be ordered initially (in all clauses). Surely, this is turning things on their head.

4.2. General considerations and conclusions. In the last sections I have mentioned a selection of facts of varied sorts that seem to be best accounted for in a theory which, like the standard theory, assumes that base structures are ordered. In this section I would like to make some general remarks about the problem.

Let us notice first that in the standard theory of the more or less interpretive sort, there is already a level of representation which is order-free in at least the sense that the order of elements is entirely independent of the order of surface structures, that is, in the semantic representations. The standard theory then entails the claim that with respect to the sorts of facts we considered in the last section, we will find differences between the behavior of structures with actual lexical items (which are ordered) and semantic structures of a parallel sort. This claim is borne out by facts like the following. Whatever the final explanation is for facts like those discussed by Postal in his crossover book, there is a sharp difference between the behavior of structures that are merely semantically related and those which are also lexically related. For example, buy and sell must be related semantically in such a way that (1) and (2) share some identical reading:

1. John sold the shares to Bill.

2. Bill bought the shares from John.

Now, if this relationship is shown by their derivation from a common syntactic (i.e., ordered) source, we should find differences like those in (3) and (4):

3. John stabbed himself.

4. ?John was stabbed by himself.

But there is no such difference in the pairs (5) and (6):

5. John sold the shares to himself.

6. John bought the shares from himself.

This differential argues against a theory in which the semantic representations are identical to base structures or one in which the base structures are order-free.

But if the semantic representations are not ordered, what distinguishes the standard theory from the theories with unordered base structures that we are considering here? As far as I can see, the only thing is the existence of a level of deep structure in which lexical elements are present in the structures and the claim made by the un-ordered base advocates that all ordering rules follow all other trans-formations. If the arguments I have given in the last section stand up (and I believe that a little scrounging could produce many other examples) then the order-free theories are disconfirmed.

As I indicated in the introduction to this paper (in the discus-sion of Shaumjan and others), proponents of order-free theories of the base often seem to take the view that there is something inherently implausible in the view that underlying structures have an abstract order that is related to the surface order of sentences. I have never been able to understand this feeling. It seems to me that there is something inherently linear in language. Order is obviously relevant in specifying the phonology of underlying elements ($\underline{top} \neq \underline{pot}$). More-over, order is obviously relevant in specifying the form of discourses. For example, the temporality of the events described in sequences of sentences is implied in the same way within sentences (this point is due to David Dowty), compare:

7. Mary got pregnant. Mary got married.

8. Mary got pregnant, and Mary got married.

Since order plays a role in units larger than sentences, and in the smallest constituents out of which sentences are constructed it seems perfectly natural to think that it plays a role all the way along in the representations of the sentences themselves. But to keep from merely begging questions we have to look for evidence, however difficult it may be to come by. On balance, it seems to me that the evidence so far supports the idea that underlying structures are ordered. But obviously the question must remain open until a whole lot more work has been done.

NOTES

1. Such a system is suggested in Peterson 1971.

2. Fillmore has apparently changed his mind and now considers the cases to be ordered (Fillmore 1971).

3. This was proved by Stanley Peters (personal communication).

4. This identification is incorrect, as far as I can tell, since I assume that Chomsky holds the view that even phonetic representation makes use of theoretical concepts not directly available to observation (see Chomsky and Halle 1968).

5. In several recent lectures, Postal has sketched a theory of grammar in which certain distinguished categories like Subject, Object, are used in order-free underlying structures.

6. Chomsky fails to note that 'free word order', if it exists is not captured by an M-system (or set system) since not all permutations are directly derivable from structures in which only sisters are freely permutable.

7. What is missing is an adequate characterization of the constraints on ordering rules, some notion of how derivations are constructed (cyclicity etc.) and a more detailed account of base categories. Sanders 1970, for example, makes free use of notions like subject, object etc. but I don't know whether they are informal characterizations or actual categories. Notice that a reformulation of base rules using the $\overline{X}$ notation (Chomsky 1970) or use of features in base categories changes radically the way in which generalizations can be captured.

8. Sanders (1970) claims that his theory makes stronger claims than the standard theory. But it seems to me that the two are incomparable. For example, the standard theory entails that two languages can differ in their base structures merely in the ordering of the elements, while Sanders' theory entails that they cannot.

9. Facts like those given in Bach 1968 or Langacker 1969b to support mirror-image rules do not support the idea that the structures on which they operate are unordered, but claim rather that significant generalizations can arise from bidirectional rules. I now have doubts about

the idea of mirror-image rules, except perhaps for anaphora rules, see Wasow 1972, Hankamer 1971.

10. All of the facts discussed in Postal 1971 would instantiate the claim that reorderings take place, if something essentially like the crossover condition is correct.

11. All analyses of languages in which the underlying order is different from the surface order count as evidence against invariant ordering (and derivatively order-free theories of the base), unless it can be shown that a better explanation is forthcoming from a theory in which no order is present in the base. I have not been convinced by the arguments given by Grover Hudson against my analysis of Amharic (Hudson 1972, cf. Bach 1970) but will deal with those questions in another place.

341

REFERENCES

Bach, Emmon. 1964. An introduction to transformational grammars. New York.

_____. 1968. Two proposals concerning the simplicity metric in phonology. Glossa 2:128-49.

_____. 1965. On some recurrent types of transformations. Georgetown University Monograph Series on Languages and Linguistics 18:3-18.

_____. 1970. Is Amharic an SOV language? Journal of Ethiopian Studies 8:9-20.

_____. 1971. Questions. Linguistic Inquiry 2:153-166.

_____. 1974. Syntactic theory. New York.

Bresnan, Joan. 1971. Sentence stress and syntactic transformations. Language 47:257-281.

Chomsky, Noam. 1957. Syntactic structures. The Hague.

_____. 1965. Aspects of the theory of syntax. Cambridge, Mass.

_____. 1970. Remarks on nominalization. In R. Jacobs and P. Rosenbaum, Readings in English transformational grammar (Waltham, Mass.).

Fillmore, Charles J. 1968. The case for case. In E. Bach and R. Harms, eds., Universals in linguistic theory (New York).

_____. 1971. Some problems for case grammar. Georgetown University Monograph Series on Languages & Linguistics 24:35-56.

Gleason, H.A., Jr. 1964. The organization of language: a stratificational view. Georgetown Monograph Series on Languages and Linguistics 17:75-95.

Gruber, Jeffrey. 1967. Topicalization in child language. In Reibel and Schane, 1969.

Hall, Barbara. 1964. Review of S.K. Shaumjan and P.A. Soboleva. Language 40:397-410.

Hankamer, Jorge. 1971. Constraints on deletion in syntax. Yale University dissertation.

Hudson, Grover. 1972. Why Amharic is not a VSO language. UCLA Studies in African linguistics. 3:1:127-166.

Jackendoff, Ray. 1972. Semantic interpretation in generative grammar. Cambridge, Mass.

Kiparsky, Paul. 1968. Linguistic universals and language change. In E. Bach and R. Harms, eds., Universals in linguistic theory (New York).

Klima, E.S. and Ursula Bellugi. 1966. Syntactic regularities in the speech of children. In J. Lyons and R.J. Wales, eds., Psycholinguistics Papers. (Edinburgh).

Kuno, Susumu. 1974. The position of relative clauses and conjunctions. Linguistic Inquiry 5:117-136.

Kuroda, S.-Y. 1969. Attachment transformations. In Reibel and Schane 1969.

Langacker, R. 1969a. Pronominalization and the chain of command. In Reibel and Schane 1969.

_____. 1969b. Mirror image rules. Language 45:575-598, 844-862.

Lyons, John. 1966. Towards a 'notional' theory of the parts of speech. Journal of linguistics 2:209-236.

Peterson, T.H. 1971. Multi-ordered base structures in generative grammar. CLS 7:181-192.

Postal, Paul M. 1971. Crossover phenomena. New York.

_____. 1972. A global constraint on pronominalization. Linguistic Inquiry 3:35-60.

_____. 1974. On raising. Cambridge, Mass.

Reibel, D.A. and Sanford Schane. 1969. Modern studies in English. Englewood Cliffs.

Ross, John R. 1967. On the cyclic nature of English pronominalization. In Reibel and Schane 1969.

Sanders, Gerald. 1969. Invariant ordering. Indiana U. Linguistics Club.

_____. 1970. Constraints on constituent ordering. Papers in Linguistics 2:460-502.

Shaumjan, S.K. 1964. Concerning the logical basis of linguistic theory. Proceedings of the ninth international congress of linguists, 155-160.

Slobin, Dan I. 1966. The acquisition of Russian as a native language. In F. Smith and G. Miller, eds., The genesis of language (Cambridge, Mass.).

Tai, James. 1973. Chinese as a SOV language. CLS 9:659-671.

Wasow, Thomas. 1972. Anaphoric relations in syntax. MIT dissertation.

THE PRESENTATIVE MOVEMENT

OR WHY THE IDEAL WORD ORDER IS V.S.O.P.

by

Robert Hetzron

In real life,[1] sentences are produced and uttered in a <u>context</u>. Most often they are part of a chain of sentences: the discourse, but they are always used in the context of reality. They presuppose certain pieces of knowledge on the part of the hearer: frequently knowledge about a specific situation in addition to trivial requirements such as familiarity with the language used and knowledge of life in general. The effects of context do contribute to the structuring of the sentence. There exist many linguistic phenomena formally describable within the sentence, but understandable only if the surrounding context is taken into consideration. Such an approach will show that some of the sacrosanct syntactic categories and distinctions are mere consequences of discourse-grammer requirements to which sentence-grammar has to adapt itself by whatever means available.

When we speak of context, we should not only take the <u>preceding</u> discourse and situation into account, but also the fact that any given sentence uttered may also contribute to the background of the <u>subsequent</u> sentences. A sentence may be restructured in such a manner that one component of it will be given a status of prominence in the short-range memory, so that it will dominate the immediate sequel to that particular utterance. The most obvious motivation for promoting an element to such a privileged status is that it is going to be mentioned or referred to in the subsequent discourse, but this is not an absolute necessity. There may be other reasons for it, such as providing an otherwise unexpressed contrast for what comes later, or, at the other extremity, it may urge the hearer/reader to remember the element in question--as a mere gesture (see (34) for Amharic), cf. fn. 7. I call the motivation for this type of prominence the <u>presentative function</u>.

The concept of presentative function overlaps a great deal with the theme/rheme analysis represented by a vast literature. I personally reject the notions of <u>theme</u> and <u>rheme</u> (or <u>topic</u> and <u>comment</u>, <u>thème</u> et <u>propos</u>) as the two ubiquitous major constituents of the sentence, at any stage of its derivation. It would take a long study to show the differences between this Functional Sentence Perspective approach (a term coined by V. Mathesius) and the one used in the present article. I will mention here just one point which is particularly important in connection with presentative. I am not operating with the concept of 'new information' as opposed to 'already known elements'. With Jespersen (1924:145) I feel that 'the "new information" is not always contained in the predicate [this term being used here in a sense equivalent to "rheme", R.H.], but it is always inherent in the <u>connexion</u> of the two elements, --in the fact that these two elements are put together...'. At issue is not the novelty of the element, but what the speaker intends to build up in the discourse (see examples (13) and (25) where this point is clearly illustrated).

I am thus suggesting that elements meant to be remembered in the subsequent context are given special prominence under the presentative function. Technically put, such elements will be endowed in the deep structure with a discourse-semantic feature [+presentative] which will have an effect on the derivational path. The clearest manifestation of the presentative function is that elements marked by it often end up, wherever they started from, in a sentence-final position. I am calling this transfer of presentative elements to the end of the sentence the <u>presentative movement</u>.

1. <u>Impersonal Quotations in English</u>

Bolinger (1970:67-8) has pointed out that in the use of quotations where the quotative verb is a passive (i.e., where the person(s) who said the sentence quoted is/are not specified), the quoted <u>that</u>-clause cannot always be initial:[2]

(1) (a) *<u>That it was an easy victory has been claimed</u>.

    (b) <u>It has been claimed that it was an easy victory</u>.

    (c) <u>That it was an easy victory has been pretty generally claimed, but I am of the contrary opinion</u>.

    (d) <u>It has been pretty generally claimed that it was an easy victory, and I am inclined to believe it</u>.

Constructions like (1b), with <u>it</u> as the surface-subject of the passive quotative verb, are always possible (cf. (1d)). On the other hand, leaving the <u>that</u>-clause in the subject position (*(1a) vs (1c)) is possible only if the quotative clause, elected to remain in final position, contains more than just trivial information. In (1a), the contribution of <u>was claimed</u> to communication is rather slim, --the actual speaker declines responsibility for the content of the quoted clause. This can be correctly expressed by the alternative (1b). Consequently, from an underlying (1a)--type structure, an extraposition rule derives (1b). This rule is obligatory if the quotative clause contains fairly neutral quotative expressions with little informational value. On the other hand, an underlying structure like (1c) may (though need not) undergo extraposition: (10d).

One can understand this behavior if one connects it with the presentative function. The linear order of the two clauses depends on what might be referred to later. The neutral <u>was claimed</u> is too weak to be subsequently used at all. Hence the incorrectness of *(1a) vs. the correctness of (1b). Only the quoted clause is likely to be referred to, is worth remembering for later use. On the other hand, further information, such as that the claim has been 'pretty general', upgrades the claim into a significant piece of information. Either one of the clauses, the quotative or the quoted one, may be slightly more important for the context.[3] (1c) contains a <u>but</u>-clause which clearly indicates that the 'quoted-quotative' order is justified because it is the general claim that is primarily challenged by the speaker. The main point is not that the speaker does not consider the victory easy (which is what is implied), but rather that he is against the consensus. In (1d), the order is 'quotative-quoted', and the <u>and</u>-clause added expresses the fact that the judgement about the victory, the content of the quoted clause, is adopted by the speaker. These fine distinctions, the relative weight of 'advancing an opinion' vs. 'the opinion itself', condition the surface-order of the two units. The clause marked [+presentative] will have now to assume the second, final position. Certain simple clauses are unable to assume the [+presentative] feature because they do not meet the prerequisites based on informational value, so that they have to give up their final position, even if they started out there, as in (1a).

In the case just presented, a whole clause is endowed with the feature [+presentative]. Furthermore, it seems that in impersonal quotations one of the elements must be presentative. Quotations are more than likely candidates for this, hence the normal order 'Quotative-Quoted', but in some cases the quotative clause has the feature: (1c). In the following, I am dealing with cases where the presentative element is a word or a phrase, i.e., a constituent of the sentence.

2.   The Expletive Preverbal Adverbs in Hungarian

Hungarian has a construction in which a static locative adverb (one of a set of six) cooccurring with a coreferential locative phrase in the same sentence is placed before the verb (Hetzron 1966). There is a restriction imposed on word-order in such constructions: the 'Expletive Adverb-Verb' group (EA-V henceforth) cannot be sentence-final (ibid., 4),[4] thus:

(2) (a)   A lány ott ült a szobában.   (Subj.-EA-V-Loc.)
          'The girl there[5] sat the room-in.'

    (b)   A szobában ott ült a lány.   (Loc.-EA-V-Subj.)
          'The room-in there sat the girl.'

    (c)   *A szobában a lány ott ült.   *(Loc.-Subj.-EA-V)
          'The room-in the girl there sat.'
          'The girl was sitting in the room.'   (see below)

How can this restriction on word-order be explained?

Let us examine the function of the expletive adverbs. First of all, they fulfill an aspectual function. The verb in (2a-b) is understood as being in the so-called 'actual aspect' (expressing that the event did indeed take place), while in the absence of the expletive adverb the aspect would be 'descriptive' (a neutral description, not factuality, see Hetzron 1966). Yet this is not enough to characterize the construction. The phrase that follows the EA-V group, the locative in (2a) and the subject in (2b), is given a type of focus and leaves a somewhat more memorable impression in the hearer/reader than the rest of the sentence. In (2a), he may visualize the 'room', while in (2b), even more clearly, the presence of 'the girl' constitutes the most important piece of information, --it may even come as a surprise. This is a pure manifestation of the presentative function.[6] In this light, the incorrectness of (2c) becomes completely understandable. The EA-V construction is a device for making the sentence-final phrase presentative.[7]

If no phrase follows this group, the use of the device is not justified, and the expletive adverb cannot be introduced.

To sum up, Hungarian has a special device for making an element presentative in sentences that contain a locative phrase. The element in question is brought, under the presentative movement, to a sentence-final position, and the verb is preceded by one of six static local adverbs coreferential with the cooccurring locative phrase.

3. Locative-Existential Sentences

3.1. Locative Sentences. The presentative movement illustrated in Sections 1 and 2 above is a very important language-universal that manifests itself in different manners throughout the languages of the world. One of the most spectacular attestations is in locative sentences which express the presence of a subject in a given place.

In many languages, when the subject of a locative sentence is definite, it stands before the locative phrase (Clark 1970, II). When it is indefinite, it is placed after the locative phrase (Kuno 1971). The pattern is (a) 'The man (is) in the house', (b) 'In the house (is) a man'. These are the respective glosses of the sentences below (always nonemphatic constructions):

(3) Arabic   (a)   ar-raǧulu fi:-l-bayti

           (b)   fi:l-bayti raǧulun

   Russian   (a)   čelov'ek v dom'e

           (b)   v dom'e čelov'ek

   Amharic   (a)   säwəyyäw bä-bet näw/allä

           (b)   bä-bet säw allä

   Turkish   (a)   adam evde(-dir)

           (b)   evde bir adam var

   Japanese (a)   otoko wa uchi ni iru

           (b)   uchi ni otoko ga iru

   Finnish   (a)   mies on talossa

        (b)   <u>talossa on mies</u>

Hungarian (a)   <u>az ember a házban van</u>

        ((b)   <u>a házban van egy ember</u>

Arabic has no present tense copula. Russian has a nonobligatory <u>est'</u> in (b) to make the indefiniteness of the subject explicit when it would otherwise not be so. In Amharic the copula is always sentence-final. With a definite subject: (a), either the general copula <u>näw</u> or the locative verb <u>allä</u> 'there is' may be used. The latter is the only possibility for an indefinite subject: (b). In Turkish, the copula is also final, but there are different copulas: <u>-dir</u> for (a) and <u>var</u> for (b). In (a), <u>-dir</u> may be omitted. Japanese has a final copula (<u>iru</u>, informal), <u>ni</u> is the locative particle. In Finnish, the copula <u>on</u> always assumes a medial position. For Hungarian, the nonemphatic order is given.[8] The copula <u>van</u> is always post-locative. We can see that independently of the copula placement, the pre-locative position of the definite subject and the post-locative position of the indefinite one are quite important.[9]

    In examples (3a), an already mentioned or otherwise known person's location is communicated. Examples (3b), on the other hand, are basically existential sentences (hence the special copula in Amharic, Russian and Turkish) which communicate the existence of an entity through indicating its emergence in a given place. I suggest that the 'Locative-Subject' order of (3b) is the result of a <u>presentative movement</u> that brings the originally initial subject (as in (3a)) to a sentence-final position. Thus the base-order in both (3a) and (3b) is 'Subject-Locative', but an indefinite subject, which is being introduced in this sentence, in order to be available for later mention in the discourse, is marked [+presentative] and is, therefore, brought to the end of the sentence, as in (3b). Copula-introduction follows the presentative movement, since in all the above languages its placement does not depend on whether the subject is definite or indefinite. It is always initial in Arabic,[10] always final in Amharic, Turkish and Japanese, always medial in Finnish and Russian (in the basic word-order) no matter which element stands first, and always post-locative in Hungarian, wherever the locative phrase happens to stand.

Note that in examples (3b) there is no explicit proof that the subject has ever been pre-locative in the base-structure. Such an assumption is suggested only by the improbability of needing two essentially
different deep structures for (3a) and (3b) that are identical except
for the definiteness of the subject, a feature that is attached to the
subject NP. Since the difference between (3a) and (3b) can be defined
in terms of one feature only, and in most languages the subject has to
be marked [±definite] anyhow, having two relative deep orders additionally
would be quite redundant. In languages like Russian and Finnish (fn. 9)
the feature in question is [±presentative]. Since definiteness/presenta-
tiveness seems to be the conditioning factor, word-order as a prime
cause, as a meaningful category all by itself, seems rather unlikely.
In fact, there <u>are</u> languages (not many) which have the same surface
order and same construction for both (a) and (b), such as Telugu where
the 'Determiner-Subject - Locative - Copula' order is the only nonemphatic one (<u>a</u>: 'that', <u>wokka</u> 'one/a', -<u>lo</u>: locative ending, same glosses
as in (3)):

(4) (a) <u>a: moga:ḍu inṭi-lo: unna:ḍu</u>

    (b) <u>wokka moga:ḍu inṭi-lo: unna:ḍu</u>

or the languages mentioned at the end of Table 3 in Clark 1970.

There still remains the question of which one of the two, (3a) or
(3b), represents the unmarked order, --whether a definite subject has to
be fronted or an indefinite one has to be postposed (through a presentative movement). Since (3a) expresses location, and (3b) existence-
though-location, (3a) seems to be the unmarked term from which (3b) is
to be derived.

3.2. <u>Indefinite subject fronting</u>. The tendency of delaying the mention of indefinite subjects shown in 3.1. is true, in many languages,
not only for copula constructions, but also for sentences containing
one of the verbs of <u>existence</u>, <u>emergence</u> or <u>creation</u> as their predicate.
Here, of course, the axis of the postposing movement will be the verb,
S-V → V-S, and not the locative phrase. Such a Verb-Subject order is
quite normal for newly introduced elements (marked indefinite) in the
so-called 'free word-order languages', whereas definite subjects may
occupy other positions (I give here the unmarked orders):

(5) Modern Hebrew (a) <u>ba iš</u> (slightly literary, vs. colloquial
<u>iš exad ba</u>)
'came man' ('A man came', 'There came a man')

(b) <u>ha-iš ba</u>
'the-man came'

Hungarian (a) <u>Jött egy ember</u>, but *<u>Egy ember jött</u>[11]
'came a man'   'a man came'

(b) <u>Az ember jött</u> or <u>Jött az ember</u>[12]
'the man came'   'came the man'

One may even have a semantic distinction based on word-order according
to whether the presentative reading is intended:

(6) Russian (a) <u>žil čelov'ek</u>
'lived man' ('There lived a man')

(b) <u>čelov'ek žil</u>
'man lived' ('The man was alive')

Hungarian (a) <u>Élt egy ember</u>
'lived a man' ('There lived a man')

(b) <u>Az ember élt</u> but *<u>Élt az ember</u>[13]
'the man lived'   'lived the man'
('The man was alive')

This means that in some cases in some languages, indefinite subjects of
verbs of emergence, etc., also have to undergo presentative movement,
though, in many instances, with less compulsion than in the locative
sentences of the (3) type.

Verbs of emergence, etc., may also enter into a '<u>there-Verb-Indef.
Subj.</u>' construction in English,[14] which is one way of achieving a V-S
order:

(7) (a) <u>There lived/arrived/stood a man there.</u>

(b) <u>The man lived/arrived/stood there.</u>

(c) *<u>There lived/arrived/stood the man there.</u>

Yet, in the proper context, English may also have

(8) <u>A man came</u> (e.g., <u>yesterday</u>)

which is an absolutely correct sentence and seems to defy the pressures
of the presentative function. The following examples will illustrate
why A man came should also come from a deeper (post-presentative movement) V-S construction *Came a man, as in (5a), through a subject-fronting process that is inspired by the general preference for an S-V order
in English. This means that if the concept of depth is admitted, with
the Generative-Transformational school of linguistics, into the Grammar,
the English situation is not that different from Hebrew, Hungarian or
Czech (Firbas 1966, esp. exx. 12-13) where the V-S is also the surface
order:

(9) (a)   A girl arrived whom I found very attractive.

    (b)   *The girl arrived whom I found very attractive.[15]

    (c)   There arrived a girl whom I found very attractive.

    (d)   *A vase broke that I inherited from my grandmother.[16]

    (e)   *The vase broke that I inherited from my grandmother.

    (f)   *There broke a vase that I inherited from my grandmother.

Example (9a) shows that there can be discontinuity between a relative
clause and its headnoun with verbs of emergence, if the headnoun is an
indefinite subject. It is not enough to have an indefinite subject, the
verb has to be one of the existential or inchoative-existential ones,
cf. *(9d). With definite subjects there can be no discontinuity at all,
*(9b) and *(9e). The sentences with verbs of emergence also offer an
alternative with initial there and V-S order, so that the continuity
between headnoun and relative clause is maintained (9c). This there
construction can only be used with verbs expressing existence, appearance, coming into the field of perception, the same ones that allow discontinuity between indefinite subject headnoun and relative clause:
(9a) and (9c), vs. *(9f).

The grammaticality of (9a) vs. the ungrammaticality of *(9b) can be
understood only if we assume an intermediary stage "Came a girl whom ...,
where the condition of contiguity between headnoun and relative clause
is still met,[17] followed by either subject-fronting (confined to the
noun only): (9a), or by the introduction of an expletive there: (9c).

356

This type of discontinuity is attested in many languages. The following is an illustration of the same phenomenon in slightly formal modern Israeli Hebrew:

(10) (a) <u>yešno talmid bauniversita ašer meolam lo haya bekoncert.</u>
'There-is student in-the-university Rel. never-in-the-past not was in-concert'
('There is a student at the university who has never been to a concert')

(b) *<u>Hatalmid bauniversita ašer meolam lo haya bekoncert.</u>
'The-student in-the-university Rel. never-in-the-past not was in-concert'

Sentence (10b), with its definite subject, is incorrect as a complete sentence (though it is acceptable as an NP containing a relative clause: 'The student who...'). This suggests that (10a) must have also had the order <u>bauniversita talmid</u>... 'in-the-university student...' on a deeper level.

3.3. <u>Initial particle</u>. Some languages achieve the V-S order for presentative (indefinite) subjects by introducing a special initial particle designed for this construction. In English (<u>there</u>) and Dutch (<u>er</u>), the initial particle is of a locative origin.[18] In French and German, on the other hand, the initial particle is a third person singular pronoun, neuter (<u>es</u>) in German (cf. fn. 22 below) and masculine (<u>il</u>) in French.

In 1970, R. Martin devoted an article to the transformational treatment of extraposition in French. His cases of optional extrapositions (leaving the obligatory ones aside here) are all instances of the presentative movement. Here is a contrastive example. (11b/d) are respectively derived from (11a/c) through an <u>impersonal transformation</u>:

(11) (a) <u>Un train passe toutes les heures.</u> (Martin 178)
'A train passes all the hours' (= '...every hour')

(b) <u>Il passe un train toutes les heures.</u>
'It passes a train all the hours'

(c) <u>Une loi d'amnistie sera votée bientôt.</u> (386)
'A law of-amnesty will-be voted soon'

(d)   Il sera voté bientôt une loi d'amnistie.
      'It will-be voted soon a law of-amnesty'

Such an optional impersonal transformation is limited to those cases
where (i) the subject is indefinite (379-80)[19] but individual (386),[20]
and (ii) where the verb is either intransitive and expresses sudden
appearance, existence or non-existence,[21] or a passive action (but not
of state or result). These extraposed passives are most often found in
official texts, the wording of laws, etc.

(12) (a)   *Il dégelait la plupart des rivières. (381)
           'It thawed the majority of rivers' (verb not existential)

     (b)   *Il passera ce train. (380)
           'It will-pass this train' (definite subject)

     (c)   *Il sera brisé ce vase.
           'It will-be broken this vase' (passive of result)

All this fits perfectly into the framework of presentative: announcing the existence or appearance of an element to be referred to
later. This device is not appropriate for presentativizing already-
known elements (i.e., reintroducing them as important items to be used
in later discourse), but this is a language- and construction-specific
limitation. Yet this phenomenon should not be regarded as a way of
placing the element containing the new information to the end of the
sentence. Martin himself points out (384) that in some special cases,
elements whose existence has already been acknowledged may appear in
such constructions (fn. 1. on p. 384):

(13) (a)   Il reste ce dernier problème.
           'It [there] remains this last problem'

     (b)   Il manque le dernier livre.
           'It lacks the last book'
           ('The last book is missing')

Here (where the definiteness is by entailment, cf. fn. 13), it is quite
clear that the construction is used in a reintroductory fashion. (13a)
probably precedes the discussion of the last problem (which may have
already been mentioned in the beginning, along with the other problems).
(13b) calls the attention to the last item of a known set of books,

still missing, on which the attention should now be concentrated (e.g.,
a search should be made for it). Note that for the latter verb, 'Subj.
+ manque' is also acceptable, but 'Il manque + transposed subject' is
more frequent because stating that something is missing is usually a
call for action: searching, replacing, etc.

The fact that passives of action may also enter into this construction clearly indicates that if its use with intransitive verbs of emergency and with these passives have something in common, the clue is not
novelty of the transposed subject. The limitations on the construction
may be slightly idiosynchratic and arbitrary, but the presentative function is characteristic of all the uses.

Finally, Martin points out (388) that this impersonal construction
facilitates the 'right-hand side expansion' (Il arrivera un malheur qui...
et qui...) which is the most obvious and tangible manifestation of the
presentative.

3.4. Presentational Construction in English. English also has an 'adverbial inversion that characterizes the type of sentence that might be
called presentational, in which the referent of the subject is introduced
on the scene,...' (Bolinger 1971:584). Some of his examples are ((14i)
was suggested by A. Bell):

(14) (a) Round the bend came the train.

(b) Up jumped the rabbit.

(c) On the stump sat a great big toad.

(d) In power at that time was a three-man junta.

(e) Out of the morass had risen a hand.

(f) Rounding the bend was a runaway locomotive.

(g) Standing there was my brother.

(h) Staring at me were two beady little eyes.

(i) Staring, staring were two beady little eyes.

Bolinger has established that the initial position may be taken only by
the adverbial or by an -ing phrase in the progressive. Let us compare
the above sentences with the following (also from Bolinger 1971):

(15) (a) *Standing was my brother. (cf. (19g))

(b) ?Staring were two beady little eyes. (cf. (19h))

*(15a) would only indicate posture. The addition of <u>there</u> in (14g)
implies appearance on the scene. Likewise, ?(15b) would be a statement
about some animal looking, but a further <u>at me</u>, (14h), implies the
speaker's sudden noticing. The repetition of the verb in (14i) also
makes the visualization of the scene more obvious. The acceptability
of these constructions involves a 'requirement of vividness' (Bolinger,
<u>ibid.</u>, 584). This is, again, a clear cut instance of the presentative
movement.

4. Cataphoric Predications in English

A great deal of attention has been given recently to the construction called 'pseudo-cleft' (16a/c/e) and to its relationship with the
usual expression of emphasis: 'cleft-sentences' (16b/d/d'/f):

(16) (a) What I saw there was a pink elephant.

(b) It was a pink elephant that I saw there. (not the relative!)

(c) What the pink elephant was looking for was a comfortable zoo.

(d) It was a comfortable zoo that the pink elephant was looking
for.

(d') It was for a comfortable zoo that the pink elephant was looking.

(e) The one that came out of the greenhouse was the gardener.

(f) It was the gardener that came out of the greenhouse.

Here the so-called 'pseudo-cleft' constructions are absolutely distinct
in appearance from cleft sentences. What connects the two is the fact
that they both contain a focused element that may be more important from
the point of view of communication than the rest of the sentence. In
view of the interpretation I am proposing below, I shall henceforth call
the structures represented by (16a/c/e), where the focused element is in
the final position, 'Cataphoric sentences', while retaining the term
coined by Jespersen: 'Cleft sentences' for (16b/d/d'/f).

Akmajian (1971) has stated that homologous cataphoric and cleft
sentences 'are synonymous, share the same presuppositions, answer the

same question' and proposed that 'the cleft sentence is syntactically
derived from the pseudo-cleft [=cataphoric, R.H.] sentence by a rule
which extraposes the initial clause of the pseudo-cleft sentence to the
end of the sentence' (149). His only substantial argument is based on
the limited agreement (always in number but not always in person) between
emphasized nonthird person subjects and the verb of the larger clause
(17a/b), where the (11a) pattern fits the agreement in the corresponding
cataphoric construction (17c):

(17) (a) It is me who is responsible. (10a)

    (b) It is I whom am responsible. (10b)

    (c) The one who is responsible is me.

In (17a), the use of the oblique pronoun leads to a third person agreement on the verb, but in (17b) the subject pronoun makes the proper subject agreement preferable.

    I disagree with Akmajian's thesis. In the first place, there is no
reason to assume that agreement precedes the establishment of linear
order for cleft and cataphoric constructions. The existence in Old
English of the agreement pattern (expressed in modern words):

(18) It am I who is responsible (Jespersen 1961, 25.4)

and (17b) above (which should not be neglected just because it is judged
pedantic today) show that the concordial mechanism involved here is much
more complicated. It so happens that (17a), the preferred form in modern
American English, matches the cataphoric agreement (17c), but it is not
the sole representative of cleft constructions. In Old English, a language with much freer word-order, the agreement is quite regular, like
in other constructions. I is the subject of be in the cleft-clause, and
the headword of the pseudo-relative which imposes agreement on the other
verb (here only coincidentally a copula) is it. Today there are other
principles governing agreement in cleft constructions. In the cleft-
clause itself, the agreement is imposed on be by the preceding element,
the invariable it,[22] and in the pseudo-relative clause we merely find
one more manifestation of the conflict between a nonthird person headnoun and the verb of a subjectal relative (also real relative) clause,
cf. Bloch, forthc.

Another point of a formal nature is that the cleft construction
allows prepositional phrases for the focused element (16'd), while the
cataphoric one does not:

(19) *What the pink elephant was looking was for a comfortable zoo.

(cf. Schachter 1973:28 (26b)), though this argument may be countered by
stating (cf. Harries 1973:133) that in an underlying (19) the fronting
of the focused element, which leads to (16d'), is obligatory.

Yet one may challenge Akmajian's hypothesis on much more important
grounds. In spite of the similarities, the cleft and cataphoric constructions are not always freely interchangeable and hence are not
synonymous. Consider the following:

(20) (a) What I want is a good clean-up job.

      (b) It is a good clean-up job that I want.

(20a) may be an instruction given by an employer of a supervisor,[23]
either as a first direction or as part of a set of instructions, whereas
(20b) could not be an unprecedented instruction nor part of a set of
instructions. The purpose of (20a) is to trigger a reaction, the compliance with the instruction, a typically presentative function. This
is what justifies the term 'cataphoric'. In general, cataphoric sentences may be first-instance communications, with no true presuppositions,[24] while in a cleft sentence, the second, pseudo-relative part is
presupposed (mentioned or inferred earlier), and the focused element
comes to fill a gap in an incomplete presupposition (Hetzron 1971a, 1.4).
In (20a), both my wanting something and the actual object of my wanting
may be announced for the first time, but in (20b) my wanting something
is known in advance and is no novelty at this stage and this sentence
only specifies the true identity of that 'something'.

From another angle, imagine a set of instructions (e.g., 'clean up
the room, open the windows, sweep the floor', etc.) and a summarizing
sentence, either one of the following:

(21) (a) It is this that I want! (relative)

      (b) What I want is this!

(21a) may appear either before or after the set of instructions. (21b), on the other hand, may appear <u>only</u> <u>before</u> such a set. This clearly shows that the final position for <u>this</u> in (21b) is justified by the presentative function. This makes it distinct from (21a) which, although containing a focus element, is not presentative and is thus neutral as to the relative position of the reference for <u>this</u>.

The semantic potentials of an element focused initially in a cleft construction (22a) and of one focused finally in a cataphoric configuration (27b) are not identical. Let us take Harries' examples (her (90) and a modified version of her (96) for French and Hungarian):

(27) French   (a)   <u>Celui qui est venu est François.</u>

              (b)   <u>C'est François qui est venu.</u>

   Hungarian   (a)   <u>Az aki jött, Ferenc volt.</u>
                    'That who came, Frank was'

              (b)   <u>Ferenc volt az, aki jött.</u>
                    'Frank was that, who came'

   English   (a)   <u>The one who came was Frank.</u>

              (b)   <u>It was Frank who came.</u>

The cataphoric sentences (22a) are ambiguous. They either tell who the newcomer is, or, as a secondary reading, merely announce his name: 'is' ~ 'is called'. In the cleft examples (22b), only the first, concrete meaning is acceptable. Likewise, in the cataphoric (16e) <u>the gardener</u> may either refer to a specific person, or it may introduce the gardener 'That's the one'. The cleft (16f) only the specific reading is acceptable. Compare further the following sentences (also from Bolinger, private letter):

(23)   (a)   <u>What I want is that book.</u>

      (b)   <u>It's that book that I want.</u>

(23b) may be a sequel to a statement expressing that 'I want something', or to one saying that 'I want a book', where the selection of a specific book is announced. (23a), on the other hand, can only follow 'I want something', and not 'I want a book' for the selective sense. In other words, <u>book</u> may be presupposed in (23b) and only <u>that</u> is the added element, but in (23a) <u>book</u> must also be presented as a new item.

The paired example of (20) shows that the cataphoric construction may have a _wider_ application: either first or nonfirst communication. The cleft is always nonfirst. (21) suggests that the cataphoric construction has _narrower_ application from another point of view. The focused element may not refer to preceding items, whereas in a cleft construction it may. (22) also indicates that from a third point of view the focused element in a cataphoric construction may have a _wider_ range of meaning: concrete and nonconcrete, while in a cleft sentence only the concrete acceptation is correct. In (23) the semantic range is _narrower_ in cataphora, no selective reading, though in a cleft both readings are possible. All this would indicate that the two constructions are not only not synonymous, but one is not part of the other. Each have a domain of their own where one of them may appear, and not the other: cataphoric construction as first-instance communication and cleft constructions as a final summary of an enumeration.

Technically, it would still be possible to derive cleft constructions from cataphoric ones, but this would require a cumbersome maze of conditions, making the transformation obligatory in some cases (when the focused element refers to preceding items) or blocking it in others (when no true presupposition is present), while leaving it optional in most cases. I doubt that such a technical juggling would be worth its while. And such a description would make all these conditions appear to be capricious and unmotivated.

What is then the source of cataphoric sentences? The usual treatments (cf. fn. 27 below) differ in some respects, but they all would have a high Sentence-node which will also appear as the highest node on the surface, and the predicate of which is, or contains, the focused element. This is basically wrong. There actually exists a construction of this pattern, quasi-homonymous with the cataphoric one. Compare:

(24)   (a)   What I saw there was a pink elephant.

       (b)   What I saw there is a pink elephant.

(24b) with its differing tenses is a possible sentence meaning that the speaker had seen something, but only now can he identify it as being a pink elephant: 'That thing [that I saw there] is [now I know] a pink elephant'. Note that this reading may also be drawn from (24a) as a result of a type of consecutio temporum arrangement, as in Yesterday I saw a girl. She was beautiful. Here was does not mean that she is no more beautiful, but reflects the tendency of presenting observations about lasting facts or properties in the tense of the observation. Now, while both (24a) and (24b) can render the 'now I know' acceptation, (24a), with absolutely obligatory agreement of tenses (but not aspect! '...had seen...was...') is the only possibility for a cataphoric sentence where no practical time-lag is understood between the content of the subject clause and the addition of the surface predicate. Since there are two homostructural, but distinct, constructions in (24a), one being the same as (24b), two different base structures have to be posited for them. See further fn. 27.

A simpler representation may be obtained by assuming the following. Both constructions, cleft and cataphora, as instances of focusing (mise en relief, Hervorhebung) which elevate the communicational importance of an element above the level of the rest of the sentence. Yet the motivation for such focusing may be varied. When an element is focused because it fills a gap in previous knowledge, it is brought forward[25] in a cleft construction or another type of emphatic construction. When the focusing is necessary for paving the way for later use of the same element in the discourse or for a pragmatic reaction, the cataphoric construction that moves the focused element to the end of the sentence is created. This latter type of justification is the presentative function. It does not necessarily exclude reference to the preceding context, e.g., the frequent expression:

(25) What I meant is...

where an earlier statement is rephrased or commented upon. But the points is here that by offering the comment, the clearer interpretation of his intended meaning, at the end, the speaker wants to make the present formulation of his thinking better remembered, which would automatically erase any earlier misconstruing of his statements.

We have seen that semantically the cataphoric predication is also a case of presentative function, and is thus the result of a presentative movement. The formal device used here is predication. It may be the case that cataphoric predication is mainly used in bound word-order languages with strict Subject-Predicate order, where bringing the presentative element to a sentence-final position would violate constraints on word-order.[26] The compromise such languages have to reach between the constraints on surface order and the presentative function/ movement is making the presentative element a surface predicate, which entitles it to a sentence-final position, and the rest of the sentence is reorganized accordingly so as to accommodate this type of predication through the introductory elements What.../The one who..., etc. In other words, in my opinion an element marked [+presentative] is lifted out of the sentence and moved to the end, and the rest is rearrangement of the structure.[27] The fact that the introductory element shows [α human] agreement with the sentence-final element, what... [-human] vs. The one who... [+human] provides a significant argument against the assumption that not only is the higher predication present in the deep structure (cf. (24) and discussion), but that the presentative element has never been lifted out from the sentence (Postal 1971:236, Hudson MS:26). Surely, one may suggest that the [+human] agreement is imposed on the initial element at some later stage of the derivation, and the [+human] value of the introductory pronominal element is not specified in the base structure, but then why such an agreement is necessary at all, if not to anticipate some data about the presentative element (for a similar argument, see (29-30))? Why not use a neutral What always in the beginning of the sentence, like Somali wah (see below)?[28] Such an anticipatory agreement may even go farther. Compare:

(36) I noticed something in the water.

What was swimming there was a dog.

What was floating there was a log.

The use of the verb 'swim' predicts a living being. These pieces of information offered in anticipation suggest that the reason for delaying the uttering of the agreement-imposing element is to create tension, curiosity, and such a delaying results from a shifting rather than from an original configuration.

A clear illustration of the principle that cataphoric predication is a device for circumventing word-order constraints is found in Somali (Andrzejewski 1974 and personal communication) a strict SOV language. The following is a neutral sentence:

(27) áhmed la ág waan ú diibay.
      'Ahmed money Sg.1c.particle Dative I-gave'
      ('I gave money to Ahmed')

Now, Somali has a way of emphasizing elements through a postposed
particle b-, but it still feels the need for expression presentativeness. It can achieve this by putting the presentative element to the
final (i.e., predicate) position and having the sentence be preceded by
wah 'entity, thing, person', which makes the main predication into an
apparent verbless sentence with zero copula, in conformity with the
Subject-Predicate order requirement (Andrzejewski 1964:140-1):

(28) (a) wáhaan la'ág ú diibay áhmed (Žolkovskiĭ 1971:216)
           'thing/person-I money Dative I-gave Ahmed'
           ('The one I gave money to was Ahmed')

      (b) wáhaan ahmed ú diibay la'ág
           'thing/person-I Ahmed Dative I-gave money'
           ('What I gave to Ahmed was money')

Here we should heed Žolkovskiĭ's arguments against a simplified analysis of this construction as a basic verbless sentence (1971:194-7). The
two most important points he raises are: (i) when the subject is final,
the verb still agrees with it and not with the apparent subject wah:

(29) (a) wáha yimi madahaweynaha
           'thing/person HE-came president-the'
           ('The one who came was the president')

      (b) wáha timi ergeda
           'thing/person SHE-came delegation [a feminine noun!]'
           ('What came was the delegation')

This would also suggest, along the lines of the argument above, that the
subject was moved out of its original position. (ii) The choice of the
case-marking preverbal particle also indicates foreknowledge of the
final Noun Phrase in some cases:

(30) (a) wúhuu tegey bur'o
           'thing/person-he he-went Buro' ('The place he went was Buro')

      (b) wúhuu ú tegey áhmed

'thing/person-he Dative he-went Ahmed'
('The one he went to was Ahmed')

In other instances one may say that the verb predicts the case-marker used with it. Here, however, the target of 'going' is marked by zero (~Accusative) when it is a place and by a Dative when it is a person. The use of u in (30b) indicates preliminary knowledge of the [+human] value of the target, which thus must precede the verb on a deeper level.

In his recent work, Andrzejewski (1974) also favors the view that this construction, that he labels now 'anticipative sentences', is a derived structure, on a par with emphasis. For its meaning, he offers the following statement (personal communication) '[the anticipative sentences have] exactly the same meaning as the corresponding baa [= emphatic] sentences [except that they are] more likely to occur when a completely new subject is mentioned. These are favored structures in news bulletins on the radio, also when announcing news in private and when expressing one's wishes in a shop'.

To sum up, the cataphoric predication is thus a device for circumventing constraints on word-order. It is the only way in Somali to bring the presentative element to the end of the sentence. Arguments based on agreement have been given to show that an actual movement must be assumed here and not an original final position. Such a movement is justified by the presentative function semantically present in these constructions.

The cataphoric predication is one device for avoiding word-order conflicts. Amharic uses another one for the same purpose, presented in the next Section.

5. The Amharic Resumptive Pronouns

Amharic exhibits a 'redundant' use of complement pronoun suffixes referring to a case-marked definite nominal complement, cooccurring in the same clause.[29] The following example is based on Getatchew 1971:106:

(31) (a) almaz betun bämäträgyaw ṭärrägäčč
'Almaz house-the-Acc. with broom-the she-swept'

(b) betun almaz bämäträgyaw ṭärrägäččəw
'house-the-Acc. Almax with-broom-the she-swept-it'

(c) bämäṭrägyaw almaz betun ṭärrägäččəbbät
    'with-broom-the Almaz house-the-Acc. she-swept-with-it'
    'Almaz [girl's name] swept the house with a broom'

(31a) contains no such resumptive pronoun. In (31b), the object is
fronted and is referred to by a final object pronoun (though the object
could also stand after the subject, which would practically result in
the same word-order as in (31a). In (31c), the instrumental is fronted
and is referred to by a pronoun at the end of the verb. (Here again,
the instrumental noun could very well stand right after the subject:
Almaz bämäṭrägyaw betun ṭärrägäččəbbät).

The function of these resumptive pronouns has baffled many a scho-
lar. Though they can only be used with definite complements, such definite complements do not require their presence: (36a). Note that the
definiteness has to mean reference to specific objects (Getatchew 1971:
102-3). Thus the sentence

(37) almaz mäṣhafun gäzzaččəw
    'Almaz book-the-Acc. she-bought-it'
    ('Almaz bought the book')

is grammatical only if 'the book' refers to a specific copy, and not to
any copy of a given book. Getatchew further showed that the NP to be
recalled by a resumptive pronoun has to be either sentence-initial (as
in (31b-c)) or appear right after the subject and/or time-adverbial,
i.e., VP-initial. It cannot occupy any other position. In other words,
in a structure $[NP_{subject}-NP_1-NP_2-V]$, with this surface order, only NP_1
can be recalled by a pronoun, and never NP_2. An alternative to this
order is $[NP_1-NP_{subject}-NP_2-V]$, as in (31b-c).

Getatchew has shown that in the resumptive construction the NP
recalled by a pronoun constitutes the 'relevant piece of information'.
To demonstrate this, he designed a test frame. If the verb in (31a-b-c)
is preceded by the particle kä-, the sentences become conditional if-
clauses. Now, with (31a-b-c) kä- as protases, the following types of
apodoses may be used:

(33) (a) gänzäb əsäṭatalläh^W
        'I will give her money'

(b) nəṣuh yəhonall
'it [= the house] will be clean'

(c) yəssäbbärall
'it [= the broom] will be broken'

Apodosis (33a), having the entire content of the protasis clause as reference, is grammatical after any of kä- (31a/b/c). On the other hand, apodosis (33b) picks up 'the house' as its topic, and is grammatical only after kä- (31b) which has a resumptive pronoun referring to the same 'house'. Likewise, apodosis (33c), dealing with the fate of the 'broom', can only be used after kä- (31c) where the resumptive pronoun agrees with the same 'broom'. In sum, the grammatical combinations are (with kä- added to the protasis verbs) (31a)-(33a), (31b)-(33a), (31c)-(33c), (31b)-(33b), (31c)-(33c), and nothing else. This suggests that the element recalled by the pronoun is the one likely to be talked about in the subsequent discourse, here the adjacent apodosis clause. Or conversely, if a sentence$_2$ communicates something about an element represented by an NP (in any syntactic function, not just subject as in (33a/b/c)) which has occurred in a function other than subject in the preceding sentence$_1$, one must have in sentence$_1$ a resumptive pronoun referring to the element to be mentioned later in sentence$_2$. If this element is the subject of sentence$_1$, there is no need for a special resumptive pronoun, since the subject imposes an obligatory agreement on the verb anyhow. But if this element is a complement in sentence$_1$, - after the subject-ending of the verb, there will be a complement pronoun in the proper case, number and gender in agreement with it.

This phenomenon is a straightforward manifestation of the presentative function. The purpose of the pronominal resumption is to point forward in the discourse.

The foregoing discussion has not really shown the justification for the resumptive pronoun in the combinations kä- (31b/c)-(33a). As in the presentative elsewhere, this definition should be interpreted somewhat broadly. The anticipatory focusing meaning manifested itself in its highest intensity in Getatchew's conditional constructions kä- (31b)- (33b) and kä- (31c) where the element recalled is literally used in the apodosis. Yet the semantic potential offered by the pronominal resumption may not be taken up in the next sentence in many cases. The reason

for it may be somewhat less tangible. At the other end of the scale,
the lowest intensity is found in acknowledgements found in the introduction of many books, following the pattern:

(34) lä-... məsgannaye aqärbəllaččäwalläh[W]
      'to'... my-thanks I-present-to-him[polite]-Aux.'
      ('I express my gratitude to...')

Here the person thanked will most probably never be mentioned again in
the book. The use of the resumptive pronoun constitutes a polite gesture on the part of the author suggesting that, while reading the book,
that person's gracious contribution should be borne in mind.

We have seen that the exponent of the presentative function in
Amharic is a case-marked resumptive pronoun referring to a case-marked
complement cooccurring in the same clause. In other words, in a presentative construction, the same NP is represented twice in the same
clause, the first time as a substantive and the second, quite normally,
in a pronominal shape. One may then wonder what the origin of this
reduplication may be.

On the surface, Amharic is an SOV language. Only clitic pronouns
may be postverbal.[30] To explain the emergency of the reduplicated presentative construction, I suggest the following. On a certain deep level
where the verb already occupies a sentence-final position, a transformation brings the element marked by the feature [+presentative] to a post-
verbal position. This, however, is going to be in conflict with the
strict requirement of the verb being in the final position. Therefore,
the postverbal NP, if not pronominal in the first place, is copied
either to a sentence-initial (pre-subject but after temporal adverbs!)
or to a VP-initial (immediately post-subject or after Subject-Temporal-,
but preceding all the other complements) position, and the second, original postverbal occurrence of the NP is pronominalized (cf. Getatchew
1971:109):

(35) (a) Amharic Presentative Movement

$$[_S \ X \ [_{VP} \ Y \ \begin{array}{c} NP \\ [presentative] \end{array} \ Z] \qquad]$$

| | 1 | 2 | 3 | 4 | 5 |
| | 1 | 2 | ∅ | 4 | 3+5 |

(b) Fronting-Copying

$$[_S \qquad X \quad VP \qquad \underset{[\text{-pronominal}]}{NP} \qquad]$$

		1	2	3	4	→
α	:	4+1	2	3	4	or
β	:	1	2	4+3	4	

(c) Pronominalization

$$[\text{-pronominal}] \to [\text{+pronominal}] \ / \ X \ NP_i \ Y \ [_{NP_i}\underline{\qquad}]$$

The symbol NP includes the case-marker complex (Hetzron 1970b).
Cases are spelled out after all of (40), since the case-spelling rules
are sensitive to the feature [±pronominal] (ibid.) - the adnominal and
the adpronominal cases do not have the same distribution, and the nominal and pronominal occurrences of the same NP will each carry their own
case-markers.[31]

In (40a) the VP-bracket is necessary to show that the subject and
the time-adverbials are excluded. Only complements are involved. This
transformation brings the presentative NP, from wherever it stands in
the VP-bracket, to a VP-final = S-final position. In fact, it lifts it
out of the VP. (40b) copies this NP to either the initial sentence-
boundary (option α) or to the initial VP-boundary (option β), creating
thus a double occurrence of the noun. After the realization of (40b),
there will be four nodes directly dominated by S, according to the respective orders: $[_S NP_{pres} - NP_{subj} - VP - NP_{pres}]$ or $[_S NP_{subj} - NP_{pres}$
$- VP - NP_{pres}]$ where NP_{pres} is the same both times. (40c) is a pronominalization rule based on the absolute identity of the nouns. Specification of S-brackets is superfluous here.

The fact that the NP referred to by the resumptive pronoun must
occupy a pre- or post-subject position, whereas the same NP with no pronominal resumption has no such limitations, shows that the NP with resumption had been removed from its original slot and was subsequently reposi-
tioned. This seems to me a serious argument in favor of the existence
of movement rules. For the historical counterpart of this movement,
see Section 7 below.

6. The Position of Hungarian Complements

In Hungarian, a noun may occur in one of three degrees of 'definite-ness', expressed by (i) lack of article, (ii) an indefinite article, (iii) a definite article.[32] The definite article indicates that the element marked by it is known, through having been mentioned before hand, or because it refers to a specifically known entity, to an abstract concept. It is also used for generic terms (cultural knowledge) and for elements known by entailment (Hetzron 1970a, 5.1.). The indefinite article is used for newly introduced, previously unknown entities (its function is more limited than in English). A noun with no article is used when the specific entity which eventually underlies the content of the noun is not relevant for the communication: what matters is only the presence of the class and not its actual representative. In other words, this is a nonindividual, nonsingulative form (cf. Dezsö 1969:37-8). Here are some examples representing the three degrees. They have the most neutral, nonemphatic word-order:

(36) (a) A fiú levelet ír
           'the boy letter-Acc. writes' (SOV)
           ('The boy is writing a letter' [='is busy letter-writing'])

      (b) A fiú ír egy levelet
           'the boy writes a letter-Acc.' (SVO)
           ('The boy is writing a [specific] letter')

      (c) A fiú írja a levelet
           'the boy writes-it[33] the letter-Acc.' (SVO)
           ('The boy is writing the letter')

In Hungarian, the articles are innovations. The definite article comes from a remote demonstrative and the indefinite from the numeral 'one'. The reconstructible word-order for proto-Hungarian is SOV. Thus, the SOV order and the article-less noun in (36a) are both remnants of the archaic situation. Synchronically, the article-less noun is [-individual], whereas a noun provided with either one of the articles (or other determiners) is [+individual] (Bese et al., 1970:116). One may thus state that the normal position of a [+individual] complement is after the verb in Hungarian, while [-individual] is preverbal. Thus, the decisive factor in word-order is the value of the feature [±individual]. As

a historical explanation of these facts, however, I suggest that the different word-order arrangements[34] (cf. Dezső 1969:57-9) are a trace of
the past working of the presentative function and movement. In (36a),
'letter' is just a qualifier of the verb 'write'. The two constitute
a compound, meaning 'to epistolize'. The speaker only wants to narrow
down the definition of the action performed by the 'boy', - not mere
'writing', but more specific 'letter-writing'. In (36b/c), however, the
entity 'letter' may be used later in the discourse. If it is the first
mention, (36b) is used. If it has already been mentioned, (36c) is the
appropriate construction. (36a), on the other hand, requires no earlier,
nor implies any later mention. In fact, it is compatible with earlier
mention, thus cannot simply be labelled 'indefinite', as in the sequence:

(37) A fiúnak eszébe jutott, hogy meg kell írnia a levelet a barátjának.
Sóhajtva leült az asztalhoz. Miközben levelet írt, megfájdult a
feje.
'The boy suddenly remembered that he had to write the letter to
his friend. With a sigh, he sat down at the desk. While he was
'letter-writing', his head started to ache.'

Here, the complement with no article, levelet 'letter-Acc.', is, by implication, identical in reference with 'the letter' mentioned in the first
sentence. One would thus expect the second occurrence of the same 'letter'
to be definite. This is nevertheless not the case for the sole reason
that the entity 'letter' is not necessary anymore in the subsequent context. The mere tiresome action of 'epistolizing' is assumed to justify
the headache. This clearly shows that complement pre- vs. postposing
with relation to the verb has something to do with what the speaker is
preparing for the subsequent context. If no later use of the entity is
planned, the complement is preverbal and carries no article. It is rele-
gated to the status of verb modifier, insensitive to the normal distinction [+definite].[35] It is nonspecific. If, however, the complement
noun is specific, it appears postverbally, and according to whether there
exists previous knowledge of it or not, it is marked [+definite].

For a grammar of modern Hungarian, the article-less complement is
preverbal because it is [-presentative], which feature is in correlation
with its being [-individual]. In practice, it seems to me that the fact
that the speaker does not intend to use the entity in later discourse

(i.e., it is [-presentative]) is what leads to the [-individual] realization. In other words, presentativeness (with a minus prefix) is relevant in (36a). On the other hand, the nouns with an article are not necessarily presentative in the modern usage. Their older presentative interpretation led to their postverbal positioning, but later they lost their [+presentative] specification and the relevant position-regularing feature has become [+individual]. For a true presentative counterpart of (36b/c) we have (see Section 4 above):

(38) Az asztalnál a fiú ott ír egy levelet/ott írja a levelet.
'the table-at the boy there writes a letter/there writes-it the letter'
('At the table the boy is writing a/the letter').

Here is a case where the presentative movement contributed to the development of the language and subsequently lost its original character and left the positioning as a residue only.

7.   Conclusions

In this article, I have shown the existence of a presentative function in language which means calling special attention to one element of the sentence for recall in the subsequent discourse or situation. This recall may be needed because the element is going to be used, directly or indirectly, in the ensuing discourse, because what is going to be said later has some connection with the element in question, - or because that element is relevant to what is going to happen or be done in the reality.

Here I have dealt with only one exponent, probably the most important one, of this function, the presentative movement that brings the element in question to a sentence-final, or at least to a later than usual, position. There are other exponents, such as prosody, particles (Arabic inna - when not governed by another verb, French voilà, especially in constructions of narrative style such as Voilà l'homme qui vient), or simply, special phrasing (e.g., the paraphrastic rendering of (ii) in fn. 6: Thére was the girl, laughing, in the room). Often the indefinite article is basically a presentative functive (cf. Jespersen 1924:152). This is particularly apparent in languages where basic indefiniteness is

marked by zero, and the indefinite article is used for introducing new
elements for later mention, e.g., literary Hungarian (Section 6, Hetzron
1970a:921), Amharic, etc. Last but not least, verbs expressing existence or emergence automatically imply that their subject is presentative. It is no wonder that with such verbs most languages do not always
insist on other markings of presentativeness (cf. 3.2 above).

One property of the presentative function worth noticing is that
its manifestations are of different intensity. For instance, compare:

(39) (a) Round the bend came the train. (19a)

      (b) What came round the bend was the train.

In both sentences 'the train' is presentative, but much more forcefully
so in (39b) than in (39a). The 'Locative-Indef.Subj.' constructions
(3.1.) are of very low intensity, since their basic function is to bring
the elements in question to the scene. The same is true of the Hungarian
expletive adverb constructions (Section 2.).

The devices used to perform the presentative movement are varied:
mere transportation to a sentence-final position (3.1., Section 6.),
such transportation with further word-order adjustments (3.4.), transportation with compensatory addition of an expletive element (Sections
1, 2, 3.3.), underlying transportation and subsequent fronting (3.2.)
along with leaving a pronominal element behind (Section 5.), superimpos-
ing a higher predicative structure (Section 4.).

The extent of the use of the presentative movement also varies,
bound by often arbitrary limitations: sometimes it is obligatory (ex.
(3)), for a full clause in impersonal quotations (Section 1); for indefinite nouns only (3.1., 3.3.), but also for definite nouns in Sections
2, 3.4., 4., ex. (34), 6, fn. 22 (i-ii), and only for definite nouns in
Section 5 (cf. next paragraph); only with cooccurring locative elements
(Section 3.1.) or also with a progressive (3.4.), through introducing
an expletive locative (Section 2.); only with verbs of existence/emer-
gence (3.1-2, in a wider sense 3.4., by implication in Section 2, esp.
fn. 6) and also with passives of action (3.3.); only for subjects (3.1-
2-3-4.), but also other parts of speech (Sections 2, 4.), or only for
complements (Section 5.) (see next paragraph), for any phrasal element

but with the case-marker left behind (Section 4.) or also with the case-marker taken along (Section 2.).

Some of these limitations are motivated by the more or less narrow interpretation of the presentativeness (does reintroduction qualify? Is an ellipsis like 'laughed' = 'there appeared laughing' (fn. 5) admissible?). In the case of Amharic (Section 5.), the reason for the fact that only definite complement nouns enter into the construction is obvious. The process used is pronominalization. In Amharic (like in most languages) only definite nouns match the structural description of pronominalization, and since subject-marking is obligatory, only complement pronouns, being omissible, are capable of fulfilling a special, marked function.

It is thus evident that the manifestation of the presentative function does not have the same compelling power as some other functions in language. This is mainly a function of stylistic importance, and its non-application would cause no serious impairment in the expression. Languages with convenient presentative devices may make a more frequent use of it, exploiting the extent of its use allowed. For example, English may use What I meant is... (25) as an alternative to I meant that... because it is available, but in the corresponding situation Hungarian would have a nonpresentative construction, e.g., Azt akarom ezzel mondani, hogy... 'I want to say by this that...' (where the extraposition of the that-clause is obligatory).

We may thus state that there exists a tendency in languages to put into final position elements that the speaker wants to keep available for further reference. We have seen that this tendency manifests itself in different constructions, according to the language, but always serving the same purpose. The question is then, what is the status of the presentative function in the general theory of language.

Clearly, the presentative function belongs to discourse-grammar which operates on somewhat less exact, less strict principles than sentence-grammar. In discourse-grammar, universal tendencies play a particularly weighty role. We can state that the presentative movement is a universal tendency, potentially always present in the speech-system of humans, applying whenever there is an opportunity.

Amharic, an SOV language, comes from a language type with a probable VSO order which, in turn, may have once been SVO.[36] It became SOV under the influence of the Cushitic substratum languages. However, thanks to the conservativeness of the morphological system, pronominal complements have remained postverbal, suffixed to the verbal word. Right before assuming the SOV order, proto-Amharic (or some stage of proto-Ethiopian) must have been a free word-order language with the unmarked order SOV (replacing the older unmarked order) in the process of crystallizing. But other word-orders were still acceptable. Under such circumstances, the presentative function had the ideal opportunity to step in. Temporarily, there must have been a system comparable to what we find in Hungarian (see Section 6. above). When the SOV order became a compelling surface constraint, the already established presentative construction (SVO) was safeguarded by the introduction of rules (40b-c), that is fronting-copying and pronominalization. Hungarian, on the other hand, used to be an (exclusively?) SOV language with no definite or indefinite article. When the articles were adopted, the language was already involved in a reorganization of its system, with a fairly free word-order. The possibility of a postverbal position for a complement was then expropriated by the presentative function along with the newly established category of definiteness (see Bese et al., 1970:115-6).

We can thus define language universals, such as the presentative, as tendencies lurking in the speech system, ready to stake a claim whenever a historical development loosens up the grammar (here the word-order) and opens a gate for further changes. The presentative, manifesting the tendency to bring the element that is needed later as close as possible to the string or situation where it is needed again, as most frequent in locative constructions, but it shows up in all cases where it has been given a chance to influence the direction of historical change. Once it has managed to become part of a particular grammar, it tends to persist, withstanding the erosive effect of later historical developments, as in Amharic (Section 5.). In other cases, it succeeds in sneaking in through a back-door, as in cataphoric predications where the presentative element has to be promoted to the status of predicate to attain the final position.

NOTES

1. This article is partly based on Hetzron 1971b. Before preparing the final version, I had fruitful discussions about some of the points with the following colleagues: B. W. Andrzejewski, Robert Backus, Alan Bell, D. L. Bolinger, Susan Fisher, Talmy Givón, Ali Jahadhmy, C. D. Johnson, Alan R. King, Robert S. Kirsner, Mstislav Kostruba, Charles Li, Edith Moravcsik. I express my gratitude to them.

2. The actual examples (1a-c) come from a private letter by Professor Bolinger in which he further elaborates on the topic.

3. 'A frame sentence which merely asserts what is already an assertion contains less information than the assertion itself, and therefore precedes. A frame sentence which does more than say just "I assert this assertion" does potentially contain more information than the assertion itself, and therefore may either precede or follow' (Bolinger, private letter).

4. The only exception to this restriction I found is in poetry, ibid., 1.2.

5. The expletive adverb may carry some information. If benn 'inside' were substituted for the neutral ott 'there', it would imply that the speaker is outside; with itt 'here', the speaker is also in the room; with fenn 'above, upstairs', the implication is that the room is situated on a higher level than the present position of the speaker; the opposite relative positioning as indicated by lenn 'below, downstairs'. The sixth expletive adverb: kinn 'outside' would be harder to use in this specific context.

6. Another example to make the point clearer:

    (i)   A lány nevetett a szobában.
          'The girl laughed the room-in'

    (ii) A lány ott nevetett a szobában.
          'The girl there laughed the room-in'

(i) is a neutral assertion, whereas (ii) would be the appropriate sentence for describing a situation where the speaker has been looking for the girl, and then he found her, laughing, in the room, i.e., - 'Thére was the girl, laughing, in the room'. This brings the whole scene into the room, and the sequel to the story has to start from there.

7. There need be no contiguity between the EA+V group and the final, presentative element, e.g.,

(i) Ott ült a szobában a lány.
'There sat the room-in the girl'

(ii) Ott ült a lány a szobában.
'There sat the girl the room-in'

(i) produces the same presentative effect on the subject as (2b), and (ii) is practically equivalent to (2a) in making the scene, the 'room', the focused piece of information. The presentative element may also be other than the subject and the locative phrase:

(iii) A szobában a lány ott ült szomorúan.
'The room-in the girl there sat sadly'

(iv) A szobában ott ült a lány szomorúan.
'The room-in there sat the girl sadly'

(or other orders), meaning 'The girl is sitting in the room, all sad', where the state of sadness is the element likely to be referred to later (e.g., the subsequent sentences may explain why she was sad, or also after relating events that might make her sad, the result of these events on her are shown, etc.). One caveat, however, - the presence of a presentative element does not commit the speaker to continue on the basis of that element. My claim is that (a) the presentativization constitutes the smoothest introduction to further mention of the same element, and (b) the presentative element is supposed to leave a deeper trace in the hearer's short-range memory than the rest, no matter what the subsequent sentences are about.

See Hetzron 1973:29 for another case of presentative in Hungarian.

8. Cf. Dezső 1969:31. Egy ember van a házban 'a man is the house-in' puts the emphasis on 'a man'.

9. It is very impressive that word-order depends on the definiteness of the subject-noun even in languages like Finnish or Russian, and one may add here Latin and Mandarin Chinese (cf. Lyons 1971:392-3, (6) vs.

(7) and (8) vs. (9)), which have no definite or indefinite article nor
any other generalized means to express [+definite]-ness (cf. Clark 1970,
L6). This suggests that after all [presentative] is the conditioning
factor in creating the 'Locative-Subject' order in (3b).

10. This is clearly seen in other tenses. See Hetzron 1972:723 for
evidence that Arabic has an initial zero copula also in the present
tense.

11. This order is impossible in Hungarian in a nonemphatic construction,
though one may very well have a homographic emphatic sentence Egy
EMPH_ember jött 'It was a man who came'. Yet the order 'Indef.Subj.-Verb
is possible without emphasis with other verbs: Egy ember evett 'A man
was-eating/ate', or even with verbs of emergence if they are preceded
by a preverb (an observation by E. Moravcsik): Egy ember megérkezett
'A man up-arrived' ('A man has/had arrived').

12. With definite subjects after the verb, the order may be justified
by the presentativeness of the subject, but it may also appear there
for other reasons. For instance, with definite generic subjects, one
may have Repültek a madarak 'flew the birds' ('Birds were flying') where
'birds' is definitely not intended to be used in the subsequent discourse.

13. But one may have Élt az ember, mint hal a vízben 'lived the man,
like fish the water-in' ('The man was living like fish in the water',
i.e., comfortably). The reason for the acceptability of this sentence
and of Jött as ember 'came the man' (12b) vs. the non-acceptability of
Élt az ember 'lived the man' as a complete sentence is that 'live' is a
pure existential verb, and when used with a definite, i.e., already
known, subject, it cannot be introductory/presentative, whereas 'come'
indicates mere emergency, capable of reintroducing an already known element. Likewise, in the sentence given in the beginning of this footnote,
'live' refers to manner of living, not to mere existence. 'The man' may
here be presentative in the reintroductory sense. In the latter two
cases, not existence, but (re)appearance in a new way of life or in a
location is communicated.

14. Cf. Bolinger 1971:585 - 'a there not only introduces the referent
of the subject on the scene but brings it into existence for the purpose
of this discourse', a clear definition of the presentative function. It

Dear N

rel claire

discontinuity

should be noted that <u>there</u> + V constructions other than <u>there</u> <u>be</u> are marginal in modern English.

15. For a number of American speakers this is acceptable. A. Bell gave the example: <u>The girl arrived that we had been talking about</u>. Yet, very interestingly, in the acceptable version of this sentence, the definite noun has a special stress, so that the prosody of (9a) (where no such special stress on the definite subject is required) and that of (9b) are not identical. I would not hesitate to call the special stress on the subject of (9b), for those who accept it, a 'presentative stress', a device other than linear order compensating for the nonfinal position, cf. Hetzron 1973:35-6 for the concept of 'bridged discontinuity'.

16. Some speakers do accept this sentence. In their grammar there must then be an extension of the permissibility of discontinuity along formal and not semantic lines.

17. Naturally, one could offer here a traditionalistic statement with no recourse to depth: (i) 'There can be discontinuity between headnoun and relative cause only when the former, a subject, is indefinite and the verb is a verb of existence/emergence.' But one should further note that (ii) the same sentences have a variant in 'There-V-S' which <u>would</u> exhibit contiguity. Stopping at this point would be wrong. Statement (i) is observationally adequate, but provides no explanation, so that the specifications sound arbitrary. Observation (ii) shows that they are not arbitrary at all. A linguistic philosophy admitting no depth would have no way to connect the two facts efficiently.

18. See Kirsner 1973 for Dutch <u>er</u> (with a slightly different interpretation) and Hetzron 1971b:96-9 for the presence of locative elements in special copulas for locative/existential sentences with an indefinite sentence in several languages, and for an argument why these elements are not to be analyzed synchronically as locatives.

19. An apparent exception to this is given on p. 380:

<u>Il passera le train que tu as déjà pris la semaine dernière</u>.
'It will-pass the train that you have already taken the week last'

but, as Martin points out, the definiteness is not governed here by earlier mention in the discourse. Here is an indefinite train which

382

shares schedule and destination with another one that was taken by the
hearer last week, and the definiteness refers to this property. This
is akin to what I once called 'definiteness by entailment' (Hetzron 1970a,
5.1.). Other instances of such definiteness are given on pp. 381-2, and
hereunder (13), e.g.,

> Il en résulterait les pires difficultés.
> 'It from-it would-result the worst difficulties'
> ('The worst difficulties would result from it')

20. Martin's examples:

> (i)   *Il n'arrive jamais un malheur seul. (nonindividual)
>   'It not-arrives never a misfortune alone', but
>
> (ii) Un malheur n'arrive jamais seul.
>   'Bad luck never comes by itself', yet one may have
>
> (iii) Il m'arrivera un malheur. (individual)
>   'It to-me-will-arrive a misfortune' ('I will have trouble')

21. Unlike in English where *There disappeared... is incorrect, French
allows for Il disparaît ainsi une coutume... 'It disappears thus a cus-
tom...' (Martin 1970:381) and Dutch has er verdwijnen meer bevolkingsregis-
ters 'there disappear more census-book' (Kirsner, private communication).

22. In German, introductory es does not affect agreement:

> (i) Es kam der Mann
>   'It came-Sg. the man'
>
> (ii) Es kamen die Männer
>   'It came-Pl. the men'

In French, however, the old agreement with the true subject, (iii) as in
German, was replaced, as in English, by agreement with the preceding element: (iv) (see Foulet 1967, 293):

> (iii) Old French: Il sont venu deus homme
>
> (iv) Modern French: Il est venu deux hommes

23. I am indebted to Professor Bolinger for this example. I quote from
his letter: 'Imagine a supervisor who is keeping an eye on several
groups of workmen. He leaves one group and approaches another--he is

giving instructions group by group. To the next group he approaches he says: <u>What I want you to do next is</u>... He would never say *<u>It is</u>... <u>that I want you to do next</u>. Since his instructions came out of the blue, no basis is laid for any <u>it</u>; there is no antecedent'. It is understood, of course, that the blank in these sample sentences contains an NP, and not a verb which would cause grammatical difficulties.

24. This observation was independently made by three colleagues consulted: Professors D. L. Bolinger, C. D. Johnson (native speakers of American English) and Mr. Alan R. King (British).

When Akmajian claimed that cleft and cataphoric sentences shared 'the same presupposition' (189), he was wrong. He probably did not check out his examples in a context, see also Grosu 1973:297, Figure 1.

25. Cf. Harries 1973:107, but unlike her, I do not consider the final position basic and unmarked. In Amharic, an SOV language, the regular pattern for a cleft construction is

(i)   təlantənna yä-mätta-w əssu näw
       'yesterday Rel.-came-Article he is'
       ('It is he who came yesterday')

with the emphasized element at the end (before a copula). Yet one may hear the opposite order more and more, in violation of the general word-order requirement of having the main verb in the absolute sentence-final position:

(ii)   əssu näw təlantənna yä-mätta-w
       'he is yesterday Rel.-came-Art.'

For me this is proof that the natural position for the emphasized element is in the front (cf. Hetzron 1971a 2.3.). In many languages this does not mean sentence-initial position, but appearance in a pre-tense carrier slot, e.g., in Hungarian, cf. Hetzron 1970a:902 (3).

There are, naturally, exceptions to this positioning, e.g., Italian subject emphasis where the subject emphasis where the subject is put in a post-verb position, e.g., <u>Io pago</u> 'I pay', but <u>Pago io</u> 'It is me who will pay'. Also in a number of Chadic languages, emphasized subjects are moved 'from their normal position before the verb into the predicate, usually after the direct object if there is one' (Schuh 1971:67). There may be two explanations for this, - one that such a regressive movement is restricted to subject-emphasis, and if any movement should be part of the expression of emphasis, the only possible movement from a pre-verbal position is into a post-verbal one. The other one is that functionally these cases may be cataphoric after all. Further inquiry is necessary here.

26. It is true that Hungarian has free word order, but it really has no cataphoric predications properly speaking. Examples (22a/b) above are marginal in Hungarian and in no way are they felt to constitute a special category. They are mere relative constructions.

27. I am arguing here against a mechanistic derivation which seeks a 'source' for each component of the surface sentence in the base structure, while providing no motivation for the focusing process involved. Such a theory needs that the ultimate surface S be represented already in the base (cf. ex. (29)), see Chomsky 1970:148, 209 (46), Postal 1971:236, Grosu 1973, and a manuscript by Peters and Bach summed up by Grosu (not available to me). Language can actually build a superstructure, i.e., an S node higher than the pre-existing highest one, through derivation, if such an operation will have the effect of achieving an important purpose. In fact, such phenomena have been noted in the literature and were named 'Chomsky-adjunction'.

28. I must mention here that I found speakers who did not object to

What I saw there was a fisherman.

29. Not to be confused with the type of topicalization (left-dislocation) where the pronoun refers to a sentence-initial, non-integrated noun, with no case-marker, e.g.,

yəh säw, təlantənna käbete bäfit ṭäbbəqo ayyähu-t
'this man, yesterday from-house-my before he-waiting I-saw him
('This man, I saw him waiting in front of my house')

30. This is a trace of an older word-order, with VO, cf. Givón 1971

31. For example,

kä-zzičč set məgəb gäzzah^w-at
'from=this woman food I-bought=her'

where the accusative is the adpronominal counterpart of the adnominal ablative k̲ä- 'from', in the acquisitional sense, cf. Hetzron 1970b, 1.n.

32. This is clear in the singular only. In the plural, there are only nouns with or without the definite article. There are also some con-straints on the distribution of these three degrees. The article-less noun may be a subject only if emphasized: ^{emph}Fiú jött be '[It was a] boy [who] came in' (implying a young male and not a female), and never *Fiú bejött 'boy in-came' (emphasis causes preverbs to quit their prever-bal position). In literary Hungarian, no noun with indefinite article may appear in the predicative position, though the spoken language is using it more and more also here.

33. This is the so-called definite (objective) conjugation, the result of an agreement between verb and definite object.

34. For (41a) the OVS order, and for (36b/c) other orders are also pos-sible, apart from word-orders with emphasis. The examples of (36) repre-sent the most neutral ones.

35. In fact, also to number. In (37), the boy may have remembered about the letters to be written to friends, and the singular levelet would still be correct in the last sentence, but not the plural leveleket.

36. Ge'ez is basically VSO but the typical Semitic pattern 'subject marking prefix+verb-stem+object-suffix' may be an indication of original SVO, cf. Givón 1971, 2.2.

REFERENCES

Akmajian, Adrian. 1970. 'On deriving cleft sentences from pseudo-cleft sentences', Linguistic Inquiry, 1.149-68.

Andrzejewski, B. W. 1964. The declension of Somali nouns. London: SOAS.

Andrzejewski, B. W. 1974. 'The role of indicator particles in Somali', Afroasiatic Linguistics.

Bese, Lajos, László Dezső and János Gulya. 1970. 'On the syntactic typology of the Uralic and Altaic languages', pp. 113-28, in L. Dezső and P. Hajdú, eds. Theoretical problems of typology and the northern Eurasian languages. Amsterdam: Grüner.

Bloch, Ariel, forthcoming. 'Direct and indirect relative in Arabic', in R. Hetzron, ed., Semitica Americana.

Bolinger, Dwight L. 1970. 'The lexical value of it'. Working papers in Linguistics. Department of Linguistics, University of Hawaii, 2.57-75.

Bolinger, Dwight L. 1971. 'A further note on the nominal in the progressive', Linguistic Inquiry, 2.584-6.

Chomsky, Noam. 1970. 'Remarks on nominalization', pp. 184-221 in R. A. Jacobs and P. S. Rosenbaum, eds., Readings in English transformational grammar. Waltham, Mass.: Ginn & Co.

Clark, Eve V. 1970. 'Locationals: a study of the relations between "existential", "locative" and "possessive" constructions.' Working papers on language universals, Language Universals Project, Committee on Linguistics, Stanford University, 3.11-37.

Deme, László. 1959. 'A nyomatéktalan mondat egy fajtájárol', Magyar Nyelv, 55.185-98.

Dezső, László. 1969. 'A főnévi csoport', Általános Nyelvészeti Tanulmányok, 6.25-158.

Firbas, Jan. 1966. 'Non-thematic subjects in contemporary English'. Travaux linguistiques de Prague, 2.239-56.

Foulet, Lucien. 1967. Petite syntaxe de l'ancien français. Paris: Champian.

Getatchew, Haile. 1971. 'The suffix pronouns in Amharic'. pp. 101-12 in Chin-Wu Kim and Herbert Stahlke, eds., Papers in African Linguistics (Current Inquiry into Language and Linguistics, 1), Edmonton-Champaign: Linguistic Research.

Givón, Talmy. 1971. 'Historical syntax and synchronic morphology: An archeologist's field trip', in Papers from the Seventh Regional Meeting, University of Chicago, Chicago Linguistic Society.

Grosu, Alexander. 1973. 'On the status of the so-called Right Roof Constraint', Language, 49.294-311.

Harries, Helga. 1973. 'Contrastive emphasis and cleft sentences', Working papers on language universals, 12.85-144.

Hetzron, Robert. 1964. 'Les syntagmes à totalisateur du hongrois', Word 20.55-71.

Hetzron, Robert. 1966. 'L'adverbe explétif ott et l'aspect hongrois', Linguistics, 25.34-57.

Hetzron, Robert. 1970a. 'Nonverbal sentences and degrees of definiteness in Hungarian', Language, 46.899-927.

Hetzron, Robert. 1970b. 'Toward an Amharic case-grammar', Studies in African linguistics, 1.301-54.

Hetzron, Robert. 1971a. 'The deep structure of the Statement', Linguistics, 65.25-63.

Hetzron, Robert. 1971b. 'Presentative function and presentative movement', Studies in African Linguistics, Suppl. 2, 79-105.

Hetzron, Robert. 1972. Review of Mélanges Marcel Cohen. Language, 48.719-26.

Hetzron, Robert. 1973. 'Surfacing', Studi Italiani di Linguistica Teorica ed Applicate, 2.3-71.

Hudson, Grover, MS. 'The unity of focusing transformations', UCLA, 24, November 1973.

Jespersen, Otto. 1924. The philosophy of grammar. London: Allen &
Unwin.

Jespersen, Otto. 1969. Analytic syntax. New York: Holt, Rinehart &
Winston.

Kirsner, Robert S. 1973. 'Natural focus and agentive interpretation:
On the semantics of Dutch expletive er'. Stanford Occasional
Papers in Linguistics, 3.101-13.

Kuno, Susumo. 1971. 'The position of locatives in existential sentences', Linguistic Inquiry, 2.333-78.

Lyons, John. 1968. Introduction to theoretical linguistics. Cambridge:
The University Press.

Martin, Robert. 1970. 'La transformation impersonelle', Revue de
linguistique romane, 34.377-94.

Postal, Paul. 1971. Cross-over phenomena. New York: Holt, Rinehart
& Winston.

Schachter, Paul. 1973. 'Focus and relativization', Language, 49.19-46.

Schuh, Russell G. 1971. 'Reconstruction of the syntax of subject emphasis in certain Chadic languages', Studies in African linguistics,
Suppl. 2, 67-78.

Zolkovskii, A. K. 1971. Sintaksis Somali [in Russian]. Moskva: Nauka.

ON THE EXPLANATION OF CONSTITUENT ORDER UNIVERSALS

by

Gerald Sanders

1. Explanation

Linguistics is an empirical science. This means that there must be linguistic theories, and that these theories must seek to generate scientific explanations of some coherent and reasonably natural set of facts about objects in the real world. The objects that linguistic theories are about are human languages, and the facts that are to be explained by such theories are the essential attributes of such languages and their range of possible variation and change.[1] Differences in subject matter are the only differences between the theories and explanations of linguistics and those of other empirical sciences, like physics, economics, or psychology. The logical and empirical conditions for explanatory adequacy are the same for all sciences, and the basic principles of theory construction, evaluation, and testing are identical for all empirical domains.

A human, or natural, language is an infinite set of sound-meaning pairings that could be effectively used for the purpose of human communication by the members of some human society. Each distinct pairing constitutes a distinct linguistic object--a distinct word, phrase, sentence, or discourse that is available to members of the society, by virtue of their membership, as a guide, score, or model for communicatively successful articulatory and cognitive renditions in utterances expressing assertions, questions, requests, promises, etc. Languages, and the linguistic constituents that comprise them, are thus cultural objects, rather than physical or behavioral ones. This distinguishes the domain of linguistics from the domains of such non-cultural sciences as physics, biology, and psychology. The domain of linguistics is also distinguished from the domains of other cultural, or social, sciences by virtue of the symbolic rather than non-symbolic character of the objects that comprise it. Linguistics could thus be defined as that science whose empirical domain is the set of all sets of sound-meaning pairings that are available as possible cultural bases for effective human communication. The facts to be explained by linguistic theories, then, are facts about the characteristics of this set, about the universal properties and relations of its members and their observed range of variation and change.

The standard informal notion of an explanation is any sufficiently satisfying answer to a Why or How question. Thus we consider things to be explained if we know why they are the way they are, or how they came to be the way they are. Our degree of satisfaction with a particular answer will depend on a large number of factors, including not only the nature of the answer itself, but also our individual knowledge about other questions and answers, our curiosity and patience, and our preferred strategy for ascending from lower to higher levels of explanation. One thing that will be demanded of any proposed explanation, however, is that it provide a sound basis for inferring the fact to be explained from principles that are non-analytic, not known to be false, and capable of having factual implications outside the given domain of the explanation.

Our intuitive notion of explanation is at least partially explicated by the standard definition of formal, or scientific, explanation. According to this characterization, a fact F is explained by E if and only if a statement describing F can be deductively derived from E, and E is a finite set of true statements including at least one scientific law that is necessary for the deduction of F.

A law is a true synthetic universal statement that is exceptionless and non-accidental. All empirical laws are universally quantified over a restricted domain. Boyle's Law, for example, is quantified over the set of all gasses, Grimm's Law over the set of all pre-Germanic Indo-European morphemes. The statements of a particular grammar are thus laws quantified over the set of all sentences or discourses of that language, or over certain well-defined subsets of these. The statements of a theory of language, or a theory of grammar, are quantified over the set of all natural languages, or the set of all grammars that generate such languages.

For a law, or any other statement, to contribute to the explanation of anything, it must of course be true. Under some views of explanation, however, statements are considered to be lawlike even if they are only statistically, or probabilistically, true of a set of objects or events, and assert nothing whatever about its individual members. Such statistical or probabilistic laws can serve to specify

statistical or probabilistic properties of sets, and can thus be used
to predict--and in <u>some</u> sense, perhaps, even explain--certain statistical characteristics of their subsets. They obviously cannot be used,
though, to predict or explain anything about all members of a set, or
about any one of its particular members. Thus, for example, the statement that ninety-three percent of all SOV languages are postpositional--
or, equivalently, that there are ninety-three chances in a hundred that
a given SOV language will be postpositional--might be used to explain
why in a given sample of a hundred languages, ninety-four of them were
found to be postpositional. It could not be used to explain why a particular SOV language (say, Japanese) is postpositional.

For a statistical or probabilistic generalization to have any
empirical significance at all, it is necessary that it specify an exact
numerical index of probability, for it is only in this way that such a
statement can be subject even in principle to empirical confirmation
or disconfirmation. Statements simply asserting that P is more probable
than Q, or more likely, or more natural, or more unmarked, thus have
no possible predictive or explanatory powers at all. They cannot be
used to account for either the existence of P rather than Q in any particular case, or the numerical preponderance of P over Q in any observed class of cases. Thus to determine the likelihood of an observed
preponderance being due to law rather than chance it is necessary to
know both the exact size of the observed sample and the exact numerical degree of preponderance that is hypothetically asserted to hold
for the domain out of which the sample is drawn.

These necessary conditions for the empirical significance of
probabilistic statements have rarely if ever been satisfied by the
probabilistic statements that have been appealed to in the linguistic
literature. Instead, one typically finds only such gross numerically
unspecified likelihood assertions as the following:

In declarative sentences with nominal subject and object,
the dominant order is almost always one in which the subject precedes the object.

(Greenberg 1963:61)

...other things being equal, lost plural distinctions are
more likely to be analogically restored than lost case
distinctions.

(Kiparsky 1972:201)

After a consonant, vowels are fully unmarked and glides are
fully marked.

(Chomsky and Halle 1968:408)

This principle says that elements belonging together in the
hierarchy of semantic representation tend to be lexicalized
and serialized in the surface representation in such a way
that hierarchical dependencies are directly reflected in
categorial operator-operand relationships and closeness of
constituents to each other in the surface string.

(Bartsch and Vennemann 1972:131)

We have, on the one hand, distinctness conditions, which,
as an initial approximation, state that there is a tendency
for semantically relevant information to be retained in
surface structure. Secondly, there are leveling conditions, which state that allomorphy in paradigms tends to
get eliminated.

(Kiparsky 1972:195)

Such statements of likelihood, tendency, or numerically unspecified
relative markedness or naturalness can be used at most to roughly
describe certain observed property preponderance relations in certain
observed sets of languages. They are too vague and unnecessarily elaborate and abstract to be really useful even as statements of mere
description. They have no possible predictive or explanatory uses at
all.

Even for those probabilistic statements that do include exact
numerical indices of probability, and are thus capable of generating
statistical predictions about the randomly-selected subsets of their
domains, it would seem quite inappropriate to say that such statements
could ever really serve to explain anything--in particular, anything
of the sort that we seek scientific explanations for. Thus the domains
of empirical sciences consist of infinite sets of objects or events of

a certain type, and the goal of each science is to provide a principled account of all significant properties and relations of all members of its domain set. The scientist is simply not concerned with the characteristics of finite sets, except to the extent that a good random sample may serve as a basis for confirming or disconfirming lawlike generalizations universally quantified over the entire infinite domain from which the sample is drawn. What the scientist wants to know is thus not, for example, why eighty-seven percent of all logs float in water, or why it is likely, natural, or the unmarked case for a log to float in water. What he wants to know, rather, is why those particular logs that float in water do float in water, and why those that don't float in water don't float in water. Similarly, a scientist dealing with human language will not want to know why subjects precede their unfocussed objects in eighty-seven percent of a sample of known languages, or why subject precedence is more common, natural, or unmarked than object precedence in the set of all known languages. What he wants to know instead is why English, for example, has subject precedence, and why Ibanag, for example, doesn't.

The task of linguistics, then, is simply the standard task of all empirical sciences--the task of explaining particular facts and generalizations by showing that they are necessary consequences of a given set of true initial conditions and unfalsified empirical laws. In other words, there can be no explanation without theories, and no theories without laws.

2. Explaining Constituent Orderings

It is one of the necessary empirical conditions for all terminal phonetic representations of natural-language sentences or discourses that they include explicit symbols or formal relations between symbols which are empirically interpreted into observation statements of the form "X precedes, or is initiated temporally prior to, Y", where X and Y are the interpretations of phonetic elements or element sets. Possible grammars and theories of grammar will thus differ with respect to ordering only in the manner in which these terminal ordering specifications are assigned.

Since the morphemes of any given language constitute a finite set, it would be possible to specify the correct orderings of sounds in their articulatory renditions by a finite list of lexical rules, or minimal sound-meaning equivalences, where the phonetic member of each rule simply includes the appropriate ordering specifications for the sounds of that morpheme. Or, if the phonological members of lexical rules include grouping specifications for syllable, nucleus, onset, and coda, as well as for their constituent segments, it would evidently be possible to derive the correct ordering of the phonetic elements of any morpheme from their groupings by means of a small set of general rules of phonological ordering that make no reference to the sounds or meanings of particular morphemes and serve to express all true generalizations concerning the relative order of sounds in the pronunciations of all morphemes of the language in question.

In any event, though, it is also necessary to account for the ordering of sounds in the pronunciations of words, phrases, sentences, and discourses. These orderings are also non-random, of course, and not fully determined by the ordering of sounds within morphemes or in fact by any phonological properties of linguistic objects whatever. On the contrary, it is the non-phonological properties and relations of such objects that determine the orderings that obtain between the sounds of one morpheme and those of another in their articulatory renditions.[2] In short, then, it is necessary for natural languages that at least some orderings be specified with respect to the elements and element sets of non-phonological linguistic representations and their groupings. The specification and explanation of such syntactic, or non-phonological, constituent orderings will be our sole concern in what follows, and all subsequent references to constituents and constituency relations are intended to refer only to the constituents of non-phonological representations.

An adequate metalanguage for the representation of linguistic objects will contain two and only two distinct relational elements. (See Sanders 1969, 1970.) These differ both in their formal properties as relations and in their empirical interpretations. The first is the relation of grouping, or co-constituency, symbolized by a comma between bracketed constituents. The second is the relation of

ordering, or linear concatenation, symbolized here by an ampersand between constituents. Grouping is a non-associative symmetric, or com-
mutative, relation that is interpreted into the two-place semantic observation predicate "is (cognitively or psychologically) associated
with". Ordering is an associative asymmetric, or non-commutative, relation that is interpreted into the two-place phonetic observation predicate "temporally precedes", or "is initiated prior to". Thus, for
any constituents A and B, the representations [A, B] and [B, A] are
equivalent, and the representations [A & B] and [B & A] are non-
equivalent.

All assertions about constituent orderings can be expressed by
universal statements of the form (1a) or (1b).

(1) (a) X [A, B] Y = X [A & B] Y

    (b) X [A, B] Y ≠ X [A & B] Y

The affirmative statement schema (1a) expresses the assertion that for
any sister constituents analyzable as A and B in a (possibly-null) context analyzable as X__Y, the constituent of type A is ordered before
the constituent of type B. The negative statement schema (1b) asserts
that under the same quantification and analyzability conditions constituents of type A are never ordered before those of type B. Instances
of these schemata can be used to express factual claims about constituent orderings of all degrees of generality, and may be universally
quantified either over the sentences or discourses of particular languages or over those of all languages.

The fact or generalization expressed by any particular statement
of the form (1a) or (1b) can be said to be explained then if and only
if that statement is deductively derivable from some set of true
statements that essentially includes at least one empirical law. Moreover, since the conclusion of the derivation is an assertion about constituent ordering, it is necessary that essential inferential use be
made of at least one fact or law about ordering.

Any fact or true generalization about the order of constituents
in sentences of a particular language can be explained by deductive
derivation based on laws of the form (1a) quantified over the set of
all representations of sentences of that language. Thus, for example,

the fact that the sounds of the precede the sounds of boy in all appropriate pronunciations of the English sentence The boy ran follows from
an axiomatic basis including the true law that for all representations
of English sentences [DET, N] = [DET & N]. This law, or ordering rule,
is probably not derivable from any higher order generalization about
English, though in Japanese, for which it is also true, it follows from
the more general law $_N$[X, N] = $_N$[X & N], and perhaps ultimately from
the highest order generalization that all attributes (or operators) are
ordered before their heads (or operands). The operant laws in all explanations and explanatory ascents such as these make essential reference to the distinctive features of grammatical constituents, their
grouping, or constructional relations, and perhaps, for higher order
generalizations at least, their relative constructional functions as
head and attribute. The power to express these properties and relations is thus a necessary condition that must be satisfied by any possibly adequate metalanguage for linguistic description or explanation.

The necessity of this degree of expressive power can easily be
demonstrated. Thus, for example, consider the set of distinct English
sentences that could be constructed by various orderings of the words
some, girls, gave, the, boys, walking, horses. Clearly, there is no
possible way to describe, let alone predict or explain, the way sounds
and meanings are paired in this sentence set by statements that refer
only to words or morphemes, either their phonological properties, or
their syntactic and semantic properties, or both. To specify the ordering of these words for any sentence in the set it is also necessary
to make essential reference to their relative grouping relations in
some non-phonological representation of the sentence. For example,
given the distinct semantically-motivated groupings in (2a) and (2b),
these can be associated by extremely general grouping-sensitive rules
with their appropriately ordered pronunciations, (3a) and (3b),
respectively.

    (2)(a) (((gave, (girls, some)), (horses, the)), (walking,
           boys))

       (b) (((gave, (girls)), (some, horses)), (the, (walking,
           boys))

(3) (a) Walking boys gave some girls the horses

   (b) The walking boys gave girls some horses

Grouping-dependent facts and relations such as these are characteristic of natural language, and a metalanguage that lacked the power of grouping-specification would be wholly inadequate for the statement of linguistic facts and laws, not only about constituent ordering but also about nearly all other significant properties and relations of linguistic objects. However, even this power seems to be insufficient, since there are linguistic characteristics which can be described and explained, apparently, only by means of statements that refer essentially not only to constituents and their groupings, but also to the head-attribute relations that hold between the members of such groupings.

Consider, for example, the distinct English nominal expressions bus station and station bus. Although these include precisely the same morphemes in what would appear to be precisely the same grouping or constructional relation, they are neither synonymous nor homophonous. There would thus appear to be no way to specify which ordering goes with which meaning here without referring to the different head-attribute relations in the two phrases and the general principle that all monolexical attributes, or at least all nominal ones, are ordered before their heads in English.

The need for a distinct power of head-attribute reference is much less certain, however, since it might be possible, as suggested in Sanders (1972c), to reduce all head-attribute specifications to distinctive grouping specifications. Thus if attributes are always subordinate to, or more deeply embedded than, their heads--an assumption that has some degree of independent support--then bus station and station bus would have the respective non-phonological representations $[[[N, STATION]], [N, BUS]]$ and $[[N, STATION], [[N, BUS]]]$, and the correct ordering specifications for each phrase would follow from the lawlike grouping-sensitive generalization $[[[N]], [N]] = [[[N]] \& [N]]$.

The metalinguistic prerequisites that have been referred to thus far hold for all theories of language, regardless of their possible differences with regard to the specification of ordering relations.

The range of such differences has been shown in Sanders (1970) to be
determined by the range of alternative assumptions that are possible
concerning the derivational predictability, variability, and terminal
completeness of the ordering relations that hold between linguistic
constituents. Evidence was presented there and elsewhere (e.g., Sanders 1969, 1972) in support of the claim that the most general, most
natural, and most revealing theories of natural-language grammar are
those which assume that ordering and grouping relations are mutually
exclusive in interpretable linguistic representations, and that all
linguistic ordering relations are derivationally predictable and invariant under transformation or substitution justified by any possible
rules of grammar. These restrictions, which jointly determine what I
have called the Derivational Theory of Ordering (Sanders 1970), follow
necessarily from the following logically independent universal constraints on the well-formedness of grammatical proofs or derivations:

(1) the Semantic Completeness Constraint--that all constituents of terminal semantic representations are related to
each other by grouping, and not by ordering;

(2) the Phonetic Completeness Constraint--that all constituents of terminal phonetic representations are related to
each other by ordering, and not by grouping;

(3) the Invariant Order Constraint--that if an element
token A precedes an element token B in any line of a given
derivation, then there is no line in that derivation in
which B precedes A.

These general constraints, which contribute significantly to the
natural delimitation of natural-language grammar, have been shown to
follow from metatheoretical principles of a still more general and
essentially definitional character. Thus the two Completeness Constraints can be derived simply from the general formal definition of
an interpretable representation of an empirical object as a string of
property and relational elements which are each uniquely interpretable
in the same extratheoretical mode or domain. The Invariant Order Constraint can likewise be viewed simply as a necessary implication of
the defining antisymmetric, or non-commutativity, axiom for ordering

relations. Thus to say that the constituents of any representation [X & A & B & Y] are ordered means that for any non-identical A and B [X & A & B & Y] and [X & B & A & Y] are non-equivalent. Since the lines of any grammatical derivation or proof of a given sound-meaning pairing constitute an equivalence class of linguistic representations (see Sanders 1972), it follows that different orderings of the same constituents cannot be representations of the same linguistic object, and hence cannot possibly cooccur as lines of the same well-formed derivation.

Each principle of the theory of Derivational Ordering has been shown to determine a class of possible grammars that is much smaller and more homogeneous than the class determined by its contrary or contradictory. (See, e.g., Sanders 1972c.) Considerable evidence has also been presented (e.g., Sanders 1969, 1970) in support of the claim that the particular highly-restricted class of grammars determined by these principles includes grammars for all possible human languages, and, in particular, those grammars that generate optimal explanations of all significant properties and relations of such languages. I know of no argument or evidence against this claim.[3] Thus since there is no possible theory of ordering that determines a more restricted class of grammars than the Derivational Theory, or a more restricted class of possible representations, derivations, and structural descriptions of linguistic objects, it is necessary to assume that this theory is correct until proven otherwise. Unless and until such proof can be provided, therefore, it is appropriate to consider consistency with the completeness and invariance principles to be a necessary metacondition on all possibly adequate theories of natural-language grammar.

Consistency or inconsistency with the completeness constraints is quite difficult to determine for most contemporary theories due to their frequent lack of explicitness on the matter of terminal representations, particularly with respect to the relational elements they may include. Nevertheless, it would appear that all of these theories are either implicitly consistent with these constraints or could be made consistent with them without significant effect on the nature of the grammars and grammatical explanations that they generate. With respect to the Invariant Order Constraint, however, the situation is

quite different. First, it is clear that nearly all recent generative
theories of grammar are quite directly and explicitly inconsistent
with this principle. For example, the theories proposed by Chomsky
(1965), Jackendoff (1972), Lakoff (1971), and Lamb (1966) all generate
possible grammars justifying the derivational reordering, or permutation, or constituents, and fragments of grammars of this type are frequently put forth in explicit attempts to exemplify or demonstrate the
claimed adequacy of the theory in question. Thus, if the Invariant
Order Constraint is correct, all of these theories of grammar are
false. Moreover, any modification that would bring them into conformity with this constraint would require significant modifications in
many aspects of their structures, and would have a radical effect on
the nature of the grammars and grammatical explanations generated, involving significant reductions not only in number but also in heterogeneity, derivational deviousness, and empirically unmotivated abstractness and invulnerability to factual confirmation or disconfirmation.

Otherwise similar theories that differ with respect to consistency
with the Invariant Order Constraint will thus generally differ quite
considerably in the particular explanations that they provide for particular linguistic facts. This will be true for all types of linguistic data, but will be most obviously the case, of course, for all facts
having to do with constituent ordering.

In subsequent discussion of such facts, therefore, it will be
necessary to distinguish the problems and patterns of explanation that
are distinctive to each of these two classes of grammatical theories--
those that incorporate the Invariant Order Constraint, which will be
referred to as invariant-order theories, and those that are inconsistent with this constraint, which will be referred to as variable-order
theories. It will be seen throughout that theories of the latter type
are faced with explanatory difficulties that do not arise in the case
of the former type, though many problems, of course, will be problems
for any theory of grammar, regardless of its powers and governing
metaconstraints.

The primary facts and generalizations that are of concern to linguists are those that are true not of some languages but of all

languages. Thus with respect to constituent-ordering our primary task
is that of providing explanations for such facts as are expressed by
the exceptionless universals reported by Greenberg (1963) and in many
of the papers in the series of Stanford Working Papers on Language Universals. Many of these facts involve the non-existence of natural languages with certain logically possible constituent orderings or combinations of orderings. Any explanation of these facts, therefore, will
require an appropriately restrictive delimitation of the class of possible natural languages. Such delimitation is appropriately specified
by delimitation of the class of possible grammars of such languages,
which is the central function of all empirical theories of language,
or theories of grammar. An adequate theory of this sort will thus
account for the significant characteristics of all human languages by
means of laws about the grammars that generate such languages. Such
grammatical explanation of linguistic facts presupposes a high degree
of theoretical explicitness, of course, and a highly restrictive set of
metaconstraints on the metalanguage and metatheoretical use and interpretation of grammatical theories. Real explanations can be provided,
in fact, only if every claim about grammars entails some empirical
claim about languages, and every difference between theories in the
classes of grammars they generate entails different predictions about
the nature of the set of possible human languages.

Since all facts and laws about constituent-ordering make essential reference to constituents and their groupings, and presuppose a
metalanguage with the power of expressing such reference, all theories
of grammar--of either the variable-order or invariant-order types--will
have the potential to restrict the class of possible constituent orderings by means of laws restricting the class of possible constituents,
the class of possible groupings of constituents, and the class of possible derivational changes in constituency and constituency relations.
With respect to terminal semantic representations, of course, there
are strong and quite direct empirical constraints, with the constituents
and constituent groupings of any given representation being largely if
not wholly determined by directly observable theory-independent facts
about the meaning and meaning relations of the linguistic object that
it represents. But there are clearly very few if any linguistic

objects whose ordering properties could be specified in terms of the constituents and constituency relations of its empirically appropriate terminal semantic representation. In other words, it is simply a fact about human language that all true generalizations about ordering hold not with respect to semantic representations but rather for the constituents and groupings of the superficial syntactic representations that are derived from them by the application of general processes of reduction and regrouping.

For the explanation of constituent-order universals, therefore, constraints on semantic representations can be relevant only in conjunction with a highly restrictive set of constraints on the transformation of constituents and constituency relations--that is, on the possible equivalences that can hold between one constituent and another, or between one grouping of constituents and a different grouping of those constituents. Such a conjunction of constraints would be sufficient for all explanatory purposes, however, only if there are no dependencies between the ordering properties of one construction and those of any other construction, and if for any given construction it is the case either that all of its logically possible constituent orderings are natural or that they are all non-natural. But it is doubtful whether these conditions, especially the former, actually hold for the set of natural languages.

The most natural and most direct basis for the principled explanation of constituent-order universals is clearly by means of universal constraints on the class of possible ordering rules, that is, the class of possible rules of grammar that assert language-specific laws about the ordering of constituents in particular constructions. For variable-order theories of grammar, however, such constraints can never be sufficient for the explanation of anything, since ordering properties are never fully determined by ordering rules alone in grammars governed by such theories, but rather by the conjunction of ordering rules and all rules of the grammar that might be used to justify derivational reorderings. For invariant order theories, on the other hand, all ordering properties are directly determined by ordering rules alone, since there is no possible way to suppress, modify, undo, or contradict any of the ordering assertions expressed by such rules.

For invariant order theories, therefore, it should be possible, in principle at least, to account for all constituent-order universals by means of grammatical laws restricting the class of possible ordering rules for natural-language grammar. For variable-order theories, on the other hand, it will always be necessary to assume a pair of separate restrictions--one on the class of possible ordering rules, the other on the class of possible derivational reorderings. This fundamental difference between the two theory-types in the relative naturalness and simplicity of the optimal explanation-types that they generate will be exemplified in the following section with respect to some of the particular problems of constituent-order explanation discussed there. This difference follows directly from their difference with respect to the Invariant Order Constraint, and thus provides important additional evidence of the correctness of this principle.

3.   Some Illustrative Complexities of the Task

The linguist is obligated, like any other scientist, to strive for maximally satisfying explanations of all significant facts and generalizations about the subject matter of his discipline. The burdens of this obligation are so heavy, the chances of achieving even the most temporary and moderate degree of success in the perpetual hunt for explanations are so few, that the temptation to abandon the hunt and settle for lesser game often becomes almost too great to resist. In linguistics, unfortunately, the explanatory goals of science have often been completely abandoned, with unfalsifiable speculations, dogmas, probability claims, and vague expressions of feeling or intuition taking the place of the explicit laws and rigorous logic of empirical science and its necessary commitment to the kind of intellectual integrity and hard-nosed objectivity that requires a possible test for every hypothesis and a proof for every claim. Some insight and much factual knowledge has undoubtedly resulted from these speculative endeavors, but, of course, no explanations of anything.

But the scientist obviously cannot settle for less than real explanations without ceasing to be a scientist, a seeker after truth and understanding. Moreover, it is only by trying to fully understand the universe that we can hope to partially understand it. It is only

by repeatedly proving our theories to be false that we can make any
approach to a theory that is true. But to prove anything, to achieve
any real enrichment of our knowledge of the universe, we must be willing to accept all of the severe obligations of nomological explanation,
all of the burdens of explicitness and complete testability, all of the
difficulties, in short, that are inherent to the task of constructing
and evaluating scientific theories.

With these general obligations and difficulties in mind, I would
like now to complete this partial prologomenon to the task of constituent-order explanation by presenting a few simple illustrations of the
extreme complexity of this task. In particular, I hope to show how any
serious attempt to achieve even the lowest order of explanation requires the assumption of numerous precise and highly restrictive metaconstraints on natural-language grammar, metaconstraints which have
far-reaching implications and interrelations with respect to all aspects of phonology and syntax. The necessity and conceptual fruits of
explicitness will hopefully be apparent in all cases, and the problems
that we face in the explanation of constituent order universals will
be seen to be inseparable from a host of interconnected problems of a
more general type, all related to the central linguistic problem of
determining the nature of human language and its range of possible
variation and change.

3.1. <u>Auxiliary Marginality</u>. One general way of explaining a law of
the form "If X, then Y" is to show that X is simply a special case of
Y. Thus, for example, if one were to ask why it is the case that "If
there are poodles in a house, then there are dogs in that house", the
only appropriate answer, presumably, would be simply that poodles are
a kind of dog. It is also possible to explain "If X, then Y" by showing that Z is the case and that both X and Y are instantiations of Z.
For example, if one were to ask why it is the case that "If oak logs
float in mercury, then beech logs float in mercury", a natural answer
would be that <u>all wood</u> floats in mercury and that oak logs and beech
logs are both kinds of wood.

This is the pattern of explanation that is commonly employed with
respect to ordering generalizations like those expressed in Greenberg's

Universal 16 (1963:67):

> In languages with dominant order VSO, an inflected auxi-
> liary always precedes the main verb. In languages with
> dominant order SOV, an inflected auxiliary always follows
> the main verb.

These generalizations would thus seem to follow quite directly from
the assumption that main verbs and inflected auxiliaries are in fact
constituents of the same type in all languages--that both are kinds of
predicates, verbs, operators, or whatever. This assumption is quite
plausible and clearly has some degree of independent support. Given
this, then, the marginality of auxiliaries would be accounted for by
the fact that if all predicates are marginal to their arguments then
every auxiliary will be marginal to its clausal argument and on the
same margin as the predicate of that clause.

But this is clearly not enough to qualify as an explanation of
Universal 16. It is also necessary to assume that these two types of
verbs or predicates--which clearly differ in some ways--always behave
in the same way with respect to ordering. There must be some universal principle of grammar, in other words, from which it would follow
that main verbs and inflected auxiliaries cannot be governed by different ordering principles.

The required principle cannot merely assert this restriction, of
course, since it would then be simply a grammatical translation of the
linguistic fact that is to be explained--namely, that main verbs and
auxiliaries are ordered in the same way relative to their arguments.
Thus, though the premises of (4) meet the formal conditions for possible explanations, they fail to really explain anything by virtue of
the essential equivalence of the explanadum (4d) and the explanatory
law (4c) appealed to in the explanans.

   (4)(a) Main verbs and auxiliaries are both predicates (or
       operands).

     (b) Auxiliaries take clauses as arguments (or
       operators).

(c) For any language, if one predicate is ordered at a clause margin, then all predicates are ordered at that same margin.

(d) Therefore: If main verbs precede (follow) their nominal arguments in a language, then auxiliaries precede (follow) their main verbs in that language.

To really explain (4d), Greenberg's Universal 16, it is necessary, therefore, to also explain (4c).

It would appear to be one of the necessary prerequisites to such explanation that main verbs and auxiliaries be assumed not only to be members of the same grammatical category, but also to be categorically indistinguishable in any way. Thus if either auxiliaries or non-auxiliaries constituted a natural subclass of the class of predicates, then it would be possible for main verbs and auxiliaries to be ordered in accordance with different principles--a possibility that is contradictory to the facts expressed by Universal 16. For example, assume that auxiliaries and main verbs uniquely include a set of one or more distinctive elements $\underline{V}$, and that every auxiliary but no main verb also includes the set of elements $\underline{AUX}$. There could then be possible grammars including the pairs of rules in (5a) and (6a), generating languages with the constituent orderings represented in (5b) and (6b), respectively.[4]

(5) (a) [[V, AUX], X] = [[V, AUX] & X]

   [V, X] = [X & V]

   (b) [AUX & [N & N & MV]]

(6) (a) [[V, AUX], X] = [X & [V, AUX]]

   [V, X] = [V & X]

   (b) [[MV & N & N] & AUX]

But Universal 16 asserts that there are no natural languages with these ordering patterns. If this generalization is true, therefore, any theory of language that generates grammars including the rules of (5a) or (6a) is empirically false.

Grammars that include only the second, or properly included, rules of (5a) and (6a) must be generated, of course, since such grammars generate well-attested natural languages like Japanese--with the right marginal ordering pattern [X & MV & AUX] generated by the properly included rule of (5a)--and Tagalog--with the left marginal ordering [AUX & MV & X] generated by the properly included rule of (6a). What is required of any adequate theory of language, therefore, is that it provided a principled basis for the exclusion of the properly including rules here without excluding the properly included ones. A natural way of achieving this would be to simply exclude the set of elements AUX from the vocabulary set for possible grammatical statements. It would then follow that there are no possible rules of grammar like the properly including rules of (5a) and (6a).

But even if this vocabulary restriction should prove to be tenable, it would still not be sufficient to account for the non-existence of languages with the ordering patterns (5b) or (6b). This is because there can be natural classes of constituents that are determined not by any internal characteristics of their members but rather by their distinctive function or external relationship to other constituents. Thus even if the internal structures of auxiliaries and main verbs are indistinguishable, these two constituent types might still be distinguishable by their distinctive grouping and/or ordering relations in sentences or other constructions that include them. This appears, in fact, to be the case, since auxiliaries always take clausal or propositional arguments and are hence always (semantically) superordinate to their associated main verbs. This distinctive difference in grouping relations would thus make it possible for there to be distinctive ordering principles for auxiliaries and main verbs, as in the rule pairs of (7).

(7) (a) [V, [V, X]] = [V & [V, X]]
         [V, X] = [X & V]

    (b) [V, [V, X]] = [V, [X & V]]
         [V, X] = [V & X]

    (c) [V, [V, X]] = [[V, X] & V]
         [V, X] = [V & X]

(d) [V, [V, X]] = [V, [V & X]
     [V, X] = [X & V]

Grammars including (7a) or (7b) generate languages with the non-natural
ordering pattern (5b). Grammars including (7c) or (7d) generate languages with the non-natural ordering pattern (6b). Any adequate theory
of language must therefore exclude all four of these grammar types
from the set of possible grammars that it generates.

If it is assumed that all grammatical rules are applied cyclically,
from the most deeply embedded constituents to the least deeply embedded
ones in phonetically-directed derivations, none of the rule pairs of
(7) would be possible, since the structural analyses of the properly
including member of each pair, which make reference to unordered constituents of a subordinate construction, could never be satisfied in
any line of any derivation. However, the principle of cyclic rule
application is clearly not sufficient to effect the required exclusion
of the non-natural orderings (5b) and (6b). Thus there could be grammars fully consistent with this principle that include the rule pairs
of (8).

(8)(a) [V, [X & V]] = [V & [X & V]]
        [V, X] = [X & V]

   (b) [V, [X & V]] = [[V & X] & V]
        [V, X] = [V & X]

Grammars including (8a) generate languages with the ordering pattern
(5b), and those including (8b) generate languages with the pattern
(6b). Universal 16 cannot be explained, therefore, either by constraints on the set of linguistic elements, or by a cyclic constraint
on the application of grammatical rules, or by the conjunction of such
constraints.

I know of no additional empirically-defensible lawlike generalization about grammars which would serve to exclude the non-natural
grammars (8a) and (8b). Nor do I know of any alternative law or set
of grammatical laws that would suffice to exclude these grammars along
with all of the other non-natural grammars represented in (5), (6),
and (7). If Greenberg's Universal 16 is true, it must be the case, of

course, that there is some such law or set of laws. But, regardless of its actual truth or falsity, it is clear that this universal, which would seem at first sight so easy to explain, turns out in fact to be extremely difficulty to explain. This difficulty, with all of the linguistic insights and valuable test conditions that are associated with it, could never become apparent if linguists were willing to accept as "explanations" of Universal 16 such informal speculative fragments of possible explanations as expressed, for example, by the comment, "Well, of course, main verbs and auxiliaries are ordered in the same way, since they're both verbs (or predicates, or operands, etc.)."

In all cases like this--and there are obviously many others like it--informal explanations can clearly be worse than no explanations at all, since they lead to no real increase of knowledge and merely obscure all of the real empirical questions and implications that are involved. Worst of all, the effect of such deceptively plausible pseudo-explanations is to suppress rather than stimulate further inquiry. Real nomological-deductive explanations, on the other hand, always raise new questions and open new avenues for significant empirical research. This is true even when the attempted explanation is false or inadequate, as in the case under consideration here. It can in fact be maintained, I believe, that the search for nomological-deductive explanations constitutes the only available natural source of scientific knowledge and the only possible justifiable basis for scientific research.

3.2. <u>Oblique Pronoun Precedence</u>. Another lawlike generalization about constituent ordering in natural language is expressed by Greenberg's Universal 25 (1963:72):

If the pronominal object follows the verb, so does the nominal object.

The generalization about pronominal precedence actually appears to hold for all oblique, or non-subject, nominals--indirect objects as well as direct ones, datives, benefactives, etc., as well as patients. In other words, it appears to be true simply that there are natural

languages with superficial predicates, or verb phrases, of the forms
(9a), (9b), and (9c), but none with those of the forms of (9d).[5]

(9) (a)   [X & PRO & Y & V & Z]   [X & NOM & Y & V & Z]
           (e.g., Japanese)

    (b)   [X & V & Y & PRO & Z]   [X & V & Y & NOM & Z]
           (e.g., English)

    (c)   [X & PRO & Y & V & Z]   [X & V & Y & NOM & Z]
           (e.g., Spanish)

    (d)   [X & NOM & Y & V & Z]   [X & V & Y & PRO & Z] (*)

It is the case, then, that every possibly adequate theory of grammar
must generate grammars for languages of the first three types but none
for languages of the fourth type.

This minimal condition for empirical adequacy has not been satisfied as far as I can tell by any actual theory of grammar that has thus
far been proposed. Grammars for languages of type (9d) are thus generated, for example, both by Lamb's (1966) theory of stratificational
grammar and by Chomsky's (1965) theory of transformational grammar,
both by Lakoff's (1971) theory of generative semantics and by Jackendoff's (1972) theory of interpretive semantics. If Universal 25 is
true, therefore, all of these theories are false, along with all other
linguistic theories that fail to predict the non-existence of natural
languages of type (9d). The known evidence indicates that this universal statement is in fact true, and that its truth is not accidental to the particular finite sample of languages that have thus far
been observed.

If it is assumed that the non-phonological representations of all
arguments include a set of one or more distinctive elements N, and
that the representations of all pronominal arguments but no non-pronominal ones also include a distinctive element PRO, then pronouns
will be universally and uniquely identifiable as members of the class
[N, PRO], and nominals, or non-pronominal arguments, will be identifiable as all members of the class [N] that are not members of [N,
PRO]. Given this representational assumption, along with the further
assumption that all verbal predicates and no arguments include the

distinctive element set V, the four langauge types of (9) will be respectively generated by grammars including the rules of (10).

(10) G.a. (Japanese) [N, V] = [N & V]

G.b. (English) [N, V] = [V & N]

G.c. (Spanish) [N, V] = [V & N] [[N, PRO], V]
= [[N, PRO] & V]

G.d. (*) [N, V] = [N & V] [[N, PRO], V]
= [V & [N, PRO]]

It will be observed that the general, or properly included, rule of the non-natural grammar (G.d) is also a rule of the natural grammar (G.a), which generates actual human languages like Japanese, Dakota, Basque, and the Western Desert Language. On the other hand, the specific, or properly including, rule of (G.d) is not included in any of the grammars that generate languages of natural types. To account for the given facts about pronominal precedence, therefore, it would appear to be both necessary and sufficient to delimit the set of possible grammatical rules in such a way as to exclude the properly including rule of (G.d) without excluding any of the other rules of (10).

It would be possible, of course, to effect the required restriction by mere stipulation. Thus a theory of grammar could achieve consistency with Universal 25 by simply including among its axioms the universal statement (11).

(11) For any set of statements G, G is a possible grammar of a natural language only if for any statement S included in G, S is not of the form [[N, PRO], V] = [V & [N, PRO]].

This axiom, with the appropriate subsidiary assumptions, would serve to exclude grammars of type (G.d) from the set of grammars generated by the theory, and would thus correctly predict that there are no human languages of type (10d), languages with postverbal pronominal arguments and preverbal nominal ones. But it is clear that such a theory does not provide any _explanation_ for this fact, since the crucial principle (11) is simply an ad hoc stipulation that has no

internal support and no external value or justification except with
respect to the very fact about pronominal precedence that is at issue
here. Indeed, (11) can be most appropriately viewed simply as a grammatical translation of this linguistic universal, since to assert that
there are no grammars with distinctively pronominal rules of post-
verbal argument-ordering is essentially the same as asserting that
there are no languages with distinctively pronominal postverbally
ordered arguments--which is precisely what is asserted by Universal
25. To explain this linguistic universal, therefore, it is necessary
to explain the grammatical universal (11) that constitutes its generative translation. In other words, the exclusion of the properly including rule of (G.d) cannot be merely stipulated, as in (11), but
must be shown to follow deductively from statements of a more general
and more generally motivated character.

When we compare the non-natural grammar (G.d) with the natural
grammar (G.c), the formal property that distinguishes them can readily
be determined. Thus both grammars include a pair of proper-inclusion-
related ordering rules specifying the differential ordering of a general constituent type (N) and a specific subtype of that type (N, PRO)
relative to sister constituents of a single type (V). The only difference is that in one grammar (the natural one) the subtype is asserted to precede its sister constituent, while in the other grammar
(the non-natural one) the subtype is asserted to follow its sister.
In other words, where the natural grammar specifies preposing of the
specific, marked, or properly-including constituent and postposing of
the general, unmarked, or properly included one, the non-natural grammar specifies postposing for the specific case and preposing for the
general, or elsewhere, case. This suggests that the reason why there
are no natural-language grammars of type (G.d), and hence no natural
languages of type (10d), may be simply that there are no possible
rules of grammar specifying the postpositive ordering of subclasses.
The general exclusion of such rules could be expressed in the form of
the following grammatical law of Specificity Preposition:

(12) Specificity Preposition
      For any set of statements G, G is a possible gram-
      mar of a natural language only if for any pair of

ordering statements [A, B] = X and [[A, C], B] = Y,
included in G, Y is of the form [[A, C] & B].

Any theory of grammar that includes this statement will be capable of explaining Universal 25. Thus since the principle of Specificity Preposition is neither analytic nor known yet to be false, and since it makes no reference to any of the particular linguistic or grammatical facts in question, it can legitimately serve as the operant law in an explanation of these facts. The stipulative universal statement (11), which constitutes the grammatical expression of Greenberg's linguistic law of pronominal precedence, is seen to follow quite directly here, since grammars like all other empirical theories must be free of vacuous statements, and since the properly including rules of (G.c) and (G.d) can occur non-vacuously only in grammars that also include their respective properly included rules. It follows then that if a grammar has an ordering rule with the semantically proximate member [[N, PRO], V], it will also have an ordering rule with the semantically proximate member [N, V]. It will thus further follow by the law of Specificity Preposition that the phonetically proximate member of the properly including rule must be [[N, PRO] & V], as in the natural grammar (G.c) for languages like French and Spanish, and not [V & [N, PRO]], as in the non-natural grammar (G.d). Any theory that incorporates this law will thus be capable of explaining, and not merely predicting, the non-existence of languages with postposed pronominal arguments and preposed nominal ones.

As in all other instances of explanation, the operant law here has numerous empirical implications outside the original domain of explanation. Some of these implications will be considered in the following sections. However, the adequacy of the explanation of Universal 25 that has been outlined here depends not only on the truth of the law of Specificity Preposition and the complete consistency of its full range of implications with respect to all known facts about human languages. There are also a number of crucial auxiliary hypotheses that have been explicitly or implicitly appealed to here, and it is only if each of these is also true that Universal 25 can be said to have been explained.

First, of course, there are the significant vocabulary and representational hypotheses assumed at the outset. Thus correct conclusions will follow from the principle of Specificity Preposition only if it is universally the case that non-phonological representations of pronouns include distinctive elements not included in the representations of non-pronominal arguments, and that the latter include no distinctive elements not included in the former. If the converse could obtain, for example, even in one language, the class of non-pronominal arguments would be distinctively identifiable, say, as [N, NOM], and what would follow then from the law of Specificity Preposition would be the false conclusion that there are possible human languages of type (10d). Similarly, if non-pronominal representations rather than pronominal ones included distinctive elements in all languages, it would follow not only that there are languages of type (10d) but also that there are no languages of type (10c), that is, no languages like French or Spanish. If both pronominals and non-pronominals could be associated with distinctive elements, finally, the principle of Specificity Preposition could have no restrictive power whatever with respect to the ordering of these constituents, and it would follow falsely again that there are natural languages of each of the four types in (10). It is clear then that the particular representational constraint that has been assumed, which has many independent testable implications of its own, of course, plays an essential role in the explanation indicated here. Should this assumption be proven false the whole explanation would be untenable.

But a further, and still more restrictive, representational constraint must also be assumed, a universal constraint against the use of negative variables, or class-complement specifications, in the statements of any natural-language grammar. Thus, if the power of negative variable reference were available, it would be possible to distinctively identify non-pronominal arguments even though they contain no distinctive elements of their own--namely by means of the negative variable, or class-complement specification, [N, ~PRO]. Any linguistic theory that permits the use of negative variables would thus generate, in addition to the grammars of (10), the grammars (G.e) and (G.f) of (13).

(13) G.e. (Spanish) [N, V] = [N & V]   [[N, ~PRO], V] = [V
                      & [N, ~PRO]]

      G.f. (*)   [N, V] = [V & N]   [[N, ~PRO], V] = [N,
                      ~PRO] & V]

The principle of Specificity Preposition would exclude (G.f) from
the class of possible grammars along with (G.d) of (10). This would be
quite appropriate, since grammars of type (G.c) generate languages of
the Spanish type, and do so in a much more appropriate way than (G.e)
does--namely, by asserting, contrary to (G.e), that postverbal order
is the normal, unmarked, or elsewhere, position for oblique arguments
in such languages. But Specificity Preposition is clearly incapable
of excluding grammars of the type (G.f), which generate the non-natural
language type (10d). Theories that include this law will thus be incapable of explaining Universal 25 unless they also incorporate both
the Simplex-Feature Hypothesis (Sanders 1972a, 1972b) and the hypothesis of Non-Negative Variables (Sanders 1972b), along with the particular vocabulary assumptions that have been made here about the representations of nominal and pronominal arguments.

The former two hypotheses are very general grammatical laws which
have already received considerable empirical support quite independently
of the facts in question here. (See, e.g., Delisle 1972; Sanders 1972a,
1972b). The latter universal is much less general, and its various
implications have not yet been investigated. The point here, however,
is simply that this attempt at explanation, depends crucially on the
set of representational and vocabulary hypotheses of the governing
theory of grammar. For non-vacuous theories of this sort, in other
words, all statements about the form and content of grammatical representations and rules have explanatory import and are subject to empirical confirmation and disconfirmation in precisely the same manner as
all other statements of the theory.

A theory of grammar that incorporates both the law of Specificity
Preposition and the cited representational hypotheses will still be
incapable of explaining Universal 25, however, unless it also incorporates the independent universal principle of Invariant Ordering.
Thus any otherwise adequate theory that permits variable ordering will

generate, in addition to the natural invariant-order grammars of (10),
the set of variable-order grammars in (14).

(14) G.g. (Spanish)   [N, V] = [V & N]
                        [V & [N, PRO]] = [[N, PRO] & V]

      G.h. (*)   [N, V] = [N & V]
                       [[N, PRO] & V] = [V & [N, PRO]]

      G.i. (*)   [N, V] = [V & N]
                       [V & N] = [N & V]
                       [[N, PRO] & V] = [V & [N, PRO]]

      G.j. (*)   [N, V] = [V & N]
                       [[N, PRO], V] = [N, PRO] & V]
                       [V & N] = [N & V]
                       [[N, PRO] & V] = [V & [N, PRO]]

All of these grammars are excluded by the Invariant Order Constraint,
of course, and none are excluded by variable-order theories incorporating the principle of Specificity Preposition and the given auxiliary
representational hypotheses. Thus since (G.h), (G.i), and (G.j) generate languages of the non-natural type (10d), it follows that the
principle of invariance is a necessary precondition for the adequacy
of the explanation outlined here.

This is not to say that it is _impossible_ for variable order
theories to explain Universal 25, since, given almost any fact and almost any axiomatic basis, it will nearly always be possible to expand
that basis in some way that will permit the generation of some explanation for that fact. Witness, for example, the epicyclic expansion of
the axiomatic basis of geocentric astronomy, or the various axiomatic
expansions of the phlogiston theory of combustion. It is clear though
that variable- and invariant-order theories of grammar cannot possibly
provide the same kinds of explanation for any facts like those expressed by Universal 25. It is also clear that, other things being equal,
an explanation provided by a variable order theory will necessarily
always be axiomatically more complex than one provided by an invariant
order theory. This is because the variable order theory will always

have to exclude a much larger and more heterogeneous class of otherwise possible grammars than the invariant order theory.

Thus to account for the facts in question here, an invariant order
theory needs to exclude only one out of four otherwise possible grammar types, while a variable order theory must exclude four out of eight
otherwise possible grammar types. Much more important, though, is the
fact that invariant order theories are capable of providing uniform,
non-disjunctive, and highly general explanations of ordering facts
like those expressed by Universal 25, while the optimal explanations
of such facts by variable order theories will apparently always require
the assumption of multiple sets of exclusionary principles, one to delimit the set of possible non-superficial constituent orderings specified by grammars, another to delimit the possible set of derivational
reorderings that can be specified, perhaps a third to delimit the set
of possible superficial orderings generated, or the possible relations
that can hold between superficial and non-superficial orderings.

For variable- and invariant-order theories alike it is necessary
to exclude grammars with the rules of (G.d) and no derivational reorderings of oblique arguments. One possible principled basis for
such exclusion has been presented here. And for invariant-order theories, though, it is also necessary to exclude grammars with the rules
of (G.h), (G.i), and (G.j). To achieve this exclusion the principles
that served to exclude (G.d) are of no use whatever. Additional principles must thus be sought.

It will be observed that all of the non-natural variable-order
grammars in (14) include the rule [[N, PRO] & V] = [V & [N, PRO]],
which justifies the phonetically-directed postposings of non-superfi-
cially preposed pronominal arguments. This is, of course, the variable-
order analogue of postpositional rather than prepositional ordering
for a specified subclass, and has the same ultimate effect as the latter. It would thus be reasonable to assume for the exclusion of such
reorderings a variable-order analogue of the law of Specificity Preposition. We can call this exclusionary principle for variable-order
theories the law of Specificity Reordering, and can express it as in
(15).

(15) <u>Specificity Reordering</u>

For any set of statements G, G is a possible grammar of a natural language only if for any pair of statements [A, B] = [A & B] and [[A, C] & B] = Y, included in G, Y is not of the form [B & [A, C]].

Any variable-order theory that incorporates both Specificity Reordering and Specificity Preposition, along with the stated auxiliary hypotheses about representation, will be capable of providing an explanation for Universal 25.[6] It has been seen that neither Specificity Preposition nor Specificity Reordering is sufficient for variable order theories, while the former is sufficient for all theories that incorporate the principle of Invariant Ordering. It will also be observed that Specificity Reordering is a somewhat less general and less restrictive principle than Specificity Preposition. Much more important, though, are the partially isomorphic characteristics of these two principles, their partial overlappings in both form and function, their parallelism without reducibility. Any theory that includes both of them will thus fail to capture a clearly significant generalization--namely, that which is expressed in invariant order theories by the principle of Specificity Preposition alone.

Given the irreducibility of the two specificity principles and the obvious necessity of reordering constraints in variable order theories, it would be reasonable to approach the overlap problem here by considering the eliminability of Specificity Preposition for such theories. Such exclusion would be possible if some other means could be found to effect the exclusion of grammars of type (G.d), which include no relevant reordering rules and hence cannot possibly be excluded by Specificity Reordering. A possible replacement principle is immediately suggested by the fact that (G.d) is one of only two possible grammar types that includes proper-inclusion-related ordering rules, and that the only other grammar type that does so is (G.c), which generates languages of the Spanish type, a type which is also generated by the variable-order grammar type (G.g) in full accordance with variable order principle of Specificity Reordering. There would be no harm then for such theories in eliminating (G.c) along with (G.d). And

this could be effected simply by the exclusion of all proper-inclusion-related ordering rules, or, still more generally, by simply excluding all ordering rules that are not defined solely on generic, or
whole-class, constituents. The latter principle of exclusion could be
expressed as in (16).

(16) <u>Generic Ordering</u> (for variable-order theories)
       For any set of statements G, Ǥ is a possible grammar
       of a natural language only if for any statement of
       the form [A, B] = [A & B], included in G, both A and
       B are single elements.

For variable-order theories, then, it is possible to account for
Greenberg's Universal 25 by a conjunction of the stated representational constraints and the laws of Generic Ordering and Specificity
Reordering. It is doubtful, though, that even this can qualify as a
real explanation of this universal. First, the principle of Generic
Ordering, which depends crucially on the power of derivational reordering, appears to be inherently ad hoc and unnatural in the context of
theories that include this power. Thus if both classes and subclasses
are subject to reordering, and classes are subject to ordering, why
shouldn't subclasses also be subject to ordering? Moreover, though
Generic Ordering and Specificity Reordering are formally distinct and
complementary in function, they are not really independent either of
each other or of the presupposed hypothesis of variable ordering.
Thus it has been seen that neither of these principles has any restrictive or delimiting powers of its own, and that it is only if <u>both</u> are
assumed that a variable order theory can exclude the logically possible
language type (10d) from the class of types of human language. Neither principle is subject to independent empirical test, therefore,
as evidenced by the fact that if a human language of type (10d) were
found--that is, if Universal 25 were false--this would show only that
<u>at least one</u> of these two principles is false. It would be impossible
to determine anything whatever about their individual truth values,
since each one is independently consistent both with the existence and
with the non-existence of languages of type (10d). This invulnerability to independent confirmation or disconfirmation contrasts sharply,
of course, with the direct vulnerability of the law of Specificity

Preposition in invariant order theories, which would be falsified by
a single instance of a type (10d) language.

3.3. Marked Adjective Precedence. Greenberg's Universal 19 (1963:68)
states the following law of adjectival ordering for natural languages:

> When the general rule is that the descriptive adjective
> follows [its nominal head], there may be a minority of
> adjectives which usually precede, but when the general
> rule is that descriptive adjectives precede, there are no
> exceptions.

In other words, in addition to languages in which all adjectives precede their heads (like Japanese), and languages in which all adjectives
follow their heads (like Thai), there are natural languages, like
French and Spanish, in which a small specified subclass of adjectives
precede their heads and all others follow. There are, however, no
natural languages in which a subclass of adjectives follow their heads
and all others precede.[7]

In languages of the French-type the set of prenominally ordered
adjectives typically includes something on the order of twenty-five or
thirty morphemes, nearly all of which are homophonous with semantically
distinct adjectives that are postnominally ordered. Thus the vast
majority of adjectives are always postnominal in such languages--e.g.,
French l'homme intelligent 'the intelligent man' (*l'intelligent homme),
Spanish un vino rojo 'a red wine' (*un rojo vino). The small class of
prenominal adjectives are identifiable only by their individual semantic properties--e.g., French le brave homme 'the worthy man' (≠ l'homme
brave 'the brave man'), le petit homme 'the little man' (*l'homme
petit), Spanish un pobre hombre 'an unfortunate man' (≠ un hombre pobre
'a poor (= economically disadvantaged) man'). The ultimate for this
language type is Basque, in which the class of prenominal adjectives
is reported to include only one member--the adjective euskal, meaning
'Basque' (Lertxundi y Baztarrika 1913:226).

It is clear, therefore, that the grammars of languages like French,
Spanish, and Basque must necessarily include morpheme-specific order-
ing rules like [[ADJ, UNFORTUNATE], N] = [[ADJ, UNFORTUNATE] & N], and
[[ADJ, BASQUE], N] = [[ADJ, BASQUE] & N], where UNFORTUNATE and BASQUE

are the non-phonological feature or features that are necessary and
sufficient to distinguish these particular morphemes from all other
adjectives in the language. The small set of rules of this sort that
are required will suffice to specify all prenominal adjectival orderings in the language, and all other adjectival orderings will be specified by the general, properly included, or elsewhere rule of postnominal ordering, [ADJ, N] = [N & ADJ].

Thus, according to Universal 19, there are natural languages with
grammars of types (17a), (17b), and (17c), but none with grammars of
type (17d).

(17) G.a (Japanese) [ADJ, N] = [ADJ & N]

G.b (Thai) [ADJ, N] = [N & ADJ]

G.c (French) [ADJ, N] = [N & ADJ]
[[ADJ, LITTLE], N] = [[ADJ, LITTLE] & N]

G.d (*) [[ADJ, LITTLE], N] = [N & [ADJ, LITTLE]]

It can readily be seen that this set of grammar types is an instance of precisely the same paradigm exemplified by the set of argument-ordering grammar types in (10). Thus in both cases the non-
natural grammar-types (10 G.d and 17 G.d) are distinguished from the
natural ones by virtue of their incorporation of a pair of proper-
inclusion-related ordering rules asserting that a specified subclass,
or properly including constituent, is ordered after its sister constituent rather than before it. Both of these independently non-natural
grammar-types are seen to be excludable then by the same general
principle of grammar--the universal law of Specificity Preposition.
The facts reported by Greenberg about marked adjective precedence in
natural language, which follow as deductive consequences of this law
and its associated representational hypotheses, would thus appear to
constitute strong confirmatory evidence for it, and for the general
metaconstraints on grammatical theories that it presupposes.

In this case, moreover, in contrast to the case of pronominal
precedence, there can be no question about the particular representational assumptions and rule formulations that are involved. Thus
while additional independent support is needed for the assumption that

pronominal arguments are an identifiable class while non-pronominal
arguments are not, no additional support is needed for the assumption
that some adjectives must be ordered by means of morpheme-specific
rules in languages like French, Spanish, and Basque, and that such
rules must specify the prenominal orderings for the language rather
than the postnominal ones. This is because neither the small class of
prenominal adjectives in such languages nor the vastly larger and
essentially open-ended complement class of postnominal adjectives can
be identified as a natural class, either semantically, phonologically,
or syntactically. There would thus appear to be no possible way to
correctly specify the differential ordering of, say, Spanish pobre
'unfortunate' and pobre 'economically disadvantaged' except by means
of a morpheme-specific rule of prenominal ordering for the former and
a properly included elsewhere rule of postnominal ordering subsuming
the latter.[8] The form and content of grammar-type (G.c) is thus very
strongly and directly dictated by the facts about French, Spanish,
Basque, and all other known languages with differential ordering of
adjectives. The effectiveness and naturalness of the law of Specificity Preposition in distinguishing this grammar-type from the non-
natural grammar-type (G.d) would thus appear to provide particularly
strong evidence for this principle, and might suggest that, with respect to Universal 19 at least, its truth is a necessary, and not
merely possible, precondition to the explanation of the facts in
question.

For theories with the additional power of variable ordering in
grammatical derivations, the available avenues for explanation of
Universal 19 are essentially the same as for Universal 25. Here again
it is necessary for such theories to exclude a larger and more heterogeneous class of otherwise possible grammar types than need to be excluded by theories incorporating the more restrictive and more natural
hypothesis of derivational invariance. In this case, a variable order
theory must exclude not only grammar-type (G.d) of (17), but also all
grammar-types including rules justifying the phonetically-directed
reordering of a specified subclass of adjectives from prenominal to
postnominal order. An explanation by the conjunction of Generic Ordering and Specificity Reordering would thus again be possible here, with

the same relative inadequacies of the parallel variable-order explanation given for Universal 25.

3.4. <u>Marked and Unmarked Attributive Ordering</u>. In addition to languages like Japanese, in which all nominal modifiers are ordered before their heads, and languages like Thai, in which all modifiers are ordered postnominally, there are natural languages, like English, in which adjectival modifiers are ordered before their nominal heads and all other modifiers are ordered postnominally.[9] The facts thus far are precisely parallel to the facts about Oblique Pronoun Precedence and Marked Adjective Precedence, since in all three cases there are languages with differential ordering of a subclass and its complement, with the subclass ordered before its sister constituent and the general class ordered after it. On the basis of this parallelism, it would be natural to expect that there should be no human languages in which adjectival modifiers are ordered postnominally and all other modifiers are ordered prenominally. This would be a false expectation, however, since there are languages, like Basque, that are precisely of this type.

Basque has already been seen to have postnominal ordering for all adjectives except <u>euskal</u>. Thus, <u>euskal jaya</u> 'Basque fiesta', but <u>gizon zintzoa</u> 'just man', <u>gizon ona</u> 'good man', <u>andre ona</u> 'good woman'. However, in nearly all other respects the language is governed, like those of the Japanese-type, by the general principle that all attributes (or operators) are ordered before their heads (or operands). Thus, in particular, Basque has prenominal ordering for both relative clauses and genitival attributes. For example, <u>nik ikusi nun etxea</u> 'the house that I saw' (cf. <u>nik etxea ikusi nun</u> 'I saw the house'), <u>arrizko etxea</u> 'the house of stone', <u>etxeko atea</u> 'the door of the house'.

Thus while there were natural language grammars of only three of the four logically possible types for the specification of ordering for pronominal and nonpronominal oblique arguments and for marked and unmarked adjectives, we find in this case that all four of the possible grammar-types for the ordering of adjectival and non-adjectival modifiers are natural.

(18) G.a. (Japanese) $_N[X, N] = _N[X \ \& \ N]$

G.b. (Thai) $_N[X, N] = _N[N \ \& \ X]$

G.c. (English) $_N[X, N] = _N[N \ \& \ X]$ $_N[ADJ, N] = _N[ADJ \ \& \ N]$

G.d. (Basque) $_N[X, N] = _N[X \ \& \ N]$ $_N[ADJ, N] = _N[N \ \& \ ADJ]$

But it follows from the stated law of Specificity Preposition that there can be no natural grammars of type (G.d), and hence no natural languages like Basque. Thus since unrestricted variables are implicitly included in all unclosed representations,[10] the constituent representation ADJ in (G.c) and (G.d) is equivalent to the representation [ADJ, X] and hence stands in a proper inclusion relation to the maximally unspecified constituent representation [X]. But Specificity Preposition asserts that properly including constituents can only be prepositional to their sisters, as in (G.c), and never postpositional, as in (G.d). The existence of Basque thus suffices to falsify this law.[11]

Situations of this sort are standard in empirical science, of course, and there is a standard set of patterns of inquiry occasioned by them. Thus, given the apparent falsification of an explanatory law, the first step, normally, is to make certain that the given falsifying data are in fact correct. In the present case, however, I know of no reason to believe that the facts about Basque are not correct as stated. Given reasonably strong assurance of factual correctness, then, there are essentially only three possible courses that can be taken. The first is to determine whether there might be any additional, or alternative, independent auxiliary principles which, when conjoined to the law in question, result in a theory that is consistent both with the facts that were originally accounted for by that law and those which would otherwise serve to falsify it. The second course would be to attempt to modify the original law, usually by reducing its generality, so as to achieve consistency with all of the known facts. Finally, as a last resort, it would be necessary to simply abandon the original law and begin the search for entirely different principles of explanation.

In the present case, I can think of no plausible independent auxiliary hypotheses which might serve to suppress the false implications of Specificity Preposition. However, by making a slight modification of the original formulation of this law, we can achieve an explanatory theory that is fully consistent with the whole range of facts under consideration concerning the differential ordering of subclasses and general classes in natural language.

The nature of the required modification is immediately suggested by the difference between the natural grammar-type (18d) and the non-natural types (10d) and (17d) in the nature of the properly included constituents that they refer to. Thus, while the properly included representations of the non-natural grammars consist of specified constant elements (N in (10d), ADJ in (17d)), the properly included representation of (18d) consists only of an unrestricted variable (X). This indicates that subclasses of the universal class must be excluded from the domain of Specificity Preposition, and that this law can be appropriately amended as follows so as to exclude grammar-types (10d) and (17d), which refer to proper-inclusion-related members of the non-universal classes [N] and [ADJ], without excluding the natural grammar-type (18d), which refers only to proper-inclusion-related members of the strictly universal class [X].

(19) Specificity Preposition (Amended)
For any set of statements G, G is a possible grammar of a natural language only if for any pair of ordering statements [A, B] = X and [[A, C, B] = Y, included in G, where A is a string of one or more (non-null) constant elements, Y is of the form [[A, C] & B].

This version of the law of Specificity Preposition, which is somewhat less general but at least as natural as the original, serves as an adequate basis now for the generation of highly general explanations of all of the cited facts about the ordering of oblique arguments, adjectives, and nominal modifiers in natural languages. That this law will ultimately fall, either by falsification or by reduction to laws of a still more general character, is almost certain, as it is for all the empirical hypotheses of mortal science. Nevertheless,

until such inadequacy is explicitly demonstrated, the principle of
Specificity Preposition, and its associated auxiliary hypotheses, must
be taken to be true, and the explanations that they generate must be
taken to be true explanations.

4.   Conclusions

The primary purpose of this study has been to indicate and exemplify
some of the basic metatheoretical and methodological prerequisites to
the explanation of facts about constituent order in natural languages.
It was suggested that these must include, above all else, a sincere
and unwavering commitment to the standard scientific task of constructing and evaluating explicit theories consisting of empirically vulnerable laws about all of the objects in their domains. Adherence to the
rigorous standards of nomological-deductive explanation was seen to be
difficult but extremely rewarding, and in fact the only possible natural
basis for real extensions of linguistic knowledge and understanding.

It has also been suggested that all facts and laws about human
languages can be most appropriately expressed by statements quantified
over the set of all grammars that generate such languages. To achieve
such grammatical explanations of linguistic facts, though, it is necessary that every distinct claim about grammars must entail some distinct empirically testable claim about languages. To satisfy this condition, there must be a uniform and fully explicit metalanguage for
grammatical statements and a set of highly restrictive metaconstraints
on the vocabulary, statement-types, interpretation, and inferential
use of all possible theories of grammar and all of the possible grammar sets that they generate. This will serve to establish the scienti-
fically indispensible implication relations that must hold between
empirical hypotheses and the factual observations that would suffice
to confirm or disconfirm them. It will also provide the necessary
empirical basis--often lacking in linguistics thus far--for determining whether different theories are empirically distinct, and for choos-
ing between them if they are.

Considerations have also been mentioned at various points to show
that there are sound empirical reasons, as well as the obvious

practical and conceptual ones, for selecting those grammatical theories
or metatheories that determine the smallest and most homogeneous class
of possible grammars consistent with the known facts about human language. In this way, vulnerability to falsification will be most effectively maximized for linguistic hypotheses, and research will be
productively directed towards the optimally significant task of testing those hypotheses that generate the strongest possible claims about
human language that are not yet known to be false.

The empirical and methodological values of this general view of
theory construction and evaluation have been illustrated here primarily
with respect to the highly restrictive theory of Derivational Ordering.
The metaconstraints that comprise this theory--the principles of Terminal Completeness and Invariant Ordering--each determine a smaller and
more homogeneous class of possible grammars and possibly equivalent
representations of linguistic objects than determined by their respective contraries or contradictories. Of all possible theories of constituent ordering, therefore, there is none that is more vulnerable to
possible falsification, and none that generates stronger or more restrictive claims about the grammars of natural languages and the structures of the objects that comprise them. It is thus necessary to consider this theory to be true until proven otherwise. This assumption
has already demonstrated its value by motivating significant investigations of the most likely factual bases for such proof. The results
of such research have thus far failed to disconfirm the theory of
Derivational Ordering, and have tended to show, in fact, that the
principles of this theory--particularly the Invariant Order Constraint--
are not only consistent with the known facts about natural languages,
but also necessary for their optimal principled explanation. The sample of constituent-order facts investigated here were seen to indicate
further evidence of this, and hence provide additional support for the
derivational theory.

The primary purpose of these investigations, however, has been to
exemplify the complexities and ramifications attendant upon any serious
attempt to explain facts about constituent ordering in natural language. Such attempts, whether relatively successful or not, were seen
to require the explicit formulation of a number of grammatical laws

whose logical implications and empirical test conditions range far beyond the initial domain of explanation. The attempt to provide explanations for Greenberg's universals about pronominal and marked adjective precedence, for example, were seen to offer occasions for the deductive use and empirical test of not only the proposed law of Specificity Preposition, but also the much more general hypotheses of Simplex-Feature Representation, Non-Negative Variables, and Invariant Ordering. This is the way it should be in empirical science, of course, since this kind of interconnectedness maximizes the opportunities for possible falsification, on both internal and external grounds, and facilitates the acquisition of real knowledge both from the confirmation of hypotheses and from their disconfirmation. Our primary conclusion, then, is simply that the task of providing explicit nomological explanations of constituent-order universals is, like all other explanatory tasks in empirical science, both extremely difficult to succeed in and yet impossible to not undertake.

NOTES

1. For further discussion of questions concerning the explanatory domain of linguistic theories, see Sanders (1974) and the various references cited there.

2. There may be certain marginal exceptions to the general phonological independence of intermorphemic ordering relations. Thus, for example, in English the comparative morpheme occurs before trisyllabic adjectives (more beautiful, *beautifuler), but either before or after monosyllabic ones (more tall, taller), with the postpositional (and cliticized) alternant strongly preferred. Also, in Tagolog, as reported by Paul Schachter, there are certain restrictions on the relative ordering of verbal clitics that appear to depend on their relative length in syllables. It is perhaps significant that both of these cases involve the ordering of sublexical constituents.

3. This takes into account both the very marginal and inconclusive remarks on ordering in Chomsky (1965), and the less marginal but no less inconclusive comments presented by Emmon Bach at the present conference. In neither case is any evidence presented to suggest that the invariance or completeness constraints are false or inadequate. All of Chomsky's assertions about ordering are in fact either false, invalid, or empirically irrelevant. (See Sanders 1970:496.) In Bach's case, all that is shown is that there are certain facts about certain languages that appear to be consistent with the hypothesis of variable ordering. It is not shown that these facts are inconsistent with the hypothesis of invariant ordering, or with any other principle of the theory of Derivational Ordering. It is the latter, of course, that must be demonstrated, and not merely the former, if one wishes to support the claim that invariant order theories are false or inadequate. But such demonstration appears to not even have been attempted thus far in the linguistic literature. In spite of this, though, and in spite of the fact that the set of invariant order grammars is properly included in the set of grammars generated by the hypothesis of variable ordering, both Bach and Chomsky evidently assume that the burden of proof rests with the weaker and more observationally constrained hypothesis of invariant ordering, rather than with the much stronger and

less constrained hypothesis of variable ordering, which determines not
only a much larger and more heterogeneous class of possible grammars
but also a larger and more heterogeneous set of possible representations for every sentence of every possible language.

4. All formulations and discussions of grammatical rules here presuppose the truth of the basic hypothesis of equational grammar (Sanders
1972c) and all of the various metaconstraints on grammatical theories
that are entailed by it, including, in particular, the principle of
Universally-Determined Rule-Application (Sanders 1972a, 1972c). Thus
it will be assumed throughout that all statements in particular grammars are strictly symmetrical assertions of representational equivalence or non-equivalence, and that all constraints on the inferential
use of such statements are strictly universal in character. The only
universal principles of this sort that will be relevant here are the
principle of Proper Inclusion Precedence (Sanders 1972c), which asserts
the applicational precedence of any rule with a structural description
of the form WXY over any rule with a structural description of the
form X, and the principle of Maximalization of Terminal Specificity
(Sanders 1972c), from which it follows that substitutions of phonetically interpreted elements (like the ordering element) for semantically
interpreted ones (like the grouping element) is justified only in
proofs or derivations terminating in phonetic representations, with
the opposite substitution justified only in semantically-terminated
derivations.

It should also be noted here that grammars of type (6a), but not
those of type (5a), would be excluded by the subsequently proposed law
of Specificity Preposition, in either of its formulations (12) and (19).

5. In all languages of type (9c) that I know of, the prepositional
pronominal arguments are always monosyllabic clitics that are preposi-
tionally bound to verbs under most syntactic conditions but postposi-
tionally bound under at least some such conditions. This, along with
the fact that non-clitic pronouns are always ordered in the same was
as non-pronominal arguments in languages of this type, suggest that
the real generalization here involves the ordering of clitic and non-
clitic arguments, rather than the ordering of nominals and pronominals.

In any event, it will be assumed here that the representation PRO refers only to the class of clitic pronouns, and includes features that distinguish all members of this class from all non-clitic pronouns as well as all non-pronominal arguments.

6. This would actually be true only if Specificity Reordering were reformulated as a global constraint on derivations, or as a constraint on identity deletion rules rather than on reordering rules. It is necessary, as shown in Sanders (1969), for <u>all</u> constraints on reordering to be expressed in one of the latter ways, since the derivational effect of any given reordering rule can always be achieved by the conjunctive application of a rule of identity adjunction (with ordering of the adjunct) and a rule of identity deletion.

7. There also are no languages that have no elsewhere ordering at all for adjectives--that is, where all prenominal and postnominal orderings alike would be specifiable only by morpheme-specific rules.

8. These rules would appear to be necessary, moreover, independently of all other facts about prenominal and postnominal adjectives, and regardless of what assumptions are made about their respective semantic sources. Thus, for example, it is clear that some prenominal adjectives, like <u>ancien</u> 'former' in French, are semantically adverbial rather than adjectival in character, since they take predicates or predications as their operands rather than nominal expressions. Thus, <u>l'ancien</u> <u>roi</u> 'the former king' means the same as <u>l'un qui etait anciennement un/</u> <u>le roi</u> 'the one who was formerly a/the king', and is, of course, radically different in meaning from <u>le roi qui est/etait ancien</u> 'the king who is/was ancient'. (Compare English <u>the former king</u> = <u>the one who</u> <u>was formerly a/the king</u> ≠ <u>*the king who is/was former</u>.) But even if this were always the case--which seems quite doubtful (cf. <u>le pauvre</u> <u>roi</u> 'the unfortunate king' ≠ <u>l'un qui etait pauvrement un/le roi</u> 'the one who was poorly a/the king')--it would mean at most that the class of prenominal adjectives could be identified as a natural class, distinguished by those semantic elements, or syntactic diacritics, that are uniquely associated with those adjectival predicates that take predicational rather than nominal constructions as their arguments or operands. But such a class would still constitute the marked or special-case class for attributives, and not the general, or elsewhere,

class. Thus, though the ordering rules for prenominal adjectives might be reducible in such an event to a single rule--perhaps of the form [[ADJ, ADV], N] = [[ADJ, ADV] & N]--the semantically proximate member of any such rule will still properly include that of the general rule for the ordering of adjectives and nominals, and would therefore still fall in the domain of Specificity Preposition.

9. To simplify the discussion, all facts about the ordering of quantifiers, determiners, and numerals will be excluded from present consideration. It is worthy of note, nevertheless, that all of these non-predicational attributes are ordered precisely the same as attributive adjectives in languages of types (17a), e.g., Japanese (17b), e.g., Thai, and (18c), e.g., English; in most if not all languages of type (17c), e.g., French, Spanish, they are ordered like the marked (prenominal) adjectives of the language.

10. An unclosed representation is any bracketed string of elements that does not explicitly include the null element, generally symbolized by $\emptyset$. All representations explicitly including this element are closed, in the sense that they can have no variable reference, but stand simply for the set of elements that they include. Thus, while the unclosed representation [A, B] refers to the class of representations [A, B, $\emptyset$], [A, B, C, $\emptyset$], [A, B, G, E, $\emptyset$], etc., the closed representation [A, B, $\emptyset$] refers only to those representations that include just the three elements A, B, and $\emptyset$. For further discussion, see Sanders (1972b).

11. For variable-order theories, of course, Basque also serves to falsify the counterpart principle of Specificity Reordering. The same amendment will thus be required for this principle as is required in the case of Specificity Preposition.

REFERENCES

Bartsch, Renate and Theo Vennemann. (1972). Semantic Structures. Frankfurt am Main: Athenäum Verlag.

Chomsky, Noam. (1965). Aspects of the Theory of Syntax. Cambridge: M.I.T. Press.

----------, and Morris Halle. (1968). The Sound Pattern of English. New York: Harper & Row.

Delisle, Gilles L. (1972). Universals and Person Pronouns in Southwestern Chippewa. University of Minnesota doctoral dissertation.

Greenberg, Joseph H. (1963). "Some universals of grammar with particular reference to the order of meaningful elements." In J.H. Greenberg (ed.), Universals of Language, pp. 58-90. Cambridge: M.I.T. Press.

Jackendoff, Ray S. (1972). Semantic Interpretation in Generative Grammar. Cambridge: M.I.T. Press.

Kiparsky, Paul. (1972). "Explanation in phonology." In S. Peters (ed.), Goals of Linguistic Theory, pp. 189-227. Englewood Cliffs, N.J.: Prentice-Hall.

Lakoff, George. (1971). "On generative semantics." In D.D. Steinberg and L.A. Jakobovits (eds.), Semantics, pp. 232-96. London: Cambridge University Press.

Lamb, Sidney M. (1966). Outline of Stratificational Grammar. Washington: Georgetown University Press.

Lertxundi y Baztarrika, J.M. (1913). Euzkal-Iztiya. ('Basque Grammar'.) San Sebastian: Baroja e Hijos.

Sanders, Gerald A. (1969). Invariant Ordering. Duplicated. University of Texas at Austin. (Mimeographed. Bloomington: Indiana University Linguistics Club, 1970.) Revised version in press. The Hague: Mouton.

----------. (1970). "Constraints on constituent ordering." Papers in Linguistics 2.460-502.

436

----------. (1972a). "Precedence relations in language." Mimeographed. Bloomington: Indiana University Linguistics Club. To appear in Foundations of Language 11.3 (1974).

----------. (1972n). "The simplex-feature hypothesis." Mimeographed. Bloomington: Indiana University Linguistics Club. To appear in Glossa 8.1 (1974).

----------. (1972c). Equational Grammar. The Hague: Mouton.

----------. (1974). "Issues of explanation in linguistics." In D. Cohen (ed.), Explaining Linguistic Phenomena, pp. 1-20. Washington: Winston & Sons.

VERB-ANCHORING AND VERB-MOVEMENT

by

Arthur Schwartz

0. Background, Thesis, Outline

Among the differences distinguishing those who posit logico-semantic
structure as the underlying representation of a sentence from those who
posit a lexical-syntactic structure as its underlying representation is
the nature of the mappings that relate the deep structure to the surface
structure, the so-called transformations. For the logico-semanticists,
the operations are more powerful, in that they involve manipulation of
abstract predicates, collapsing of semantic primitives, and "lowering" of
material.

Another perspective on this debate leads to the matter of weakening
linguistic theory by means of substantive constraints on tranformations.
I made one such attempt a few years ago (1972) with respect to movement
transformations. There, notions like "nucleus" and "constituent" were
used--so that the constraints made no reference to lexical categories like
N, V, P, etc. In this paper, I would like to show how such constraints
can be narrowed even further.

Following on Greenberg's classification (1966) of SVO, VSO, and SOV
attributes, both Lehmann (1973) and Steele (1973) have sought to simplify
the typology to, roughly, a Modifier/Modified parameter under the rubric
VO versus OV (with some implicit primacy given to verb phrase structure
over noun phrase). What this reduction does is to collapse the SVO and
VSO types, a conflation which seems desirable in view of the number of
characteristics shared by these systems (e.g., prepositions, WH-fronting,
auxiliary before the main verb, etc.) and the current depreciation of the
notion "grammatical subject".

I have argued for a distinction between SVO and VSO in terms of VP-
constituency: specifically, that SVO is distinct from VSO and SOV systems
by just that attribute; and that, in fact, the construct VP was peculiar
to SVO organization. Since that proposal (1973), data on the relatively
infrequent VOS system (sometimes called Subject-Final) have suggested to
me that if my arguments for VP-constituency were valid, they had to be
extended to VOS systems as well: in short, VP-constituency is a trait of
any system whose underlying order is VO. In this respect, then, SVO and
VOS stand against VSO and SOV.

In the present paper, I will again argue for a distinctive attribute
of SVO systems. The principle is a corollary of an earlier proposal
which claimed that VSO and SOV systems involve a decision about the posi-

tion of the verb (predicate, generally), whereas SVO do not. (The rarer VOS system falls together with VSO and SOV under this parameter.) The corollary to this dichotomy between verb-anchoring systems and the SVO system is that verb-movement of any kind obtains only in the latter.

The organization of this paper is as follows: in section 1, I take the base order of contemporary literary Spanish as problematic--i.e., that a case can be made for either SVO, VSO, or VOS. In section 2, interrogatives in VSO and SVO are examined: in the clearest instances, SVO WH-questions are distinct from VSO; however, some SVO systems--in their interrogative forms, look like VSO. It is only in the forms of embedded interrogatives that SVO fall together and contrast as a group with VSO. In section 3, Spanish interrogatives ultimately lead us to accept Spanish as an SVO system of the second type: like other such systems, it converges with VSO in independent questions. But it can be shown that is employs a verb-fronting rule, and this kind of rule is found in SVO systems only. The basic SVO character of Spanish is substantiated by the behavior of the enclitic pronouns. In section 4, this principle of verb-fronting as an SVO diacritic is applied to contemporary standard German, where the evidence again points to SVO as the underlying order. The dependent clause pattern of SOV turns out to a generalization of the verb-fronting thesis: namely, verb-movement is uniquely SVO, all other systems being verb-anchoring. In conclusion, I point out that dependency theory is the most suitable expression of this empirical constraint.

1. The Base Order of Spanish

In taking Spanish as a problem case, and then showing that it must have SVO as a base, I do not wish it to appear a new or terribly important discovery; neither do I wish it to seem a mere exercise. What I want to demonstrate is that its SVO character, while unequivocally sensed in terms of intuition, has quite a potent rival in a supposed "straw man" like VSO; and that it takes some arguing to show that it really is (still) SVO. If we just consider the variety of surface word orders, Spanish appears indeterminate. VOS is a possibility because of declaratives and interrogatives like the following (page numbers refer to Ramsey 1956):

    (1)(a) no era grande la distancia que separaba a la
            not was great   the distance that separated the

quinta del monasterio
cottage from monastery
"The distance separating the cottage from the monastery
was not great." (539)

a poco que se descuidara, le rebosarian de la boca
hardly   off guard (past)   flood (plural) from mouth
  confidentias
  secrets
"Scarcely was she off guard, secrets would come flooding
from her mouth." (563)

mi esposa, a quien ya   le empezaba a doler la
my wife, to who already   begin   to hurt the
cabeza, se retiro
head   retired
"My wife, whose head was already beginning to ache,
withdrew." (203)

(b) que   quieren decir estas senales?
what want   say   these   marks
"What do these marks mean?" (512)

de que le sirve a usted llorar?
what   serves to you   crying
"What good does crying do you?" (514)

muerto yo, que vendran a ser mis hijos?
die I   what   come to be my children
"When I die, what will become of my children?" (540)

But VSO is also possible, for the same reasons:

(2)(a) tiene usted la camisa toda ensangrentada
have you the shirt all   bloody
"Your shirt is all bloody." (192)

no comprendia   el buen sacerdote los malos corazones
not understood the good priest   the evil   hearts
"The good priest did not understand hard hearts." (496)

no comprendo lo que quiere usted decir
not understand what which want you   say

"I don't understand what you mean." (512)

(b) que estaban haciendo los muchachos en el patio?
what were doing the boys in the courtyard
"What were the boys doing in the courtyard?" (362)

ha escrito usted hoy a su senor tio?
have written you today to your uncle
"Have you written to your uncle today?" (321)

visito usted la Biblioteca Nacional en Quito?
visited you the Library National in Quito
"Did you visit the National Library in Quito?" (324)

And, of course, SVO data--which I will not cite--are as abundant in main clause indicative declaratives. I have not sought statistical preferences because sooner or later notions of markedness must decide where the "most natural" form prevails; and even then, matters are not clear. For example, subordinate clause behavior is usually conservative: at any one time, where we have a contrast between main clause and subordinate clause evidence, we still cannot tell whether subordinate clause behavior is a relic and the innovating main clause has established itself as the underlying pattern; or whether subordinate clauses still reflect the basic character of the language in the face of relatively new options appearing in the less constrained main clause. Modern German is a classic instance of this dilemma (see section 4).

But aside from finite clause behavior, Spanish supplies further arguments for each of the three possible base orders. VOS is just what is required for nominalizations like el abrir la puerta Juan (lit. the opening the door John) "the opening of the door by John; John's opening the door"; it should also be noted that these lack a VSO alternant. VOS and VSO have both types of interrogatives (yes/no and WH) as well as a number of imperatives to substantiate a V-initial hypothesis. Like such systems, Spanish also has a very close bond between the auxiliary verb and the main verb: in ha escrito usted hoy a su senor tio?, the auxiliary ha cannot be separated from escrito--*ha usted escrito...?; *ha hoy escrito usted...?; etc. It also requires WH-fronting in interrogatives (except for echo or incredulous questioning): this strictness is more closely associated with verb-initial systems, unlike SVO--like English and French--which sometimes relax this requirement. In support of SVO, however, is the overwhelming

native speaker preference in simple declarative clauses; for example,
Juan compro el coche "John bought the car" is clearly preferred to compro
Juan el coche when these are offered in isolation and independent of discourse effects, and the same prejudice prevails when negation is introduced (S. Kattan, personal communication: in subordinate clauses, VSO patterns become more acceptable).

Thus, when the evidence is summed up, nothing conclusive emerges; and
one is led to feel, in this state of indeterminacy, that perhaps setting
up a contrast between SVO and VSO systems is indeed an artifact; that VO
(contrasting with OV) is--after all--the significant relation in any study
of underlying order.

2. SVO and VSO Interrogatives

SVO systems allow or require WH-fronting generally. Hebrew, for example, keeps the declarative order intact except for the obligatorily initial question-word:

> (3) ma   ata   oxel?
>   what you   eat
>   "What do you eat?"
>
>   efo   hu   gar?
>   where he   live
>   "Where does he live?"
>
>   lama   ata   soel   oti?
>   why   you   ask   me
>   "Why do you ask me?"

In yes/no questions, Hebrew simply imposes a contrasting (rising) intonation over the declarative order:

> (4) ata   soel   oti?
>   you   ask   me
>   "Are you asking me?"
>
>   ata   holex   le-exol?
>   you   go   to eat
>   "Are you going to eat?"

```
ata  lo  mar  ziy?
you  not Mr.  Ziv
"Aren't you Mr. Ziv?"
```

Other SVO systems may be quite like Hebrew in their WH-interrogatives--
for example, Finnish and Indonesian:

(5)(a) Finnish
```
mita  tama  on?
what  this  is
"What is this?"
```
```
mita  te   sanotte?
what  you  say
"What did you say?"
```
```
kuinka  tama  sana  aannetaan?
how     this  word  is-pronounced
"How is this word pronounced?"
```

(b) Indonesian
```
apa(kah)  engkau  membatja?
what      you     read
"What are you reading?"
```
```
dimana(kah)  mereka  tinggal?
where        they    live
"Where do they live?"
```
```
siapa(kah)  saja  memukul?
who         I     hit
"Who do I hit?"
```

(except that Indonesian also allows the WH-word to remain in position--and
in that case the emphatic particle -kah cannot be used). But such SVO
systems differ from Hebrew in their yes/no question formation. In addition to a question intonation over declarative order, Finnish allows a
constituent-fronting under -ko encliticization: in the unmarked type, -ko
will cause the finite verb to be fronted; in the marked, other constituents
may be put in focus:

(6) tulee-ko han?
```
     comes     he
     "Is he coming?"
```

kirjoja-ko mies myy?
books   man   sells
"Does the man sell books?"

paljon-ko kello on?
much   time   is
"What time is it?"

Indonesian also has an unmarked yes/no form--like Finnish and Hebrew,
simply the declarative order under a rising intonation (but unlike them,
it can use an S-initial particle apakah to signal the unmarked yes/no
form). For emphasis, Indonesian uses the same -kah seen above in WH-interrogatives:

(7) ke-rumah itu-KAH anak ini   pergi?
     to house the   boy   this go
     "Was it to house that this boy went?"

     ki-LA-kah mereka tinggal?
     in LA   they   live
     "Is it in LA that they live?"

     oleh dia-kah buku itu   di-batja?
     by   him   book that was read
     "Was it by him that that book was read?"

Roughly, then, such SVO systems form WH-interrogatives with least distur-
bance to the underlying order: e.g., S V O+wh → O+wh S V; S V O Adv+wh
→Adv+wh S V O; etc. In yes/no questions, there may be a fronting of
some high-lighted element, but the finite verb is not distinctive: e.g.,
S V O+ko → O+ko S V; S V O Adv+ko → ADV+ko S V O; S V+ko O → V+ko S O;
etc.

In contrast, VSO systems will generally have the WH-constituent
directly in front of the verb or verbal complex. For example, Squamish
(Kuipers, 1967: 146-7); Samoan (Marsack, 1962: 62-3); and Berber
(Penchoen, 1967: 15.2f)--

(8) Squamish   sta'm k°i sna'?-s
                     what   is-called
                     " What is it called?"

                     tm-ta'm na‿ƛ'i'q ta‿x°ali'tn
                     when   arrived   white man

"when did the white man arrive?"

c-x° ? 'nca-s k° ci n-sa't
   where   you-put my-shot
"Where did you put my ammunition?"

Samoan   'o ai e te manatua
                 who you Pres remember
                 "Whom do you remember?"

                 o le fea niusipepa sa e faitau ai
                 which   newspaper Past you read
                 "Which newspaper did you read?"

                 aisea   sa   e   le   fa'atali
                 why   Past you not wait
                 "Why didn't you wait?"

Berber   matta h.nnid
                 what you-say
                 "What did you say?"

                 mani had-af.n   1.hd.mt
                 where Fut they-find   work
                 "Where will they find work?"

                 m.lmi had-b.rhan
                 when   Fut they-stop
                 "When will they stop?"

And what such systems typically share in yes/no interrogatives is a particle either in S-initial position (e.g., Samoan pe/po), or encliticized to the first constituent (Squamish -?u, Kuipers 160; Berber -sa, Penchoen 15.7). In general, then, SVO and VSO systems contrast in WH-questions schematically as follows:

        S V O: WH S V ... ?
        V S O: WH V S ... ?

(although when the subject nominal is questioned, there may be the same surface form--WH V ... ?).

    However, other systems are not so transparently SVO in their interrogatives. French, for example, requires Finite Verb-Fronting in its yes/no questions:

> (9) mangent ils maintenant
>   eat   they now
>   "are they eating now?"
>
>   a-t-il vu   le film
>   has he seen the movie
>   "has he seen the movie?"
>
>   êtes vous venus hier
>   were you come yesterday
>   "did you come yesterday?"

although it does allow "declarative" order if the S-initial est-ce que
is used. English also has Finite Verb-Fronting, but more restricted
than the French (i.e., have, be, and the modals can, may, etc.).

Both languages similarly have WH-Fronting, though not obligatorily
in some dialects:

> (10) avec qui parleras   tu anglais
>   with who will-speak you English
>   "who will you speak English with?"
>
>   où   sont ils allés
>   where are they gone
>   "where have they gone?"
>
>   comment faisons nous ceci
>   how   do   we   this
>   "how do we do this?"

Notice that the finite verb must follow the fronted WH-constituent,
suggesting that the verb-fronting characteristic of yes/no questions
also occurs here. Thus, such SVO systems as English and French appear
to be VSO in their interrogative forms--

A		B
S V O+wh	→	O+wh V S
S V O	→	V S O
V S O+wh	→	O+wh V S
V S O	→	V S O

when (if?) they employ a verb-fronting process. And, indeed, given surface forms like those in column B, together with a sufficiently varied declarative order, we could not be sure what the underlying order might be. (That colloquial Spanish also allows an S-initial particle que in yes/no questions further confounds the SVO/VSO distinction.)

So far, we have seen a VSO/SVO convergence in surface forms in main clause interrogatives. It remains to ask whether they go separate ways under embedding. And, indeed, taking Berber and French as representative of the types under discussion, we can see the underlying distinction emerge:

(11) ttutlan   f-matta illan... (13.1)
      they-speak on what that-is
      "they speak about what occurs..."

u-s-qqar.n-š mam.k ha-s-g.n n.γ matta ha-s-g.n (13.2d)
not-him-say   how Fut-him-do or   what Fut-him-do
"they do not tell him how or what they will do to him"

ud-ssin.n   la mani la ma-dg   had-af.n 1.hd.mt (13.8d)
not they-know nor where nor what-in Fut-find work
"they didn't know where or in what they would find work"

j'ai oblié   comment le prêtre a dit la messe
I-have forgotten how the priest has said the mass
"I have forgotten how the priest said the mass"
(cf. *...comment a dit le prêtre la messe; or,
     *...comment a dit la messe le prêtre)

je ne sais pas comment la police est allée à Paris
I not know not how the police are gone to Paris
"I don't know how the police went to Paris"
(cf. *...comment est allée à Paris la police; or,
     *...comment est allée la police à Paris)

(Forms like <u>...où est allée la police</u> and <u>...ce qu'a fait la police</u>
cannot be taken at face value; where a complement follows the main
verb, the subject must be restored to its position before the finite
verb.) That is to say, the suspected SVO system manifests (typically)
a <u>WH S V</u>.... pattern, whereas the VSO manifests a <u>WH V S</u>.... In fact,
the divergence is even greater with certain V-initial systems: cf.
Tongan (Shumway, 1971)--

    (12) declarative: 'e 'alu 'a Mele he mahina kaha'u (384)

                                Fut go   Mary the week   next

                                  "Mary is going next week"

    main clause WH: 'e 'alu 'afē 'a Sione (162)

                                  Fut go when   John

                                  "when is John going?"

    embedded WH: 'oku 'ikai te u 'ilo pe 'e ha'u 'afē 'a Sione (163)

                            Pres Negative I know if Fut come when   John

                            "I don't know whether John is coming"

where the verb-initial character of the system persists under all forms.
But the SVO systems that were somewhat misleading in their main clause
interrogatives because of a (putative) verb-fronting process now look
more like the most distinctive of SVO systems (e.g., Finnish, Hebrew,
Indonesian).

3. SVO Systems and Verb-Fronting

    We return to Spanish now, to look at interrogatives. As we saw
in section 1 (the data cited as (2) on pp. 441-442), main clause interrogatives look like VSO forms. Somewhat disconcertingly, embedded forms
confirm a V-initial hypothesis, if not VSO specifically:

    (13) sabe usted a dónde ha ido Paco (218)

            know you to where has gone Frank

            "do you know where Frank has gone?"

ha visto usted qué efecto ha causado a los dos (el)
have seen you what effect has caused to the two (the)
"did you see what effect their seeing each other again

   volverse a ver (346)
   returning to see
    had on both of them?"

se comprenderá fácilmente cuánto impacientaba a ambos
   understand-Fut easily how-much irritated to both
"it will be easily understood how much this delay

   esta tardanza... (386)
   this delay
   irritated them both"

If our conclusions of section 2 are valid, Spanish is VSO since WH-questions should show underlying SVO order most conspicuously under embedding; clearly Spanish shows an inclination toward ...WH V... (as did, for example, Berber).

Before giving up the chase, however, we should note one aspect of V-fronting in SVO systems: when it is used to characterize yes/no interrogatives, it is also so used in the WH-type; and where it is missing in one, so is it in the other. This strict correlation in just those SVO systems that resemble VSO in interrogatives yields a powerful diagnostic: such SVO systems will never be "inconsistent" in their WH-interrogatives. For example, English will admit

   (14) they will see what?   (no WH-fronting; no V-fronting)
      or what will they see?   (WH-fronting; V-fronting)

but not *will they see what? (V-fronting; no WH-fronting) or *what they will see? (WH-fronting; no V-fronting). In contrast, VSO systems can be "inconsistent" in this respect--e.g., Samoan:

   (15) sa latou o mai ma ai (62)   (no WH-fronting)
      Past they come with who
      "with whom did they come?"

```
sa   e  sau  anafea i  Apia (63)        ("partial" WH-fronting
Past you come when  to Apia             to post-verbal posi-
"when did you come to Apia?"            tion)

o anafea na  fa'auma ai e               (WH-fronting to
  when Past finish    by                 S-initial position)
"when did they finish the

 i latou le   galuega (120)
   them  the   work
 work?"
```

so that if we tried to ascribe a verb-fronting rule to Samoan, we would
be forced to view it as operating independently of WH-fronting.

With this contrast between "consistent" SVO interrogatives and
"inconsistent" VSO, we again consider Spanish. We find that it does not
admit of "inconsistency":

```
(16)  *ha   dicho usted qué  cosa
       have  said  you  what thing
      "what did you say?"
      (cf. qué cosa ha dicho usted?) (126)

      *ha   ajustado usted a quiénes
       have  hired    you    whom
      "whom have you hired?"
      (cf. a quienes ha ajustado usted?) (126)
```

What this means, then, is that Spanish has a Verb-Fronting rule that is
inherently linked to WH-Fronting, and when the latter does not occur,
neither does the former. And since Verb-Fronting is idiosyncratic to
SVO systems, Spanish is underlyingly SVO.

Once we concede this thesis, other facts fall into place. One
example should suffice. The behavior of the enclitic object pronouns
seems rather random vis-a-vis indicative and imperative moods. In the
subjunctive used as an imperative, the object pronouns must be encliti-
cized--just as in the ordinary imperative-- if the verb is an initial
in the clause (Ramsey, p. 97):

> (17) deje-la usted
> leave-her you
> "let her alone"
>
> digan-me ustedes lo que les parece
> tell-me you (pl) what to-you seems
> "tell me what you think"
>
> busquémos-lo por este lado
> seek we-it on this side
> "let us look for it on this side"

Each of the forms in (17) is unacceptable if the pronoun object precedes the verb: *la déje usted; *me dígan ustedes...; etc. However, when the verb is not absolutely initial, then the pronouns cannot be encliticized but must now precede the verb:

> (18) propicia se te muestre la fortuna
> favorable you show fortune
> "may fortune prove kind to you"
>
> malos demonios te lleven
> evil demons you carry (away)
> "may the devil take you"
>
> no me los den ustedes (441)
> not me them give you (pl)
> "do not give them to me"

The ordinary imperative shows the same alternation in the contrast between affirmative and negative: the pronoun placement is obligatory--

> (19) guárde-se usted de caer (506)
> protect-self you from fall
> "take care not to fall"
>
> no se meta usted... (509)
> not self put you...
> "don't interfere..."

I would like to stress the obligatory conditions of this behavior:
the pronouns must encliticize when the imperative verb is clause-initial;
they must precede, when it is not (regardless of what the first constituent may be: que, no, Subject NP, predicate adjective, etc.). What
is striking is that these pronouns show a similar alternation when the
verb is in the indicative mood: the verb not clause-initial, these
pronouns precede; the verb clause-initial, the pronouns can be found
encliticized--

>   (20) dígo-lo porque crea   en...   (95)
>   (I)say-it because (I)believe in...
>   "I say it because I believe in..."
>
>   mandó-les   que se   detuviesen (95)
>   ordered-them that self stop (pl)
>   "he ordered them to stop"

or not:

>   (21) le miran   como padre   (45)
>   him regard   like father
>   "they regard him as a father"
>
>   se   formará la parada a las diez (341)
>   self form-Fut the parade at the ten
>   "the parade will be formed at ten (o'clock)
>
>   los casó   el obispo (502)
>   them married the bishop
>   "the bishop married them"

How can this "option" in the indicative be accounted for? The explanation is obvious enough: the indicative form of the verb in (20-21) is
not clause-initial in the same sense as it is in (17). The pronouns
can precede the finite verb because "basically" the verb is not clause-
initial: the subject (nominal or pronominal) is there. With suppres-
sion of the subject pronoun or movement of the subject nominal, the
verb comes to "look" clause-initial. The encliticization obligatory
for the imperative is extended optionally to the indicative:

(22) ellos le miran...   →   Ø le miran...   →

     el obispo los casó   →   los caso el obispo   →

     la parada se formará...→ se formara la parada   →

     (opt) miran-le...

     (opt) casó-los...

     (opt) formará-se...

We see, then, that the pre-verbal pronouns in (21) are not really exceptional. If there is anything to be explained, it is rather the option
of encliticizing when the declarative turns out in one way or another to
be clause-initial, an option denied to the yes/no interrogative in
spite of a similarly superficial clause-initial appearance. At the
moment, I have no idea how such differences are to be accounted for.

Having established that Spanish, not being VSO, must be SVO does
not illuminate the precise way in which VSO and VOS surface orders
arise. We still have to argue for Verb-Fronting rather than, say,
Subject-Postposing. The only argument I know of for deriving a VSO...
order from SVO... by Verb-Fronting (rather than some other process) has
to invoke a constraint against "lowering (Schwartz 1972). What the
constraint rules out is moving the subject NP into its sister VP-constituent:

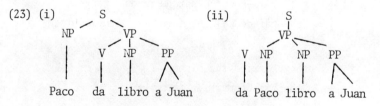

(23) (i)   (ii)

One might propose that Subject-Postposing, when it interrupts a
phrase, nullifies the constituency relations within the phrase: thus,
Paco da el libro a Juan "Frank gives the book to John", with the
structure of (23i) above, would re-structure into (24):

(24)

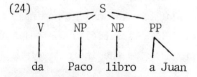

I know of no strong evidence for the constituency claims implicit in (24): in fact, (23ii) and (24) differ only in the type of constituent composed of da, Paco, el libro, and a Juan after restructuring. What can be pointed out in this regard is some evidence that VO base configurations can be reordered to OV and still preserve their VP-character.

The data for this claim comes from contemporary Mandarin (C. Li, personal communication). First, we can demonstrate VP-constituency (and also the SVO nature of the language) by noting emphatic frontings like

(25) wo neng chu Junggwo   chu Junggwo, wo neng
      I   can   go China   go China   I   can
      "I can go to China"   "go to China, I can"

The Ba-construction, if it derives from a movement of the post-verbal object to pre-verbal position, does not nullify VP-constituency: the various tests that would establish VP-structure (auxiliary verb position, bu-placement, interruptability by time adverbials, etc.) all show that ba NP V constitutes a unit.

The evidence that VP-constituency is retained after the basic VO relation is disturbed is found, again, in emphatic frontings of the verbal complex:

(26)(i) zhang-san neng shui   zai zhuang-shang →
         John   can sleep at bed   on
         "John can sleep on the bed"

         Z. neng zai zhuang-shang shui
         J. can at bed   on sleep
         "John can sleep on the bed"

   (ii) Z. neng zai zhuang-shang shui →
         J. can at bed   on sleep
         "J. can sleep on the bed"

         zai zhuang-shang shui, Z. neng
         at bed   on sleep, J. can
         "sleep on the bed, J. can"

      Z. neng shui zai zhuang-shang → shui zai zhuang-shang, Z. neng

As (26i) indicates, a verb like <u>shui</u> "sleep" allows its locative complement to either precede or follow. But either form, the basic VO or the
derived OV, allows fronting--as (26ii) indicates. The inference,
therefore, is that VP-constituency (like other constituent types: cf.
attributive adjective movement within the NP in English) does not
cancel by simple reordering within the phrase.

We are thus left to inquire into the idea of "nullification by
interruption", and are immediately beset with a number of difficult
questions. Why can't all phrases tolerate interruption, and thus
"disintegrate" into their immediate constituents? (E.g., <u>we all went to</u>
<u>the store</u> → *<u>we went to all the store</u>.) What is the structure of
"successful" interruptions in which (somehow) the original constituency
is still sensed? (E.g., <u>they all went to the store some time yesterday,</u>
<u>I think</u> = (?) → <u>they all went--some time yesterday, I think--to the</u>
<u>store</u>.) Is there a sliding scale of valence or bonding with which to
"measure" constituency strength? Are any aspects of this scale universal? And so on. Whatever the answers to those questions, there are
clearly different kinds of interruptions. The basic issue is whether a
Subject-Postposing that "breaks up" the Verb-Phrase should be posited;
and, further, whether that "interruption" can be subsumed under a more
general class of constituency nullification. My own inclination, obviously, is not to allow a postposing of that sort. This is not to say
that Subject-Postposing is not to be found in Spanish: assuming one
such process does not preclude one like Verb-Fronting (cf. English
<u>there</u>-forms of the type <u>there emerged from the left temple a crimson</u>
<u>spot</u>; <u>there obtains at 30,000 feet a different kind of condensation</u>;
etc.). Subject-Postposing in Spanish would account for the many <u>VO...S</u>
orders, both declarative and interrogative. Although I am not prepared
to specify the mechanics of the process, I see nothing to rule out a
movement that could be either clause-final or post-VP. And such a
formulation would still tolerate the view that question forms like
<u>VSO...?</u> and <u>O+wh VS...?</u> involve Verb-Fronting (perhaps even VP-Fronting
of a restricted sort: <u>es viejo su hermano de usted?</u> literally, is
old your brother of you, "is your brother old?"; <u>que estaban haciendo</u>

los muchachos en el patio? literally, what were doing the boys in the courtyard, "what were the boys doing in the courtyard?").

4. Verb-Anchoring and Verb-Movement

What has been shown for Spanish is that, like English and French, it is an SVO system that uses Verb-Fronting as one of its signals of interrogation. When Verb-Fronting occurs, apparently (i) it occurs in SVO systems only; and (ii) if it is used to mark one interrogative form (the yes/no type), it will be so used for the other. As for the first observation, with respect to Verb-Fronting, I am inclined to generalize the constraint: to my knowledge, verb-movement of any kind is found only in SVO systems. This constraint does not necessarily follow from the proposal that every other system is Verb-Anchoring; but the two constraints are plausibly in support of each other. SVO language-learners do not "make a decision" about the position of the verb, and so the verb is "movable"; learners of V-initial and V-final languages view the verb as a fixed point, and so do not "imagine" it as movable.

The restriction of V-movement to SVO systems is a useful investigating tool. For example, if we know that Turkish is SOV basically, then surface forms like SVO (common when the object is sentential) come about by complement postposing rather than some other device. Or, in the case of German, if we are faced with a choice of SVO or SOV as the base order, then SOV → SVO by verb-movement is not a possible maneuver. Our survey of interrogative forms in SVO and VSO systems has some bearing on the German problem, since German does have the surface forms O+wh V S...?; V S O...?; etc. As noted earlier, these forms can belong either to VSO or SVO. But since German is hardly a candidate for VSO, it must be SVO--the order of the simplest indicative declarative sentences. Then the SOV order must come about either by complement preposing or by verb-movement. The predictions of derived constituent structure are clear: if it is complement movement to pre-verbal position, VP-constituency should be preserved (cf. the Mandarin evidence above, pp. 455); but if the movement involves the verb, then the target must be S-final rather than VP-final position since the nucleus of a phrase does not move within its phrase (the so-called Fixed Nucleus Constraint, cf. Schwartz 1972).

458

(27) (A) Complement Pre-posing

(i)   (ii)

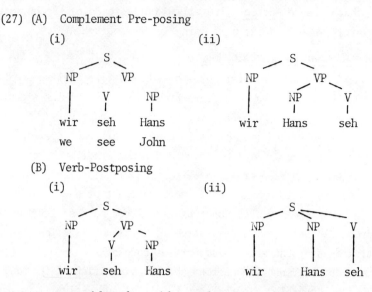

(B) Verb-Postposing

(i)   (ii)

Before we even consider the evidence that bears on the predictions implicit in (27Aii) and (27Bii), consider more complex predicates and what complement pre-posing would entail. For example, double complement verbs like <u>give</u>, <u>offer</u>, <u>send</u>, <u>teach</u>, etc., would require the movement of both complements, simultaneously to boot since there is no independent evidence for moving each separately. But simultaneous movement of non-constituents-forming elements violates the Unit Movement Constraint. Clearly, the process becomes troublesome and inordinately intricate when we go beyond the simplest cases. Verb-movement, then, seems to be the alternative. The predicted structure of (27Bii) asserts that the original VP-constituency is not preserved in the SOV structure of dependent clauses. This prediction is indeed borne out: given unemphatic forms like (28)--

(28) (A) (i)   der Mann muss das Buch gelesen haben
              the man must the book read   have
              "the man must have read the book"

(B) (i)   der Mann muss das Buch lesen
              the man must the book read
              "the man must read the book"

how can we explain the unacceptability of (29Aii) and (29Bii)?

(29) (A) (ii) *...das Buch gelesen muss der Mann haben
the book read   must the man   have
(cf. ...das Buch muss der Mann gelesen haben; or,
...gelesen haben muss der Mann das Buch)

(B) (ii) *...das Buch lesen muss der Mann
the book read   must the man
(cf. ...das Buch muss der Mann lesen; or,
...lesen muss der Mann das Buch)

As we saw in Mandarin, derived OV configurations in themselves do not preclude VO-constituency: German OV order, however, comes about not by adjunct movement, but by Verb-Postposing. Thus, das Buch gelesen and das Buch lesen are not constituents.*

A concluding remark: just as I argued in the case of the Fixed Nucleus Constraint (1972), so here too linguistic theory is inadequate to the extent that its constructs fail to incorporate empirical constraints. Verb-Anchoring can be expressed directly in dependency terms--

(30)

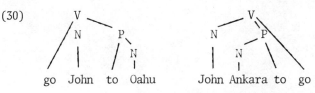

because the formalism rules out the possibility of moving the verb within its phrase, i.e., the statement of such a concept is "improper" as defined by the formal system. SVO organizations are different; a structure like

(31)

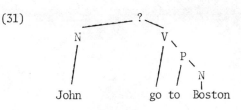

allows either (32i) or (32ii):

460

(32) (i) V-Fronting   (ii) V-Postposing

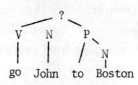

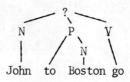

Such contrasting representations as (30) and (31) force a reconsideration of "S"-structure (cf. Chomsky's bar notation, 1970). The question mark in (31) and (32) indicates my own indecisiveness at this point.

NOTES

*   In checking the German situation further, I have found that forms like (29) may not be totally unacceptable, but clearly more difficult to accept then either of the alternatives given parenthetically in the text (i.e., das Buch muss... or lesen muss...). I am not sure whether the semi-acceptability of aber das Buch lesen muss der Mann for some speakers should not be handled by a notion like markedness with respect to the Unit Movement Constraint; or whether the intuited sense of a "compound" (i.e., something like Buch-lesen) indicates that our problem here is really related to something else going on in German. For example, it is possible to say gestern im Garten habe ich das Buch\gesehen, where two S-level adverbials, gestern "yesterday" and im Garten "in the garden", basically non-constituents form a "unit" as defined by the finite verb habe being in "second position". Native speakers inform me that there is no understood conjoining here (as if from gestern und im Garten) but rather than the two adverbials "form a single unit". If such a process must be allowed somewhere in a German grammar, then the problem presented by das Buch lesen... may not actually constitute a counterexample to the claims advanced in this paper. Notice, moreover, that something similar will have to be done for English constructions like only yesterday in the garden did we see an oriole, where the non-constituents yesterday and in the garden have both been fronted. Since both phrases are in the scope of only, the fronting of each independent of the other seems unlikely.

  At any rate, I should mention that underlying SVO order for German on the basis of word-order typological considerations has been arrived at independently by O. C. Dean, Jr. (forthcoming). Details are not at my disposal, but the position of the finite verb apparently plays a central role in Dean's arguments.

References

Chomsky, N. (1970) "Remarks on Nominalization". Readings in English Transformational Grammar, ed. R. A. Jacobs and P. S. Rosenbaum, 184-221. Ginn and Co. Waltham, Mass.

Dean, Jr., O. C. (forthcoming) "Word Order Typology and the Position of the Verb in German". Ph.D. dissertation, Department of Linguistics, University of Georgia.

Greenberg, J. (1963) "Some universals of grammar with particular reference to the order of meaningful elements". Universals of Language, ed. J. Greenberg, 73-113. MIT Press. Cambridge, Mass.

Kuipers, A. (1967) The Squamish Language. Mouton & Co. The Hague.

Lehmann, W. P. (1973) "A structural principle of language and its implications". Language, 49:47-66.

Marsack, C. C. (1962) Teach Yourself Samoan. English Universities Press. London.

Pencheon, T. (1967) "Etudes Syntaxiques du Parler Berbère (Chaouia) des Ait Frah (Aures)". Ph.D. dissertation, University of Paris. Published in 1973 as Etudes Syntaxiques d'un Parler Berbere by the Instituto Orientale Naples.

Ramsey, M. (1956) A Textbook of Modern Spanish. Rev. by R. Spaulding. Holt, Rinehard, Winston. New York.

Schwartz, A. (1972) "Constraints on movement transformations". Journal of Linguistics, 8:35-85.

——————. (1973) "The VP-Constituent of SVO Languages". Syntax and Semantics, vol. I, ed. J. Kimball. Academic Press. New York.

Shumway, E. (1971) Intensive Course in Tongan. University of Hawaii Press, Honolulu.

Steele, S. (1973) "The positional tendencies of modal elements and their theoretical implications". Ph.D. dissertation, Department of Linguistics, University of California, San Diego.